# BUCCANEERS
## OF THE
# CARIBBEAN

———❧❧❧———

## How Piracy Forged an Empire

## JON LATIMER

Harvard University Press
Cambridge, Massachusetts
2009

Library of Congress Cataloging-in-Publication Data

Latimer, Jon. Buccaneers of the Caribbean : how piracy
forged an empire / Jon Latimer.
p. cm.
Includes bibliographical references and index.
ISBN 978-0-674-03403-7 (alk. paper)
1. Buccaneers—Caribbean Area—History—
17th century. 2. Privateering—Caribbean Area—
History—17th century. 3. Adventure and adventurers—
Caribbean Area—History—17th century. 4. Seafaring
life—Caribbean Area—History—17th century.
5. Caribbean Area—History, Naval—17th century.
6. Imperialism—History—17th century. 7. Spain—
Colonies—America—History—17th century.
8. Great Britain—Colonies—America—History—17th
century. 9. France—Colonies—America—History—17th
century. 10. Netherlands—Colonies—America—
History—17th century. I. Title.
F2161.L38 2009
972.9′03 dc22
2009007389

# CONTENTS

# ILLUSTRATIONS AND MAPS

## SECTION ONE

The Port of Seville in 1498, detail showing an expedition setting out for America, by Alonso Sanchez Coello, oil on canvas (Museo de America, Madrid / The Bridgeman Art Library)

Piet Heyn, 1629 copy after a lost 1625 original by Jan Daemen Cool (Scheepvaart Museum, Amsterdam)

A buccaneer in the West Indies, engraving, 1686 (Private Collection / The Bridgeman Art Library)

The Buccaneer Was a Picturesque Fellow, by Howard Pyle, oil on canvas, 1905 (Delaware Art Museum)

The Dutch Retreat from San Juan de Puerto Rico, 1625, by Eugenio Caxes, oil on canvas (The Prado Museum, Madrid)

The Recapture of the Island of St Kitts, by Eugenio Caxes, oil on canvas (The Prado Museum, Madrid)

Robert Rich, 2nd Earl of Warwick, by Daniel Mytens the Elder, oil on canvas, c.1632 (National Maritime Museum, London)

La Isla Tortuga (Archivo General de India, Seville)

The fortifications at Araya (Archivo General de Indias, Seville)

Vice-Admiral Sir Christopher Myngs, by Sir Peter Lely, oil on canvas, 1665–6 (National Maritime Museum, London)

## SECTION TWO

Sir Henry Morgan, coloured engraving after illustration from *The Buccaneers of America*, by John Esquemeling (Peter Newark Historical Pictures / The Bridgeman Art Library)

Henry Morgan captures and sacks the town of Puerto del Principe, Cuba, in 1668, illustration from *The Buccaneers of America* by John Esquemeling, published 1699 (Peter Newark Pictures / The Bridgeman Art Library)

Captain Morgan defeats Spanish warships blocking the mouth of Lake Maracaibo in 1669, illustration from *The Buccaneers of America* by John Esquemeling, published 1699 (Peter Newark Pictures / The Bridgeman Art Library)

Henry Morgan and his Pirates ill-treating the citizens of Maracaibo on the Spanish Main in 1669, engraving (Private Collection / Peter Newark Historical Pictures / The Bridgeman Art Library)

Francis L'Ollonais, coloured engraving, 1684 (Private Collection / Peter Newark Historical Pictures / The Bridgeman Art Library)

Henry Bennet, 1st Earl of Arlington, after Sir Peter Lely, oil on canvas, c.1665–70 (National Portrait Gallery, London)

Charles II, by Samuel Cooper, oil on canvas (The Trustees of the Goodwood Collection / The Bridgeman Art Library)

George Monck, 1st Duke of Albemarle, by Sir Peter Lely, oil on canvas, 1665–6 (National Maritime Museum, London)

*Extorting Tribute from the Citizens*, by Howard Pyle, oil on canvas, 1905 (Delaware Art Museum)

*An Attack on a Galleon*, by Howard Pyle, oil on canvas, 1905 (Delaware Art Museum)

William Dampier, by Thomas Murray, oil on canvas, c.1697–8 (National Portrait Gallery, London)

A true and perfect relation of that terrible Earthquake at Port Royal in Jamaica, which happened on the 7th June 1692, broadsheet (British Library / The Bridgeman Art Library)

## MAPS

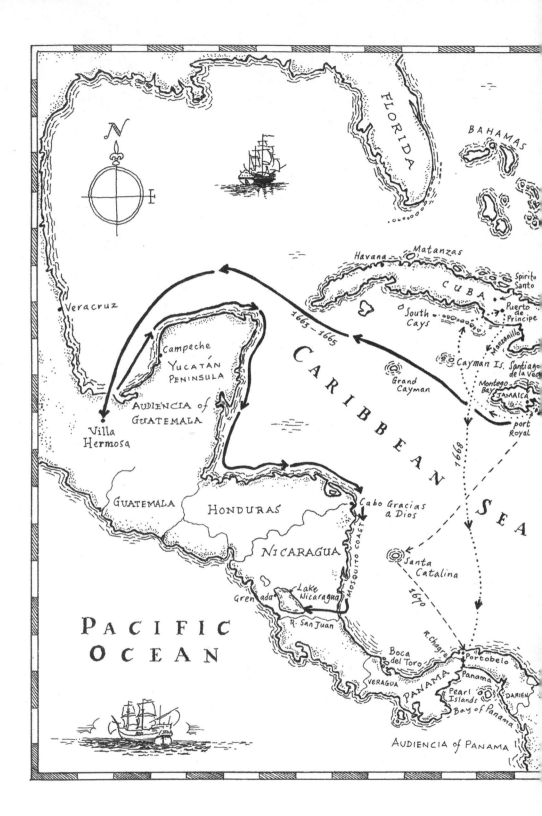

FLORIDA

BAHAMAS

N

E

Veracruz

Havana    Matanzas

CUBA

Spirito
Santo

Puerto
de
Principe

South
Cays

Campeche

Yucatán
Peninsula

1663 - 1665

Manzanillo

Cayman Is.  Santiago
de la Vega

Grand
Cayman

Montego
Bay
JAMAICA

AUDIENCIA of
GUATEMALA

C A R I B B E A N

port
Royal

Villa
Hermosa

1668

GUATEMALA

HONDURAS

Cabo Gracias
a Dios

S E A

NICARAGUA

Santa
Catalina

Lake
Nicaragua

Grenada

R. San Juan

1670

PACIFIC
OCEAN

R. Chagre

Boca
del Toro

Portobelo

VERAGUA

Panama

PANAMA

Pearl
Islands

DARIEN

Bay of Panama

AUDIENCIA of PANAMA

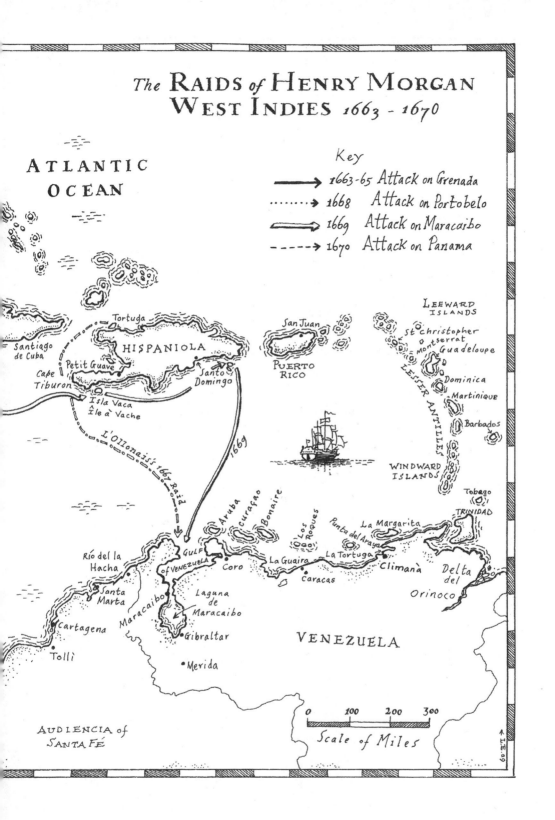

# The RAIDS of HENRY MORGAN WEST INDIES 1663 - 1670

ATLANTIC OCEAN

### Key

| | | |
|---|---|---|
| ⟶ | 1663-65 | Attack on Grenada |
| ·····⟶ | 1668 | Attack on Portobelo |
| ⟹ | 1669 | Attack on Maracaibo |
| − − −⟶ | 1670 | Attack on Panama |

Santiago de Cuba

Tortuga

HISPANIOLA

Petit Guave

Cape Tiburon

Isla Vaca Île a Vache

L'Ollonais 1667 Raid

Santo Domingo

San Juan

PUERTO RICO

LEEWARD ISLANDS

St christopher
Montserrat
Guadeloupe

Dominica

Martinique

LESSER ANTILLES

Barbados

WINDWARD ISLANDS

Tobago

TRINIDAD

1669

Aruba
Curaçao
Bonaire

Los Roques

Punta del Araya

La Margarita

La Tortuga

La Guaira

Caracas

Climaná

Delta del Orinoco

Río del la Hacha

GULF of VENEZUELA

Coro

Santa Marta

Maracaibo

Laguna de Maracaibo

Gibraltar

VENEZUELA

Cartagena

Tolú

Merida

AUDIENCIA of SANTA FÉ

| | | | | |
|---|---|---|---|---|
| 0 | 100 | 200 | 300 | |

Scale of Miles

# ACKNOWLEDGEMENTS

Any historian owes a debt to those who have gone before, and this work is no different. Among those to whom I am indebted are Kenneth Andrews, David Cordingly, Peter Earle, Cornelis Goslinga, Karen Ordahl Kupperman, Kris E. Lane, David F. Marley, Carla Rahn Philips and Irene A. Wright. Once again my thanks to John Hall of Swansea University for his support and encouragement, and to Professors John France and John Spurr of the History Department and Dr Steve McVeigh in American Studies; to Ian Glen and the library staff at Swansea University, and Carmarthen Library, the British Library and the National Maritime Museum. For the maps I am greatly indebted to my old friend and cartographer, Leslie Evans, and thanks also to Ian Drury and Bea Hemming at Weidenfeld & Nicolson and, as ever, to my agent, Andrew Lownie.

# INTRODUCTION

Before their eyes in sudden view appear
The secrets of the hoary deep, a dark
Illimitable ocean without bound,
Without dimension, where length, breadth, and height,
And time and place are lost; where eldest Night
And Chaos, ancestors of Nature, hold
Eternal anarchy, amidst the noise
Of endless wars, and by confusion stand.

John Milton, *Paradise Lost*

The decisive decade for European exploration of the world was the 1490s, when Christopher Columbus, acting on behalf of the king and queen of Spain, reached the West Indies and the Caribbean Sea became the setting for what Germán Arciniegas called a grandiose drama similar to the transition from the third day to the fourth day in the Creation myth, for space was discovered that seemed to the Europeans of the fifteenth and sixteenth centuries to be limitless. The Mediterranean suddenly shrank into a lake and their horizons widened, as the Caribbean became the focus of a New World.[1]

The term 'Caribbean' usually pertains to the sea, comparable in size to the Mediterranean, that stretches from the islands known as the Greater Antilles – Cuba, Española (Hispaniola, now Haiti and the Dominican Republic), Jamaica and Puerto Rico – south-east through the great arc of the Lesser Antilles extending from the Virgin Islands down to Trinidad. It then carries on west and north along the coasts of South and Central America to the Yucután Channel, which separates Mexico from Cuba. These islands together with the Bahamas are known as the West Indies. It is a region of tremendous cultural and political diversity, the product of several centuries of history since European colonisation and rivalry began to be played out in the region. The Caribbean islands are volcanic in origin and are, in effect, the tops of an undersea mountain range rising to more than 5,000 feet on

Mount Diablotin on Dominica. Although there is little of the plateau formation that would make agriculture easy, the soil is very fertile and the climate warm and fairly uniform all year, being tempered by the north-east trade winds (which actually vary between north-east and south-east) that blow almost continuously. For, unlike the inner sea, the Caribbean is very much a part of the Atlantic Ocean, with treacherous and dangerous currents. Heavy rainfall occurs in summer and autumn, while the hurricane season that lasts from June to November often leaves trails of destruction across the islands, inhibiting shipping which tends to stick to well-known sea lanes.

The effect of the wind and current system on navigation for sailing ships was to impede and circumscribe it. This served to restrict contact within the region, and particularly to isolate east from west, which in turn affected how the region was colonised. Ships leaving Spain would follow the Moroccan coast as far as the Canaries where they would take on water. They would then pick up the north-east trade winds to cross the Atlantic in about a month, arriving at the Windward Islands* (usually between Dominica and Guadeloupe). The return journey made use of the Gulf Stream via the treacherous Florida Straits picking up south-west trade winds to Europe, taking perhaps two or three months and possibly broken by a stop at Madeira or the Azores. The Lesser Antilles are therefore well to windward of the Greater Antilles and continental South America (the Main, known as Tierra Firme) and act almost like a row of fortresses separating the Atlantic from the Caribbean, while remaining relatively safe from attack themselves from ships having to beat into the wind from the Greater Antilles. But these tiny islands held no easily exploitable riches for the Spanish, no gold or silver, and were inhabited by warlike Carib natives. Not wanting them for settlement and not realising their importance for defence, the Spanish ignored them.[2]

Throughout the period but especially early on, Spain treated the New World as a source of income for little or no work or investment. By 1600 she had already shipped three times the total quantity of gold

* The prevailing wind is more south-easterly than north-easterly, making passage from south to north easier, hence the southern group of the Lesser Antilles from Martinique southwards are known as the Leeward Islands and the northern group from Dominica northwards are known as the Windward Islands.

and silver existing in Europe when Columbus sailed; but during the same period her trade and industry withered and unemployment became so bad that the church and state provided practically the only jobs. A vast bureaucracy controlled the ships, bullion and trade of the Indies, and the people were governed with an iron hand which guaranteed that nobody in the New World used their own initiative, but instead sought permission from Spain first, a procedure that often took more than a year. Gold from Nueva España (New Spain, modern Mexico) was gathered for shipment at Veracruz while silver from Ecuador, Chile, Bolivia and the great Potosí mines in Peru was brought up the Pacific coast (known at the time as the South Sea) then loaded on to mule trains to be carried across the Central American isthmus to the Caribbean (or North Sea) where it was transferred on to silver fleets for carriage to Spain. At first it was taken to Nombre de Dios in Panamá but later, when it was found that the River Chagres allowed half the journey to be made by boat during the rainy season, it went to Portobelo.[3] But both of these ports were shallow, and the great defensive harbour for Tierra Firme was built at Cartagena in modern Colombia, some 250 miles to the north-east.

The rendezvous for treasure ships from Nueva España and the Main was Havana in Cuba, whence they would sail for home in convoy usually exiting the Caribbean through the Florida Channel, or the Windward Passage between Cuba and Española. And as Havana and Cartagena became nodes for the bullion trade so the Spanish largely turned away from other areas, ignoring minor ports or channels to windward. Into this New World foreigners soon came, looking for trade as well as plunder, for although the pope moved quickly to defuse rivalry between Spain's and Portugal's existing claims on the world, he could not solve the rivalry between Spain and the rest of Europe, which manifested itself from the early sixteenth century when Spain – which had only just completed the expulsion of the Moors from her own territory – failed to incorporate this vast and heterogeneous new region into the realm. This was hardly surprising, since so much of Spain's energy had been expended in the long wars against the Moors, action that would continue into the new century.

To the Spanish all foreign interlopers were always simply *piratos* (pirates) or *corsarios luteranos* (Lutheran corsairs). The irony is that her own conquest of the Americas was a huge act of piracy by modern definition – an act of robbery on or by descent from the sea. What is attempted here is to tell the story of a particular group of pirates, or rather privateers – that is to say, 'private men-of-war', meaning both ships carrying commissions or letters of marque from a legitimate government and the men that sailed in them. By the middle of the seventeenth century these privateer–pirates had become known to the English by the name 'buccaneers'. (The French term was *flibustiers*, derived in turn from the English 'freebooter', meaning a soldier who served for booty rather than regular pay; the Dutch term was *vrijbuiters*, or *zeerovers* – sea rovers.) For as Kris E. Lane has noted, no other group of pirates in history 'has been more celebrated, hated, romanticized, demonized, or otherwise misrepresented than the late-seventeenth-century buccaneers'.[4] But the definition of piracy has always been prone to different national historical perspectives and, very often, bias. And just as the English terms 'buccaneer' and 'pirate' have become interchangeable since the seventeenth century, so the difference between a privateer and a pirate has always been opaque, and buccaneers were motivated by what has always most interested pirates down the centuries – plunder.

Even contemporaries understood that the buccaneers were a phenomenon of greater significance, and by the time buccaneering reached a conclusion in 1697 these hardy adventurers had helped to set three more European nations – English, French and Dutch – on the road to empire, and to subsequent worldwide rivalry. This process grew from an early addiction to plunder, originating in the wars of religion of the sixteenth century, in the Dutch struggle for independence from Spanish rule and, for Elizabethan England, in the long war with Spain (1585–1603). All this took place against a backdrop of a steady decline in Spanish fortunes, something which has not just been recognised by historians after the event, but which formed the context in which policy-makers operated at the time.[5] By the time the brethren of the coast, as the buccaneers called themselves, rose to prominence in the middle of the seventeenth century, Spain had fallen a long way. And for some forty years they fought a sporadic private war with her, maintaining tenuous alliances with non-Spanish Caribbean colonies – symbiotic arrangements that provided them with a place to dispose of plunder and obtain supplies, while the colonists gained protection from the Spanish.

The early part of the seventeenth century was a chaotic period in Europe: the northern Netherlands were asserting their independence from Spain, and entering what would become known as the Golden Age; France was embroiled in religious wars which were followed by the rise of King Louis XIV, the Sun King; and the British Isles were in turmoil, culminating in the Cromwellian dictatorship and the Restoration. But it was England's achievements – for among the British nations the Welsh were subsumed into England, the Scots excluded, and the Irish suppressed and exploited – that were most significant in the Caribbean during the latter half of the seventeenth century. Eric Williams, the historian who later became prime minister of Trinidad and Tobago, described the West Indian islands as the 'hub of Empire'.[6] Indeed, by the end of the seventeenth century England's West Indian possessions were regarded by such contemporaries as Charles Davenant, Josiah Child and Dalby Thomas as her most profitable overseas investments.

By Adam Smith's time at the end of the eighteenth century, sugar dominated the Caribbean economy; sugar plantations were an economic success, even if a dismal social failure, and the British empire was firmly established. But Adam Smith got it wrong: the prosperity of Britain's Caribbean possessions was not due to 'the great riches of England of which a part had overflowed'.[7] Initially it was down to Spanish silver, stolen or traded for by foreigners in defiance of what was then still the greatest empire in the world. Only later would the islands generate further wealth, wrung from the sweat and blood of Africans to help fuel the industrial revolution that would propel Britain towards victory in the Napoleonic Wars, a conflict in which French rivalry in the Caribbean was effectively ended, and which in turn enabled Britain to expand her empire across the globe ultimately to cover a quarter of its land surface.

The rise of the buccaneers of the Caribbean, therefore, was an essential part of the rise of Britain, and it coincided with the decline of Spain, first as the dominant player in European and Mediterranean politics and later as an economic superpower, which weakened her ability to defend her American colonies and left them vulnerable to buccaneer depredations. John Lynch argues that Spain lost her colonial wealth due not so much to foreign encroachment as to Spanish America appropriating it for herself; that between 1600 and 1810 Spanish America in effect preserved her own territory and defended imperial communications and was the guardian of empire, so this is also the story of the recession of Spain within the Hispanic world rather than the recession of that world.[8] Certainly England's most fruitful periods of colonisation (1624–30 and 1655–60) both came during wars with Spain, while at other times the lack of central control over the colonies allowed English enterprise in the Caribbean to flourish, and the local mode of warfare was just another form of this. Because the buccaneers were something more than mere raiders, and the term should be understood in that context, their operations were designed not to profit by Spanish decline but to exploit opportunities whenever they arose.[9] They always maintained, or tried to maintain at any rate, a thin veneer of legitimacy which supposedly raised their activities above mere piracy. And two factors separate the buccaneers from other privateers through history: first was their tendency to band together and work towards common objectives, with a strong democratic element in both their command and their reward structures; second was their propensity for amphibious operations – they were always as much concerned with raiding onshore as with taking prizes at sea, and when it suited them they also indulged in hunting and cutting dye woods, or smuggling and other forms of illicit trade with Spanish settlements. For trade was the dominant political theme of the period and was probably a more important factor than any other in generating conflict. Spanish silver would prove to be, in effect, the gunpowder on which worldwide trade exploded like a Roman candle.

# 1

## A NEW WORLD

Drake he's in his hammock an' a thousand mile away,
 (Capten, art tha sleepin' there below?)
Slung atween the round shot in Nombre Dios Bay,
 An' dreamin' arl the time o' Plymouth Hoe.
Yarnder lumes the island, yarnder lie the ships,
 Wi' sailor lads a-dancin' heel-an'-toe,
An' the shore-lights flashin', an' the night-tide dashin'
 He sees et arl so plainly as he saw et long ago.

Sir Henry Newbolt, Drake's Drum

The world changed for ever when Christopher Columbus stepped ashore in the Bahamas on 12 October 1492, after a seventy-day voyage across the Atlantic. Subsequently he sailed south to Cuba and east before returning to Spain to report his discoveries. A second voyage took him to Dominica and along the West Indian island chain to Española and Jamaica where he landed on 5 May 1494 in St Ann's Bay, and it was these mountainous islands that would become the principal bases for the buccaneers. Meanwhile in May 1493 Pope Alexander VI hurried to solve the problem of Spanish–Portuguese rivalry by dividing the world in two. He attempted this at first with his *Inter caetera* bull separating their claim 300 miles west of the Cape Verde islands, and then with the Treaty of Tordesillas of 7 June 1494, which established the 'lines of amity' at approximately 45° west.[1]

Spain now claimed the New World entirely and exclusively, and with papal blessing regarded it as God's gift to exploit for the greater glory of the Catholic church, as much as for the temporal glory of the Crown of Castile. However, not only did this inexactly defined meridian unintentionally put Brazil in the Portuguese section, it encouraged both nations to believe that they had religious authority to all land without a settled Christian government, and that they could monopolise trade with these territories.[2] And just as these claims were never universally accepted by the rest of Europe, so the religious upheaval of the Reformation during the following century would undermine them completely. Meanwhile, still searching for a sea passage to India and the spice islands of the east, Columbus travelled along the Venezuelan coast and into the Gulf of Darién on his third and fourth voyages. In 1497 John Cabot discovered North America, and in 1498 Vasco da Gama sailed around the Cape of Good Hope. Although Columbus had failed in his stated mission of finding a route to the east, the Spanish authorities were not slow to act upon his achievements; in 1502 a permanent settlement was established on Española and another colony was founded at Bulboa on the American mainland near Panamá. Española was the first, and for sixteen years the only, Spanish colony – the heart of the Spanish empire – and it became the key to its history.

For the first two decades of Spanish rule the colony was run by a commercial company controlled by Columbus and the crown as joint partners, but by 1510 gold production had reached a peak. Thereafter the economy declined, and many Spaniards departed looking for other sources of gold, and for Indians to exploit. The crown had established the Casa de Contratación at Sevilla in 1503 to regulate trade with the New World, thereby investing Sevilla with a monopoly in that trade which, during the sixteenth century at least, would remain largely effective.[3] Since Sevilla lies sixty miles up the River Guadalquivir this ignored the enormous and excellent anchorage at Cádiz, but it also reserved the riches of the Americas for Spain. Eventually the loss of numerous ships on the bar at Sanlúcar de Borromeo at the river mouth saw the regulations modified, but American trade remained managed by the crown and merchants of Sevilla exclusively for their joint benefit and not for that of the colonies. Apart from one interruption in the 1550s the city enjoyed a huge increase of shipping that continued until the second decade of the seventeenth century. In America the enterprise was run on authoritarian lines as towns sprang up to exploit the accessible gold, but it also created the conditions for massive contraband trade and this would increasingly undermine the business.[4] But it was the expedition which followed that would really transform the New World and begin to shape it to a European vision, bent to the will of a group of military adventurers who either lacked or ignored specific instructions. Their sovereign was immensely puzzled by the process, and actually suspected some of them of planning to secede and set up independent states; he was mollified only by the immense wealth in gold and silver they sent back to Spain.

In 1519 a small force of 600 soldiers under the command of Hernán Cortés landed near the modern town of Veracruz in Mexico. Armed mainly with swords, pikes and crossbows, a few small guns and thirteen muskets, the expedition was accompanied by sixteen horses. It marched inland through steamy coastal jungle and up mountain passes to the high plateau of central Mexico, with Cortés using a mixture of diplomacy and force to obtain supplies from the villages they encountered. He learned that the country was ruled by the Aztecs, a warlike people who extracted tribute in the form of food and forced labour from the villagers. The Aztec civilisation was highly developed with advanced agriculture, hieroglyph writing and stunning architecture, particularly the temples, where human sacrifices were carried out that horrified the invaders. But the Aztecs did not possess the wheel, nor did they use horses or oxen, and the discovery that the country was rich in gold and silver which Aztec craftsmen worked into beautiful jewellery and ornaments was compelling to Cortés and his men, and within two years they had conquered it. Cortés besieged and took the Aztec capital, Tenochitlan, built on islands around the shores of a lake, destroyed it and began to build what would become Mexico City. The Aztec king, Montezuma, was stoned to death by his own people, but, for the subjects of what was now Nueva España, tribute to the Aztecs was simply replaced with tribute to the kings of Spain, as ever increasing quantities of gold and silver were shipped home.[5]

The conquistadores thus gave their lord, generally referred to as the Holy Roman Emperor Carlos V (Charles V to the English), possessions of a new sort, since his existing European territories already constituted an empire. But overseas territories added a new complexity to a variegated political entity held together only by the allegiance of his subjects rather than by a common language or institutions. The European world was in turmoil and a new religion was springing up, leading to war that would spill across the Atlantic as Spain's European rivals began to seek a share of the glorious wealth of the Americas. If licensed private warfare in the form of buccaneering came to fruition during the Stuart and Commonwealth periods, its origins can be traced back to the time of the Tudors. By 1522 French privateers were causing so much damage to the Spanish Atlantic trade that the crown imposed a tax – the *avería* – to pay for its defence.[6] But such taxes, and the imposition of responsibility for defence on to the victims of piracy, did little to ease the problem and sowed the seed of discontent.

In England after 1525 the attitude of England's King Henry VIII to naval matters began to change, not out of some newfound love of sea power, but driven by the exigencies of his foreign policies. During the early part of his reign he employed ships only in an auxiliary capacity, but the failure of various adventures increasingly forced him to rely upon them as a fundamental pillar in defence of what remained a weak and unstable country, a strategy that Scotland had already adopted. Foremost among the factors driving this change was the succession question. Desperate to secure an heir, Henry began considering divorce from Catherine of Aragon. But it seemed unlikely that Pope Clement VII would grant this; he was virtually a prisoner to Carlos V, who was not prepared to sacrifice his aunt Catherine, especially as this might free Henry to marry a French princess. Soon afterwards Henry became infatuated with Anne Boleyn, and the stage was set for the breach with Rome which was to have such far-ranging consequences.

On 25 November 1527 came the first recorded breach of *Inter caetera* when an English ship, *Mary Guilford*, appeared off Española's capital Santo Domingo looking for water and provisions. She had been, apparently, part of an exploratory expedition towards Newfoundland in search of a passage to the Far East, although Henry was also curious about the source of Spain's new wealth, having recently changed sides in the great struggle between the Habsburgs of Spain and the Valois of France. Carlos V was under no illusions about the significance of this impudent intrusion into Spanish territory, flouting as it did both his and papal authority, and within a year he had received reports that a French ship had raided San Germán on the western end of Puerto Rico, a true portent of things to come.[7]

Henry's turbulent love life brought him two daughters, a third wife in Jane Seymour, and at last, in 1537, a male heir. That year French pirates were once more harrying Spanish shipping and settlements in the Caribbean, including Havana in Cuba, Santo Domingo and the growing ports of Cartagena and Nombre de Dios.[8] By now Henry had broken with Rome and dissolved the monasteries, gaining a considerable cash windfall, but at the cost of increasing isolation from the continent. And although he lived and died a Catholic in all but name, he had effectively prepared the country for more virulent forms of Protestantism and undermined the legitimacy of his successors.[9] Scotland remained both Catholic and allied to France, a potential source of instability in the north, and when France and the Holy Roman Empire went back to war in 1542, Henry was determined to strike at the heart of the Franco-Scottish alliance. He agreed to participate with Carlos V in a combined invasion of France, and in December 1544 he issued a proclamation allowing unrestricted warfare at sea. This, however, led to unintended consequences; Spanish ships sailing between Spain and Spanish Flanders found themselves prey to English pirates, often backed by courtiers and others close to Henry, and the Spanish retaliated in kind. English piracy, not for the first time, was causing Spain serious problems.[10] And not only did English merchants begin heartily to dislike Spanish officials, but the pirates themselves began to cast greedy eyes on Spain's overseas empire and the trade that it created. But they were not the first to do so.

French Huguenots (Protestants) had been raiding the West Indies since the 1520s and in 1537 Jean d'Ango of Dieppe took nine ships from a Spanish treasure convoy; in 1543 French pirates captured the port of Cartagena. When war officially resumed between France and Spain in 1552 it made the Caribbean a significant theatre of international war for the first time, and by the end of this round of hostilities the French had taken Santiago de Cuba (1553) and Havana (1555), as well as Cartagena again in 1559.[11] In that latter year France and Spain concluded the Treaty of Cateau-Cambrésis with a clause which stated that fighting west of the Azores or south of the Tropic of Cancer would not give cause for war in Europe, a provision crisply rendered as 'no peace beyond the line'. This recognised both that the Spanish would not admit that anybody was entitled to challenge papal authority on the matter, and that nobody else would take it seriously.[12] Meanwhile Henry died in 1547 and there followed a period of upheaval and setback while England was effectively ruled by Edward Seymour, Duke of

Somerset, acting as lord protector and regent to the young King Edward VI. But Somerset's foreign policy was as disastrous as Henry's had been; when England withdrew from the war in 1550 the country was practically bankrupt, utterly isolated, exhausted and threatened with economic and political crisis.[13] And in 1553, before Edward had the chance to show he was not the reincarnation of Henry V, that the Hundred Years War really was over, he died, aged just fifteen.

The succession of Henry's staunchly Catholic elder daughter Mary added religious turmoil to the mixture. Her ill-fated marriage to Felipe (Philip), Carlos V's widowed son and, soon afterwards, King Felipe II of Spain, proved a disaster both personally and for the nation. Her death in November 1558 was greeted with relief, and the succession of her sister Elizabeth with popular approval. But Elizabeth's grasp on power was, and would remain, precarious: England's only sure defence was the sea and her ships; only they could hold France and Spain at arm's length, and for every pirate bent on plunder or explorer seeking adventure, there were a thousand Englishmen reliant on the cloth trade and determined on peace with Spain.[14] 'Bend your force, credit and device to maintain and increase your navy by all the means you can possible,' the secretary of state was advised in 1560, 'for in this time, considering all circumstances, it is the flower of England's garland . . . and your best and best cheap defence and most redoubted of your enemies and doubtful friends.'[15]

An efficient navy and good luck allowed Elizabeth to neutralise the greatest threat to her position; in December 1560 King François II of France died and was replaced by the ten-year-old Charles IX, severing the dynastic connection between France and Scotland.[16] By the following year the Spanish had regularised the system of bullion convoys that had first been first organised in 1526 to bring American treasure safely back home. At first there had usually been one convoy per year, but from 1555 the idea evolved for two fleets, one for Nueva España and one for Tierra Firme due to leave every year in April and August respectively, under compulsory escort by warships of the *armada de la guardia* paid for out of the *avería*. Although a schedule was established for such convoys, in reality the New Spain fleet (*flota*) generally left Cádiz in July reaching Nueva España in September, and the Tierra Firme fleet (later called the *galeones*) would depart some time between

March and May and, having reached Cartagena in about two months, then take another two months to move along the coast to Nombre de Dios where it would spend the winter. During the sixteenth century the fleets generally returned separately, although both would try to make it through the Florida Channel by the end of August.[17] From the sixteenth century until well into the eighteenth, it was a dream of both English and French to capture the phenomenal wealth of a treasure fleet, and it would become a dominant theme in English naval strategy, though neither ever succeeded in achieving it. If anything, the bold acts of corsairs and privateers showed the effectiveness of the Spanish colonial system in the sixteenth century, requiring more and more daring moves to penetrate its defence.[18]

In Europe, with France embroiled in civil war until 1564 and Elizabeth supporting the Huguenot faction, naval operations were marked by the first extensive issuing of letters of reprisal – providing a thin veneer of legal cover to English and French pirates against merchant shipping of all countries. So the established connections between Protestantism and piracy grew, reinforced by Elizabeth's proclamation of 1563 permitting general privateering.[19] But in Elizabethan terms the word 'privateering' is not strictly appropriate. It was only coined in the following century to describe a legal status just then emerging from obscurity. In sixteenth-century England, there were only two ways by which the law allowed private vessels to capture other ships for profit. First was by general proclamation against a named enemy in wartime, to which in principle captures were limited, although there was no means of enforcing these terms. And given that Elizabethan local government was in the hands of unpaid nobility and gentry, it was extremely difficult for the crown to prevent a breach of the law should these notables choose to effect one; the elder Sir Walter Raleigh, vice-admiral of Devon, was an active pirate, and Sir Edward Horsey, captain of the Isle of Wight, was a patron to pirates of all nations, and made the island a base for Channel pirates.[20]

The second way derived from England's medieval marcher law by which a merchant, traveller or shipowner who had been robbed in the territory of or by subjects of a foreign prince in peacetime, but was unable to obtain redress through the courts of that country, could be authorised by a court (the court of admiralty in the case of a shipowner) to recoup his losses up to a specified sum by seizing the property of subjects of that country. For this purpose he was issued with a letter of reprisal or *lettre de marque*.[21] This was, however, very different from the 'letter of marque' issued from the seventeenth century onwards by an admiralty court in time of war to provide private vessels with legal safeguard to cruise against enemy shipping, and subsequently to sell the prizes once they had been condemned as enemy property by the court. This is the classic definition of privateering as practised in wartime, while the letter of reprisal was issued only in time of peace. But sixteenth-century 'peace' embraced numerous undeclared wars, civil wars and rebellions which gave grasping and unscrupulous author-ities the excuse to issue letters indiscriminately, and the English lords admiral were notoriously willing to permit activities from which they derived a 10 per cent cut.[22] In Scotland letters of reprisal were inheritable property that could remain in force for generations; Captain Patrick Blackadder was still taking Portuguese prizes in 1561 thanks to a letter granted in 1476.[23]

Although England and Spain were at peace during the 1570s, con-tinuous encroachments by English pirates and adventurers – John Hawkins and his family notable among them from the late 1560s – progressively undermined good relations, a situation complicated by Elizabeth's ambiguous involvement with these exponents of private enterprise.[24] For Hawkins certainly acted with at least the tacit approval of his sovereign, and trade was always the prime interest of this most respectable of pirates. Before Hawkins, English ships had ventured into the Caribbean at least twice, but these were isolated incidents of little significance.[25] Spain's American colonies had been importing slaves since the beginning of the century, with Española being the main market after the first three decades of Spanish rule gutted not only the island's accessible gold, but its native population as well. The gentle Arawak people Columbus found there had numbered at least a million, but by 1520 they were almost extinct and settlers increasingly looked to slave-grown sugar for their prosperity.[26] Smuggling was soon well established as the Spanish authorities tried to restrict trade to Sevilla via the enforced monopoly with heavy taxes on exports. But this was counter-productive as it forced up prices, and the Spanish could never hope to exclude all foreign interlopers, nor prevent their own citizens

dealing in cheaper contraband, most of which arrived in caravels*
from the Canary Islands where Spanish merchants traded freely with
Portuguese, Italian, Flemish, French and English merchants.[27]

Hawkins' first expedition in 1562 saw him sail to Africa to buy slaves
which he took to the Caribbean and there made a tidy profit. When
he repeated the journey in 1564 he found the reception much less
welcoming as the officers who had traded with him had been punished,
and in 1568 he met a visiting Spanish *flota* at San Juan de Ulúa and was
lucky to escape alive. He decided it was time to quit this dangerous
business, although he felt he deserved recognition for trying to open a
new line of enterprise, and subsequently put a slave on his coat of
arms. However, a cousin of his who also survived the fighting at San
Juan was the uncompromisingly Protestant Francis Drake, who would
choose a much more aggressive response to the situation in poorly
defended America.[28] For although the savage thoroughness with which
Spain extirpated the French Huguenot settlements in Florida showed
her determination when roused, she concentrated her efforts in Europe
where the forces of Protestantism were rising, and did little to protect
America where neither crown revenues nor sovereignty were seriously
threatened by bit-part raiders.[29]

The Netherlands at this time formed a complex congeries of states
and towns loosely federated in seventeen provinces under the sovereignty of Carlos V. Although various strains of Protestantism had
begun to make an appearance the majority of the population remained
Catholic. Discontent had nevertheless been growing for some time
in the Low Countries as Carlos V's religious intolerance dismayed
Flemings, Hollanders and Zeelanders unable to understand such sen-
timents in a fellow Netherlander. And by separating the seventeen
provinces from their many ties in Germany Carlos made a serious
blunder; in entrusting them to his son, Felipe II of Spain, he made
another, for given his political and religious aims this was the last man
on earth suitable to rule the Dutch. The personal union with Spain
was, according to one historian, 'an unmixed evil'.[30] By now the Dutch

---

* Caravels were small two- or three-masted lateen-rigged vessels that were fast and handy for
fishing or fighting. As they progressively grew in size they carried a mixture of square and
lateen rigging. (See Clinton R. Edwards, 'Design and Construction of Fifteenth Century
Iberian Vessels: A Review', *Mariner's Mirror*, 78 (1992), 419–32.)

were developing into a significant power as stripped-down fat-hulled herring buses and *vlieboots* (fly-boats) became ubiquitous, dominating the North Sea, Baltic and Iberian trade with Dutch freight rates among the lowest around. These ships were manned by skeleton crews on minimal rations and wages, as Dutch thrift combined with Calvinism encouraged reinvestment of savings and profits over conspicuous consumption among the burgher–oligarchs, producing a distinctive maritime culture.[31]

When Willem of Orange raised the first makeshift forces of rebellion to rid the country of Spanish rule and religious persecution in 1568, it was easily defeated by the Duque de Alva. But what appeared to be a little local difficulty for the Habsburgs was, in fact, the beginning of what would become known as the Eighty Years War, or the Dutch Revolt, which would transform this unexceptional corner of northwest Europe into a nation that would rival the Spanish in the Caribbean, and make Amsterdam the most important commercial centre in the world.[32] And it would fall to a fleet of maritime vagabonds, the so-called Sea Beggars, to lead the liberation after they fled the terror unleashed on heretics by Alva. Known as *pechelinguas* to the Spanish, a word supposedly derived from the important port of Vlissingen (Flushing), the Sea Beggar fleet quickly grew, making a North Sea that already swarmed with English and French pirates even more unsafe as Willem issued *kaperbrieven* – letters of marque.[33]

Privateering would provide both a grounding in seamanship and necessary funds for war, but Alva did not understand the importance of the war at sea, and neglected the defence of the coastal towns; the success of the Beggars in turn fed the discontent necessary for the rebellion to succeed. Spanish persecution drove the richest merchants and the ablest artisans northwards, and when Felipe exulted in the capture of Antwerp in 1585, he did not know that within two years 20,000 people would emigrate, creating a loss of money and intellect from which the port city would take two centuries to recover. By 1590 one-third of Antwerp's houses were for sale as international business relocated northwards or went bankrupt. By 1648 the Bourse, once a babel of noise, with every tongue of Europe to be heard there, was silent, transformed into a library.[34]

Meanwhile, although the Portuguese controlled the coast of Brazil and Spanish rule was firmly established throughout the Caribbean basin and the Central American Main, settlements remained small and scattered along the seaboard, with a only few larger towns inland. Thus, apart from a few hides and dyes, and the gold and silver it yielded, the Spanish empire was poor and unproductive. By the 1570s the production of gold was already in decline, but silver was increasing, especially from the great Potosí mine of the Andes. The silver was carried north along the Pacific coast to the city of Panamá, then by mule-train through the jungles of the isthmus to Nombre de Dios for collection by a convoy to carry it back to Spain. Between 1570 and 1577 there were at least thirteen English expeditions to the Caribbean as the English openly adopted the search for plunder, at first joining and then outstripping the French; all this was undertaken without licence, authority or letters of reprisal and was, therefore, a campaign of outright piracy.[35] The raiders were very keen to cut the Spanish silver route at what appeared to be its most vulnerable point – the crossing of the Panamanian Isthmus at Nombre de Dios.

In 1571 this became Drake's target, although he attacked too late in the year when the silver had departed, and his actual assault miscarried. Undaunted, he made contact with escaped slaves – *cimarrones* – and mounted a successful raid on a mule train in February 1573, earning fame and riches. Although the quantity of silver he secured amounted to no more than 5 per cent of the annual shipment, the moral effect of this success was to have enormous repercussions in both Spain and England.[36] Other raiders followed unsuccessfully in Drake's footsteps, and the Spanish suppressed the *cimarrones*. But in 1578 Drake passed through the Straits of Magellan into the Pacific to raid Peru and Ecuador, then crossed the Pacific and returned to Plymouth in 1580. He brought with him booty worth perhaps £600,000 on which the investors in the expedition, including the secretary of state Sir Francis Walsingham, the earls of Leicester and Lincoln and other aggressive Protestant courtiers, not to mention Her Majesty the Queen, made a 4,700 per cent return. It was therefore hardly surprising that Elizabeth knighted the 'master thief of the unknown world' on his own deck, since her share enabled her to pay off her entire foreign debt and still leave £42,000 to invest in the new Levant Company.[37]

In the twenty-first century it is difficult to imagine the truly astonishing nature of this feat; only Magellan's ship had ever achieved it before, and Magellan had not survived to tell the tale. If anyone was likely to repeat such a voyage it would surely be another Portuguese, a Spaniard or perhaps a Frenchman, the recognised masters of oceanic navigation. The Scots had more experience than the English of open-ocean voyaging, having developed close links with Dieppe and Le Havre where a brilliant school of Huguenot navigators, adventurers and pirates flourished. The Scots were involved in raiding the Caribbean by 1547 at the latest, and in 1567 accompanied a French raid on Burburata in Venezuela.[38] The first English ship to cross the equator had done so only in 1555, and no Englishman was capable of navigating unaided to the Caribbean when Elizabeth ascended the throne in 1558, with only one capable of it ten years later. Drake's achievement, barely a decade further on, excited the unrestrained admiration of the greatest navigators of the day. But, more important, it created a political firestorm; suddenly the entire country was inflamed 'with a desire to adventure unto the seas'.[39] And the extreme vulnerability of the Spanish empire had been laid bare, just as the threat of Spanish power was growing and political developments on the continent were increasingly threatening England.

During the 1580s the pressure on England mounted steadily. France, the natural counterweight to Spain, was now in religious and political turmoil; the Dutch rebellion was being gradually reduced by Alexander Farnese, Duke of Parma (although the seven northern United Provinces declared their total independence in 1581, and fought on); Ireland was in revolt; and the death of the last king of Portugal saw Felipe II occupy that country, adding to Spain's wealth. Felipe's annual revenue was some ten times that of Elizabeth, and, convinced – almost certainly wrongly – that Felipe had committed himself to an attack on England, in 1584 the queen pledged aid to the Dutch rebels and accepted a plan from John Hawkins to raid the Caribbean. Once more financed by private investors, but also carrying Elizabeth's commission, Drake seized Santo Domingo on Española, the oldest Spanish city in the New World, on the last day of 1585. He sailed a month later to capture Cartagena, and on 4 April came within hours of intercepting a *flota* carrying £700,000 bound for Spain, creating a profound shock among the Spanish. A wretched pirate from an insignificant northern island had demonstrated Spain's real vulnerability, and such impudence would have to be punished. Far from deterring war by bold action, Elizabeth had provoked it.[40]

The following year Drake was once more at sea, this time leading an expedition to lurk off Cape St Vincent in Southern Portugal, long notorious for pirates, and known to Spanish sailors as the 'cape of surprises'. Although he achieved little by way of material damage, admitting that he had done no more than 'singe the King of Spain's beard', the humiliation was too much for that prince to bear. Protesting that 'with this corsair at sea in such strength, we cannot protect any island or coast, nor predict where he may attack', Felipe resolved that the only way to eradicate this threat was to root it out at source.[41] But this was a war that neither side wanted: Elizabeth sought only a compromise that would keep Spanish armies out of the Low Countries and preserve her throne; for Felipe, England was a natural ally he would never have attacked unless he believed his own interests to be under mortal threat. However strongly he felt about the Catholic faith, he had, until now, resisted all blandishments by the Pope or Catholic exiles to act.[42] As the two countries lacked any land boundary at home or overseas it would be a naval war, though neither side had any experience of such an undertaking. The story of the Armada and its subsequent destruction has become one of the iconic tales of English history, and while the cause of its failure has been shrouded in myths ever since, it was unquestionably a catastrophe for Spain that both emboldened the English to make fresh attacks and put fresh heart into Spain's enemies elsewhere. If there is a moment when the tide of Spanish expansion began to turn, then 1588 is that moment.[43]

Flush with the euphoria of victory, the English continued the war with a series of grand expeditions, often aimed at capturing a treasure fleet, but without success. Felipe now took steps to remedy his lack of sea power, building many ships in the ten years following the Armada and creating a nascent admiralty board, or Junta de Armadas, in 1594.[44] In 1595 Drake proposed another major expedition to the Caribbean, comprising twenty-seven ships, six of which were provided by the queen, who also stumped up two-thirds of the necessary money, some £33,000. This force raided the Río de la Hacha and Santa María in Venezuela and took Nombre de Dios, but the troops were beaten back by the Spanish as they attempted to cross the isthmus, and as the fleet approached Portobelo Drake succumbed to dysentery, dying on 28 January 1596. Although it was later intercepted by a Spanish fleet, the expedition managed to return home with little damage. But the failure of this mission showed that the West Indies were effectively out of range of a large-scale Elizabethan expeditionary force.[45] However, it did help spur the Spanish crown's first attempt at building an *armada de barlovento* or Windward Squadron to defend the Caribbean, although this came to nothing when the initial shipbuilding programme exceeded its budget.[46]

Far more significant was the successful raid on Cádiz by a combined Anglo-Dutch force under Lord Howard of Effingham in June 1596. This was a monumental catastrophe for Spain, a humiliation of unprecedented magnitude, and Felipe's response was to order a retaliatory assault on England.[47] A second Armada of 126 ships was assembled in remarkably short order, but on 28 October it was caught on a lee shore off Galicia; thirty large ships were lost and the remainder were driven into port. The following year another attempt was made by the Spanish, who this time assembled 136 ships carrying 9,000 troops. It approached to within thirty miles of the Lizard before being struck by another powerful storm on 12 October 1597, which sank twenty-eight of the vessels. Meanwhile news of this expedition took the English court completely by surprise.[48] But the significance of these major ventures must be seen in the context of the continuous erosion of Spain's position by a host of lesser men, for, as James Williamson noted, British maritime achievement rested 'not only upon the great names which History records in her most lurid passages, but also upon the accumulated exploits of the infinite number of small men, but for whom the Drakes and the Hawkinses, the masters of the sea, would never have been'.[49]

Fortunately for Elizabeth and England, Felipe was dying and Spain's finances were on the verge of collapse. The war drew to a close through exhaustion on both sides, with distractions taking place elsewhere, such as the rebellion in Ireland of Hugh O'Neill, Earl of Tyrone. In 1598 the crown passed to Felipe III, a man of pacifist leanings who longed to end the seemingly interminable wars. With the succession in 1603 of the pious and pacific King James VI of Scotland as King James

I of England, the 'wisest fool in Christendom' was wise enough to seek peace, and a conference was soon convened headed by Lord Howard on the English side. Supported by Sir Robert Cecil, Howard proposed that England be allowed to trade freely with the Indies and to set up bases in the Caribbean to that end, although he knew that Spain would never accept this; eventually the English moderated their demands as James made plain his desire to avoid foreign conflicts. For her part Spain wanted peace with England in order to isolate the Netherlands and concentrate on subduing the rebels of the United Provinces, so Felipe III was prepared to make concessions. When the Peace of London was signed in 1604 the Spanish agreed that England could trade anywhere except America, and secured a commitment from James that he would punish by death any of his subjects who sailed to the Indies.[50]

Throughout the Spanish war the vast majority of privateering effort had been concentrated in European waters, against shipping bringing the valuable Baltic commodities – grain, timber, copper and naval stores – on which Spain depended. Although attacks on Hanseatic, Dutch, Scottish, Polish, Swedish and other neutral ships created diplomatic difficulties, and also damaged English trade, they took a heavy and unremitting toll on Spain's merchant fleet, particularly affecting the Basque and Cantabrian ports on which that fleet was based. Spain had not recovered her strength of the 1570s even 300 years later, and this would clearly affect her ability to support her American empire in the seventeenth century.[51] Although only a small number of privateers operated in the Caribbean, they could be supported over a season and, of more than 150 voyages during the course of the war, most sailed individually or in small groups, of rarely more than four. Between 1585 and 1603 there are known to have been at least seventy-four ventures sent to the Caribbean, comprising a total of 183 ships. Unable to protect her own trade or damage the enemy's, Spain could do nothing to prevent her colonies on the eastern Main swiftly becoming dependent on foreign trade. The cumulative effect on Spanish trade and settlements away from the major cities was literally devastating; by the war's end much of the Spanish Caribbean was depopulated and in a state of ruin, leaving local trade largely in English, Dutch and French hands.[52] Plunder and trade were never separate activities, and by 1600

Española's trade was dominated by English and Dutch smugglers.[53]

The most significant development from the 1590s onwards was the rise in Dutch maritime trade that amazed contemporaries and still baffles posterity. 'The prodigious increase in the Netherlands in their domestic and foreign trade, riches and multitude of shipping', wrote Sir Josiah Child in 1669, 'is the envy of the present and may be the wonder of future generations.'[54] Much to the consternation of Spanish officials who were trying to fortify major ports and protect bullion fleets against Elizabethan privateers, less easily controlled items such as hides, sugar, ginger and canafistula (a purgative drug similar to senna) were being shipped to the Netherlands from the Caribbean, and ever more seizures were being made in the eastern Atlantic as well. Between 1592 and 1596 seven Dutch contraband ships were said to have stopped off at the island of La Margarita off the coast of Venezuela.[55] By this time the smugglers were working through *tangomangos*, or middlemen, usually individuals working alone who in return for large commissions took orders and transmitted them to the smugglers, and who when caught simply paid their fines and carried on, ignoring the authorities. On Española, for example, controls had been imposed on salt so that only sufficient quantities to produce a specific amount of leather were supplied, and the sale of leather was subsequently controlled; but beyond the control of the capital the whole island collaborated in the export of leather – the entire population was involved.[56]

However, privateering was to have another, equally profound effect: it transformed the English merchant fleet and the merchant class that owned it. If, before the war, England's mercantile prosperity was intimately bound to the cloth trade by means of Antwerp, now her fleet had both the skills and the ships to undertake long-distance trade and a newfound desire to use them. When Felipe II married Mary in 1558 he sent Stephen Borough to study at the navigation school of the Casa de Contración in Sevilla, and Borough returned with the standard Spanish textbook, Martin Cortés' *Arte de navegar* which was immediately translated. The competence of English navigators improved noticeably from then on, spurred by piracy and privateering. From the 1590s when English privateers began to appear in great numbers in the Mediterranean, they made little attempt to distinguish between enemies like

Spain and neutrals like Venice, and soon earned England a reputation as nothing less than a pirate nation.[57]

The war produced such a large class of skilled navigators that English scholars were now making rapid original advances in mathematics and navigation, so that in the course of a generation they passed from being pupils of the Spanish to being teachers of the Dutch, although navigation was still a very inexact science.[58] England might remain, according to the Earl of Essex, 'little in territory, not extraordinarily rich and defended only by itself', but twenty years of war had radically transformed not merely her outlook, but her very maritime fabric.[59] At the same time the men of Dieppe, Le Havre, Cherbourg, Saint-Malo, Brest and La Rochelle descended in increasing numbers on 'Pérou', to barter Normandy linens (known as *rouens* in French, or *ruanes* in Spanish) for hides from Española.[60] And if the Spanish and Portuguese regarded interloping, smuggling and piracy in the Americas as all one and the same thing, it was hardly surprising that foreigners chose not to distinguish them. Even if the only intention was trade, foreign ships must needs be armed and ready to fight if there truly was 'no peace beyond the line'. Spain simply could not expect to keep the New World or the Caribbean to herself.

# 2

## TOBACCO AND SALT

What vertues in the *noble weed* do rest,
What *Constitutions* it agrees with best,
And what *diseases* it will cure, is now
Thy Task, my *Muse*, Rub my contracted brow,
And waken all the heat that's in my Brain,
To adde a *Genius* to another strain.
*Tabaco, King of Plants* I well may call;
Others have *single* virtues, this hath all.

Raphaël Thorius, *Hymnus Tabaci* (Hymn to Tobacco)

During the sixteenth century Spanish American trade was so important that 'all of European life and the life of the entire world ... could be said to have depended' on it.[1] But the exploitation of immense riches in precious metals would eventually prove a curse in disguise for Spain; the concentration on production from the mines focused crown attention to such an extent that the industry which alone could keep and absorb such wealth was neglected. War with the Netherlands drained the resources of Castile and her empire as her 'bullionist' commercial system, designed to maintain her monopoly, instead undermined it and inhibited development.[2]

If, in the early decades of the sixteenth century, the resources of Andalusia and Castile were sufficient to provide most of the needs of the Spanish colonists, as they became increasingly self-sufficient in primary products so the demand for manufactures, textiles and metal goods grew. Many of these were brought into Sevilla from Italy, Germany, France, the Netherlands, England and elsewhere, and accounted for an increasing proportion of outward-bound cargoes. These goods rose rapidly in price with taxes levied on top at every stage of the journey, so that by the time it reached faraway Chile a

packet of paper cost 100 pesos,* the equivalent of fifty head of cattle.³
Naturally goods could be acquired far more cheaply from original
sources, leading the *audiencia* (appellate court) at Santo Domingo as
early as 1549 to plead with Carlos V to license Flemish vessels to come
to Española to trade.⁴ But the eyes of the crown and the merchants
were fixed firmly on the treasure; they demanded quick returns and
were uninterested in investing in the colonies in any way, thus steadily
undermining them. Spain did not realise her good fortune, for though
the French, Dutch and English wanted booty and profit by trade they
did not covet one square foot of Spanish territory – at least, not yet.

Since trade in the Caribbean was poorly serviced, inevitably
someone filled the gap. From the middle of the sixteenth century this
was via the Canary Islanders, partly through a system of licences
(*asientos*) and later through smuggling. When the smugglers turned
out to be French and English this produced a different order of indignation from the authorities, especially as these interlopers were just as
likely to plunder as to trade. Smugglers brought slaves and all sorts of
manufactured goods, and were usually welcomed by monopoly-weary
colonists, but it still involved risk on the part of the smugglers, since
no Spaniard wanted to be denounced as a traitor by carrying on illegal
trade. In 1568 a certain Captain Borgoing of Le Havre, an experienced
smuggler who even carried a licence on this voyage, put into La Margarita Island north of Venezuela seeking pearls. A Spanish *vecino* or
urban householder called Carillo, who normally engaged in such trade,
invited the French ashore with guarantees of safety. But ten or twelve
days later, seemingly out of pure capriciousness or possibly as the result
of some insult, he attacked them with other settlers. Some sixteen
Frenchmen were killed and their bodies strung up along the coast for
show, demonstrating that the colonists were not the only ones taking
risks from such trade.⁵ Only the main ports were fortified so these were
paired with smugglers' retreats, like Baru near Cartagena and El Garote
near Portobelo.⁶ But because there was practically no direct contact
between metropolitan and secondary ports, *rescates* were quick to fill

* The peso, or Spanish silver dollar would become famous as the 'piece of eight' from its
other Spanish name, the *real de a ocho*, worth eight reales, with sixteen 'pieces of eight' or
128 reales being worth a gold piece or doubloon.

the gap caused by lack of supply and exorbitant prices, and the Spanish were not alone in suffering this way. In 1619 the governor of Bermuda, Nathaniel Butler, complained that the island's company sent only one ship that year, and barely a month after its departure he was forced to authorise trade with a Zeelander from Middelburg who had corn, shoes, clothing and other vitally necessary items.[7]

At the turn of the century the French probably had the largest share of the trade, and in describing the situation in 1604 at Manzanillo, the port of Bayamo in southern Cuba, the governor of Jamaica reported a veritable international smugglers' convention. An eyewitness informed him that:

> there are nine ships of Flemings, French and English engaged in contraband, and in Guanalhibes in Española another five, and that the French plunder with one hand and trade with the other, and that the mouth of the River Cauto in Bayamo is occupied so that no ship may leave without safe-conduct from the smugglers ... Those who are most strongly established there are Pompilio the Genoese; Cavallon, a Frenchman; Captain Arceo, a Frenchman; Abraham, a Fleming; Jacques, a Fleming; a Lombard captain; one Mota, who is married in Puerto Príncipe [Cuba], a Portuguese who has joined the French and lives by robbery; and two Englishmen who are selling goods taken from ships bound from Spain to Havana.[8]

The Spanish authorities' ambivalent attitude to the colonists was reciprocated, illustrated by the word *rescates*, often used in the singular and as a term of abuse. It has no simple translation but lies somewhere between trade and criminal enterprise, and might mean exchange, barter, smuggling or ransom; in due course the word *rescatadore* would become synonymous with pirate.[9] And *rescatadores* could expect brutal treatment if caught. In 1604 the Venetian ambassador to England reported that the Spanish had captured two English ships in the West Indies.

> They cut off the hands, feet, nose and ears of the crew and smeared them with honey, and tied them to trees to be tortured by flies and other beasts. The Spanish here plead that they were pirates, not

merchants, and did not know of the peace. But the barbarity makes people here cry out.[10]

Such cruelty would eventually come back to haunt the Spanish.

In 1604 they made a plan to depopulate the northern part of Española by removing its people to the area around Santo Domingo, prompted by the revelation that Protestant Bibles were among the items being brought in by the smugglers. On 2 August 1605 the governor suddenly appeared at Bayahá on the north-western coast of the island and read a *cédula* (royal proclamation) issued in January. In it His Catholic Majesty complained of 'inveterate and pernicious traffic' with foreign smugglers and ordered the residents to transfer to the south of the island, and, to enforce the order, soldiers were on hand to torch the buildings. The process was then repeated at Puerto Plata, Monte Christi and La Yaguana while the inhabitants ran riot, and the Dutch tried to provoke them to rebel.[11]

The consequences of this forced migration were terrible. Of the 110,000 head of cattle only 8,000 could be rounded up, and shortage of pasture meant that only 2,000 of these survived, producing a severe meat shortage as the rest ran wild. A third of the population of Bayaguana died from starvation and disease, and in 1609 the remains of the town were razed to the ground. It became necessary to hold mass before dawn so that those without clothes could hide in the darkness, and many homeless people resorted to cattle-rustling as vast areas of the island were abandoned, later to be occupied by French and English evicted from other places and giving rise to the buccaneers.[12] A similar policy was carried out in Nueva Ecija, and severely damaged the economic development of what is now Venezuela, as the short-sighted determination of Don Francisco Gómez de Sandoval y Rojas, Duque de Lerma and his puppet, King Felipe III, to maintain a *mare clausum* (closed sea) would only undermine Spain's position. By refusing to develop her colonies Spain would have to supply them herself, but this she could not do, therefore defeating the very point of her holding them. By 1608 the governor of Caracas, Venezuela, Sancho de Alquiza, was complaining that shortages were so bad he had no paper on which to write his letters of complaint.[13]

Now that the English were making peace with Spain it was left to the Dutch to inflict on her the final defeats that would bring the long wars to a close, albeit a temporary one. In 1606 they destroyed a powerful Portugese fleet off Malacca, and the following year a Spanish one off Gibraltar. Thus ended a period in which, while maintaining the finest tradition of the Sea Beggars, they had been transformed from rugged pirates into a national fleet that Spain could not defeat. As the fighting along the Flanders frontier became bogged down in inconclusive stalemate, Prince Maurits of Nassau could smirk: 'So you come to negotiate with the Beggars?'[14] This astonishing success was symptomatic; it was the Dutch and not the English who would break the back of Spanish sea power in the early part of the seventeenth century. The seas of Europe were already familiar with their banner of horizontal bars of red, white and blue, and it was soon swarming over other seas where it heralded the startling emergence of a new empire. Fortified by their Protestant faith in a world before rationalism, the Dutch thanked the blessing of providence for their freedom.[15] For now the chief stumbling block to a truce was their insistence on the right to trade in both East and West Indies. Their negotiators, headed by veteran statesman Johan van Oldenbarnevelt, were left in no doubt that the price of full peace and recognition of their republic was the sacrifice of Dutch ambitions in the Indies, and the inhibition of moves to set up a West India Company. These obstacles were avoided only with a carefully worded Article V that allowed the Dutch to trade with the peninsular ports as far as the line of Tordesillas, and left a relatively free hand in the east but implied that the Americas remained a Spanish preserve, to penetrate which they needed the express permission of Felipe III.[16] But the article contained a proviso that this restriction would not be valid in countries 'that chose to grant permission, even beyond the stipulated limits'. This was practically guaranteed to generate further conflict, since the Dutch interpreted the willingness of colonies to accept contraband as third-country permission to trade.[17] Both before and after the truce, they sailed westward carrying cutlery, wines, cheese, butter and African slaves, returning with sugar, tobacco, hides, ginger, canafistula, pearls, sarsparilla, cochineal, indigo, dyewoods and cacao, or nothing at all if their luck fell that way. Whatever rights they might have acquired under the truce, in the Caribbean they

remained pirates, foreigners and heretics with whom business could only be conducted surreptitiously.

The conclusion of the Truce of Antwerp in 1609 was a tacit admission of defeat by Lerma and Felipe III, and was soon seen as a political humiliation; it was a recognition that the United Provinces was a free and independent nation, one that already demonstrated considerable prosperity.[18] Although the Spanish crown did not formally abandon its claim to sovereignty over the northern Netherlands until 1648, it was a claim the world did not take seriously. But neither had a single square foot of territory been wrested from Iberian control in the New World, and while foreigners might be a nuisance, it still remained for them to seize the basis of an empire.[19] But while attempts by the French, Dutch and English to break the Spanish monopoly in the Americas had failed, at least superficially, Spain was seriously weakened by those wars driven by dynastic or religious zeal, particularly in the Low Countries. At home she was forced into a humiliating reliance upon Hanseatic and even Dutch vessels, which ensured a large increase in north European shipping in Andalusian ports bringing an abundance of Scandinavian timber and northern manufactures. These products were key elements in the further expansion of Sevilla's monopoly with the Americas between 1609 and 1620, which was characterised by a growth in exports, or rather re-exports.[20] Furthermore, illicit trade with foreigners at Sevilla and Cádiz, and in the New World itself, had seen Spain's gold and silver drain away and her real wealth decline, while domestic craftsmanship had withered. Although there was as yet no question of losing control of the main Indies trade routes, Spain's power was being eroded at the margins and, with practically all sources of revenue mortgaged to the hilt, her strength was an illusion.[21]

In England the smooth accession of King James I to the throne was managed by the Cecil–Howard faction that dominated English politics. As Cecil in a private capacity and Howard, now Earl of Nottingham, in a public capacity as lord admiral represented the powerful privateering interest, this introduced a measure of tension. The king disliked pirates as much as he did any other men of violence, and he soon stopped the mounting campaign of privateering on both sides of the Atlantic, and relieved the pressure on the Caribbean, enabling

the Spanish to target smuggling with both physical measures and diplomatic pressure in London.[22] In October 1605 the Spanish again decided to build the *armada de barlovento*, a special squadron of eight galleons and four sloops to defend the Windward Islands, and Felipe III launched an aggressive, if not very successful, campaign against pirates, illegal traders and smugglers and the colonists who collaborated with them. He authorised the colonists to keep confiscated merchandise, and at the same time drastic measures were taken to remove entire populations who protected smugglers, a policy that devastated whole regions. The naval structure was altered and fortifications were built.[23]

London merchants, if not the seamen of the West Country, could at least react to this campaign by transferring their interest to trade in the Mediterranean through the Levant Company, or in the Far East through the newly formed East India Company. The almost total cessation of hostilities between the Dutch and Spanish in 1607 also greatly reduced the Dutch presence in the Caribbean, giving Spain a brief respite if not solving her fundamental economic and defence problems. But the cost of war in Europe was prohibitive; Spain found that the 130,000 ducats* needed for Caribbean defence was beyond her and the *armada de barlovento* was abandoned at Havana in 1609.[24] But piracy was a residual problem just about everywhere, including around the coast of Britain. The new Venetian ambassador fell prey to them on his way to England in 1603, and the king's brother-in-law, Christian IV of Denmark, suffered likewise in 1614. Captain John Smith explained why so many men turned to piracy:

> King James who from his infancie had reigned in Peace with all Nations had no imployment for those men of warre so that those that were rich rested with what they had; those that were poore and had nothing but from hand to mouth, turned Pirats; some, because became sleighted of those for whom they had got much wealth; some for that they could not get their due; some, all that lived

---

* A ducat was a small gold coin of Italian origin in common use throughout Europe, originally worth half a doubloon, but all currency conversions were subject to considerable variation over time.

bravely, would not abase themselves to poverty; some, vainly, only to get a name; others for revenge, covetousness, or as ill.[25]

Indeed, the period 1608–14 was something of a golden one for English and Dutch pirates in the north Atlantic, operating on a large scale and over a wide area; but thereafter the appearance of Barbary corsairs from Algiers and Tunis served to focus minds on the problem, even if a suitable solution remained elusive.[26] 'With regard to the mass of the populace, which has amassed such wealth by privateering, and among the common people in particular,' noted the Venetian ambassador in 1620, pirates 'are not held in ill-repute.'[27] But piracy now started to decline dramatically.

The Dutch–Spanish truce signalled the start of a period of relative calm in the Caribbean, with only occasional alarms caused by French and English pirates raiding and trading in the Greater Antilles. *Rescatadores* were always to be found along the thinly populated coasts of western Cuba or Jamaica. In 1606 a Spanish official wrote to the king in exasperation of the colonists of Española: 'They are the most disloyal and rebellious vassals that any king or prince in the world ever had, and if your highness were to appear among them, they would sell your highness for three yards of Rouen silk or even for nothing.'[28] There never was any shortage of intruders looking for trade or plunder. Haunting the islands and coasts, they patrolled the sea lanes on which the colonies depended for their trade and livelihood – frigates, caravels and round ships that carried sugar, hides, tobacco, ginger, sarsparilla and pearls bound for Spain, and linens, manufactures and other goods inbound. In the summer of 1609 a French man-of-war allegedly of 150 tons, with a crew of 130 including Englishmen, took a Canarian prize in the Virgin Islands, and set the company ashore at St Christopher (St Kitts) which seems to have been used as the vessel's temporary base. French pirates were also reported to be operating off Cuba. This may have been one of several ships including English and Dutch vessels that appeared at this time in the bay of Isla Vaca (Cow Island) off Española to supply arms and ammunition to a secret settlement of rebels supposedly three leagues* inland, of mixed blacks, whites and mulattos known as *genta levantada*.[29]

* A league is three miles.

From before the end of the sixteenth century tobacco was the ruling colonial product in the New World; it was used for barter and as payment in kind to defray rents, wages and taxes. In Bermuda in 1621 brides were sold for 100 pounds of tobacco apiece.[30] Prices in the 1590s ranged from 12 shillings to as much as 90 shillings per pound, but towards the end of the century the market for tobacco in north-west Europe expanded considerably, being especially strong in England as early as 1597.[31] By the time King James published *A Counter-Blaste to Tobacco* in 1604, it had become in his adopted country far more than a mere aristocratic fad or apothecary's cure-all. 'No, it is become in place of a cure, a point of good fellowship, and he that will refuse to take a pipe of Tobacco among his fellows ... is accounted peevish and no good company.'[32] Officially valued for customs purposes at half a mark (6s 8d) per pound in the new Book of Rates issued by the English Treasury in 1604, by 1610 it was a major import commodity with an annual value estimated at over £60,000; a year later a Spanish observer noted that English consumption had risen to 100,000 pounds per annum, worth approximately £100,000.[33] Serious tobacco smuggling out of Trinidad got under way soon after peace was declared between the English and Spanish governments. Reports from the authorities in Venezuela during the final years of war expressed alarm at the dominance of tobacco cultivation over all other forms of agriculture, and dismay at the increasing number of English, Dutch and French pirates attracted by it.

By 1607 smuggling was in full swing, and in December the governor of Cumaná reported that 'now tobacco is cleared from all these provinces except San Tomé and the island of Trinidad ... a great quantity of goods is smuggled and that English and Dutch ships are never lacking there'.[34] Thomas Hickory estimated that in 1608–9 some twenty vessels called to collect tobacco from Trinidad and between summer and spring of 1609–10 thirty foreign vessels arrived in Port of Spain.[35] An attempt was made to colonise Guiana (modern Guyana) for tobacco cultivation between 1609 and 1612; and Robert Harcourt, who took part in this venture, predicted a brilliant future, claiming it 'will bring as great a benefit and profit to the undertakers, as ever the Spaniards gained by the best and richest silver mine in all the Indies'.[36] But most attempts at settlement failed within two or three years, and the increasing infiltration into the area finally produced a strong Spanish reaction. The Dutch and English established a substantial tobacco trade based on the Orinoco and Trinidad to avoid anti-smuggling measures at Cumaná which was well established by 1609, and by 1611–12 Trinidad was said to be the outlet for all the tobacco in Venezuela, and the inlet for European wares to Cartagena and beyond.[37] Letters from the Spanish ambassador in London stressed the increasing numbers of English ships involved as the 1611–12 season saw this lucrative trade reach its climax, so that worried members of the Junta de Guerra del Consejo de Indias (War Council of the Indies) reported in March 1612 that 'great quantities of enemy ships of different nations, particularly Dutch and English, resort to the island of Trinidad to contraband with the residents for the fruits of the soil and above all tobacco … and all this is done so freely that ordinarily there are ten or twelve ships there'.[38]

Trinidad was not the only focus of smuggling operations, however. In 1612 the governor of Cuba complained that:

> all these years these coasts have been infested with small pirate vessels, from which our majesty's subjects who live by trade and navigation have suffered much damage, and it is understood from some who have been robbed and put ashore that they are becoming as attached to *rescates* as to pillage.[39]

In the same year the Junta de Guerra proposed an expedition of 4,000 men be sent against the English colony at Virginia, but nothing was done about it; Bermuda seemed far more threatening due to its proximity to the homeward route of the silver fleets. But Felipe III played down the threats, partly from his own pacific inclinations, but also because of Spain's weakness. Three years later he finally dismissed the matter; it was not so much because of the cost involved in expelling the intruders from the Caribbean as that the previous forty years of war had emptied the treasury.[40] And as Gómez de Sandoval deplored the naval weakness of Santo Domingo, Española was said to be awash with French and English vessels which had been chasing every sail approaching or leaving port for a month, but, lacking gunpowder, the authorities were powerless to intervene. That year French pirates took prizes off Havana and raided near Campeche in the Gulf of Mexico, and in 1618–19 pirates took nine frigates plying the ports of eastern Cuba in just ten months.[41] Most of these intruders were involved in smuggling at Trinidad or San Tomé with raiding engaged in as a by-product, and only by a small proportion. The authorities cracked down on tobacco smuggling in 1612 after which the English, French and Dutch began to spread scattered tobacco factories and plantations south of the Orinoco as far as Maranhão in northern Brazil. Little is known about this enterprise, but a French Capuchin monk, writing from Maranhão in 1613 where a French group had established itself a year earlier, thought the settlement could supply tobacco 'because at this time the Spanish have broken off the trade that was done at Trinidad, whereas this here is as good as the said island of Trinidad'.[42]

Three years later Sir Walter Raleigh, who had published a book in 1595 entitled *Discovery of the Large, Rich and Beautiful Empire of Guiana, with a Revelation of the Great and Golden City of Manoa (which the Spaniards call El Dorado)*, was finally released from gaol and authorised to make a journey in search of the fabled city, though strictly prohibited from indulging in acts of piracy.[43] The following year he set up a company to finance the expedition and sailed with fourteen ships and 2,000 men to Trinidad where he put his plan into action on 7 November, leading six vessels to take the capital, San José de Orduña, while his son and Lawrence Keymis sailed up the Orinoco to storm San Tomé. Although Raleigh was successful, his son was not and was killed facing fierce resistance from the inhabitants before the Spanish retreated into the jungle, sending for assistance from Bogotá. On 29 January Keymis ordered a retreat, only to be hounded for nine days by the inhabitants reinforced by Indian bowmen. He eventually reported back to Raleigh having lost 250 men. In despair, Keymis shot himself, although it is possible that it was Raleigh who pulled the trigger. Raleigh then tried to persuade his captains to take the Indies fleet but he was universally opposed, and some of them deserted, so that in April he ordered the fleet to sail with its small booty of tobacco and some jewels looted from the church. But his misfortunes were far from over; his captains continued to desert and he reached Bermuda with only two ships left. Approaching Europe he tried to dock in France but a mutiny forced him into Plymouth, and on returning to London he was arrested and tried on evidence presented by the Spanish ambassador. With the death sentence passed against him in 1603 deemed still to hold, he was duly hanged on 29 October 1618.[44]

The Spanish also brought pressure to bear on James I to forbid a planned expedition by Roger North to the Amazon two years later. North was prepared to defy the ban, having his own powerful backing, but he was imprisoned for a few months on his return, and the end of the Dutch–Spanish truce in 1621 served only to strengthen Spanish resolve to exclude all foreigners from the region. In 1623 the Portuguese attacked in such force that Dutch planting in the delta collapsed entirely.[45] What alarmed the colonial authorities most of all was not so much the loss of trade as the presence of foreigners dominating portions of the area and apparently spreading their influence. In eastern Venezuela the situation was, if anything, worse, as tobacco was a valuable commodity commanding a rapidly expanding market. The demand for tobacco after 1612 prompted a 'tobacco rush', with Virginia leading the way as annual exports rose from 60,000 pounds in 1619 to 500,000 in 1628 and 1.3 million ten years later. By that time Bermuda, St Christopher, Barbados, Nevis, Antigua, Maryland, Martinique and Guadeloupe were also producing tobacco. In the customs year of 1621–2 (Michaelmas to Michaelmas) the official value of tobacco imported to London alone was £55,306, but almost certainly much more entered without being recorded – that is, was smuggled – and the total national import must have exceeded 166,000 pounds.[46] It remained a luxury item until the rapid spread of production in the 1620s and 1630s dropped the price dramatically to a few pence by 1630, and to no more than a penny a few years later.[47] Thus it provided a major driving factor in colonisation and much of its history, especially economic and social, is encompassed in this progression, because planting tobacco meant planting a colony. European capital preferred quick returns, and the merchants of London, Bristol, Dieppe, Le Havre, La Rochelle, backed by the credit afforded by roving Dutchmen, saw tobacco boom for two decades, giving the Caribbean a boost with the establishment of many new English and French colonies.[48]

As the English sought tobacco, so the French looked to import Rouen linen for which there was great demand, and to export hides. But hides were of little economic value to the Spanish, compared to bullion, dyes or sugar. What most interested the Dutch, however, was salt to support the North Sea herring industry, 'the mother of all commerce' as an old Dutch saying has it, as well as the butter and cheese industries. The herring fleet grew from 150 vessels in 1550 to over 4,000 a century later, and the demand for salt grew proportionately. Near Cumaná in Venezuela a narrow isthmus known as Punta del Araya offered probably the finest salt pan in the world. The first Dutch salt ships arrived in 1599 and by 1605 at least 768 arrived, some with trade goods to indulge in *rescates*, but according to Spanish reports 611 came empty to gather salt.[49] Then a Spanish fleet comprising fourteen galleons and four smaller ships carrying 2,500 men commanded by Luis de Fajardo, a veteran of recognised ability in the struggle against both heretics and pirates, left Lisbon on 11 September supposedly bound for Flanders. Instead they headed for the Caribbean and on 6 November they easily routed the interlopers – who were mostly Dutch, plus a few English and French – and took nine Dutch ships in a first assault. They then stormed ashore at Araya and killed some 400 Dutchmen.

Fajardo remained in the area for a month, sweeping up another seven vessels including a 100–tonner and a twenty-six-man crew who killed fourteen Spaniards before being forced to surrender.[50] Fajardo treated his captives as 'pirates and corsairs', for, although the Dutch had not engaged in raiding, like the other foreigners they had been contrabanding along the coast at Cumaná and elsewhere. Dutch accounts, especially that of Velius van Hoorn, stressed Spanish cruelty. Following a *cédula* issued on 6 July of that year Fajardo 'treated skippers and crews very roughly; some were hanged cold bloodedly after they had been prisoners for some time. Some were drowned, some had their legs broken.'[51] The immediate cost to the Dutch was put at 100,000 florins, but they were not intimidated, and barely a year later complaints were once more flowing regarding Dutch interlopers.[52] The Spanish expedition now sailed to Española, which it reached in January 1606, and went ashore to subdue the remaining settlers who had refused to move to the south of the island. While at anchor Fajardo learned of a large gathering of smugglers at Manzanillo Bay on Cuba, and sent his second-in-command, Juan Alvarez de Avilés, with six galleons to engage twenty-four Dutch vessels (again accompanied by about six English and French ships) off Cabo Cruz.

On 7 February Avilés attacked and during the mêlée his galleon was grappled by a Dutch ship under Abraham du Verne. The Dutchman's magazine then exploded, taking both vessels to the seabed, and the outcome of the skirmishing was inconclusive. The remaining smugglers and salt diggers scattered, and the Spanish expedition limped homeward having scarcely made a dent in the enemy traffic, for according to one contemporary chronicler the news of the Araya massacre 'turned many to raiding who otherwise would never have thought of doing so'.[53] In 1607 a powerful Dutch fleet caught Avilés at anchor off Gibraltar and destroyed him and his entire fleet, burning twelve warships and fourteen lesser craft. In their wrath the Dutch threw bound captives into the sea and slaughtered survivors in the water. Thus was Araya avenged, and with peace in 1609 came the opening of the salt pans at Setúbal in Portugal to Dutch traders that largely undermined the economics of acquiring the mineral from Venezuela.[54]

The salt example does, however, serve to illustrate the problems and remedies employed by the Spanish in both foreign and colonial policy. In an empire as large and far-flung as Spain's, it was impossible to ensure that salaried law officers were maintained in every place where her monopoly and power might be challenged. One tactic she employed, as seen here, was the sudden reversal of an apparently laissez-faire attitude into brutal repression, applied not only to foreign trespassers but even occasionally to recalcitrant officials and colonists – although this only heightened distrust among the colonial population. A second tactic which produced less obviously tangible or immediate results was the paying of informants to betray their peers, a policy that further served to sow distrust among settlers and prevent them gaining a measure of cohesion in opposition to crown authority. And although the Fajardo expedition had succeeded in expelling the Dutch from the salt pans, they merely moved along the coast and began bartering for tobacco.[55] It was unsurprising that the Spanish king was wary of these foreigners. When he bought shipbuilding materials from the Dutch in 1612 and gave permission for their delivery to Havana, not only did the materials prove entirely unsatisfactory but a clerk on board the freighter, who was said to be an old pirate, took the opportunity to sound and chart the harbour.[56]

In 1618 the brief lull in the Caribbean came to an end as what would become the Thirty Years War broke out in Europe, producing an increase in the number of pirate attacks. La Margarita was raided that year and Cartagena reported that seventeen ships were lying off Cape San Antonio with more off Cuba. The Junta de Guerra, already aware 'that the enemy was infesting the Islas de Barlovento', decided in August to send two ships with a reinforcement of soldiers; but this seems to have had no effect. Cuba was increasingly beset along its southern coast and ports along that littoral were cut off from Havana, preventing it from exporting its produce, notably copper from the Santiago district.[57] In August 1620 the governor of Havana lamented: 'This last year the damage they [the pirates] have done is greater, because they have appeared on the coast in greater number than in previous years ... and I have verified that the largest of the ships does not exceed 200 tons in burden, the typical size being 100–300 tons.' A couple of 200-ton warships would be sufficient to deal with these invaders, he thought, but six months later he was still raging that he lacked the strength to prevent them ranging the length of his coasts. He added that their activities were expanding to Santo Domingo and Puerto Rico, using as bases the islands of Nevis and Virgin Gorda, 'which are the enemy's safe places and anchorages, where most years they winter, preparing and careening* their ships and fortifying their spirits'.[58]

When Felipe III died in 1621 he was succeeded by his son, the dissolute young Felipe IV, a curious character who mixed religious bigotry with a love of music and bullfighting. Real power, however, passed to his favourite, Don Gaspar de Guzmán, Conde-Duque de Olivares, who acted more like a father figure than chief minister and embarked on an ambitious attempt to retrieve the crown's now some-what battered reputation, aiming to return the king to the illustrious heights of his sixteenth-century forebears.[59] To start with they decided to dispense with the Dutch truce, as it seemed to Olivares that there was nothing to prevent the Spanish armies in Flanders from sweeping through the United Provinces. James I would not make trouble as he still hoped to marry his son to the Infanta; France was on the verge of

---

* Careening involves cleaning the hull of clinging sealife and recaulking the timbers with tar.

civil war; and the fighting in Bohemia would soon engulf Germany. But Olivares fatally underestimated the growing strength of the Dutch, and when war resumed between Spain and Holland in April the illicit Caribbean salt trade soon also resumed at full throttle.

As early as September 1621 Diego de Arroyo Daza, governor of Cumaná, learned that six Dutch ships were anchored at Ancón de Refriegas near Punta de Araya. They went about their business as though they had never been away, wrote Arroyo, and although he was able to stop them obtaining fresh water from the Bordones river and immediately issued a ban on *rescate*, he pointed out that the ship which should have brought supplies to the colony had not arrived, and he could not ensure that the population would comply.[60] The following year Arroyo Daza fortified the pan himself, building the Castello Santiago del Arroyo de Araya on the hilltop of Cerro de Daniel, named after Dutchman Daniel Moucheron who had earned this dubious honour by being hanged on the summit.[61] On 27 November forty-three Dutch salt carriers appeared, and though rather taken aback by the new defences, proceeded to bombard them for two days before landing a thousand men. Arroyo led a stout defence in which the Dutch admiral and four captains were among those killed, and the Dutch retreated disheartened, harassed by native archers.[62]

A few weeks later in January 1623 another fleet of forty-one Dutch ships arrived and blasted away to no avail, and six Dutch cargo vessels were taken by a Spanish fleet of fourteen ships under Admiral Tomás de Larraspuru, while a number of others engaged in smuggling in the area were forced to flee. A further 106 ships from various quarters attempted to load at Araya but met an identical refusal, and no more attacks occurred as it was apparent that the port was now closed. Besides, they had by now developed other sources in the Caribbean.[63] Unfortunately this rivalry produced a lasting legacy of bitterness: when the Dutch raided La Margarita in May 1623 they massacred most of the 1,200 inhabitants and razed the town to the ground, while a hundred women and children survived and were subsequently sold into slavery with the Barbary corsairs.[64] But what interested the Dutch most besides salt was hides from Cuba and Española, tobacco and dyewood from the Indians of Venezuela and Guiana, and they also took prizes where they could and continued the illicit trade in manufactures.[65] To facilitate all these ventures a great commercial enterprise was in the offing in Amsterdam. Soon it would provide a Dutchman to make more trouble in the Caribbean than the Spanish could handle.

# 3

# PIET HEIN

Piet Hein, Piet Hein,
Piet Hein zijn naam is klein, Zijn daden benne groot,
Zijn daden benne groot,
Hij heeft gewonnen de Zilvervloot.
Hij heeft gewonnen, gewonnen de Zilvervloot,
Hij heeft gewonnen de Zilvervloot.*

Traditional Dutch song

Pieter Pieterszoon Hein (or Heyn) was born at Delftshaven in 1571, the port of Delft near Rotterdam. As a boy he joined his father who skippered a merchant vessel, and enjoyed an adventurous boyhood and early youth, being imprisoned three times by the Spanish – in Spain, the Spanish Netherlands and the West Indies – and at one stage being forced to row in the Spanish galleys alongside his father. In 1607 he entered service with the Dutch East India Company (Verenigde Oostindische Compagnie, formed in 1602 and usually referred to by its Dutch abbreviation as the VOC). He returned home five years later as master of an East Indiaman, married the widow of a colleague and settled in Rotterdam. Now a rich citizen, he was elected alderman in 1622, and having completed the customary year in office he was then asked to become second-in-command of an expedition to Brazil, marking the start of an extraordinary career fighting the Spanish and Portuguese in Africa and the Americas.

Under its charter the VOC had a monopoly of trade and navigation east of the Cape of Good Hope and west of the Straits of Magellan for an initial twenty-one years. The governing body or court of seventeen directors (the Heren XVII) had powers to conclude treaties of peace or alliance, to wage defensive war and to build strongholds and

---

* 'Piet Hein, Piet Hein, His name is short, his deeds are great, he captured the Silver Fleet.'

fortresses in its region; it could employ civilian, naval or military personnel who would swear allegiance to the company and to the States-General (the Republic's parliament), and it would as frequently resort to the sword as to the pen. One of the main reasons that forced the Spanish to accept a breaking of the Iberian monopoly was the success of the VOC, and this suggested that similar methods might work in the west. The driving spirit behind moves to found a West-Indische Compagnie (West India Company – WIC) was Willem Usselinx or Usselincx (1567–1647), a Calvinist refugee from Antwerp and prolific pamphleteer.[1] Usselinx was fiercely proud of his Flemish background, and was convinced that the north had been of no consequence until the Flemish immigration. He believed that Dutch agricultural colonies could be settled in the New World and would provide the mother country with a valuable and expanding export market. A strong religious strain ran through his proposals, leading him to deprecate the use of slaves as both inhuman and uneconomic.[2] The idea of a WIC had first been mooted in 1606, but the practical difficulties seemed too great and the matter was dropped, much to Usselinx's annoyance because he thought it promised 'the greatest traffic in the world'. And once the truce with Spain was signed in 1609 his ambitious plans were shelved, since American produce could be obtained more easily and safely (if not more cheaply) via Spanish and Portuguese ports rather than direct from the Caribbean.[3]

In 1619 van Oldenbarnevelt was executed on the back of a trumped-up charge of high treason that marked the triumph of the militant Calvinist war party led by Prince Maurits. Both the prince and the *predikants* of the church were anxious for renewed war with Spain, if not for the same reasons. For their part, the Spanish were quite ready to accept a renewal of hostilities; the truce had provided a useful breathing space in Flanders, the war that had just started in Germany appeared to be going well, and it seemed that the German Protestant princes would be unable to render any useful assistance to the Dutch. The Spanish also hoped that a resumption of war in Europe would distract the heretics from their overseas meddling. By 1621 when the Dutch–Spanish truce ended, pirates had painfully demonstrated the vulnerability of Spanish possessions away from the main bases. With war once more on the cards, the proposals for a WIC were dusted off, warmly supported by both clergy and burgher–oligarchs, and the company received a charter from the States-General on 3 June that year. But this was no mere commercial enterprise; it was also a political association designed to injure the enemy and develop revenues and territories at his expense. And from Brussels the Infanta Isabel sent Felipe IV detailed plans showing that the company had designs on Matanzas Bay and Havana, reckoned to be the centre of the Indies trade.[4] However, the central board of nineteen directors (Heren XIX) took much longer than the VOC to come up with working capital – two years as opposed to one month, although the sum subscribed was greater at 7 million guilders against 6.5 million – but in the meantime little was done to improve Spanish defences.[5]

At sea the years between 1618 and 1623 were very difficult ones for Spain, her naval strength having declined to its weakest point in 1616 although it made a considerable recovery thereafter.[6] By 1620 it was clear that Spain could not afford renewed hostilities with the Dutch, as the continent was racked with war; royal finances had been badly mismanaged by corrupt officials and the crown faced enormous debts just as the American bullion trade slumped dramatically.[7] But the menace of the Barbary corsairs in the Mediterranean and the eastern Atlantic, combined with the Dutch blockade of the Iberian coast, provided a stimulus to naval rearmament. However, with the threat that would be posed by the Dutch West India Company yet to materialise, Spain failed to provide adequate protection for her Caribbean colonies, and infiltration continued without let or hindrance, but also with a new aim: colonisation.

The first official gathering of the Heren XIX was at Amsterdam on 3 August 1623. The WIC was modelled in many ways on the VOC, but its offensive role in the war for Atlantic trade was strongly emphasised from the beginning, so that it differed radically from Usselinx's original, largely peaceful plan.* The charter gave the company a monopoly on all Dutch trade with the Americas and West Africa; it was similarly authorised to make war or peace with indigenous powers, to create

---

* Disappointed with the terms adopted, which went against his ideals, Usselinx instead entered the service of the King of Sweden hoping that the northern court would realise his plans.

and maintain naval and military forces and to exercise judicial and administrative powers in the areas it controlled. The WIC was devised primarily for war on two basic premises: the national government was reluctant to expand warfare 'beyond the line', and the merchants were willing and able to accept it as a profitable and Protestant duty. The company was a vehicle for the pursuit of profit through war, and would resist all efforts at negotiation with Spain as this would curtail its business, even when the Spanish showed willingness to reach an accommodation.[8] But the first ships it sent to sea were purely trading vessels, and the problem remained of where to strike the first blow.

Although Usselinx retained supporters for founding colonies where the Spanish held little or no control, such as Guiana or Chile, majority opinion was more belligerent: some advocated cutting the Panamanian Isthmus and the Spanish empire in two, in order to seize the bullion from Peru and Mexico; others suggested taking Havana or another part of Cuba suited to intercepting the *flotas* in the straits of either Florida or Yucután; still others wanted a more daring plan to capture a port on the Iberian peninsula itself, anticipating the British seizure of Gibraltar some eighty years later. But the proposal that found favour with both the Heren XIX and the States-General was a plan to conquer Brazil, where sugar output was estimated at 5 million guilders per annum, and relatively weak defences cast an irresistible lure.[9]

An expedition to capture Bahía de Todos os Santos (San Salvador, or All Saints Bay, off northern Brazil) was duly fitted out in 1623. Comprising twenty-six ships carrying 450 guns and 3,300 men under Admiral Jacob Willikens, previously an Amsterdam fishmonger, with Piet Hein as vice-admiral, this force took the town without opposition on 10 May 1624. The news provoked joy in the United Provinces and dismay in the Iberian peninsula where, for once, Madrid and Lisbon reacted in a spirit of unity and co-operation, for the Spanish suspected that the true aim of the expedition was not Brazilian sugar but Peruvian silver. King Felipe IV felt that Spain's prestige as a naval power was at stake and ordered a huge combined fleet consisting of twenty-six Portuguese ships under Francisco de Almeida and thirty-seven from the Spanish Armada del Océano reinforced by other regional squadrons commanded by Juan Fajardo de Guevara. Under the overall command of Fadrique de Toledo, the fleet carried a total 945 guns, 3,200 sailors and 7,500 soldiers who arrived at Bahía at Easter 1625 to find the Dutch in disarray. Although they had expected a strong reaction, the Dutch had failed to organise a relief expedition, with the result that the Hispano-Portuguese fleet expelled their incursion, taking 3,000 prisoners in the process. Willikens had returned to Holland with eleven ships the previous July and had sent Hein with seven ships to Angola, having decided that in order to hold Brazil the Dutch would have to control the provincial slave trade in West Africa.[10]

Finding the Portuguese defenders on their guard, Hein had been unable to secure the Angolan port of Luanda and when he returned to Bahía on 18 April 1625 he encountered the combined fleet. Faced with such overwhelming power he was forced to continue northward, reaching Holland at the end of July.[11] The Heren XIX were not unduly worried, believing that their garrison in Brazil would be able to hold out quite easily until relief arrived, not knowing that it had surrendered just twelve days after Hein sighted the combined fleet. Thus when the Dutch relief fleet reached Bahía on 26 May with thirty-four ships and 6,500 men under Admiral Boudewijn Hendricks, burgomaster of Edam, it managed only some inconclusive skirmishing. Hendricks decided to lead eighteen ships to try and capture San Juan de Puerto Rico some 3,000 miles to the north-west. This had been under consideration by the Heren XIX for some time, since its position at the entrance to the Caribbean made it ideal for the distribution of contraband; alternatively Hendricks could try and intercept a silver fleet or attack Havana. But spies had reported Dutch intentions and the Spanish authorities were suitably alert.

On Puerto Rico the governor, Juan de Haro, prepared his defences; San Juan had a garrison of 350 men with good artillery. Unfortunately Haro miscalculated. He expected the Dutch to attack the battery at El Boqueron but they instead sailed straight into the bay, passing Castello San Felix del Morro practically unscathed. Diego de Larrasa described how Hendricks 'entered with such self-confidence as if he were in Holland or Zeeland, due to the poor or non-existent dexterity and low number of the [Spanish] artillerymen. The artillery was in such a sorry state that many pieces became jammed at the first firing, since the carriages were so old and some of them had been loaded four years earlier ...'[12] Hendricks was able to bombard San Lázano Point and then landed to sack the city, whose inhabitants had fled into the nearby woods, carrying with them their most precious possessions and forcing the governor to make a stand in El Morro. But the Dutchman took it and then laid siege to San Juan. On 27 September Hendricks issued an ultimatum to surrender, which Haro refused. In an attempt to break the blockade the governor organised a sortie of eighty men which achieved some success, as they were able to gain the fort of El Cañuelo at the entrance of the bay, giving them control of it. Hendricks tried desperately to retake it, eventually succeeding some three weeks later.

On 21 October Hendricks again demanded surrender, threatening to burn the city if Haro refused. Instead, Haro replied:

> I have studied the paper you sent me, and if all the powers of Holland were here today in Puerto Rico, I would rejoice, for then they would witness the courage of the Spanish. And if you burn the city, we have courage enough to build new houses, for there is still timber in the hills and materials on the land. And today I am in this fort with enough men to burn all your ships. So send me no more missives, for I shall not reply to them . . .[13]

Hendricks burned the city the following day, but shortly afterwards the defenders received reinforcements from Santo Domingo. Realising that his efforts would come to naught, the admiral raised the siege and set sail on 1 November. But as he departed his fleet suffered serious damage from the Spanish guns, causing one of the Prince of Orange's ships, the *Mendeblick*, to beach. Desperate to recover her, the Dutch sent five launches, only to encounter six Spanish launches dispatched to secure her capture. With no time to save the ship the Dutch mined her and finally withdrew on 2 November; but they set the fuses too long and the Spanish managed to prevent her destruction.[14]

The city had been recovered but considerable damage had been wrought by the invaders. Besides the fort another ninety-six buildings had been burned and a further forty-five stone buildings destroyed; the churches had been pillaged, with slaves, jewels and archives stolen – even Bishop Balbuena's library had been sacked. But Hendricks had lost a warship and a launch together with 200 men killed and fifteen captured. These unlucky prisoners, Haro informed the governor of Santo Domingo, would be sent 'straight to hell, unless they choose to go to heaven'.[15] The difference was but small, as they were all to be hanged, though eleven had agreed to convert to Catholicism which supposedly ensured their passage to heaven. Haro, however, had also been severely wounded and died soon afterwards.[16] For his part Hendricks first retired for a month to the Bay of San Francisco on the north of the island to recover; he then sailed to La Margarita and seized and abandoned a number of towns; he went on to Coche, Cumaná and Araya, where he attacked the castle of Santiago with gunfire and engaged in a skirmish with the twenty-five defenders before turning north. On 14 June he was at Cabañas on Cuba, as a slave called Matheo Congo reported to Havana; the Dutch burned a ship under construction there and killed the pigs and hens, before sailing onwards, a menacing fleet of about two dozen ships.[17] But, hoping to intercept a *flota* between Florida and Yucután, they attempted nothing. Then Hendricks contracted a fever, and died, disappointed, off the coast on 2 July 1626. Of his original force only some 1,500 men remained, and his successor Adrian Claesz could not maintain discipline: the remnants of the fleet returned to Holland having accomplished little save the capture of a few merchant ships.[18]

The disasters suffered by the Dutch at Bahía, Puerto Rico and Elimina in West Africa in 1625 came as a severe and nasty shock to the W I C. But the company still had some fight left in it. By the end of May 1626 Piet Hein was at sea once again with fourteen ships carrying 1,675 men and 312 guns with a plan to reinforce Hendricks and help to capture a *flota*. Only in August when he reached his cruising ground off Yucután did Hein learn that Hendricks had died and his fleet had departed. When he then met a well-armed Spanish fleet of forty ships under Tomás de Larraspuru off the island of Tortuga near Española on 9 September he did not feel strong enough to confront it. Had Hendricks been there, he bitterly recorded, 'I would have taken the whole fleet. It grieves me that I had to let so beautiful an opportunity slip through my hands only because of a lack of assistance.'[19] Thus only by what the Spanish regarded as a God-sent miscalculation did he fail to attack either or both of the vulnerable Mexican fleets, one sailing from Veracruz and the other heading for that port at the time.[20]

The Dutch avoidance of contact with Larraspuru's warships was attributed by the Spanish to cowardice, but in fact it made perfect business sense; profit not glory was what the Dutch were seeking. Hein's orders were quite flexible, however: it had been envisaged that he might not meet up with Hendricks, and in that event he was to proceed to Brazil and await further orders. On the night of 2/3 March 1627 he reached Bahía and sailed straight into the harbour, despite fierce fire from the shore batteries. There he captured or destroyed twenty-six merchantmen including many Baltic traders.[21] On 8 July another Dutch force attacked two galleons escorting a few merchantmen up from Honduras that had been reinforced by a hundred musketeers and ten guns, including one bearing the august name of *Carlos V*; they captured the flagship and the treasure it carried, and drove the other aground. This ship's colour was saved only by an infantryman called Francisco Isidro, one of a relief column sent overland to help. He stabbed a Dutchman who had just killed the colour-bearer, and wrapped it around his body before jumping into the sea. He then rescued the commander of the expedition, Alvaro de la Cerda, and three sailors who could not swim, by pushing them ashore.[22] But another seventeen Spanish merchantmen had been taken by Dutch cruisers in the Atlantic to give a total of fifty-five prizes, and the booty thus taken provided the WIC with a welcome boost to its coffers. These successes went a long way to atone for previous disappointments and gave the WIC a second wind.

The plan to capture a *flota* was based on the understanding of its regular operation at the time. From Sanlúcar, the port of Sevilla, and from Cádiz, the Tierra Firme fleet – now known as the *galeones* – and that of Nueva España – *flota de San Juan* – would sail at different times. Normally the former departed in April and comprised eight powerful galleons of around 600 tons carrying twenty-four to twenty-eight guns and escorting twenty or so merchantmen via the Canaries to enter the Caribbean between Trinidad and Tobago en route to Cartagena and Portobelo, where they would load Peruvian silver. In July it would sail via the Yucután Channel to Havana, passing Cape San Antonio in early to mid-August. The Nueva España fleet consisted of four galleons with around fifteen merchantmen, and sailed later in the year, usually entering the Caribbean between Guadeloupe and Dominica in early

August. It then split up, with two galleons going to Trujillo in Honduras and the others to San Juan de Ulúa in September where they unloaded and spent the winter, loading in turn gold, silver, cochineal, indigo, tobacco, hides, wood and many other products. It would depart in June for Havana to rendezvous with the Honduran ships and await the Tierra Firme fleet. Reunited, the whole caboodle would depart at the end of August, sailing home via the Florida Channel and the Azores to Sanlúcar and up the Guadalquivir river to Sevilla's Puerta de las Mulas where Casa de Contratación officials took over.[23]

In order to exploit this routine the Heren XIX formed a fleet of thirty-one ships carrying almost 4,000 men and 689 guns, which was ready by the end of May 1628. Hein was promoted to general with orders to make another attempt on the silver fleet 'that brings to Europe the golden rod that chastises and demoralises the whole of Christendom, a rod whose might may be defeated by twenty-four well-armed warships and twelve despatch boats provided with cannon and munitions, crewed by valiant sailors . . .'.[24] He left Texel in May and reached the island of St Vincent on 12 July, taking great care not to be observed, before arriving off Cape San Antonio at the beginning of August. Meanwhile, a second Dutch fleet of twelve ships was operating in the Caribbean under Pieter Adrienszoon Ita, and had already secured valuable prizes. The appearance of these fleets prompted the Spanish authorities to send messages warning the *flotas* not to sail, but Hein was familiar with this precaution and intercepted the dispatches, capturing six boats, sinking another and forcing the last to return to Havana. However, the dispatch to Cartagena reached its destination and the Tierra Firme fleet did not sail, although the Honduras squadron under Alvaro de la Corda and the fleet from Nueva España set out as planned.

On the morning of 1 August 1628 Ita attacked Corda, and after a terrible fight forced him and his vice-admiral to beach their ships and try to disembark their crews. As they did so Corda was wounded and drowned, and his ship surrendered with half his men killed.[25] Governor Lorenzo de Cabrera of Havana sent out two frigates to support Corda, but these were driven back into harbour. This Honduran fleet carried hides, ginger and silver, but one ship could not be refloated and had to be burned. Ita then learned that the Tierra Firme fleet was approaching and, deciding that his twelve ships were no match for this, withdrew north. His withdrawal in turn caused the Spanish to make a grave error, as they wrongly concluded that all Dutch ships had left the area, though Hein's fleet still cruised undetected in the Florida Straits. When his fleet was finally observed on 22 August and Governor Cabrera sent dispatch boats to carry warning, few were able to reach their destinations.[26]

Hein now lay in wait for the Nueva España fleet. He had by now also received reinforcements and his fleet comprised ships mostly over 300 tons, with his flagship *Amsterdam* over 1,000 tons and his second-in-command's over 800. Possibly in order to rein in his known intrepidity, the Heren XIX had appointed the 'prudent' Hendrick Corneliszoon Loncq to this position. Hein organised his large fleet in three lines, each of two squadrons, with a fourth line of one squadron. On 8 September he captured a vessel belonging to the Spanish fleet and learned that the rest were on their way. They had departed Veracruz on 9 August but a storm had scattered them somewhat, although most had reformed. A few hours later the main fleet appeared, eleven ships escorted by four galleons commanded by Juan de Benavides and his admiral, Juan de Leoz. Taken by surprise, the Spaniards' best hope was to get into Havana, but this was blockaded by Hein, or else to run the ships aground and unload the silver and try to defend it from land. But the Dutch had the weather gauge* giving them the advantage in manoeuvre, so Benavides tried to run for Matanzas which lay ahead and where defences were being prepared.[27] But it seems that the pilots with Benavides were less familiar with the bay's shoals than they claimed, and several of the larger ships grounded, stranding the treasure well offshore and leaving most of their guns pointing the wrong way.

For the first and only time, this operation – so often attempted by French, Dutch and English – was crowned with success. From Havana Benavides reported to his king that on sighting the Dutch, and:

---

* The weather gauge was a position later defined as 'the situation of one ship to windward of another, when in action & co[mpany]'. It gave several immediate advantages: the smoke of battle cleared more quickly from that side of the ship and blew on to the enemy, but most importantly it gave the holder the ability to choose the timing and range at which an action would be fought.

seeing that I was determined to proceed and resolved to die in the attempt, my men urged me to avoid the risk and save Your Majesty's silver ... and heeding the advice of those in a position to give it, I agreed to seek refuge in the port, thinking that by leaving the enemy little room for manoeuvre I could save the silver, or at least the men, and burn the ships, the treasure remaining where it might be saved. I reached the bay when night had fallen, although it was light as day. Although there the wind usually drops at night, on this occasion it freshened, and the enemy came so close that I had to disembark the men as fast as I could, planning to defend myself on land and burn the ships. But the men fled in disorder when I was still at my captain's post giving orders. When I set foot on land I was alone. The enemy immediately boarded our ships, firing many rounds. And thus they seized everything.[28]

In fact, few shots were fired as it seems the Dutch were at first reluctant to board the Spanish vessels, until a boy got on board and started whistling a tune they all knew. Certainly no Spaniards were killed but all were put ashore, including Admiral Leoz who, having had time to change his uniform, went unrecognised.[29] Hein secured the silver uncontested and transferred it to his own ships; then he burned the Spanish fleet apart from the galleons which he took as prizes, and released the prisoners, sailing for Europe on 17 September. Knowing that he risked attack in the English Channel he entered Falmouth, and having obtained an escort duly reached Holland on 9 January 1629.

The booty amounted to over 177,000 pounds of silver worth 8 million guilders which was brought back to Hellevoetsluys on 10 January 1629 following a long and stormy journey. There were also 66 pounds of gold, 1,000 pearls, nearly 2 million hides plus substantial amounts of silk, musk, amber, bezoar and many other precious rarities. It was an unmitigated disaster for Spain, whose armies in the Netherlands and Germany were awaiting their pay and in need of provisions and warlike supplies. Worse, her Genoese, Venetian, Milanese, Florentine and Neapolitan bankers were awaiting interest, and in some cases principal as well, and being forced to default on loans was something her international bankers would never forgive. From now on Spain's security, the silver of the apparently bottomless mines, was only as good as the ships that carried it, and interest rates soared as bankers adopted risks normally associated with marine insurance under-writers.[30]

The States-General received congratulations not only from the ambassadors of France, England, Venice, Denmark and Sweden, but from the pope, the Italian Urban VIII, who was not on good terms with Felipe IV.[31] In Spain the news caused lasting indignation. 'Who', declared Pedro Gutierrez Ortíz in 1637,

> can hear of this and not seize high heaven in angry hands? Who, at the risk of a thousand lives if he had them, would not avenge so grievous an affront? ... The Hollander has so degraded us that commonly, in adjacent kingdoms, where formerly they called the Spaniards unchained lions, they now call us embroidered Marias with braided hair and padded legs![32]

Benavides and Leoz were arrested and imprisoned in the castle of Carmona while awaiting trial; Benavides was eventually executed at Sevilla on 18 May 1634, while Leoz died in an African prison having unsuccessfully sought reinstatement.[33]

In contrast the United Provinces went absolutely wild with joy, and the sale of booty yielded some 12 million guilders for the WIC which, once the company had paid its outstanding debts and the costs of the expedition, left a profit of some 7 million guilders. Hein's success represented almost as much profit as the company had earned in total over the previous thirteen years, during which it had taken a total of 547 Spanish and Portuguese ships. Shareholders received a 75 per cent dividend and the Prince of Orange some 700,000 guilders as 10 per cent due to him as captain-general's and admiral-general's prize-money. The directors contented themselves with a modest 1 per cent gratuity and gave the same to Piet Hein, which paled in comparison to the 31,000 florins given to Jacob van Heemskerk for taking a Portuguese *caváca* in the east.[34] Meanwhile the officers and men received an additional seventeen months' wages, but unhappy with so paltry a return many rioted in the streets of Amsterdam.[35] The silver fleet was, according to the English ambassador to The Hague, 'the greatest prize that was ever taken from the Spanish, and being added to the fleet of Honduras taken in the beginning of August in sight of Havana, and verie many other prizes taken most by the shippes of the West India Company ... will amount to above twenty hundred thousand pounds of sterling, all taken within the space of a year'.[36] But Hein was disillusioned with the treatment he and his men had received, and put forward some extravagant demands as condition of re-employment. When these were rejected by the Heren XIX he was appointed commander-in-chief of the Dutch navy, only to be killed in action against three Ostend privateers on 18 June.[37]

Hein prompted numerous hopeful imitators, but none was anything like as successful. In 1629 Cornelis Corneliszoon Jol – better known as 'Pie de Palo', or 'Peg Leg', thanks to the wooden left leg that replaced his own lost in a sea battle when aged twenty – sailed with twenty-seven ships to Havana. But all he achieved were some minor acts of pillage and his dreams of capturing either the fleet or the city came to nothing. Equally frustrated was Adrian Janszoon Pater's attack on St Thomas in Guiana. He attempted to build a fort and start a settlement there for which he offloaded building materials, but guerrilla attacks by the locals cost him 200 men in the space of a few days. Bitterly frustrated, he decided to attack Santa María, which he approached with 3,000 men on 16 February 1630. The city was evacuated while an 'imposing' Spanish force prepared to defend it, some fifty men in three trenches and in the fort another nineteen men manning four bronze and two iron guns.[38] After a bitter two-hour artillery duel Pater disembarked and the Spanish abandoned their trenches and the fort, leaving just Cristóbal Matute and four men to defy the Dutch horde. Pater demanded they surrender, and Matute agreed providing the city was not burned, whereupon he took up his walking stick and followed his four unarmed men out of the fort to meet the astonished attackers. On 5 March Pater sailed for Brazil, but his ship caught fire and he drowned after jumping overboard on 12 September.[39]

In all three WIC fleets scoured the Caribbean in 1630 under Ita, Pater and Jan Gijbertszoon Booneter, but they extracted little profit and during 1631–2 several more costly expeditions were mounted, likewise yielding meagre results.[40] In 1632 the Caribbean was thrown open to any Dutchman willing to mix in with the Spanish, although besides providing his ship with armament and ammunition, the enterprising merchant would also have to cough up 20 per cent of his profits and carry a WIC 'super-cargo' to ensure he complied with various regulations.[41] 'Peg Leg' Jol was once more unsuccessful in 1632, although he managed to capture a few minor prizes while awaiting the silver fleet, and the following year he struck an alliance with a renegade former Havana slave called Diego de Los Reyes, better known as Diego el Mulato, or Diego Lucifer, in order to attack Campeche in Mexico. Diego, who had turned against his former masters in 1629, became an outstanding leader of Dutch sea rovers. He was described by the renegade English Catholic priest Thomas Gage, who was robbed by him in 1637:

> This mulatto, for some wrongs which had been offered unto him from some commanding Spaniards in Havana, ventured himself desperately in a boat out to sea, where were some Holland ships waiting for a prize. With God's help getting unto them, he yielded himself to their mercy, which he esteemed far better than that of his own countrymen, promising to serve them faithfully against his own nation, which had most injuriously and wrongfully abused, yea, and whipped him in Havana . . .[42]

That Diego was swiftly promoted to captain suggests that the Dutch recognised and valued ability over colour and nationality, at least in terms of Caribbean warfare. He was also symptomatic of the mixed-race rebels that would increasingly feature in pirate crews as the seventeenth century progressed, particularly among the buccaneers, European renegades and seamen who had much in common with former slaves and mixed-race Spanish subjects.[43]

The combined assault on Campeche took place on 11 August with eleven ships and two sloops carrying 500 men, with the invaders demanding 40,000 pesos in return for sparing the city. But as the defenders claimed not to have such a sum it was put to the torch.[44] In 1633 a squadron under Jan Janszoon van Hoorn pillaged Trujillo in Honduras, and sacked San Francisco in Campeche Bay, taking nine ships and a large stock of logwood* and cacao.[45] But the main WIC player between 1634 and 1641 was Jol. Despite being responsible for one of the greatest acts of piracy of all time, Hein was respectfully known to his Iberian foes as *el almirante*; Jol, however, was only ever referred to as *el pirata*. But he was not completely lacking in Hein's qualities, even if two legs was one of them. He was immensely brave, and operating alone in 1634 he took three prizes; in 1635 he took eleven, and a year later he took fourteen.[46]

At the same time progress was made obtaining salt from alternative sources to Punta de Araya; for five or six years pans were used at La Tortuga off Venezuela and on San Martín in the Windward Islands, where a rock-salt mine of excellent quality was established. At both sites the WIC erected forts, but in 1631 the substantial installations on La Tortuga, capable of handling thirty or forty ships at a time, were destroyed by a Spanish expedition comprising forty Spanish soldiers and a hundred native archers under Benito Arias Montano, governor of Caracas, who thus achieved a notable minor victory.[47] Nevertheless the Dutch returned soon afterwards and production soon reached 12,000 *fanegas* (a *fanega* being approximately 12 gallons) per week. The formidable Arias Montano, newly appointed governor of Cumaná, attacked again the following year, bringing with him the famous Italian engineer Juan Bautista Antonelli, who devised a means of flooding the pan, thus rendering it useless [48]

Meanwhile the Dutch turned their attention to San Martín, which they may have been using as early as 1627, although Spanish complaints began registering only from 1631 onwards when eighty Dutch carriers arrived in two squadrons, each protected by three men-of-war. The Dutch left thirty men behind to build a fort, unaware that there were already fourteen Frenchmen living there.[49] A much larger assault was planned for San Martín by the Junta de Guerra as Olivares declared that there would be no quarter for 'the pirates and the rebels [Dutch] in the Indies'.[50] In June 1633 a force of 1,300 men under Lope de Hoces,

* Logwood – *Haematoxylum campeachianum* – is an unspectacular tree with crooked branches and twisted trunk found upon the coasts of Campeche, Honduras and Yucután, the cutting and removal of which was forbidden to any but Spanish subjects. It became highly prized by European ink-, textile- and furniture-manufacturers, for a large splinter steeped in water produces a rich dark-red dye the colour of blood.

Marqués de Cadereyta, one of Spain's finest naval commanders, was detached from a regular Peru fleet bound for Panamá, and following a short siege compelled the Dutch garrison of eighty men to surrender.[51] The Spanish then left their own garrison of 250 men under Cebrián de Lizarazu, and four months later Arias Montano surprised and took another Dutch fort recently erected on the mainland at the salt pan near to the Unare estuary, killing twenty-one Dutchmen and destroying the installations, even burning their wheelbarrows.[52] Lizarazu was supposed to be supplied from Puerto Rico or Santo Domingo, but found himself largely abandoned; his men lacked water if it did not rain and food if they did not fish, and the garrison was short of powder and carriages for its guns.[53]

Faced with a never ending quest for a safe haven to produce salt, the Heren XIX decided in April 1634 'to approve the taking of the island of Curaçao in order to secure a place from which to obtain salt, timber and other products'.[54] This was carried out by an expedition under Johannes van Walbeeck and a pirate called Pierre Le Grand, with little resistance being offered by the Spanish governor, Lope López de Morla, for the Spanish population amounted to only thirty-two including the governor's twelve children. The occupation was soon extended to Aruba, where the Dutch had been exploiting a low-quality salt pan for ten years, and a year later to Bonaire.[55] The Spanish war council met in January 1635 to consider reconquest, but its plans never amounted to anything; lack of men and ships precluded evicting these latest invaders, although Bonaire was briefly retaken in 1642. The Dutch on Curaçao would become a permanent fixture, an ulcer on the no-longer-healthy Spanish American body politic.[56]

The outbreak of war with France in 1635 added to Sevilla's trade problems, and the Dutch capture of Curaçao persuaded Olivares once more to revive the idea of the *armada de barlovento* with eighteen galleons and four smaller vessels, to be based on taxes raised in Nueva España, but it would not be until 1641 that any ships were ready.[57] Meanwhile the *rente de los naipes* – a tax on the manufacture and sale of playing cards which had been a crown monopoly since Felipe II, and was organised as a contract or *asiento* – was raised from six to eight reales in 1635 in order to fund it. There was thus another tax subject to abuse and another item liable to smuggling.[58]

In 1638 Arias Montano learned that eight Dutch vessels were once more working the salt pans at La Tortuga and requested aid from the governor of La Margarita, who provided him with fifty soldiers, fifty Indians and six canoes. Arias Montano was able to set off on 4 April with a total force of 150 soldiers, 200 Indian archers and oarsmen in thirteen canoes. They were spotted by a Dutch vessel which sounded the alarm, but they managed to land and storm the fort, beheading forty defenders while the remainder fled for their ships. The fort was destroyed and the salt pans flooded once more as Arias Montano gained a notable victory.[59] However, 'Peg Leg' Jol was once more in the Caribbean that year, and when the governor of Havana gained word of his presence he sent warnings to Veracruz and Portobelo. The report reached Veracruz in time but not Portobelo, whence the Tierra Firme fleet had already set sail under Carlos de Ibarra. Hunter and prey met on 30 August when the Dutch were anchored in Pan de Cabañas, but Jol's attack was unsuccessful, and though he tried again on 3 September he failed to capture a single Spanish ship, and lost a great many men in the process.[60] He was forced to withdraw and his fleet was severely damaged by a hurricane, while de Ibarra retired to Veracruz on 24 September to pass the winter. Having regrouped, the fleets of Tierra Firme and Nueva España set sail for Spain taking an unusual route, avoiding both Havana and the Azores, and arrived to a rapturous welcome at Cádiz on 15 June 1639.[61] But Jol's presence in the area caused great alarm to the Spanish, and a permanent sense of siege when defeat at the battle of the Downs in October ended Spanish naval dominance of the north Atlantic for all time.

The Portuguese rebellion against Spain which began in 1640 heralded a period of crisis for the WIC, and from this time onwards it would deteriorate from a mighty war-machine to a common smuggling and slave-trading organisation, a process stemming in large part from its conquest of Brazil.[62] In 1640 Jol tried again to attack Havana with thirty-six ships but succeeded only in losing six when the fleet was scattered by a storm before he could launch an attack, and the Spanish subsequently recovered much booty including seventy-two guns.[63] At the same time the Dutch tried to establish a new settlement on the Unare estuary, bringing with them a prefabricated timber fort that was assembled in just seven days, only for them to be thrown out by Juan de Orpín, governor of Cumanagoto, and the salt pan was flooded once more.[64] In 1644 a large Dutch fleet under Peter Stuyvesant invited the demoralised garrison of San Martín to surrender, which they did after a brief resistance sufficient to satisfy honour. The Dutch occupied one-half of the island, later sharing it with the French.

With merchant interests developing, the impetus to raiding among the Dutch slowly decreased as during the 1640s they emerged as the principal carriers of the Caribbean: English and French settlers as much as Spanish ones saw Dutch trade as liberating them from their home nations because, quite simply, they got a better deal from it.[65] Nevertheless, the Spanish remained deeply fearful of large-scale attacks for many years after Matanzas, and spent enormous sums on naval escorts for treasure ships. During the 1620s the tonnage of the *armada de la guardia* amounted to 37 per cent of the total fleet compared to 12 per cent in 1601, and in 1632–3 cost upward of a million ducats, but it met no enemies and lost no ships to storms. Thus the *avería* was a tax which consumed that which it was designed to protect, and it was hardly surprising that merchants faced with an imposition of between 23 and 40 per cent in order to fund these protective fleets (and this covered only around 20 per cent of the total cost, the rest coming from the royal treasury) resorted increasingly to fraud or preferred to take their chances with the pirates.[66]

For their part, the Dutch were beginning to encounter problems that previously plagued the Spanish and Portuguese; colonies were far from being simple milch cows of empire, but in fact soaked up ever growing amounts of money for their administration and protection, and this was especially true of Brazil which remained in Dutch hands until 1654. But as the empire in South America collapsed and it seemed the WIC was a spent force, an English contemporary noted that 'upon the unhappie Civill War that broke out in England they [the Dutch] managed the whole trade of the western colonies and furnished the islands [Barbados and St Christopher] with negroes, copper, stills, and all other things appertaining . . . for making of suger'.[67]

Having tried their hand on San Martín, then settling St Eustatius (1635) and Saba (1640), it became clear to the Dutch that Curaçao would be the jewel in the WIC's crown, despite being barren and unsuitable for plantation agriculture, for its location and the superb natural harbour at Willemstad made it ideal for barques and long-boats engaged in clandestine trade with Venezuela and New Granada (Colombia). By March 1661 the Spanish ambassador at The Hague was warning Madrid that the Dutch had 'established large stores with every kind of merchandise there which they deliver during the night, using long boats, taking back silver bars and other goods'.[68] However, the WIC was doomed as an enterprise; a war-machine run by merchants was never seriously likely to succeed, especially as it was increasingly at odds with the VOC. If its rise had been meteoric, its decline would span thirty years with Curaçao its base. Too arid for plantations but ideally situated for distributing slaves, Willemstad became a slave emporium driven by refugees from the fall of Luanda and of Brazil in 1654, an increasingly forlorn outpost.[69]

Although with the Treaty of Münster peace was sealed between Spain and the United Provinces in 1648, finally ending the Eighty Years War, many Dutch adventurers would simply ignore the new settlement and carry on raiding and smuggling. But Piet Hein's one-off success remained unique, and could not be compared with the cumulative effects of raiding that steadily drained Spanish resources, or with the later war against the buccaneers. Dutch operations under the aegis of the WIC were different from these subsequent campaigns in two ways: first, they were not organised in an ad hoc and 'democratic' fashion by the participants, since the men were not self-styled adventurers, but rather *varendvolk* (common seamen of a proletarian sort); secondly, the participants could not expect to earn a significant share of any booty. This goes a long way to explaining why Dutch forays into the Pacific were failures, and reveals Hein's success as anomalous. Furthermore, if Dutch piracy was a business, then it highlighted a fundamental and irreconcilable conflict between labour and management that led not only to crew riots but to the creation of a new wave of privateers, as the Dutch found themselves in increasing competition with the English and French.[70]

# 4

## BRETHREN OF THE COAST

Then said the souls of the gentlemen adventurers —
Fettered wrist to bar all for red iniquity:
  'Ho, we revel in our chains
  O'er the sorrow that was Spain's;
Heave or sink it, leave or drink it, we were masters of the sea!'

Rudyard Kipling, *The Last Chantey*

As early as 1577 John Dee, Queen Elizabeth's Welsh astrologer, predicted the rise of an 'incomparable British Impire' based on the mythical conquests of King Arthur and Prince Madoc of Gwynedd, who supposedly discovered America in 1170. But the concept failed to strike a chord with the queen or with merchants and adventurers.[1] Then Francis Bacon, prophet of New Atlantis and breaking with the traditions of scholasticism, became an advocate of emigration; but he warned that 'planting of countries is like planting of woods', and would take time to produce results. He also noted that colonisation centred not on the 'propagation of the Christian faith', but on 'gold, silver, and temporal profit and glory'.[2]

At the beginning of the seventeenth century the British empire did not exist. Even the term 'Great Britain'\* was a nebulous one – embraced by a Scottish king of England to describe his heterogeneous realm. As the century developed it remained very much an English enterprise in which the Welsh were quietly included, while the Irish and Scots generally were not, at least for another century or more. At the same time English and Scots involvement in Ireland, in particular the plantations of Ulster and Munster, distorted transoceanic activity and settle-

---

\* Although James favoured the term Great Britain, Scotland and England remained constitutionally separate. The Scottish navy would disappear during the civil wars of mid-century, and the Royal Navy was financed from English revenue, so the term 'English navy' remains appropriate at this stage.

ment, so that the Scots and Irish were restricted to populating rather than promoting such schemes. So the early colonies were strictly speaking English rather than British.[3]

The first attempt to establish a colony in North America had been Sir Walter Raleigh's Virginia in 1585, named after the queen, in what is now Roanoke, North Carolina. But this was evacuated after only one year, and completely abandoned in 1587 as all England's energies were concentrated on the war with Spain. By the time peace was concluded with the Treaty of London in 1604 Raleigh was in gaol for plotting against the new king. When James I signed the treaty he recognised all territory effectively occupied by the Spanish, but not that which remained unoccupied. The official Spanish view of the treaty was that the omission of America reinforced Spain's exclusive rights to the New World, and that any Englishman found there would be treated as a pirate.[4] The first attempt to plant an English colony in the Lesser Antilles was by a group of some seventy men who landed on St Lucia in 1605. They had originally intended to reinforce an attempt by Charles Leigh to set up a colony on the Wiapoco river (or Guayapoco, north of the Amazon), but their ship *Olive Branch* could not beat down the South American east coast against adverse winds and currents, and they anchored at St Lucia to seek provisions. Although they were greeted by friendly Caribs, there was insufficient food available to continue the voyage, and a violent row ensued between the colonists and the ship's company with the colonists agreeing to settle the island instead. This, however, provoked a reaction from the Caribs, who attacked soon afterwards and massacred most of the settlers. Nineteen survivors managed to escape and reach the mainland, where the Spanish learned of their sad tale.[5]

The idea of a colony continued to attract Plymouth and London merchants who persuaded the king to issue a charter to the Virginia company which in 1607 sent an expedition that founded Jamestown in Chesapeake Bay. The colony struggled to begin with – of 104 men and boys, 51 had died by the following spring – and it endured a precarious few years teetering on the brink of failure before the settlers began growing tobacco for export, after which things gradually improved. But the founding of Jamestown did not affect the Caribbean in the way the Spanish feared it would, seeing it as a potential nest of pirates for which it was not used.[6] In 1613 a Canarian owner–master claimed to have been attacked and robbed off the coast of Puerto Rico by a Chesapeake man-of-war, but the governor of Havana was unconvinced, and it may have been an attempt by the Canarian to cover up his lack of an official register.[7] Nevertheless Jamestown did affect the Caribbean indirectly, as it diverted Spanish attention from more direct threats; yet the Spanish failed to do anything about it, believing it would fizzle out of its own accord. Eventually it flourished, and Maryland followed in 1622, with slaves providing the labour, and sugar and tobacco the wealth. The one action the Spanish did take, however, affected Caribbean security in the long term.

English colonisation of the Caribbean islands was both preceded by and causally linked to privateering in Spanish waters. In 1606 a proposal was made and accepted by the Spanish crown to garrison and fortify Guadeloupe or a nearby island, in order to quell the Caribs who posed an increasing threat to units of the treasure fleets thanks to English and French ships providing them with firearms in exchange for tobacco. The proposed garrison of 150 men would have to come from Florida, halving the garrison there. But with Virginia being only 300 miles from Florida, and with progress in evangelising the Florida Indians progressing better than expected, the scheme was postponed and effectively shelved. Guadeloupe and the other Lesser Antilles were left to the Caribs, and ultimately to the French, Dutch and English. Further plans for colonising the Lesser Antilles soon appeared; an Anglo-Dutch syndicate attempted to colonise Grenada as a tobacco-producing enterprise in 1609 when a group of 208 Londoners were landed – not perhaps the best-suited people for establishing plantations. The ships carrying them continued on to Trinidad and, on their return, found the colony all but destroyed by disease and took off the survivors.[8] The Virginia company also produced a subsidiary that colonised the Somers Islands (Bermuda) after Sir George Somers was shipwrecked there in the same year. Three men who stayed behind when the others got away found a huge lump of ambergris worth thousands of pounds, and systematic settlement began in 1613.[9]

Despite a ban on attacking the Spanish Main from English ports, enterprising English captains took to using remote harbours such as Barnstaple and Dartmouth, or accepting commissions from foreigners

like the Prince of Orange. Among the adventurous merchants supporting such ventures were the Courteen brothers of London and
Middelburg with their associates Ralph Merrifield and Marmaduke
Rawdon of London. Privateering was therefore probably the most
important source of capital for the infant colonies of the West Indies.[10]
During the early 1620s English Parliamentary leaders began to encourage the king towards an attack on the Spanish Caribbean. In March
1624 Sir John Eliot asked Parliament: 'Are we poor? Spain is rich. There
are our Indies.'[11] Renewed war between the two countries in 1624
following James I's intervention in the Thirty Years War saw a fresh
wave of foreign penetration of the Caribbean leading to settlement;
the principal cause of the shift toward colonisation by the French,
Dutch and English was the soaring price of tobacco in northern
Europe.

Dutch naval spearheads had made it possible for north Europeans
to penetrate the area, and it was no coincidence that all three had
arrived in the Lesser Antilles by the early 1620s since all three had, at
least temporarily, settled their religious strife and made peace with
Spain, even if they did not accept her suzerainty in the region. They
also adopted the 'mercantilist' premise that cash crops would be their
New World 'mines'.[12] Wind and currents favoured the strategic colonisation of the Lesser Antilles, and also made them ideal jump-off
points for assaults on the Spanish empire, as Armand Jean du Plessis –
'Iron Armand', the great Cardinal Richelieu of France – was happy to
admit.[13] But the most immediate and important driver was the search
for good tobacco land. Captain Thomas Warner, having been unsuccessful in Guiana, first put in to St Christopher, which lay off normal
Spanish navigational routes, in 1622 and a year later without gaining
permission from the crown he set out to found a tobacco colony.[14] He
first sailed for Virginia in search of recruits for his enterprise, but found
only four or five, with the result that the party amounted to only about
fifteen people including Warner and his eldest son Thomas, then aged
thirteen, who joined his father on 28 January 1624. Captain John Smith,
writing soon afterwards, recorded that:

at their arivall they found three French-men who sought to oppose
Captain Warner, and to set the Indians upon us; but at last we all

became friends and lived with the Indians a moneth. Then we built a Fort and a house, and planting fruits, by September we made a crop of tobacco; but upon the 19th of September came a hericano and blew it away.[15]

The Caribs had been willing to trade and allow visits, even temporary residence, as long as Europeans respected their customs, gardens and women.[16] At first the Indians remained friendly – the little colony could not have survived had they been otherwise – and despite the failure of a first crop of tobacco a second one thrived when a reinforcement, the *Hopewell* under John Jeaffreson, arrived in March 1625. In due course Warner returned to England in this vessel with all the available tobacco, physical proof of the success of the enterprise, although it is unclear whether this occurred before or after the arrival on the island of a new French party.[17]

In 1596 the twenty-one-year-old Pierre d'Esnambuc, impecunious son of Nicolas Belain, sieur d'Esnambuc et de Canouville, had entered service with a friend and native of Rouen, Urbain de Roissey, sieur de Chardouville, assuring himself that in six years he would surely waylay some rich prize or take possession of a fertile island.[18] But the years had rolled by and the friends could barely cover their expenses, although they did learn the art of navigation and obtained commissions in the navy. In 1625 they were sailing a small brigantine with forty men and just four guns when they fell in with a 400-ton Spanish galleon off the coast of Cuba carrying thirty-five guns. Undeterred by this disparity, de Roissey decided to attack. After three hours of unequal combat, with his ship badly damaged and most of his crew killed or seriously injured, he drew off, and the Spaniard, unable to catch the obstreperous Frenchman, sailed away greatly shaken by the punishment he had received. Badly wounded himself, de Roissey needed a port in which to repair his ship and recover. He obviously had to avoid Spanish territory, so he decided to head eastward. He reached St Christopher some two weeks later at the end of October, dropping anchor off the northern part of the island in the shadow of Mount Misery near Pointe de Sable.[19]

There he found the existing English settlement growing tobacco, and the possibilities appealed to d'Esnambuc, who now assumed leadership of the enterprise. To the survivors of his crew he could add a group of stragglers who, driven from Guiana, had found refuge on St Christopher, making a total of some eighty men. But this would not be sufficient for an independent colony and he would have to return to France for more. In the meantime, he reached a protective alliance with Warner against the Caribs. It was just as well, for soon afterwards the Caribs on neighbouring islands gathered a large number of canoes carrying some 500 warriors to attack the Europeans. Captain John Smith recalled that 'we bade them be gone, but they would not; whereupon we and the French joyned together, and upon the 5th of November set upon them, and put them to flight'.[20] Having successfully defended their new colony Warner and d'Esnambuc agreed to return to their respective countries to secure funds for its joint development. Six months after his arrival, d'Esnambuc and de Roissey were ready to leave for France, arriving home in the summer of 1626 whereupon they earned a handsome reward for their cargo of tobacco.

The two adventurers bought a coach and horses together with clothing suitable for men of their new station, and travelled to Paris to sell their idea to an expectant public. By dint of lavish spending they convinced a number of notables to share the enterprise, but the power in the land, Richelieu, had recently decided that the best way to proceed would be to follow the Dutch pattern of large trading companies to protect against the risks of small investors falling foul of freebooters. As de Roissey and d'Esnambuc arrived in Paris the cardinal had just launched the Company of the Hundred Associates to take over the nascent colonies in Canada; they persuaded His Eminence that St Christopher and the surrounding islands also presented a wonderful opportunity, and that they were just the men to exploit it.[21] So they cut a deal to form a company of St Christopher with Richelieu as the largest shareholder, to colonise the island plus Barbuda and any others between 11° and 18° north not possessed (the charter did not say 'claimed') by another Christian prince.[22] At the same time Warner applied for and obtained patent protection for growing tobacco from the crown for the colonisation not only of St Christopher, but also of Nevis, Montserrat and Barbados. He also opened negotiations with the lord treasurer, the Earl of Marlborough, to secure proprietary rights to the islands, but these went instead to James Hay, first Earl of Carlisle, as both were men of great wealth and influence at court, the economic titans of the age. Before this arrangement was concluded, however, Warner sailed from England armed with his patent as lieutenant of the king, and letters of marque authorising reprisals against the Spanish.[23]

Meanwhile Captain John Powell, a veteran trader and pirate in the Caribbean, was returning from Brazil when he dropped anchor on the leeward side of Barbados on 14 May 1625. He erected a cross and, drawing upon the 'traditional ceremonies of possession', claimed the island for King James I by inscribing a tree. His men then left other 'Marks of their possession for the Crown of England' before proceeding to St Christopher and then home. On reaching England Powell told his employer, Sir William Courteen, of the 'goodness of this island', which confirmed previous glowing reports and began a conflict of interest between Courteen and the Earl of Carlisle.[24] Courteen formed a syndicate including Powell to fund three ships 'with Men, Ammunition, Arms, and all kind of Necessaries fit for Planting and Fortifying' a settlement on Barbados. This venture saw Powell's brother Henry land on the island on 20 February 1627 with eighty men in the *William and John* at the present site of Holetown, and his nephew, also John, appointed governor.[25] The preparations for the second and third ships were completed by John Powell soon afterwards, and the *Peter* and *Thomasine* departed in early April. Soon housing was built and, with help from Arawak Indians, crops were planted, notably tobacco and corn.

On St Christopher Indian trouble had now broken out among formerly friendly natives alarmed by the increasing numbers of white men who, interested only in growing tobacco, had failed to provide themselves with sufficient food and were greedily eyeing Carib gardens. Fortunately for the settlers, soon after Warner's return an Indian woman called Barbe revealed to him a Carib plot. Despite having brought 400 men from England he felt that even reinforced by the French they would be no match for the Indians, and he decided to fall upon them while they were engaged in a drinking bout, killing a large proportion of them including their chief, Tegreman, reputedly in his hammock.[26] Knowing that the Indians were expecting reinforcements, Warner built barricades and set watch. When a large body of war canoes appeared carrying more than 3,000 warriors, the colonists held their fire for a deadly volley that sent the survivors into ignominious retreat. Soon afterwards the Caribs attacked the French, who received immediate support from the English, after which began the expulsion of the natives from their islands apart from a few women retained as slaves.[27]

For his part d'Esnambuc had gone to Le Havre armed with his new authority and raised 322 men for *La Catholique*, while de Roissey secured 210 men in Brittany for *La Victoire* and *La Cardinale*. They sailed on 27 February 1627 arriving at Pointe de Sable on 8 May, but matters were so badly managed that provisions ran low and almost half the men succumbed to disease. Five days later the two European contingents signed a treaty dividing the island between them, with the English taking the centre and the French the two ends. They agreed to aid each other against the Spanish or natives as necessary, and to regulate their own trade; no Englishman could land without permission of the English governors, nor any Frenchman without permission of the French, and Dutchmen would require permission from both. But the most remarkable clause restrained them from conducting hostilities against each other even if their home nations were at war, unless specifically ordered by their governments in which case due notice should be given. This clause was inserted by the colonists because England and France were then at war and all could see the folly of becoming involved in actions so far removed from Europe faced by hostile natives and Spanish. This did not prevent mutual distrust and local disputes from arising on a regular basis, but the Spanish threat remained strong, so that this local treaty was repeatedly renewed until 1662. In the meantime, to counter the Spanish threat, the English built Fort Charles, armed with twenty-two guns, while the French built Fort Richelieu in the north with fourteen guns, and Basse-Terre in the south with eleven.[28]

For the Spanish threat was very real. In the 1620s and 1630s the Spanish crown, under the direction of Olivares, was convinced that only the centralisation of power could overcome its gross inefficiency and weakness. Given that only 20–25 per cent of crown revenue came from American bullion, and with barely one-third of the crown's 16 million European subjects – mostly Castilians – shouldering the burden of this bellicose foreign policy, the overruling of local laws and institutions was designed to strengthen the effective exercise of king-ship. America was regarded as being almost integral to Castile and her bullion would underwrite Olivares' ambitions, which included cutting fraud and foreign penetration by means of increased government inter-vention and suppression of inter-colonial trade.[29] In the opening years of Felipe III's reign the crown had expected 2 million ducats a year of American silver, but this had halved by 1616 and by 1620 had been reduced to 845,000 ducats, as long-term changes in the relationship between Spain and the Americas kicked in. Peru and Nueva España approached self-sufficiency in foodstuffs, and were increasingly reliant on northern European manufactures, albeit shipped via Sevilla. Oli-vares failed to grasp that the way to conserve the wealth of the Indies was through trade, domestic and international, which would prevent the exploitation of Spain by foreign merchants bent on draining the country of its silver.[30]

In 1625 he came up with a scheme for a common defence pro-gramme – the Union of Arms – to bind the monarchy's disparate parts together, and he extended this to the New World in 1627, a move that stretched the finances of the Americas to the limit. Dissatisfaction grew as he drove Spain towards a belligerent and ultimately disastrous foreign policy, and while Americans complained that justice and good government lay in ruins, Olivares ploughed on regardless.[31] When news of developments on St Christopher reached Madrid, following hard on Piet Hein's capture of the silver fleet, Don Fadrique de Toledo was given orders to expel all foreigners from the Caribbean. But Richelieu learned of this plan and was able to send nine French royal ships under François de Rotondy, sieur de Cahouzac, to defend St Christopher at a time when the impecunious Charles I could not.[32] Cahouzac left France in June 1629 and reached the island in August, much to the delight of the French colonists who immediately instructed the English to retire to their own quarters, after they had apparently exceeded their bound-aries.[33] Edward Warner, acting as lieutenant-governor in his brother's absence, sought a three-day stay hoping to solicit aid from some English ships, but the French granted him just fifteen minutes and Cahouzac then captured six English ships, putting them completely at his mercy and forcing the English to withdraw.

Having thus arranged matters and established a small colony on St

Eustatius, and in the continued absence of the Spanish fleet, Cahouzac concluded that his presence was no longer required. With disastrous consequences he decided to allow his captains to roam the Caribbean privateering, and was himself soon bound for the Gulf of Mexico. Soon afterwards, in August 1629, the Spanish fleet left the Iberian peninsula, and when it arrived at Nevis on 16 September it took eight English ships completely by surprise. Nevis had recently been planted by Anthony Hilton, who was originally sent to Virginia by some English merchant-adventurers but happened to stop off in St Christopher and became determined to set up his own plantation. Following sponsorship by a different group of Anglo-Irish merchants and after raising a small crop of tobacco, he was persuaded to go to London where he found backing from Thomas Littleton, who had a patent from the Earl of Carlisle granting him Barbuda, or any other small island he might select. Hilton chose Nevis and landed on 22 July 1628, but the colony had barely got its start when the Spanish arrived. The island's mainly Irish indentured servants then refused to fight, so the planters were forced to ask for terms the following morning.[34]

Indentured service was an extension of a long-established English practice. Most young people left home and entered service, usually on the land, working on a series of annual contracts devised at hiring fairs throughout the country. Servitude was a stage of life offering youngsters the chance to learn basic skills necessary to set up on their own, and both parties were obliged to observe the conditions of the contract throughout the year. Theoretically servants were free for only one day of the year when they attended the hiring fair where they could meet their peers and compare notes; bad masters would find it hard to attract servants so the system supposedly offered some protection. Servants might work for a decade before being in a position to afford to set up on their own, usually as a tenant, though even this limited independence was beyond the range of many.[35] However, in the colonial setting the situation changed since the master paid the servant's passage, and the latter was obliged to work longer in order to pay off the initial investment.

Life was extremely hard for the poor commoner in the West Indies, especially indentured servants whose quality of existence was little better, if at all, than that of slaves. Yet they were not necessarily misled into slavery. Service was intended as a credit mechanism by which they could borrow against the future rewards of their labour, to repay the costs of their passage and resettlement. It offered an attractive and mutually beneficial option, at least superficially, for those without means of their own. The colonial world offered a refuge for those who sought to escape, adventure for those so inclined, and a 'last resort of scoundrels'.[36] The incentive was that in the Americas freedmen (those who had worked out their contracts) would be offered land of their own. But very often the terms of the contract would prove to be quite different to that agreed in England, and many found themselves trapped in contracts of seven years or more, at the end of which they were forced to sign on again simply in order to eat.[37]

Two days after capturing Nevis, Fadrique disembarked troops on St Christopher, having missed Cahouzac by only a few days; it was a powerful force comprising thirty-five galleons and fourteen merchantmen besides the eight English ships seized at Nevis. The Spanish landed at Basse-Terre, where de Roissey was in command with reinforcements of 900 men. The French defended valiantly until forced to surrender under honourable terms, after which the Spanish moved on to secure Fort Charles and then Fort Richelieu, taking a total of 2,300 prisoners, 129 guns and 42 stone mortars, 1,350 muskets and arquebuses, together with large quantities of powder and ammunition. The forts were destroyed and the prisoners released on condition that they return to Europe and never set foot in the Caribbean again; their tobacco crops and warehouses were then destroyed, the fruits of four years' hard labour.[38]

Some of the French set sail for Antigua, but were forced to seek shelter from a storm on San Martín, where they suffered dreadful privations for lack of water. De Roissey returned to France and was thrown into the Bastille by Richelieu for his failure. Other Frenchmen dispersed to found colonies on Montserrat, Saint-Barthélemy and Anguilla. The English fared better, agreeing to an orderly retreat; but they were warned that should the Spanish return from Brazil to find them still there they would be put to the sword. As soon as the Spanish sails had disappeared over the horizon, however, they began rebuilding their settlement, and in 1630 d'Esnambuc returned to restart the French one. Others among the expelled settlers found their way to Tortuga just a few miles off the north-west coast of Española, where they joined the renegade group of cattle-hunters known as *boucaniers*, or devoted themselves to tobacco cultivation and trading with Dutch smugglers as the WIC offered them protection, promising 'not to allow them to perish, providing them with everything they needed in exchange for leather obtained from hunting livestock'.[39] Thus, far from stamping out alien invasion, the consequences of the Spanish assault on St Christopher would have entirely unintended consequences, not only failing in its primary task of eliminating foreign encroachment, but actually helping to spread it across the Caribbean as a whole.

The island of Tortuga offered little to recommend it beyond its natural rocky defences; shaped like a turtle, hence its name in Spanish (Île de la Tortue in French), it is less than fifty miles in circumference. The population was made up of renegade Europeans, former indentured servants, combined with marooned sailors and other marginalised individuals who found refuge there from the late 1620s onwards. These mostly French hunters operated along the north and west coasts and along the south coast as far as Bahía de Neiba but concentrated on the plains, now evacuated by the Spanish, where grasslands and open woods favoured livestock and which had previously supported dense native populations. Much of what we know about these men, the original buccaneers, comes from the famous account of Alexander Exquemelin, *The Buccaneers of America*. First published in Dutch in 1678, it was translated first into German, then into Spanish, English and French, with later Italian and Russian editions.[40]

Exquemelin's tales of blood-spattered hunts with pigs and cattle slaughtered with wild abandon belie the way these *boucaniers* got their start in uninhabited regions, which was thanks to two factors of which they were probably unaware. First, the natives of their new lands, mostly peaceful Taínos, had disappeared nearly a century earlier, killed by disease imported by the Spanish or hauled off to work in the mines.[41] Meanwhile the livestock introduced by the Spanish – cattle, horses and pigs – had flourished in the absence of predators, either natural or human. Thus, although the country appeared to be wild, it was not natural, although it would take just thirty years for these men and packs of wild dogs to render the fauna so scarce that Père Jean-Baptiste Labat and others lamented an ecological disaster.[42]

The early buccaneers described by the French Jesuit historians Labat, Pierre François-Xavier de Charlevoix and Jean-Baptiste du Tertre were an odd bunch to say the least. The Abbé du Tertre, writing some years later, described them as being:

> an unorganised rabble of men of all countries, rendered expert and active by the necessity of their exercise which is to go in chase of cattle to obtain their hides, and from being chased themselves by the Spanish who never give them any quarter.
>
> As they would never suffer any chiefs, they passed for undisciplined men who for the greater part had sought refuges in these places and were reduced to this way of life to avoid the punishment due for the crimes which could be proved against many of them [in Europe] . . . I have seen some of these who had lived this miserable life for twenty years without seeing a priest or eating bread.[43]

They lived a life based on hunting and curing the meat of the feral cattle and pigs, known as *viande boucanée* from the Taíno-style wooden frame or *boucan* on which the meat was smoked. The local Indians had developed this technique because, having no knowledge of salting meat, they saw a whole carcass go bad in twelve hours in the tropical heat. They dug a shallow pit capable of holding a good fire and drove four long stakes into the corners which met at the top to form a V-shape structure. From this they suspended a frame like a farm hurdle made of hardwood such as lignum vitae, which grows all over the Greater Antilles, or of greenwood.

The fire was then lit and stoked so as to produce a slow heat and the meat cut into strips and laid on top of the frame to cure in the heat and smoke. When cured it was called *boucan* by the Indians. The whole 'kitchen', pit and frame, was also called a *boucan*, and the technique earned these renegades the name *boucaniers*. But at the time the term had the mundane meaning of 'cowkillers' and it was not until much later that the word 'buccaneer' – the bold and colourful free-spirited, cutlass-wielding corsair, with a gleam in his eye and a pistol in his belt – came into use. Buccaneers did not use salt to produce their *boucan* unless it was intended to be kept for a long period or if it was pork; and occasionally, in order to give the meat a particular relish, the skin of the animal was cast into the fire which gave the flesh a fine red colour.[44] The meat they produced – what the English called jerked-meat or jerky, itself a corruption of the American Spanish *charqui* – desite being dry and stiff as a board was of excellent flavour, although this would fade after some months. It was sold in bundles of a hundred strips for six pieces of eight, and was traded, along with tobacco and crude sugar, with passing English, French and Dutch smugglers for the various manufactured items the *boucaniers* needed, including powder and shot, and alcohol of which they were very fond.

As befits hunters everywhere they paid considerable attention to their weapons, long-barrelled and broad-stocked muskets which were the finest of their type available, from the great French gunsmiths of Dieppe and Nantes. These matchlocks and later wheellocks represented the forefront of Renaissance artistry, being hand-crafted and heavily ornamented, with working parts formed into the shape of dolphins and scenes from Roman mythology etched on to the barrels. Creating such weapons in the days before mass-production was a task for numerous craftsmen – designer, stockmaker, barrelsmith, inlayers and engravers – and French gunsmiths were Europe's best, producing lighter weapons than their competitors, for which the *boucaniers* were prepared to pay large sums of money. These most treasured possessions were cleaned obsessively and the *boucaniers* became famous for their skill at arms. By contrast the Spanish were usually equipped with much cruder arquebuses, slower to fire and less accurate, and often putting them at a distinct tactical disadvantage both on land and at sea.[45]

Having no government the *boucaniers* lived by a loose code known as the *coutume de la côte*. They lived in pairs in an arrangement called *matelotage* that had legal implications suggesting a kind of same-sex marriage. Normally they would spend around six months of the year hunting in the interior of Tierra Grande, as the now depopulated north coast of Española was then called, and living in simple shacks built on stilts thatched with palm-fronds, know by the Taíno word *barbacoas* (or *ajoupas*), and sleeping under improvised mosquito nets, often with bonfires burning to windward with green leaves to provide smoke and keep the insects at bay. Meat and bones were cast casually aside where the men lived so that flies swarmed, but worse were the sandflies and mosquitoes biting all day long, but especially in the hours just before sunset until just after dark and at dawn, and it was not uncommon for a man to be driven demented by fifty or a hundred bites at a time, so to protect themselves they smeared their bodies in lard. However, the tropical heat was usually bearable and varied by little more than ten degrees.[46] But disease spreads easily in the heat and humidity of the tropics, and at a time when the connection between mosquitoes and malaria was unknown, nor the importance of hygiene, it carried away far more men than bullets ever did in a region where life was hard enough at the best of times, and a man would be exhausted by a task that in a moderate climate would leave him only tired.

These adventurers wore coarse clothing, usually comprising a pair of rough linen trousers and a loose shirt, with caps, shoes and belts fashioned from rawhide. At the end of the hunting season they would congregate for trade fairs so soaked by blood from the slaughter of animals that one contemporary described them as looking tarred.[47] Elsewhere on Española the Spanish who settled outside the towns lived a similar lifestyle, and Exquemelin later described the people of San Juan de Goave, west of Santo Domingo, as mostly hunters and butchers who were for the most part of mixed blood – people of black and white parentage, known as mulattos, or of Indian and white descent, called mestizos. The village produced a great quantity of hides and tallow, 'but nothing else is produced there on account of the great dryness of the soil'.[48]

Unlike the Spanish, however, the non-Spanish interlopers established trade ties with passing non-Spanish vessels and then began attacking those of the Spanish and at this point the jerky-makers also became sea-raiders. With increasing frequency as their numbers grew they would set out in long dugout canoes, in groups of perhaps twenty or so, to attack Spanish coastal trading barques laden with hides and tobacco that plied the coasts of Cuba and Española. They would either throw the crews overboard – for there was no love lost between them and the Spanish – or possibly swap the prize for a canoe, and return to divide the spoils equitably between them. The plunder was sold to merchants on Tortuga where the captured barques would be converted into pirate vessels and guns, powder and ammunition could be obtained. In such barques they could strike further afield, to the coasts of Yucután and the Bay of Campeche. It was a simple and adventurous, if somewhat barbaric, life.[49]

The *boucaniers* who thus took to the sea became known as *flibustiers*, which may have derived from the English 'freebooter' and Dutch *vrijbuiter*, one who plundered freely; it has also been said to have derived from 'flyboat', the English translation of the Dutch *fluyt*, typically a single-decked, square-rigged, shallow-draft vessel with three masts designed to be handled by a small crew.[50] After a while the two words became interchangeable and later, when planting was encouraged by the authorities, those who tended the land were known as *habitans* and anybody who worked for them or the hunters were known as *engagés*, and together they were known as the *corps des avanturiers*. But it would be quite wrong to assume that the *flibustiers*, or buccaneers as they became known to the English, were necessarily great seamen. What both *flibustiers* and *boucaniers* had in common was their skill with small arms, being very accurate shots. But their preferred vessels – barques or sloops – were very simple and required a minimum of seamanship. Freebooters, a softer word than pirate implying something slightly better than a common robber, derives from the tradition of soldiers serving for booty only rather than for regular pay, which in the centuries leading up to the seventeenth had been the most common form of engagement. Buccaneering, as opposed to earlier forms of privateering, was essentially locally based and is conventionally dated from around 1640.[51]

All these adventurers lived together 'with very good understanding', according to Charlevoix, for 'they had established a kind of Democratic Government; each free person had a Despotic authority in his own habitation, & every Captain was sovereign on board; as long as he was in Command, but one could depose him'.[52] The buccaneers referred to themselves as *les frères de la côte*, the brethren of the coast, and lived by a code or 'custom of the coast'. This embodied a distinctive and remarkably democratic concept of justice and class conciousness, a stand against 'the great' men of the age, whether shipowners, masters or other authority figures.[53] Indeed, the crew of a buccaneer ship was 'just about the most democratic institution in the world in the seventeenth century'. A Mexican who later spent five years imprisoned on Jamaica said they were 'very happy, well paid and they live in amity with each other. The prizes that they make are shared with each other with much brotherhood and friendship.'⁵⁴ J. S. Bromley commented on the similarity between the buccaneer and the *picaro*, the rogue-hero of the seventeenth-century Spanish novel, noting that authorities agree on their:

> self-will, caprice, dislike of work; on their disordered and unwashed clothing, their habit of singing while companions tried to sleep and shooting to make a noise; on their blasphemies and debaucheries. So long as they had cash to spend, it was difficult to persuade them to the sea ... Living from day to day, at the mercy of events, the picaresque rogue is seldom his own master for long, yet living on his wits he can assert his independence and turn the table on masters no more virtuous than himself.⁵⁵

By combining the freebooting traditions of European mercenary soldiers with those of oppressed sailors, the brethren of the coast became a sanctuary for all manner of outcasts – social misfits, military deserters, runaway slaves and indentured servants, those escaping debts and other responsibilities – to create a myth of independence embodying the very ideals of liberty, equality and fraternity that would destroy the *ancien régime* little more than a century later.⁵⁶

The first definite system of government among the disparate European inhabitants of Tortuga was set up by Anthony Hilton after Fadrique evicted him from Nevis. On his return to England in 1630 Hilton was once more determined to set up on his own colony, and thanks to wide consultation with sea captains he settled on Tortuga as being a place with little likelihood of Spanish interference.⁵⁷ This was just as well, since in 1633 another English settlement was destroyed at Punta de la Galera on the north-east tip of Trinidad by Don Juan Alvarez de Eulate leading three Spanish companies and fifty Indian archers. Alvarez was probably not exaggerating when he reported to the crown that the service he had rendered would save great expense 'because it is certain that if the enemy had succeeded in fortifying themselves, as they were doing, and if the relief ship they were expecting in April had arrived, His Majesty would doubtless have been obliged to send an armada to drive them from that place'.⁵⁸

In France Richelieu prepared for a final showdown with Spain and by 1635 had reorganised the French Company of the Indies into a new company, the Company of the Islands of America, led by his *homme de confiance*, François Fouquet.[59] French expansion to Martinique and Guadeloupe came from a combination of land hunger in the islands and domestic politics, but without the company's official sanction d'Esnambuc led an expedition with his nephew, Jacques Dyel du Parquet, from St Christopher that established a post on Martinique, insisting to Richelieu that this would threaten the Spanish empire. This pleased the cardinal, in part because both Martinique and Guadeloupe were Carib strongholds, separated by another in Dominica. D'Esnambuc then asked for permission to conquer the latter because he claimed 'the English have a grand design' upon it and had landed forty men there in 1635, although the Caribs forced them to leave.[60]

Richelieu then persuaded the francophile Italian Pope Urban VIII to sanction sending French Capuchins, Dominicans and Jesuits to the 'Spanish' Caribbean. On 14 February 1638 Philippe de Loinvilliers de Poincy, Knight of the Order of St John and a squadron leader in the French royal navy, was appointed captain-general of the American Isles as replacement for d'Esnambuc who had died on St Christopher in late 1636, having by then founded colonies on Martinique and Guadeloupe.[61] By the late 1630s, with growing populations creating land hunger, the French, Dutch and English all launched initiatives to seize Tobago, Grenada, St Lucia and Barbuda, but were usually thwarted by the local Caribs. It was the French, however, rather than the natives, who were the ultimate beneficiaries of resistance to English encroachments. Being numerically weaker they often pursued a policy of diplomacy, and by the mid-1640s relations were sufficiently good to enable a Dominican priest called Raymond Breton to live on Dominica.[62]

The Spanish, however, remained implacably opposed to any foreign settlement, especially on Tortuga, and sent Carlos de Ibarra to put all the 300 mostly English settlers there to the sword. This operation took place in 1639 and once more those settlers who managed to escape took refuge on Tierra Grande until the Spanish had gone.[63] Meanwhile de Poincy arrived at St Christopher in February 1639 accompanied by his second-in-command, François Levasseur, who would cause immediate problems for the new governor. Levasseur was a Huguenot banished after the siege of La Rochelle and, to avoid having to expel him, de Poincy decided to send him to regain control of Tortuga, which had been repopulated by 300 men from Nevis under Roger Flood of the recently formed Providence Company.[64] At the end of May 1640 Levasseur embarked with fifty men, all Huguenots from Normandy, and sailed for Port-à-Margot, a small island off Española. During a period of three months he established contact with the *boucaniers* and increased his forces by another fifty men, and on 31 August he landed and captured the island. Initially he continued to submit to de Poincy's authority and was appointed governor, and the first article of the covenant by which the island would be governed, dated 2 November 1641, guaranteed equality of religion and set down the regulations. Special attention was paid to the division of profits, with one-tenth going to the crown and the remainder divided in two, one for the company and one shared between Levasseur, de Poincy and the officers.[65]

Having gained control of a private fiefdom, however, Levasseur had no intention of abiding by any covenant. Now over forty years old and highly experienced in the art of war, he chose a good site, La Roca, on a rocky promontory overlooking the harbour on the south-east of the island, and built a fort which he called his 'dovecote'. From then on he ignored de Poincy and his orders, and repelled a force of forty men sent from St Christopher under de Poincy's nephew, the seigneur de Loinvilliers, to oversee his actions. He imposed Protestantism as the official religion, burned the Catholic chapel and began persecuting its adherents. And when the Spanish made an assault in 1643 with ten ships and 1,000 men, La Roca stood firm, and the attackers were forced to retreat.[66]

# 5

## SUGAR AND SLAVES

Par las Indias de Castilla
No daré una blanca ya,
Que el inglés acá ni allá
No deja pasar barquilla.
De la plata es la polilla,
De España la confusión,
Barrón de la religión,
Asombro del que navega,
Gallo sue turba y que ciega
Hoy totallmente al León.*

Avisos de don Jerónimo de Barrionuevo[1]

Elsewhere in the Caribbean, foreigners were becoming steadily entrenched; the difficulties experienced in Virginia and Massachusetts had shown that establishing a successful colony was a very risky business. But with Barbados apparently thriving rapidly after its establishment, it was also clear that a great return might be expected in short order.[2] The rise of the buccaneers has sometimes been attributed to the strategic designs of kings and their ministers, yet far more important was the failure of tobacco in Barbados where, despite starting well, the crop soon deteriorated to such a degree that it proved to be 'so earthy and worthless that it would give little or no return', while Virginia's product was proving to be excellent.[3] As the colony struggled to establish itself, the issue of proprietary rights had created a considerable legal wrangle between Sir William Courteen and the Earl of Carlisle.[4] Eventually the dispute was settled in favour of Carlisle, but over the following years the island's status would be confused by

---

* In exchange for the Indies / Not a farthing shall I give / Since neither here nor there / The English let past a boat. / And as moth to flame, / The English are to silver, / To Spain they bring low spirits, / To the church they bring a stain, / Wonder to he who sails, / A rooster which doth peck / And leaveth the lion blind.

Robert Rich, second Earl of Warwick, who wanted to purchase it, and Carlisle appointed Henry Huncks as governor, duly confirmed by King Charles I, who had succeeded his father James I in 1625.[5] By 1635 the population included some 4,000 payers of poll tax and the island took 20 per cent of all emigrants to America and the Caribbean; three years later there were 764 planters with ten acres or more. But most were struggling to make a living as Barbados tobacco became so notoriously inferior to that of Virginia that Peter Hay, one of the biggest planters, was bluntly informed in 1637 that, 'of all the tobacco that cometh to England', his was the worst.[6] As an alternative some tried planting cotton, but over the course of the next decade or so the island's economy would, like everyone else in the Caribbean, depend far more on Dutch than on English traders.[7]

When Charles I authorised a privateering war against Spain following his accession, Puritan grandees were very happy to combine the search for profit with the opportunity to strike against the enemy of Protestantism. The Earl of Warwick was among those who had participated most eagerly. A Puritan and longstanding opponent of the Stuart kings, he followed in his father's footsteps by maintaining a private navy.[8] Two of his ships, the barque *Warwicke and Somer Ilands* under Captain Sussex Camock and the *Robert* under Captain Daniel Elfrith of the Somers Island Company, were directed to attack Spanish shipping and settlements anywhere in the Caribbean after he obtained privateering commissions from the duc de Savoie. In 1629 Camock and Elfrith discovered two islands fifty miles apart, Santa Catalina (Providence) and San Andreas (Henrietta), a hundred miles off the Mosquito Coast of Honduras between Cabo Gracias a Dios and the San Juan river, facing some 300 miles of low sandy shore studded with mangrove swamps. During the sixteenth century Central American trade had been geared towards the Pacific and, with the exception of Honduras, with its weakly defended port at Trujillo, there remained a thousand miles of coast and islands uninhabited by the Spanish. While Camock stayed behind with thirty men to explore San Andreas and defend it, Elfrith hurried home in the *Warwicke* with the news. Soon afterwards a few Englishmen took up permanent residence at Cabo Gracias a Dios, and the Dutchman Abraham Blauvelt sailed south to make contact with Sumu Indians and other tribes (Blauvelt was still living there as late as 1663 and the town of Bluefields was named after him). There they discovered sarsparilla which they shipped home in increasing quantities as it became famous as a cure for scrofula, elephantiasis and venereal disease.[9] In, return the Sumus gained rum, European clothing, cattle and pigs, and eventually firearms. But the rum drove many into alcoholic degeneracy and their free mixture with Europeans and Africans literally changed them into a new people described by ethnologists as Samba-Miskitas.[10] Often servants and slaves escaped together, so appalling was the condition of both, and following the Spanish capture of St Christopher many escaped to the Mosquito Coast where they joined the native population and began to cut logwood.[11]

Elfrith travelled via Bermuda where he had estates, and whose governor, Captain Philip Bell, was his son-in-law. Bell sent a persuasive letter onwards with Elfrith to businessman Sir Nathaniel Rich, who was also the Earl of Warwick's cousin, as both men could see the potential of an island 'lying in the heart of the Indies & the mouth of the Spaniards'.[12] A commercial company was established, the Company of Adventurers to the Island of Providence. Many factors added to the great emigration of English people during the 1630s. Economic hardship pushed many to seek a better life, exacerbated by the misconceived war with France and Spain in the late 1620s that placed an increasingly heavy strain on the relationship between king and Parliament, while war weighed heavily on a people struggling with inflation, harvest failure and industrial depression. But many were fleeing the drive towards a new Arminian religious conformity, especially Puritans, and the uneasy relationship between civilian and military authority was another factor, one mirrored on the far side of the ocean where defence against the Spanish was of prime importance. The Providence venture was partly designed to offer shelter to English Puritans, but it is also clear from the people who provided backing that it was never intended merely as a haven from religious persecution. The end of war with Spain in 1630 did not end the personal antagonism that motivated Warwick who, with his brother, the Earl of Holland, began planting this colony in the 'privity' of the king long before the charter was granted the same year.[13]

Santa Catalina is a volcanic peak rising to 1,190 feet above sea level with a hot climate all year round and, while subject to heavy rain in the autumn, is liable to be dry for up to five months in the summer. The island was chosen because it was regarded as one of the best in the Caribbean; it was small, very fertile with a good climate, and possessed of a fine natural harbour that could be easily fortified. Furthermore, situated off the Mosquito Coast, it lay roughly equidistant from the ports of Cartagena and Portobelo, close to the route followed by Spanish vessels travelling to Veracruz or Havana, making it an ideal location for raiding activities. Meanwhile Bell assured Rich that tobacco would make it valuable, even if the island failed to yield any gold or silver. The first settlers arrived under Bell on Christmas Eve 1629, and Elfrith joined them soon afterwards, as did Captain Samuel Axe. Meanwhile investors in the project and additional settlers were sought in England, and the first group of a hundred departed London in *Seaflower* in February 1631, while Axe supervised the construction of Fort Warwick overlooking the main harbour, where the city of New Westminster was to be built. Not that defence preparations went smoothly.[14]

The formation of the Providence Island Company would provide a clear link between the activities of the Elizabethan seadogs and Oliver Cromwell's Western Design that was to follow (see Chapter 6), and would mark a transition in colonial policy.[15] The company was not only the exact contemporary of the Massachusetts Bay Company, it was intended to be *the* great Puritan venture and attracted the same type of solid Puritans as the New England colony, among both its settlers and its backers; but it faced problems not encountered by the mainland colonies, particularly the constant threat of attack from the Spanish. As a West Indian colony its economy was reliant on tobacco as a plantation crop, but this failed to make satisfactory returns, and for ideological reasons the planters were refused ownership of their lands by the venture's backers, which contributed to failure by forcing them to rely on human property in the form of slaves at a rate unprecedented at this stage of colonial development. This supposedly godly society, therefore, came to rely on privateering and slavery, and was planned by a group of gentry and aristocrats who shared strong religious convictions and had ties of blood and marriage. Their core was a group of Puritan grandees determined to spread the word of reformation, and besides Warwick, Holland and Nathaniel Rich included the Member of Parliament John Pym, William Fiennes (Lord Saye and Sele), Robert Greville (Lord Brooke), Edward Montague (Lord Mandeville), Sir Benjamin Rudyerd, Sir Gilbert Gerard, Sir Thomas Barrington and Oliver St John. For these men 'providence' meant aligning themselves with God's great purpose, and since providence had already endowed them with positions of wealth and influence, it infused them with great confidence in their enterprises.[16]

Warwick, Pym, Saye and Brook were the executive leaders of the company, and besides considerably increasing their own wealth at the expense of Spain they would learn to work together in a manner that would prove invaluable to the cause of Parliament in the years to come.[17] Ironically, while John Pym would present the military impositions on English counties as one of the main grievances of the Short Parliament in April 1640, throughout the 1630s he expressed frequent outrage when colonists objected to the military obligations imposed by the Providence Island Company.[18] Unsurprisingly, the combination of religious settlers and military men was never likely to promote harmonious government, nor could it produce unity of purpose in defence matters; the settlers thought the company should provide servants to build public works such as defence posts, and resented having to contribute.[19] By 1632 the colony appeared to its sponsors in England to be on a firm footing, but this was too good to last, and by the time *Seaflower* returned to London somewhat later than expected, the letters she carried revealed a situation little short of mutiny in the new colony led by no less than the chaplain, Lewis Morgan. It also transpired that Elfrith had invited Diego el Mulato on to the island; a small number of Dutch had been found living there when the English arrived, and the presence of these privateers greatly worried many of the planters who feared it would bring the wrath of the Spanish down upon their heads. But the company remained confident that these problems could be overcome as it prepared a second ship, *Chastity*, to carry more settlers, including women.[20]

However, things did not run smoothly. The island's tobacco production was singularly disappointing and to sustain themselves the colonists turned increasingly to trade with the Indians of the Mosquito Coast.[21] They established trading posts at Cabo Gracias a Dios and

Darién, where the Indians might bring valuable commodities in exchange for manufactures. Providence would then provide storage until they could be shipped back to England, and firm alliances with the Samba-Miskita Indians would prove to be one of the few lasting benefits of the Providence venture as the island's long-range planning increasingly focused on the mainland.[22] By 1634 the company was already looking to replace Bell as governor, although the event that most radically changed the island's economy was the successful repulse of a Spanish attack in July 1635. Captain Robert Hunt was chosen and departed on the *Blessing* in March 1636, with the island now expected to serve as a base for privateers and to open up new channels of development. Inevitably, conflicts sprang up between the planters and the privateers, who were authorised to take men from the island to serve with them.[23]

While Providence was being developed specifically to support privateering, Tortuga proved satisfactory to its settlers; but as they were poor Hilton and his followers decided to apply for protection to the Providence Island Company and gained its backing, with Tortuga being formally named Association Island. Friendly relations were soon established with the *boucaniers* on the island and on Española, but when Hilton died in 1634, to be replaced by Christopher Wormeley, an Irish renegade called John Murphy made his way to Santo Domingo and persuaded the governor that the capture of Tortuga would be a simple matter. Tortuga was duly raided in 1635 by 250 Spanish soldiers under Rui Fernández de Fuermayor, who spoiled an otherwise impressive arrival by running his ship aground. But Wormeley appears to have lived up to his name by hurriedly piling whatever possessions he could into some vessels in the harbour and sailing away, abandoning the remaining colonists to their fate. Fuermayor duly made clear his displeasure by hanging 195 colonists and seizing thirty-nine prisoners and thirty slaves.[24] The Spanish assault had temporarily cleared out Tortuga, but he failed to leave a garrison, and before long a new French colony was established with settlers who had escaped from it to Tierra Grande. But Providence Island's greatest fame as a nest of piracy came after Tortuga's clearance which separated it from the company's control and as a result enabled the company to obtain letters of marque from Charles I to launch retaliatory raids. At a subsequent meeting to discuss the settlement of Association Island on 23 May 1636, it was noted that, apart from the fertility of the soil and other attributes, it derived advantage 'by a neighbourhood to Hispaniola [and] the fair opportunity of gaining prizes'.[25]

As a result of this Thomas Gage, in recounting his journey along the Mosquito Coast in 1637, declared:

> The greatest fear that possessed the Spanish in this voyage, was the Island of Providence ... whence they feared lest some English ships should come against them with great strength. They cursed the English in it, and called the island a den of thieves and pirates, wishing the King of Spain would take some course with it, or else that it would prove very prejudicial to the Spaniards, lying near the mouth of the Desaguadero, and so endangering the frigates of Granada, and standing between Portobel and Cartagena, and so threatening the Galeons, and the King's yearly and mighty treasure.[26]

Certainly it was proving a lucrative venture. In 1638 the company ship *Providence* was returning from the West Indies when she was surprised and taken by a Dunkirker off the English coast. In testimony to the admiralty court concerning the case, her cargo was valued at no less than £30,000.[27] And in January 1640 the case of *Warwick and Secretary con Grove* came before the court which demonstrated that while in the West Indies the *Warwick* had taken 'great quantities of gold, plate, money, diamonds, pearls, jewels, and other goods and commodities' of astonishing value.[28]

When the Spanish finally made their long-feared attack in July 1635, it came after that on Tortuga and therefore with warning. Samuel Axe, who had been trading on the mainland, returned to Providence to help with preparations having accepted Dutch letters of marque. The Spanish therefore felt justified in wiping out a nest of English pirates.[29] The Spanish fleet was commanded by Captain Gregorio de Castellar y Mantilla, who first anchored outside New Westminster and sent an emissary to demand the island's surrender. Governor Bell refused, citing his responsibility to King Charles I, upon which the Spanish decided to attack at a point between the main island and its small western outlier, which the colonists regarded as very inaccessible and had therefore not fortified. Still they were able to drag heavy guns to the heights overlooking the Spanish approach and in due course forced the 'torn and battered' Spanish, who struggled against the prevailing winds and currents, to retreat 'in haste, and disorder'.[30]

Despite these developments in the Caribbean Spain and England remained at peace, and in December 1635 a conference had been convened to discuss this instability. But the Spanish attack changed the entire situation. It was at this time that the Providence Island Company heard of the attack, and appealed to the king through the Earl of Holland for letters of marque which would allow the island itself to sponsor privateering, as many investors had been keen to do from the outset. It was a proposal, however, that set the island's military – some godly and some not – against the more pious civilian population. When the request was granted by the king on 21 December, it signalled a significant shift in foreign policy.[31] For some years Charles had been following a pro-Spanish policy, despite Spain's role as the hammer of Protestants in the German wars. His beloved wife, the French Catholic Henrietta Maria, was the centre of an influential group of courtiers including Holland who favoured an alliance with France, although the granting of letters of marque would prove to be as far as the policy went.[32] Meanwhile the Spanish still had to consider what to do about Providence Island. In December the Junta de Guerra de Indias (War Council of the Indies) agreed that the English had no right to be in the region at all and could be eliminated legally; the dilemma that remained was how to prevent them simply occupying another of the myriad islands in the Caribbean unless the crown was prepared to commit major forces to sweep them out.[33]

However, it would take another five years before the depredations of the Providence privateers reached such a level that the commander of the *flota* allowed diversion of his ships for the task, and it would lead to scattering of the settlers precisely as the junta had predicted. In the meantime not only was the company granted letters of reprisal, but it could issue commissions to others, the only English agents that could do so at the time. Soon partnerships were formed with merchants such as Maurice Thompson, who shared 20 per cent of their takings with the company in return for using the island as a base, thereby increasing the profitability of the island for investors, who maintained a blithe

The popular Dutch admiral Piet Heyn proved Spain's most dangerous adversary in the early years of the seventeenth century, and gained enduring fame when he captured the entire Spanish silver fleet.

(*Previous page*) Seville was the centre of Spanish trade with the Americas throughout the sixteenth century; here an expedition is shown setting out for America.

Pag 84

Two very different depictions of a buccaneer:

*(Above)* The original buccaneers, or *boucaniers*, were hunters and butchers by trade. The name derives from their method of smoking meat learned from the indigenous population on Hispaniola.

*(Right)* Howard Pyle's illustration of a buccaneer for *Harper's Monthly Magazine* in 1905 shows a more familiar swashbuckling image, laden with firearms.

In 1625, a Dutch fleet of eighteen ships commanded by Boudewijn Hendricks attempted to capture San Juan de Puerto Rico. Despite being vastly outnumbered, the Spanish garrison resisted, forcing Hendricks and his men into retreat.

Fadrique de Toledo successfully oversaw the expulsion of the French and English settlers from the island of St Christopher (St Kitts) in 1625.

Robert Rich, second Earl of Warwick, a Puritan and longstanding opponent of Charles I, maintained a private navy and led an unsuccessful privateering expedition against the Spaniards in 1627.

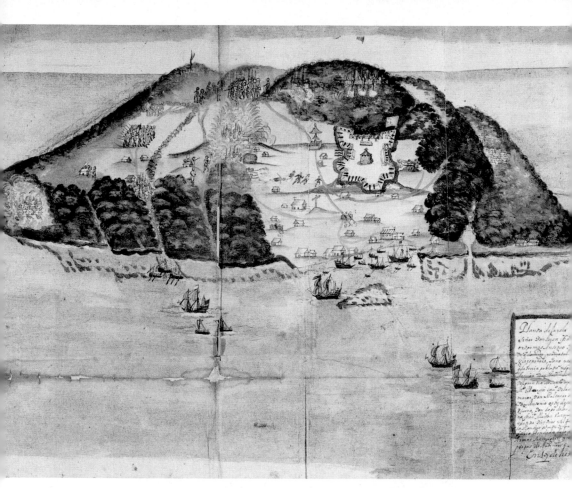

The heavily fortified island of Tortuga became the unofficial headquarters of the 'Brethren of the Coast'.

Punta del Araya in Venezuela was the scene of many battles. The fortifications shown here were built to protect the town's highly prized salt pans.

Sir Christopher Myngs, the bold and resourceful commander in chief
of the British station in Jamaica.

assurance that the godly experiment was somehow insulated from the repercussions of privateering. By linking themselves to the great Elizabethan seadogs to carry on a private war, the military faction sought to inhibit the persecution of European Protestants by interdicting the flow of Spanish American treasure, but at the cost of undermining the civilian basis of the colony. And in response to the reluctance shown by many colonists to fulfil their obligations, regarding them as an infringement of English rights, the company responded with the absolute loss of freedom for an increasing number of African slaves.[34]

So it was that the Providence Island experiment entered 1636 in a spirit of renewal, and Captain Robert Hunt, a godly man, was selected to replace Bell as governor. While Bell's experience was largely Caribbean, Hunt had served with Protestant forces in the Netherlands and at the siege of La Rochelle. Privateering offered new opportunities but would also mean an increased danger of Spanish attack, and the company ensured that additional soldiers, armaments and ammunition were shipped out. But Hunt proved to be a dismal failure as governor; he allowed factionalism to flourish and the subsequent persecution of Bell, and soon the company decided that a firmer and more experienced hand was needed.[35] In 1638 the island saw a huge influx of military men with the appointment of a new governor, the sixty-one-year-old Captain Nathaniel Butler, an 'ancient soldier at sea and land' who had commanded ships in expeditions to Cádiz, the Île de Rhé and La Rochelle during the 1620s, and who had succeeded Bell as governor of Bermuda and rebuilt its fortifications.[36] Providence Island's new council of war comprised Butler and Captains Axe, Robert Hunt and Andrew Carter, and the functions of government were increasingly delegated to them, as Butler clearly regarded the island as first and foremost a privateer base. A further grievance for the civilian population was the introduction of foreign values, because much privateering was done on the basis of consort arrangements with the Dutch, who were the most knowledgeable operators in the region. Butler himself was dismayed by the far superior information Dutch mariners possessed, as he discovered on his own frustrating and fruitless privateering voyage to the Mosquito Coast.[37]

On this trip beginning in May 1639 Butler met a turtling expedition out from Providence whose members informed him that Captain

William Jackson, a privateer financed by Maurice Thompson under a Providence Island Company licence, had captured a slave ship at Trujillo, in ransom for which the town had paid 'eight thousand weight of indigo, two thousand pieces of Eight, and two chains of Gold'. Butler duly proceeded to Trujillo which he took easily, 'but found it miserably poor and utterly empty . . . having all of the [inhabitants] run away one way and conveyed their goods out another way'. Butler prevented his disgruntled men from burning the town, and all they captured was a frigate; in exchange for that ship's sail he gave the town's representatives 'a worser boat from us'.[38] He then made for Cape San Antonio at the western tip of Cuba, but a series of errors both destroyed any hopes of success and brought the crew to the verge of dehydration and starvation; navigational miscalculation saw them make landfall 'according to expectation' only once in two months, and the ship's officers began talking of 'conjuring and ill presages'. The English ignorance of the Caribbean was embarrassing to Butler, whose chart even mislocated Jamaica, but he did attempt to lay the groundwork for future plans. He wrote an appraisal of the Cabo Gracias a Dios as a possible plantation site, noting the widely held view that the Moskito Indians hated the Spanish and loved the English.[39]

With relations throughout the colony now in turmoil Butler proceeded to make his way home in March 1640, leaving Captain Carter as his temporary replacement. When in May the Spanish made a second attempt to evict the English from the island, Don Melchor de Aguilera, captain-general of Cartagena, had renewed his pleas that Providence Island – that 'den of thievery' with its excellent harbour, so close to both Cartagena and Portobelo that the flow of food and other supplies was being interrupted – convinced Don Juan de Vega Basan and Don Rodrigo Lobo of the Peru *flota* to do something. They detailed Don Antonio Maldonado de Texada to intervene with a combined force of around 700 soldiers. On the evening of 30 May some 300 Spanish approached a landing site between Black Rock Fort and the mouth of the Black River 'singing with a dreadful and formal tone *pero, diabolo, cornuda, sa sa sa*', only for Carter to embarrass his soldiers by 'ducking at every shot', before fleeing to Fort Warwick.[40] But fire from the forts forced the Spanish to land at a very difficult spot facing slippery rocks and a sheer cliff face. Their numbers were limited because several of the landing boats had been damaged in a storm while the fleet had been assembling near Cabo Gracias a Dios. And despite being assured by Aguilera that the English would 'fly away like so many sheep at the very sight of the enemy approaching', the attackers were cut down and only two were left unwounded.[41]

Carter then compounded his cowardice by ordering the slaughter of the prisoners, and although the Spanish themselves carried orders that all the men of the colony were to be put to the sword, and the women to be prizes for them, this went too far for the company and it ordered Carter home as soon as it became aware of this violation of the standards of civilised warfare.[42] The company gave thanks for the deliverance of its colony, which offered 'further arguments of hope that God hath reserved it for some special services to his own Glory and the honor of this Nation', but chose to replace Carter with Captain John Humphrey, appointing Captain Thomas Fitch as his deputy. The commissions were to prove the last correspondence of the Providence Island Company; its members were all closely involved in much more important developments at home where arguments over divine providence were approaching a cataclysmic showdown between king and Parliament. Meanwhile Humphrey tried to encourage immigration from the struggling Massachusetts colony. The Spanish authorities were aware of this plan, which may well have added to the urgency of their desire to rid the island of the troublesome English; their own colonists meanwhile chafed in impotent anger at their enemy's continued depredations.[43]

These led the Spanish ambassador to the Court of St James's, Alonzo de Cárdenas, to complain that Warwick, Saye, Brook and Pym, having received letters of reprisal for supposed losses, had been sending ships of war annually under captains who abused their commissions to rob and harass his Catholic Majesty's subjects. On 11 July 1640 he presented another bitter complaint, stating that he:

understands that there is lately brought in at the Isle of Wight by one, Captain James Reskinner, a ship very richly laden with silver, gold, diamonds, pearls, jewels, and many other precious commodities taken by him in virtue of a commission of the said Earl [of Warwick] from the subjects of his Catholic Majesty ... to the infinite wrong and dishonour of his Catholic Majesty, to find himself thus injured and violated, and his subjects thus spoiled, robbed, impoverished and murdered in the highest times of peace, league and amity with your Majesty.[44]

It is not clear that King Charles took any action to rein in his subjects, and this lack of any effective response may well have contributed to the Spanish determination to stamp out this nest of vipers lurking in their midst.[45] On special royal orders General Francisco Díaz Pimienta assembled a fleet of seven large ships and four pinnaces with attendant boats to carry 1,400 soldiers and 600 seamen from Cartagena. It arrived off Providence on 19 May 1641.[46]

Pimienta was not going to make the same mistakes as previous expeditions and he reconnoitred carefully, concentrating on the relatively unfortified eastern side of the island. Many of his subordinates advised landing in the half-moon bay in the south-east, but the general saw the English furiously digging trenches and emplacing two guns there, while Andrew Carter – still awaiting his replacement – later admitted that he had pinned his hopes on this being the objective. But when adverse winds ruled out the eastern side of the island altogether, Pimienta boldly aimed at the main harbour of New Westminster, banking on being able to get there more quickly than the English could move overland; he further decided that the pinnaces could answer for the artillery of the forts, and chose to leave his large ships out of the action to preserve them for carrying silver back to Spain. The attack was launched on 24 May and Pimienta was impressed by the defences, but his plan quickly succeeded and he moved to occupy the governor's house on the hill while his men fanned out to quell any remaining resistance. Once the Spanish flag was seen above the governor's house, however, the English flags were lowered over the forts and a flag of truce sent to negotiate a surrender. Pimienta chose to spare the lives of the English, and on 25 May he formally took possession of the island and celebrated a Catholic mass in the church.[47]

Among the booty taken were sixty guns and a great deal of equipment that had been stockpiled for a new colony to be established on the Mosquito Coast. The 381 slaves were taken and sold at Cartagena, both their numbers and those of the 350 English settlers being far fewer than the Spanish had expected. The English had been fearful of rebellion, so many had already dispersed to the Mosquito Coast, St Christopher, Tobago and Ruatán in the Bay of Campeche (where they were overrun the following year).[48] Pimienta stated that the women and children were to be quartered among the inhabitants of Cartagena who had asked for them with pleasure, and they were sent on to Cádiz and thence to England at their own expense, a marked contrast to the brutal treatment of Spanish prisoners by the English governor.[49] The general also respectfully refused to comply with the royal order to destroy the island's defences, pointing out their considerable strength and noting the need to keep out the Dutch, who had expressed an interest in acquiring the island. He was confident that a small, self-sufficient garrison of 150 men could hold it and left Don Gerónimo de Ojeda in charge. All of this was confirmed by royal *cédula* in 1643, and Pimienta was rewarded with a knighthood of the Order of Santiago.[50] For now, with civil war engulfing England, there was no possibility of any sort of expedition to reclaim the island. But the Spanish had not yet seen the last of the Providence Island Company, for it was under one of its commissions that Captain William Jackson embarked on his second long privateering voyage in 1642, with Samuel Axe as his vice-admiral.

Despite the fall of Providence and the onset of civil war in England, Warwick was not deterred from continuing his private war with Spain. Indeed, his hostility to that kingdom was so open that when he was appointed lord high admiral in 1642 many saw in this appointment an ulterior motive on the part of Parliament, and Cardenas viewed it with considerable alarm lest it portend an expedition against Spain. He had good cause to be worried. In September 1642 Jackson set out to punish the Spanish enemy with a good old-fashioned English show of force, deliberately in the style of Drake, carrying a commission granting him complete freedom of action. He commanded three ships 'well appointed and furnished with all manner of warlike provision and necessary habiliments', and 'arrived at Barbados where he published his intent against the Spaniards'.[51]

Jackson immediately sent a ship to St Christopher to gain recruits and had no difficulty raising 500 men himself on the usual privateering terms of 'no purchase, no pay'.* He then began fitting out three pin-naces, which being small ships of ten or twelve tons were ideal for landing raiding parties. They set sail on 11 November for the Testigos in Venezuela where they rendezvoused with the ship from St Christopher, making a total of some 1,100 men, divided into eight companies carried in seven ships, including one of 350 tons (twenty-eight guns), another of 240 tons (twenty guns) and a third of 140 tons (sixteen guns), together with the three pinnaces and a merchant ship 'for the more convenient accommodation of the men'.[52] That plunder was the voyage's exclusive purpose was clear from the testimony of a Scottish participant, Robert Adam; the ships carried nothing but provisions, gunpowder and shot.[53]

On 24 November the fleet set out on its adventure, but despite his great strength Jackson avoided the major settlements and went for smaller, less well-defended ones, although these were also less pros-perous. Starting with the island of La Margarita he proceeded to sack several towns on Tierra Firme and in Central America, including La Guaira, Puerto Cabello and Maracaibo, where Jackson lost a ship and eighty-nine men. But the expedition was most notable for a brief skirmish on Jamaica in which forty Englishmen were killed and the ransom of Santiago de la Vega (modern Spanish Town near Kingston). The raid yielded a disappointing booty of 200 cattle, 10,000 pounds of manioc-flour bread and only 7,000 silver pesos. Jamaica possessed no gold, which largely explains why the Spanish were not very interested in it, despite its being arguably the most beautiful of the Greater Antilles. Nevertheless the peaceful Taínos had been enslaved by the Spanish under the strange tributary institution of the *encomienda*, and by the 1520s were almost extinct. Some provisional settlements were made on the north coast, such as Sevilla la Nueva, which was attacked by French pirates in the 1540s, and a capital of sorts was established at Santiago de la Vega. But by the early seventeenth century the island's economy was moribund and by the early 1630s direct contact with Spain had ceased.[54] The only energy to be found was displayed by its wild fauna rather than its human population, while the only threat

---

* 'Purchase' was a word used by pirates and buccaneers meaning booty or plunder, but the term survives in marine insurers' salvage agreements in the form of 'no cure, no pay', meaning no pay without success. (D. Pope, *Harry Morgan's Way*, p.108.)

to this balance was from feral animals introduced by early settlers. However, the natural beauty of the island did prompt twenty-three of Jackson's adventurers to maroon themselves voluntarily there in order to live among the Spanish and their livestock.[55] Some 200 disgruntled participants in the expedition had already obtained permission to settle on Barbados.

From Jamaica they sailed to attack Trujillo in Honduras. Indeed, so devastating was this assault that 150 years later the governor-general of Guatemala, in an historic return to the coast, marvelled at its extent and wondered who might have carried it out.[56] But in the Gulf of Mexico the expedition lost three more ships wrecked on rocks and on departing the Caribbean to head for England yet another vessel was lost to a Dunkirker.[57] The overall value of the booty taken was so small that it may have covered no more than one-twentieth of the total costs, and this lack of success helps explain why so few large expeditions were ever mounted. Local knowledge and a local base were essential, and it was easier to make money through peaceful trade where this was possible, although official Spanish reluctance meant it usually took the form of smuggling. Away from the main ports individual Spanish ships were allowed to trade by *permiso* (permit), but by leaving the safety of the convoys such ships were vulnerable to pirates, and as the numbers of the latter steadily increased so the numbers of *permiso* vessels declined, opening the way for smugglers who were often the self-same pirates that attacked *permiso* vessels.[58]

Following Jackson's raid one Spanish official lamented in 1644 that the population of Jamaica was now 'so terrified and nervous that if two ships are seen off port, without waiting to know where they are from, they remove the women and their effects to the mountains. The time they waste in doing this gives the enemy the opportunity to return and occupy the town without resistance ...'[59] More importantly, it highlighted the real weakness of the Spanish in the Caribbean and would help fix Oliver Cromwell's gimlet eye upon it, for as one anonymous participant who wrote an account as 'Mercuris Americanus' observed, the success might result in 'some noble design against the professed enemies of our religion, which will prove not only acceptable to God but beneficial to the Commonwealth and to every particular adventurer in the same'.[60] And as Richard Norwood, a church minister in the West Indies, put it, Jackson had shown 'what might be done in the West Indies'.[61] Indeed, his raid presaged England's rise as a major player in the region, for within five years of his return the Dutch would sign a peace treaty with Spain, and although they would continue to be a significant factor in the Caribbean, theirs would henceforth be a commercial policy. That of confrontation would be taken up by England, for the French would remain entangled in internal divisions for another decade or more. Unsurprisingly Jackson's expedition provoked bitter protests from the Spanish government, and shortly after his return to England Cárdenas presented a fiercely worded petition to Parliament demanding the captain's arrest and punishment and the confiscation of his unlawful spoils. When this failed Cárdenas went to the court of admiralty, but to no avail.[62]

By 1640 the English had gained a demographic advantage over other European nations in the Caribbean, and up to 1660 the islands attracted more settlers than the mainland colonies of the north, suggesting that they offered better prospects for both material and social advancement.[63] This was despite the failure of tobacco on Barbados, because a superior alternative crop was being developed. Sugar was now being cultivated by one of Barbados's more enterprising planters, Colonel James Holdip, and when other planters saw his success they quickly followed suit. The reorganisation of the economy of Barbados and the Leeward Islands in the next two decades became known as the 'sugar revolution' and sugar replaced tobacco, cotton and indigo as the principal crop; by 1650 Barbados's sugar crop alone would be valued at £3 million.[64]

Before 1640 most plantations were small – no more than a few acres – but as these failed so they would be sold to wealthier neighbours and increasingly they were replanted with sugar. Sugar cultivation needed more land but also required more labour and equipment; landowners started to enclose tenants by buying or forcing them out, making the island unattractive to propertyless Europeans, and replacing their labour with African slaves because the work was intolerably hard to a free labour force, especially at harvest time. Workers had not only to clear the lush tropical vegetation but to sow, tend and harvest the sugar cane, crush the juice in a mill and boil it before it fermented, all in enervating heat. In 1641 Barbados had only a few hundred slaves, but by 1645 it had 5,680 and by 1698 there would be 42,000.[65]

Vast profits enabled successful planters to absorb the costs associated with slavery, and consequently many planters simply tore up the indentures of whites who were surplus to requirements, saving themselves the costs of feeding relatively useless men and at the same time avoiding paying them the lump sum they would be entitled to if they completed their service. Given that most indentured servants would be paid off with at best a few hundred pounds of tobacco, few could ever aspire to becoming planters themselves. Besides, many of them never aspired to anything of the sort, being convicts transported as an alternative to more draconian punishments, and including large numbers of Irish and others whose politics did not fit the new Commonwealth as it developed during the late 1640s.[66] Such behaviour was undoubtedly ruthless, but it was easily justified by Charles Jeaffreson at Nevis who declared that if the criminal prison at Newgate and the debtors' prison at Bridewell 'should spew out their spawn into these islands, it would meet with no less encouragement, for no gaol bird can be so incorrigible but there is hope for conformity here, as well as preferment . . .'.[67]

If they took ship hoping to find opportunities on other islands, unemployed whites soon discovered that Nevis, Antigua, St Christopher and San Martín had no desire for them, because their own young men were suffering from the same problems. A direct result of the transformation to a slave economy was a mass of unemployed whites looking for opportunities; the expansion of buccaneering was therefore closely connected with displaced men already in debt, and often desperate men at that, while escaped slaves could also make a better life on board a ship. Thereafter the buccaneers became a broad mixture of original *boucaniers* and men drawn from every walk of life by the promise of easy riches. But as William Dampier later noted, there was never any shortage of artisans among their ranks: 'We had Sawyers, Carpenters, Joyners, Brickmakers, Bricklayers, Shoemakers, Taylors &c.'[68]

In summer 1645 the Barbados planters boldly decided to maintain their present government and ignore the commissions of both sides in the civil war; they refused to declare for Parliament, but at the same time Carlisle could not influence matters, having declared for the king and been captured early in the conflict. Although Carlisle did not lose his patent, it became inoperable as he had no means of enforcing it. Deeply in debt and aware of his impotence in the matter, he leased the proprietorship for twenty-one years in exchange for half the gross revenue to Francis, Lord Willoughby of Parham,[69] Meanwhile efforts were made to prevent the conflict at home from dividing the island in a similar way. According to Richard Ligon, anybody who uttered the words 'Roundhead or Cavalier' had to treat 'all those who heard him' to a meal, so some did it 'purposely' to 'enjoy the company of one another'.[70] But this aloofness from domestic troubles could not be maintained, and as Parliamentary forces won more battles, so Royalist sympathisers increasingly fled to the island. In 1646 Humphrey Walrond (or Waldron) decided to try and make Barbados a Royalist enclave; he purchased a substantial plantation and began to rally sympathisers together with his brother Edward.[71]

Shortly after hearing the news of Charles I's execution in early 1650, the brothers organised a Committee of Safety and persuaded the island's Assembly to impose a loyalty oath and mobilise the militia. A crisis soon developed, transforming the once peaceful island into one where mounted Royalists rode about swearing they would 'sheath their Swords in the hearts of those that will not drink a health to' Charles II, and 'another to the confusion of the Independent [Puritan] doggs'.[72] Just as the Walronds assumed control Willoughby arrived, and soon showed himself adept at moderating the various factions. First he sent planter George Marten to secure a commission from Parliament and sought to reassure the moderate faction, led by a young Devon man called Thomas Modyford. Modyford had only recently arrived in Barbados, the first of five sons of a former mayor of Exeter; this 'restless spirit' was a cousin of George Monck, Cromwell's general, but was himself a Royalist and travelled with a few thousand pounds to escape the Puritan grimness that was then settling on England. Eventually he paid Major Hilliard £7,000 for half an estate comprising some 500 acres (for the whole of which Hilliard had paid £400 seven years earlier). About 200 of these acres were devoted to sugar and the rest to tobacco, ginger and cotton.[73]

In July Willoughby asked the Assembly to confirm his commission from King Charles II by publicly supporting the crown, but by now the mood had changed and they refused; in August he stripped the Walronds of their civil and military positions and called for new Assembly elections. But as he sought to consolidate his position Parliament was finally moving to punish the planters for embracing the Royalist cause, and mounted an expedition under Sir George Ayscue, Daniel Searle and Michael Pack with orders to reduce Barbados 'to the obedience of the Commonwealth'.[74] Ayscue's fleet did not approach the island until 16 October and, after it had seized fifteen mostly Dutch ships it found there and engaged in a brief artillery duel with the defenders, both sides established their positions. Willoughby refused to yield, and the fleet, with only 1,000 men against the 6,000 available to the defence, and running short of supplies, could do little more than launch raids.[75] In late December Modyford, who had risen quickly in local politics, headed an attempt in the Assembly to reach an accommodation, and when this failed he decided to act unilaterally. Ayscue was prepared to deal with any moderate elements, and Modyford as colonel of the Windward Regiment offered to lead 2,000 men in support of Ayscue if he should try to take the island by *coup de main*. Ayscue duly informed Willoughby of the regiment's defection on 5 January 1651. The following day he landed, and Willoughby prepared to meet the new combined force with some 3,000 men of his own, but heavy rain over the next three days prevented a decisive meeting and the plummeting morale of his troops persuaded him against pressing the matter. On 11 January the two sides agreed to the generous terms offered by Ayscue.[76] When the Assembly reconvened it ordered Willoughby to leave and only return with Parliament's blessing. Daniel Searle was appointed governor.

It seemed the island was finally secure when lookouts on the east of the island spotted part of a Royalist squadron approaching under the late king's nephew Prince Rupert, who had sailed from France knowing that the island had declared for the crown. But when Rupert learned that it had surrendered he sailed on, trying unsuccessfully to obtain provisions from other English and Dutch islands, although he did manage to get a few things from the French, and continued cruising with his brother Maurice. Finally, having been caught in a hurricane during which his brother's ship disappeared, he returned to Europe. But because nobody actually saw Maurice's ship sink, his fate remains a mystery to this day, and for a long time it was rumoured that he had been captured and imprisoned by the Spanish.[77] For although the King of Spain reserved the right to hang any Englishman found in the Indies, he very rarely did so. Normally they would be taken to the prisons of the Casa de Contración at Sevilla and after a short spell of incarceration, allowed to escape. This meant that they could not be said to have been pardoned and also forestalled any attempt by Arthur Hopton, the English ambassador, to petition for their release.[78] The ease with which they obtained their freedom impressed the ambassador who in 1639 wrote: 'In all things concerning His [Catholic] Majesty's subjects, I find all be, and particularly in the Conde [Olivares], respects that I think the subjects of no other king or ally of their's have found, this much I hold myself bound to testify.'[79] Frenchmen were given no quarter, but the English and Dutch were spared for fear of reprisal by England and the United Provinces, and when urged to take a stronger line in 1645 Felipe IV demurred.[80]

At last Barbados could finally settle back into the serious business of growing sugar and making money, but the fundamental problem with high-volume plantation production, particularly sugar, was that as the market flooded it drove down prices. High production levels therefore failed to maintain the economic rhythm, and from the beginning all the sugar islands were involved in trade with other colonies. Yet when Barbadians proposed free trade they meant not only with Scotland and Ireland but with Dutch and Spanish smugglers.[81] And with Spain exhausted, English attention increasingly focused on the Dutch who, of all nations in the seventeenth century, drew the greatest profits from illegal New World trade. This extraordinary success aroused unbridled jealousy among the middlemen of other nations who appealed to their governments to oust them. As the discovery of their ships by Ayscue's Barbados expedition demonstrated, they dominated Caribbean commerce throughout the British civil wars, and the Navigation Acts of 1651 and 1660 were specifically designed to prohibit their operations, by requiring all colonial trade to be carried in English ships (Scotland being regarded as foreign).[82] However, these acts depressed the island economies considerably. 'Free trade is the life of all Colonies,' Lord Willoughby would later complain: 'Whoever he be that advised his Majesty [Charles II] to restrain and tie up his Colonies in points of trade is more a merchant than a good subject, and would have his Majesty's island be nursed up to work for him, and such men.'[83] As a result, until a new web of illicit commerce could be developed, these acts would shift economic momentum to a place where the profits to be made from buccaneering provided a lure to almost every section of West Indian society, England's newly acquired colony of Jamaica.

# 6

## THE WESTERN DESIGN

Reader, behold presented to thine eye
What us Columbus off'red long ago,
Of the New World a new discovery,
Which here our author does so clearly show;
That he the state which of these parts would know,
Need not hereafter search the plenteous store
Of Hakluyt, Purchas and Ramusio,
Or learn'd Acosta's writings to look o'er;
Or what Herrera hath us told before,
Which merit not the credit due from hence,
Those being but reckonings of another score,
But these the fruits of self experience.

Thomas Chaloner, 'Introduction' to Thomas Gage,
*The English-American, or A New Survey of the West Indies*

Throughout the first half of the seventeenth century the Spanish in the Caribbean were hampered by continual defeat in Europe, while a Castilian government with a Castilian worldview failed to grasp the importance of the sea. Referring to the Peace of Westphalia in 1648 which ended the Thirty Years War and the long Dutch struggle for independence, the chronicler of Spanish Jamaica, Francisco Morales Padrón, wrote simply, 'it is best not to speak of it'.[1] These long wars left Spain absolutely exhausted; there was no money in the treasury and no credit to be had; her industry had withered to almost nothing and for several years the merchants at Veracruz and Sevilla had been requesting that the Council of the Indies cut down on the number of merchant ships – and therefore of merchandise – sent to Nueva España. The warehouses at Veracruz were piled high with goods sent out years before that nobody would buy because of the exorbitant prices, massively undercut by smugglers.[2]

The First Anglo-Dutch War concentrated the minds and energies of the English state after 1652, and when the Treaty of Westminster ended the conflict on 26 April 1654, some saw an opportunity to combine with the Dutch in a Protestant-republican crusade against international Catholicism, and Spain in particular.[3] Six days earlier Cromwell and the Council of State, appointed as the executive of the Commonwealth by the Rump Parliament following the execution of Charles I, discussed the feasibility of launching an expedition against the Spanish Americas. Cromwell, now endowed with absolute power as Lord Protector, defined the issue at first as one of finding employment for the navy and a large army about to be reduced in size anyway. Before the Council were two basic choices: to attack either France or Spain with the other's support. Cromwell regarded Spain as the more dangerous nation to the Protestant cause with the added benefit that a war with her would be profitable, especially with American treasure as a reward for victory. He was unambiguous about his imperial aspirations:

> we have command of the Spaniard's fleet, that he can neither come nor go nor come, and so he hath absolutely lost benefit of the Indies. Then we have the advantage of Hispaniola (a country beyond compare as they describe it) for the transplanting as much of our people from New England, Virginia, the Barbadoes, the Summer Islands [Bermuda], or from Europe, as we see requisite ... as our settlement at home.

The Council then discussed various possible targets, with Española topping the list alongside Cuba, Portobelo and Panamá, all important to the *flotas*.[4]

Before he could take any steps to attack France where he was always keen to help the Huguenot cause, Cromwell would have to come to terms with Spain, and he has been accused of deviousness in negotiating with Spain in Europe while simultaneously planning to attack the Americas – certainly that became the Spanish view.[5] But while an Anglo-Spanish alliance briefly seemed possible during 1654 it never materialised, as Spain did not have the money to offset the expenses of an English expedition to France, nor would she make any concessions on the two issues that might have compensated for it: tolerance for Englishmen in Spain, and trading rights with Spanish America. Besides, Cromwell's preference was for an accommodation with France, if he could just manoeuvre Charles II out of that country, and the offer of an alliance with Spain was only an expedient made in a fit of annoyance with France when she refused to recognise the republic. In fact, his religious zeal and his economic plans for England's greatness always brought him back to the same point: an attack on Spain.[6]

At the time the writings of popular authors such as Thomas Gage – a former Catholic priest whose 1648 publication *The English-American, or A New Survey of the West Indies*, created a sensation – and translations of the works of Bartolomé de Las Casas and Thomas Campanella reinforced the current of anti-Spanish feeling already prevalent in seventeenth-century England – the 'Black Legend', the perception of Spain as a cruel and treacherous nation bent on world domination and the elimination of Protestantism.[7] Within the army in particular, Spain was seen as a more Catholic country than France and therefore the more natural target for Englishmen as God's chosen instrument to chastise the Anti-Christ. 'What peace can we rejoice in', demanded Major-General Charles Fleetwood and his officers, 'when the whoredom, murthers and witchcraft of Jezebel are so many?'[8] And better still, Gage wrote, 'the Spaniards cannot oppose much, being a lazy, sinful people, feeding like beasts upon their lusts, and upon the fat of the land, and never trained up to wars'.[9]

Gage deliberately set out to catch the attention of the leadership of the New Model Army, to persuade them to undertake an expedition against Spanish America. He dedicated his book, which was headed by a laudatory poem by Thomas Chaloner, to General Lord Fairfax, a dedication read as a call to action. Gage believed that his adventures in America as well as his conversion were no accident, but an opportunity to provide useful service to a now more completely reformed England to spread the Gospel across the Atlantic. He urged Fairfax to consider a design to conquer American lands, and invoked Henry VII's famous lost opportunity in not sponsoring Columbus. He added that Fairfax need not worry about the legitimacy of the plan, as Spain had no right to the Americas. But if 1648 was no time to be suggesting the launch of a transatlantic campaign, by 1654 the situation had changed dramatically. Cromwell was under the delusion that English traders needed formal Spanish recognition to operate in the Caribbean, when the reality on the ground was somewhat different; but it served as a useful instrument of Protestant propaganda, as were recent attacks on English ships and citizens, examples of 'popish treachery' that were alluded to in the manifesto issued by Cromwell in October 1655. In reality, however, control from Madrid was extremely weak, and Cromwell probably believed that his efforts – first excessive demands and then war – were for the ultimate good of English traders, even if his policy betrayed a complete misunderstanding of actual conditions.[10]

It has been a matter of debate to what extent Cromwell saw his policies as the logical culmination of thirty years of development and struggle, rather than a mere throwback to the days of Elizabeth.[11] He undoubtedly felt it was given to him as lord protector to make the reformed religion secure against all future developments, and to protect that goal he must ensure England's security from foreign invasion and sedition. Until Spain was detached from her source of American silver the danger to England would continue. But as a direct government activity, as opposed to Elizabethan freebooting, such a scheme represented a sharp and distinct change in policy.[12] Certainly Spain's weakness was no reason *not* to attack her. As the century progressed so the flow of treasure from her colonies had slowed dramatically. It seemed that God had brought her low just at the moment when true Protestants were victorious in England in order that the final blow could be struck and the Anti-Christ vanquished once and for all.[13]

In this vision Cromwell was supported by New England clergymen, and via the Reverend William Hooke he began corresponding with John Cotton, regarded as a leading interpreter of Biblical prophecies. In 1651 Cotton told him 'that to take from the Spaniards in America would be to dry up the Euphrates', thus fulfilling the prophecy of Revelation 16:12 which heralded the last days: 'And the sixth angel poured out his vial upon the great river Euphrates; and the water thereof was dried up, that the way of the kings of the east might be prepared.' Cotton argued that the pope's attack on episcopacy in England was the pouring of the fifth vial and that the very culmination of history was accelerating, an interpretation that appealed to Cromwell.[14] General paranoia about popery was widespread in seventeenth-century England, while virulent anti-Spanish propaganda also stressed the demonology of the Inquisition and its oppression of native peoples. The infamous account of Spanish depredations by Bartolomé de Las Casas, *Tears of the Indians*, was regularly reprinted in Protestant states at war with Spain, and was translated afresh by John Milton's nephew in 1656.[15]

Thomas Gage was also an important influence on Cromwell, though exactly how important is not clear from the lord protector's documents. Certainly he was considered significant enough to be assigned to the expedition in an official capacity, being appointed in November 1654 as a regimental chaplain (a position more akin to a Red Army political commissar during the Second World War than that of a modern army chaplain).[16] Another notable adviser to Cromwell was Colonel Thomas Modyford, who proposed the capture of Trinidad and the country around the mouth of the Orinoco river, reasoning that as this lay to windward of Spain's territories on the Main it would require an expedition from Europe to recapture any English colonies established there.[17] But the principal impulse behind the expedition was, in any case, not religious but economic: paying the largest standing army in England's history to date was exhausting the treasury, while collecting the necessary taxes made the government less popular than that of King Charles I.[18] Yet it was well known that Spain derived fabulous wealth from gold and silver taken from the Americas, and nothing seemed easier than to cut off the flow of treasure and thus solve England's financial crisis with a single blow.[19]

When Cromwell again proposed an attack in the West Indies to the Council of State on 20 July 1654 it provoked sharp divisions. It would represent the first deployment of state military resources in the pursuit of colonisation beyond Ireland, and debate revolved around the feasibility and justification of such a scheme.[20] Major-General John Lambert argued forcefully that success was 'improbable'. Such a scheme would not 'advance the Protestant cause', he said, and would distract men and attention from more immediate concerns in Ireland. Cromwell countered that the expedition would cost no more than outfitting the ships and, probably thinking of Drake and Piet Hein, added that it would provide a great opportunity for profit. He believed that six fast-sailing ships, 'six frigotts nimble', raiding the Bay of Mexico would be enough to find booty to pay for the expedition and infuse new funds into the Commonwealth.[21] Finally, after much hesitation, a decision was made to this end, and the 'Western Design' was born. Preparations were already well in hand when in August Cromwell summoned the Spanish ambassador, Cárdenas, and informed him that England's continued friendship would be conditional on Spain accepting religious tolerance and trade rights. The ambassador's reply was that to accept these demands 'was to demand of his Master his two eyes'.[22] Indeed, rather than give way, which in the seventeenth century amounted almost to asking a nation to surrender its independence, Spain was prepared to risk war.[23]

Shortly afterwards Cromwell appointed Admiral William Penn and General Robert Venables as commanders of the expedition and ordered them to work out a plan in complete secrecy.[24] Besides the military and naval commanders, civilian commissioners were appointed: Edward Winslow had previously travelled to Massachusetts on the *Mayflower*, but had since returned and advised Cromwell on various matters; his official job description now included 'the compounding of delinquents' as administrator of London's appalling debtors' prisons, and many unfortunate inmates would find themselves impressed into the expedition.[25] Gregory Butler had served with the Earl of Essex and Sir William Waller during the civil war before migrating to the West Indies, and Daniel Searle had been governor of Barbados since Ayscue's expedition to restore the island to the Commonwealth. The commissioners were instructed to secure English interests 'in those Countries, which now lye open and exposed to the will and power of the King of Spaine . . . and also for getting ground and gaineing uppon the Dominions and territories of the said Kinge there'.[26] But while Venables was named first in the preamble to the commission, Penn's name appeared first in the body of the document and in the instructions to the commissioners, confusing the chain of command.

The central plank of the plan would be the deployment of 3,600 regular troops and settlers from Barbados and St Christopher, sufficient to take and hold Santo Domingo or Puerto Rico or Havana or Cartagena, or even all four of them.[27] Although the secret of the expedition's destination was to be kept from everyone, rumours that it would be Spanish America were circulating as early as May 1654.[28] Indeed, the demands for manpower, especially seamen, saw the press gangs out in

Oliver Cromwell in the 1650s

force. Recruiting and collection of warlike stores were entrusted to Major-General John Disbrowe (Desborough), Cromwell's brother-in-law, while supply of provisions was largely overseen by another West Indian hand, Martin Noell. But from the beginning the preparation was plagued by corruption and profiteering and it was completed hastily and inefficiently, which would severely hinder the expedition.[29] The 2,500 men assembled in England in five regiments were mostly from existing units, whose colonels took the opportunity to purge their ranks of their worst soldiers making them formidable in numbers only, and made up to strength by scouring the gaols.[30] The men were:

> Hectors, and Knights of the blade, with common Cheats, Theeves, Cutpurses and such like leud persons, who had long time lived by the sleight of hand and dexterity of wit, and were now making a fair progresse unto Newgate, from whence they were to proceed towards Tiborn; but considering the dangerousnesse of that passage, very politickly directed their course another, and became Souldiers for the State.[31]

Indeed, far from being republican idealists bent on liberating heathens from the yoke of Spanish perfidy, they were motivated only by fear of the gibbet and the lure of plunder.[32]

A sea regiment was later formed from among the sailors on the expedition, but the plan envisaged that the fleet call first at Barbados where more men were to be recruited, then at St Christopher for the same purpose, so that extra arms would have to be provided. But there appears to have been no proper division of the stores, arms and food taken on board the ships which would lead to bitter disputes between the two services.[33] Among the officers of the expedition were many former servants of the Providence Island Company. Andrew Carter, who showed a remarkable ability to recover from repeated disgrace after being forced to leave the Parliamentary army in Scotland through drunkenness, now commanded a regiment with the rank of colonel; Lewis Morris would raise a regiment in Barbados; and Kempo Sabada, a Dutch mariner who served Providence Island as a pilot, would operate in the same role.[34] Indeed, Cromwell lamented the loss of Providence since it would have provided an ideal jumping-off point for attacking the mainland and for 'the hindrance of the Peru trade and Cartagena'.[35]

As the force assembled at Portsmouth during December discipline was on the verge of breakdown, and many men had to be forced on to the transports. But in spite of mutinous stirrings the expedition departed on 24 December 1654, and made an uneventful passage to reach Carlisle Bay, Barbados on 29 January 1655.[36] There Penn ordered the immediate seizure first of eighteen Dutch merchantmen trading illegally with the colonists and later of a ship carrying 244 slaves, which did nothing to commend the expedition to the colonists. Not that members of the expedition were impressed by their hosts. Henry Whistler, who was sailing-master of Penn's flagship *Swiftshure*, thought the island the dunghill on which England threw her rubbish, as the people were either rogues or whores.[37] Despite this mutual distrust, Modyford – as speaker of the Assembly – invited Venables to address the members and appeal for the 4,000 men he needed.

There was also much controversy over Venables being accompanied by his new wife, with some saying he was more concerned with prostrating himself before the throne of Venus than harkening to the dictates of Mars, and that his decisions were influenced by her. Certainly when he set about recruiting islanders he did so indiscriminately, so that he soon had 3,000–4,000 volunteers. But many of them, being either elderly or patently unfit, were poorly suited to joining an army, and despite measures to avoid the recruitment of indentured servants, since 'their indentures were not being writ on their foreheads', several of them together with freemen in debt took the opportunity to escape their bonds.[38] But they were, complained Venables, 'not to be commanded as Souldiers, nor to be kept in any civil order; being most prophane debauch'd persons that we ever saw, scorners of Religion, and indeed, men kept so loose as not to be kept under discipline, and so cowardly as not to be made to fight'.[39]

Yet if the men he recruited seemed poor human material, this was due to ill-treatment, insanitary conditions and a bad diet exacerbated by too much rum. And not only the men drank to excess. Gregory Butler's consumption appalled his brother officers, even in the hard-drinking world of the seventeenth century. Winslow reported how Butler 'got drunk ... and ran shouting thro' the Town ...'.[40] He later disgraced himself at St Christopher and 'was so drunk that he fell from his Horse and vomited', leading Venables to call him 'a drunken sot'.[41] Meanwhile the stores ships had yet to arrive and it was decided to strip Barbados of arms as well as men, with all the island's blacksmiths put to work to make 2,500 ten-foot-long half-pikes made from 'cabbage stalks' – wood from the cabbage tree.[42] These were issued to a regiment formed from among the Irish on the island who had risen in rebellion in 1650, and now the virulently anti-papist Puritan Daniel Searle saw an excellent opportunity to be rid of them. But they were never drilled together and their commanding officer, Lieutenant-Colonel Lewis Morris, was 'not very cheerful in the designe', having a young wife 'who hath been very importunate with him to leave the vayage'.[43]

A muster of the troops, now formed into seven regiments, shortly before they sailed onwards gave the total as 6,973, to which a further 1,200 were added at St Christopher. Besides the infantry there was a troop of horse (fifty-six strong), a small artillery train (fifty men), a company of scouts (sixty), a company of firelocks (160 men armed with muskets equipped with flintlock mechanisms that were more reliable than the matchlock weapons generally issued), and a company of a hundred *reformados* – officer supernumeraries who served as volunteers. But Venables was taking a serious risk in sailing when still short of provisions, especially when the quality of his command was so low; he must have been expecting little or no resistance. By the time of his departure, most of the surplus food of Barbados had been consumed, and the army apparently feared the navy would abandon it on a hostile shore, because at a council of war held on 18 March the following resolution was passed: 'That it be proposed to General Penn and his officers, that as the land forces do promise never to desert the Fleet, that General Penn and his officers mutually engage with the Land forces not to leave them until their Supplies come, which if they should miscarry, then to transport them back to England'.[44] On 31 March the expedition sailed for St Christopher, arriving on 6 April to be saluted by both English and French batteries. The men who had already been recruited in the Leeward Islands embarked, and they sailed for Española on the same day in three squadrons.[45]

It certainly appears that whatever security measures had been put in place had failed; the Spanish already knew all about the expedition, had correctly predicted its destination and had taken appropriate measures.[46] Don Bernardino de Meneses Bracamonte y Zapata, Conde de Peñalva, was made president and captain-general of Española, and was sent to the island with 200 soldiers. Peñalva sailed on *La Concepción* and arrived at Española on 29 March with his son, Don Gutierre. After a careful inspection of the Santo Domingo garrison which identified only 170 of the 300 men as effective, Peñalva drafted every man and boy over fourteen years old into the militia and summoned help from inland and from Puerto Rico. He formed a makeshift company of fellow noble passengers on *La Concepción* and found adequate arms in good order with which to equip the defenders, mostly lances which would serve the Spanish well in the brutal irregular fighting to follow. He assessed the town's fortifications as inadequate and was especially worried about Santo Domingo's vulnerability from landward, but he took every possible precaution by dispatching infantry and artillerymen under Captain Damian del Castillo Vaca to reinforce Fort San Gerónimo and the line of the River Jaina.[47]

As the English fleet approached the island the senior officers on board held a series of councils of war. The army officers were keen to launch a direct assault on Santo Domingo, but Penn was reluctant to risk his ships in an unknown harbour. It was therefore agreed to land some six or seven miles to the west, or leeward, near the mouth of the River Jaina. Despite trying to remain below the horizon to gain surprise, the fleet was spotted by Spanish lookouts on 13 April. Next morning it divided, with Penn planning to make a diversionary landing east of the town. But the first of a series of mixups occurred when Venables discovered he had no pilot to guide him to his landing site, and with the wind behind it the fleet was eventually carried some thirty miles beyond the town to leeward of Point Niaso. At least the landing was unopposed, and by 4 p.m. a column was on the march, continued next morning across savannah which the Spanish fired to drive the cattle away. The heat was intense and the men had no water bottles, so they helped themselves to oranges as they passed the trees before encamping for the night, having covered an estimated eighteen miles that day.[48]

The march resumed in the morning and reached the River Jaina, but lacking a guide the troops were at a loss to find a ford, and marched inland until they discovered one by chance some twelve miles upstream. If one aim of the scheme had been to bring Protestant enlightenment to the realms of Spain's colonies, it seems the greatest blow that was struck was when the soldiers 'brought forth a large statue of the Virgin Mary, well accoutered, and pelted her to death with oranges'.[49] On 17 April they continued through a cocoa plantation where they were joined by the two regiments which had been due to make a diversion but had been unable to land east of the town. The combined troops had seemingly lost their way when they found an old Irishman whom they forced to serve as a guide. But when they failed to reach their expected destination Venables ordered the man to be hanged despite the protests of several members of his staff, but this matter was of little concern to someone who had spent five years serving in Cromwell's notoriously brutal suppression of Ireland.[50]

Nevertheless, the army finally approached Santo Domingo, only to be held up by the guns at Fort Gerónimo as the forlorn hope* was put to flight with a loss of some twenty men, during which abortive attack Venables hid behind a tree and the Sea Regiment came to the rescue. The English retired and, as the Spanish followed up, they found evidence that the enemy troops were suffering dreadfully from shortage of water, which caused more of them to die than were killed in action. They also found much discarded loot, despite English orders to the contrary, and were disgusted and appalled by the desecration of their statue; they now knew they were fighting not only for their homes but for their religion.[51] For the next six days the English remained inactive as the senior officers wondered what to do and conditions in the camp deteriorated. Henry Whistler described the results graphically:

> But the lieing heare did doue the armie more hurt then thayer marching, ffor the fresh meat, and the abundant of frut they did eate, and lieing in the raine did case most of them to haue the Bluddie-flux, and now thayer harts wore got out of thayer Dublates into thayer Breches, and wos nothing but Shiting ...[52]

* In early modern European warfare the use of a vanguard called a forlorn hope (or *enfants perdus*) was a common tactic, a body of picked men or volunteers, usually numbering a hundred, who led the storming of a fortified position. It was the most dangerous position, but carried great honour, and often involved the right to plunder.

III

While the 'bloody flux' – dysentery – attacked them from within, the Spaniards grew increasingly bold without, raiding outposts and killing a number of stragglers. These raids were often launched by cowkillers, a mixed group of mostly half-breeds and former African slaves employed to slaughter feral cattle. Equipped with lances they were very effective in the woods against the unsteady English troops, many of whom were put to flight simply by hearing the cry 'the cowkillers are coming'.[53]

Not until 24 April were the English ready to attempt another assault on the town, by which time the Spanish had collected reinforcements and had strengthened their defences. Late in the afternoon the English dragged two field guns and a mortar forwards, stopping about two miles short of the objective but without water, as the wells had been stopped up. They continued in the morning led by a forlorn hope of 240 men, followed by the *reformado* company, the firelock company, then the troop of horse. As they approached Fort Gerónimo they could see that the Spanish had cleared the woodland behind it, and came under sustained fire from seven guns in the fort before being charged by cowkillers and regular Spanish cavalry, who had apparently been lying in wait for them. The forlorn hope was swiftly routed, throwing the *reformados* into confusion, and though the latter defended themselves valiantly, by the day's end only eighteen out of fifty-five survived; among the casualties was Major-General Heane.[54] The firelocks offered only a ragged volley before making off as the Spanish turned their attention to the troop of horse. Having scattered this, they continued against Venables' own regiment which led the main body, hacking their way in and killing a major and three captains, and taking five company colours to add to the three taken from the *reformados* and firelocks. Only now did the exhausted Spanish draw off, weary of killing according to one eyewitness.[55]

The English camped near by that night, and a detachment prepared to assault the fort. But, by now disheartened, Venables ordered a retreat in the morning and, along with the dead, buried the mortar in the hope of retrieving it later. But by 28 April the English were back at the Jaina river, utterly demoralized and suffering severe privation as they were cut off from shipboard supplies. Men going inland in search of cattle were driven back by cowkillers, frightened even by the sounds of leaves rustling in the wind or fiddler crabs scuttling along the ground.[56] Recriminations soon followed. Adjutant-General Jackson who commanded the vanguard was court-martialled and condemned on a charge of cowardice. He was cashiered and had his sword broken over his head, and put to swabbing the wards of the hospital ship.[57] The English had nothing left to do but leave the island in disgrace, and by 2 May most of the army had boarded ship, a process completed by the next day. They set sail on 3 and 4 May only after a final tragic and wasteful episode characteristic of the whole expedition. Unable to load the remaining cavalry mounts, the army slaughtered a hundred horses on the beach. Francis Barrington, a veteran dragoon officer of the Irish campaign, was horrified. He considered there to be enough valuable horseflesh to sweep clean any of the Spanish Antilles, and was revolted by the brutal massacre. The episode inspired him to close his letter home with a frank condemnation of his general and the conduct of the expedition.[58]

At least the embarkation was completed without interference by the Spanish. Peñalva offered a reward of 400 pesos to the messenger who might successfully carry warning of the English fleet to Jamaica, though it was found that Penn had wisely assigned a squadron to patrol offshore to prevent such communication. In one last effort to warn Jamaica, Peñalva sent men by canoe rather than ship, but their canoe leaked and the voyage was abandoned. Española had remained Spanish thanks to prior warning and time for preparation; Spanish Jamaica would have no such advantage. Meanwhile Peñalva set about the other necessary task of ritually celebrating the victory.[59]

Early on Monday 7 May, Admiral William Penn fired a gun and flew a jack from the ensign staff of the *Swiftshure* marking the start of a day of humiliation and fasting, to seek God's blessing on the forthcoming attempt on Jamaica, and his forgiveness for the sins leading to the defeat before Santo Domingo. Richard Rooth wrote a personal prayer in his journal, beseeching the Lord's guidance and protection. That day also saw the death of Edward Winslow who, according to a letter from Robert Venables, succumbed to a fever, although Gregory Butler believed he died of grief for the loss at Santo Domingo.[60] On the afternoon of 9 May, two fishermen hunting turtles in the vicinity of Morante Point on Jamaica caught sight of the fleet and quickly took to their canoes to carry the warning to Santiago de la Vega. The next day at dawn the fleet came in view of Caguaya (Cagway), the port of Santiago. The Spaniards counted fifty-six ships (there were only thirty-eight) and numerous smaller vessels as the governor, Don Juan Ramírez de Orellana, raised the alarm and dispatched his *maestre de campo* (colonel), Don Francisco de Proenza, to Caguaya to identify the ships. Penn's ships sailed in under their own flags, and Proenza sent word to Santiago that the fleet was English.[61]

Direct contact between Jamaica and Spain had ended twenty years before, and without warning and without reinforcement, the island was profoundly vulnerable. Each English soldier was issued with fourteen rounds of musket ammunition, rations for three days, one day's supply of brandy and six yards of match cord for his musket. At 6 a.m. on 10 May, Penn approached Caguaya and at 9 a.m. ordered a signal gun fired to prepare the assault. Unfortunately some of the ships ran aground following his orders to stand in closer to shore. Once they were all anchored Penn landed the army, and as the sailors on the loaded boats began pulling for shore, the Spanish opened fire. The English fleet took advantage of their shallow-draught vessels in the harbour to return it, and silenced the Spanish batteries, allowing the soldiers to get ashore.[62] The Spanish fled, abandoning not only their fortifications but their guns, and Barrington believed God had blessed the army, as in his military eye the defenders of Caguaya were in a far stronger tactical position than at Española, having coastal fortifications and artillery to meet soldiers riding in exposed boats. But the 180 Spanish militiamen abandoned their defences without making any sort of effective resistance on the road between Caguaya and Santiago. The army arrived at the town the following day at 2 p.m. to find it likewise abandoned, but with its valuables and supplies evacuated.[63]

As the English troops approached Santiago a Spaniard named Antonio de Salinas met them on horseback bearing a flag of truce, possibly a handkerchief. He communicated an offer of such supplies and provisions as the fleet might need. Based on their experience with William Jackson the Spanish misunderstood English intentions, believing that as in previous raids they came to plunder, refit and go on their way; they also assumed Venables to be a mercenary officer.[64]

When he demanded thirty head of cattle with goats and sheep, this only reinforced their impression; but when thirty cattle were duly delivered, there being no goats or sheep, the Englishman appeared to lose his cool. Not thirty but 300, he insisted, since how could thirty cattle feed 16,000 men? And in light of what seemed to him a joke he also demanded thirty saddled horses and the governor's authorisation of surrender, for which he would brook no delay.[65] Venables demanded to meet the governor or suitable official and Orellana sent Don Francisco de Carvajal, his *sargento mayor*, to discuss terms. When Carvajal said they would meet to discuss things 'as soon as it suited the service of God, the Kingdom and the Church', the Englishmen burst out laughing, and Gage, who was interpreting, said that God had no need of their services as he was in Heaven, and the English had come to serve not Felipe IV but their own interest, which was best for the island. When Carvajal protested that the island was Spanish by dint of papal authority and 140 years of occupation he was told bluntly by the Protestant that 'law does not give possession, only force of arms'.[66] Eventually a surrender was negotiated on 15 May and a spectacular parade was held in which nine victorious regiments displayed thirty-six colours. Had the treaty terms been followed they would have given the English immediate control of the island: the Spanish were to leave all slaves and property on Jamaica, taking only two suits of clothes apiece, and to prepare for transportation to Nueva España.[67]

In an effort to enforce the treaty the English took hostages, and when they refused to submit Venables threatened to hang the governor, which had little effect; nor did he carry out this threat. As the army was hungry, a constant theme on Jamaica, the soldiers grew restless and began striking out on their own in search of food. This proved fatal for some as the Spanish had begun organizing resistance in the surrounding countryside. The efforts of musketeers to shoot cattle frightened off the herds, making it difficult for the army to round them up, and the soldiers resorted to other expedients to bolster the meat supply, falling back on dogs, horses and donkeys. Francis Barrington expressed a definite preference for the latter, and wrote that he 'did eat heartily of it'.[68]

This brief peaceful period of the English invasion ended when scattered Spanish resistance broke out near the town. The Spanish retreated to the south-west of Santiago, into the Guatibacoa region, the location of many Spanish cattle ranches. Proenza made certain of the safety of the people of his household, and then took a position on a bridge two leagues from the town with a force of 130 musketeers and lancers and fifteen black archers. English stragglers roaming the countryside in search of food provided easy prey for his scouts, and from a young man of Barbados named either George or Nicholas Paine, who served the expedition as an interpreter and was spared when he pleaded for his life in Spanish, they heard encouraging news: they did not face an invincible fleet, but one soundly beaten on Española. Somehow, Paine may have been returned to the English or have escaped, because he was later hanged for indicating the army's vulnerability to the Spanish.[69]

After a week's negotiations Spanish emissaries agreed to surrender, leaving the ailing governor as a hostage, but the remaining Spanish defenders turned down the offer of transport if they would lay down their arms. They refused, claimed John Daniel, because many were Creoles without resources elsewhere, and were resolved to die in Jamaica sooner than become paupers in another colony or in Spain. Daniel concluded that the English would have a hard campaign clearing them out, comparable to the irregular war in Ireland, but Venables and Butler hoped that Spanish forces would be too weak to make a stand on the island; they also hoped to prevent any Spaniards escaping to Cuba.[70] When Colonel Anthony Buller made a patrol of the island late in May, he captured two Englishmen who had been living there and questioned them about why so many Spaniards had not surrendered. Priests told frightening tales that the English had denied God, they said, and planned to slaughter the population after putting out the eyes of any who approached their lines. Some Spaniards also continued to claim that the English were there only for food, and would be gone in three or four months.[71] And food was increasingly scarce, so that the army had to use cassava as a substitute for bread. Even when stores ships finally reached the island on 19 May they brought enough bread for only twenty-two days at half-rations, and the fleet had only enough for three months' further service. A call for help was sent to New England, but increasingly the men suffered from dysentery just as they had on Española. Being no respecter of persons the infection heavily afflicted the officer corps, and by 14 June only five field officers 'were in health', leaving the army with inadequate leadership.[72]

The Council of State signalled the godliness of the Design with cruel impracticality when on 9 June 1655, unaware of the failure before Santo Domingo, it ordered 2,000 Bibles to be sent to an army lacking tents, water bottles and adequate rations.[73] At the same time Penn prepared to return home, leaving just a small squadron under Vice-Admiral William Goodson at Jamaica, a decision reached only after *Discovery* (thirty guns) blew up following a fire. It then took some time for Penn to get ready and he departed on 25 June. But the fleet enjoyed no better luck on the return voyage. *Paragon* suffered a similar fate to *Discovery* when she exploded thirty miles off Havana with the loss of a hundred men, and the fleet became increasingly scattered as it approached home. Penn notified Cromwell of his presence at Spithead on 31 August, and was immediately sent to the Tower for deserting his post without permission.[74] Not long after Penn's departure for England, Venables – fearful of what his fellow commander might report to the lord protector and stricken with dysentery – abandoned the Design as well. Venables' illness impaired his ability to command, and a council of war on 7 June agreed to grant him authority to return home, departing on 4 July. When he reached England on 9 September he too was committed to the Tower, but was released a month later along with Penn.[75]* On Jamaica meanwhile, Cromwell's instructions relating to a change of command were opened, and Gregory Butler was nominated to take over, but this arrangement proved unsatisfactory all round, especially when Butler himself expressed a desire to return home. Major-General Richard Fortescue was appointed in his place, but by now the system of commissioners had completely broken down, and with the death of Thomas Gage the army was also desperately in need of chaplains. The future command arrangements of the expedition would require Cromwell's close attention.[76]

When news reached Madrid that Jamaica had been lost, Felipe IV

---

* Penn was restored to the Admiralty in March 1660, in time to organise the fleet that brought the restored King Charles II back to England in May. He was knighted on 9 June and became a key adviser to the king's brother, James, Duke of York, in the administration of the Restoration navy. His eldest son, the Quaker William Penn (1644–1718), founded the colony of Pennsylvania. Venables was never employed again by either Cromwell or Charles II and retired to Cheshire, where he lived quietly with his second wife Elizabeth in a loveless marriage.

was convinced he had doomed the nation. The news hit him 'like an avalanche', noted one historian. 'Panic spread through Seville and Cadiz, and curses loud and deep of the falsity of heretics rang through Liars Walk and the Calle Mayor.'[77] But in England nobody was rejoicing; word reached Cromwell of the failure against Española on 24 July and he had shut himself alone in his room for a day to begin a process of self-examination that continued to the end of his life. Popular reaction to the news of defeat was swift, widespread and hostile, and by October the lord protector found himself in an official war with Spain.[78] The New Englander Robert Sedgwick knew why. 'God is angry,' he wrote to John Winthrop Jr. 'What God will do with this design I know not. I was willing some time to believe that God was in it, but he yet seems to disown us.'[79] Cromwell was shattered by the defeat in Española, and though he never accepted that defeat entailed the divine endorsement of Spain, he accepted it as a rebuke of England: the goals advocated by Puritan grandees for more than thirty years were, it appeared, not God's goals after all, and Cromwell's refusal of the crown in 1657 sprang in large part from this sense of sin and failure.[80] A godly and stable settlement could never derive its income from privateering, but with Providence Island's godly settlers long dispersed, only the privateering remained.[81]

Yet the Western Design was in many ways epochal: it opened a new era for England and the world by marking the beginning of the true expansion of the British empire. David Armitage defined it as 'the imperial moment of the English republic' as it forsook the more peaceful approach of the Stuarts. He also highlighted the eschatological motivations for conquest of Spain's American empire: a belief among Puritans in England and New England that the downfall of Spain would hasten the millennium. Although Cromwell saw an assault on Spanish America as a limited naval war that would add to England's wealth in trade without leading to war in Europe as well, continental war did break out with Spain, for despite the capture of Jamaica and Dunkirk the republican empire-building campaign was a failure.[82] But the Western Design would have profound consequences in the long term, helping to determine the economic policy not only of the Protectorate, but of the Restoration, and it would become an example taken up in the eighteenth century to inspire a new round of assaults on Spain in the West Indies, determining Britain's relationship to and dominance of the mercantile system to the end of that century.[83] The capture of Jamaica would provide the buccaneers with the perfect base from which to develop their business.

# 7

## BUCCANEER ISLANDS

These men were that breed of rovers whose port lay always a
little further on. If they lived riotously, let it be argued in their
favour that at least they lived . . . We think them terrible. Life is
terrible. But it was not so terrible to them; for they were
comrades, with the strength to live their own lives. They may
laugh at those who condemn with the hate of impotence.

John Masefield, *On the Spanish Main*[1]

If England's colonies had been left to fend for themselves during the
civil wars, it appeared for a while as if all the French colonies would
be brought under central control. But the imperial plan would turn
sour for the Bourbon absolutists as surely as it would for their Stuart
and Habsburg cousins, as war with Spain degenerated into civil war
(the Fronde, 1648–53) and France fell under the regency of Anne of
Austria. With the Company of the Islands of the Americas facing
bankruptcy her chief minister, the Italian landlubber and aesthete,
Jules, Cardinal de Mazarin, cut naval spending and colonial control
drained away.[2] In 1648 he decided to sell Guadeloupe and its adjacent
islands – Saint-Barthélemy, Marie Galante and the Saintes – to their
governors, and two years later Martinique went the same way, followed by St Lucia and Grenada, while de Poincy bought French St
Christopher on behalf of the Knights of Malta.[3]

For its part Tortuga enjoyed a period of prosperity. A place of
safety had been created for illicit trade, where the buccaneers could
sell hides and buy merchandise from the smugglers. Tobacco plantations, warehouses and depots were set up, and although the governor François Levasseur did not openly collaborate with privateers,
he allowed them to operate freely making Tortuga a sort of free-
trade republic governed by decree, generating enormous profits by
taxation on trade agreements made on the island and enforcing his

will through a reign of terror. He was assisted by two godsons, Thilbaut and Martin, whom he designated his successors, and he built a prison at La Roca which he called Purgatory from which convicts descended into 'Hell', a machine of his own invention, on which victims were tortured until maimed or crippled for life. Such despotism could not go on unpunished, however, and in 1652 the chevalier Timoléon Hotman de Fontenay, Knight of the Order of St John, reached St Christopher on a frigate of twenty-two guns hoping to recruit men to replace his exhausted crew. De Poincy had been looking around for some time to find a man capable of dealing with his renegade subordinate, and de Fontenay appeared to be just the man. He had gained considerable experience in the Mediterranean campaigns and on 29 May the two men signed a covenant similar to that which de Poincy had signed with Levasseur when he had appointed him governor of Tortuga eleven years previously. An assault force was duly assembled and sailed, only to receive news on its arrival of the tyrant's assassination.[4] Thilbaut's relationship with a prostitute who was also a renowned beauty had provoked such constant reproach from his godfather that he hatched a conspiracy. One morning as Levasseur went to inspect the warehouses he was attacked by seven or eight men armed with muskets. Their shots hit the mark, but it was not, in fact, the governor but his reflection in a mirror. As he turned to his black sword-bearer to prepare to defend himself, Thilbault rushed forward and cut him down.[5]

Having no forces with which to resist, the conspirators agreed to accept de Fontenay's authority in exchange for Levasseur's worldly goods and a promise never to investigate the circumstances surrounding his death. So de Fontenay took possession of the island in the name of the company and reinstated the Catholic religion. The change of regime encouraged many people to return as rules for harmonious existence were established once more. In order not to antagonise the Spanish, de Fontenay decided not to colonise Tierra Grande, but he did actively foster privateering, taking the Mediterranean version as his model. The Spanish learned of the change from English and French prisoners, and a report sent to Felipe IV concluded that 'the English and French enemies, with over 1,000 men, made landfall on the north side of the island [Española], in twenty-two towns on the best sites. Unhindered they went from place to place stealing cattle, taking much meat and many pelts from the people in villages close to the north and in particular from Tortuga, where the islanders have their fort . . .'[6] The colony was made up of some 700 French settlers (and probably other Europeans), and some 450 slaves, about half being Africans and half local Indians.[7]

On 18 August 1653 Andrés Pérez Franco, captain-general of Española, died and was replaced temporarily by the thirty-three-year-old Juan Francisco Montemayor Cuenca, who swore to retrieve the situation. He convened a number of *juntas* through which he proposed to intervene and made preparations to this end. On 8 December he wrote to the king outlining the need to deal with the French and the measures that would be necessary to do so; but without waiting for royal approval he collected a force and set sail. Despite losing three of his five vessels in a storm, he arrived off the coast of Tortuga on 10 January 1654 where his two lead ships were fired upon from Levasseur's old fort. So Montemayor and his infantry commander, Gabriel Roxas del Valle Figueroa, decided to land about a league to the west.[8]

Eight days later, following a brilliant Spanish manoeuvre which saw the erection of a battery of eight or ten large guns on a hill across from La Roca, the French capitulated, and 350 men surrendered, with twenty-five being released from gaol. Eventually some 500 people were sent from the island under safe-conduct passes while Thomas de Fontenay, the governor's brother, was held hostage. Among the booty taken were seventy guns including four of bronze, worth some 20,000 ducats, for the loss of two Spaniards killed and between twenty-five and thirty defenders. In order to retain control of the island a garrison of 150 men was left under Baltasar Calderón Espinosa, who repulsed two French counter-attacks, one led by de Fontenay after his brother had been released. His small force of just 130 men and a few Dutch had had to retreat after twenty days of hard fighting. Tortuga might have become another *presidio*, or permanent dependency like San Agustin in Florida. Instead, despite Montemayor's successful efforts, with the arrival of Bernardino de Meneses Bracamonte y Zapata as the new captain general and president of the *audiencia* of Santo Domingo, Tortuga was evacuated on 8 April 1655, and soon it was once again teeming with buccaneers.[9]

First into the void was an English merchant, Elias Watts, who sailed from Jamaica with the intention of starting a colony and found the island deserted. After settling with his family and a dozen others he returned to Jamaica and obtained a commission from the governor before returning with another 150 men, who began planning raids on Tierra Grande with the aid of French survivors from the de Fontenay disaster. Watts led his motley bunch of 400, most of whom were buccaneers, back on to Española at Puerto de la Plata on Palm Sunday, 1659. They made for Santiago de la Vega some twenty-two miles inland, taking the governor and inhabitants by surprise, holding the governor hostage and plundering at will. Bracamonte complained that he had just had word of peace between Spain and France, to which the buccaneers retorted they had an English commission, and advised him to prepare to die. As he was saying his prayers they had second thoughts and instead demanded a ransom of 68,000 pesos. But on returning to the coast they were ambushed by the local militia and were allowed to pass only after threatening to slit the governor's throat. On the coast they released their hostages and made it back to Tortuga, where their booty amounted to 300 pesos each.[10] No good came of it, however, as the leader of the Frenchmen returned home on an English ship whose captain threw him overboard, and none of the other participants prospered from their ill-gotten gains.[11]

The success of Watts in settling on Tortuga excited envy in France; after all the island had previously been French. On 26 November 1659 one of the original settlers from twenty years previously, an adventurer called Jérémie Deschamps, sieur du Moussac et du Rausset, obtained a royal commission as governor. But knowing that Watts was popular and that this commission would be insufficient by itself, he went to London and inveigled an order authorising Jamaica to recognise him as governor providing he granted English colonists equal rights to French ones. He then returned to La Rochelle, collected thirty men and set off for Jamaica. When Watts learned of what had happened he panicked, seized a ship in the harbour and loaded his family and property on board before sailing to New England, never to return. The French arrived the following day. Following two abortive attempts to reclaim the island for the English Tortuga officially came under French jurisdiction. But it remained a base for buccaneers and merchants of all nationalities, even though by this time Jamaica had developed its own reputation as a haven for buccaneers.[12]

Not only had England been convulsed by civil war in the 1640s but Spain faced rebellions in Catalonia and Portugal which, coming on top of the Thirty Years War, placed an intolerable burden on the resources of the state, and by the middle of the seventeenth century she was in full retreat in Europe with France increasingly the dominant power. Thus, although the Treaty of the Pyrenees (1659) was not an especially harsh settlement for Spain, it marked the end of the Habsburg dominance of Europe.[13] Similarly the fall of Jamaica had created something of a crisis in the Spanish Caribbean, as officials worried about their ability to defend key islands and seaports. At the same time, war with England closer to home distracted Castilian Spain from attending to colonial concerns.[14] In Jamaica herself London's main objective between 1655 and 1664 was consolidation of the island as an English possession. In a letter confirming him in his appointment as commander, Cromwell wrote to Fortescue:

> I doe commend in the midst of others miscarriages, your constancy and faithfulness to your trust in every [situation] where you are and [your] takeing care of a company of poore sheepe left by their shepherds; and be assured, that as that which you have done hath been good in itself, and becominge an honest man, so it hath a very good savour here with all good Christians and all true Englishmen, and will not be forgotten by me as opportunitie shall serve ... We think it much designed amongst us, to strive with the Spanyard for the mastery of all those seas.[15]

But to Vice-Admiral Goodson he wrote that the war was one not of dominion but of religion. 'The Lord himself hath a controversy with your enemies; even with that Roman Babylon of which the Spaniard is the greatest underpropper. In this respect we fight the Lord's battles.'[16]

On the island the Spanish organised themselves as well as possible and Proenza, feverish, partly blind and with an abscess on his foot, named Don Cristóbal Arnaldo de Isasi as his lieutenant-general. Isasi busied himself arranging ambushes, and enjoyed some early success. But the Spanish desperately needed reinforcements which were not forthcoming, although they knew the English were also suffering, as their early appeals for more settlers from Barbados, St Christopher and Nevis had been rejected.[17] John Daniel, however, was impressed by Jamaica's potential; the Spanish had left sugar mills, maize and rice behind, while salt, fish, fowl, tobacco, 'rare fruite' and forests flourished. Daniel reported hearing that spices – cloves, mace and cinnamon – grew on Jamaica, and also believed the rumours of gold and silver mines. Showing some business enterprise, he thought that silk worms could be introduced. All of this led him to conclude that the English were better off with Jamaica. Española would have been too large to hold and the topography would allow too many Spaniards simply to retreat into the hills and forests and carry on the battle. Moreover, Española's position windward of Cuba would prevent English ships from returning to the island after raiding, whereas Jamaica was ideally situated for galling the Spaniard, and was very fertile. Thomas Modyford on Barbados wrote on 6 July 1655 that Jamaica was more suitable for colonisation than Española. He believed that Jamaica had an excellent harbour and asserted that the island enjoyed a particularly useful situation for an attempt on a *flota* as it sailed between Cartagena and Havana. Provided that England continued supplying the army, and English frigates patrolled the Caribbean, he thought that nothing could prevent Jamaica from becoming a viable colony in three or four years, one that would provide a base for further bold actions against Spain.[18] But as things stood it remained far from viable, and could not even support the army as it was.

The fleet that brought the English in May 1655 had soon departed and, as the total Spanish population had not exceeded 2,500, the area currently planted with food crops was totally inadequate to support an army three times that size. It was now too late to plant crops because the summer months in Jamaica are dry, and in any case turning the army into farmers was hampered by a lack of tools and seed; isolated farms would be vulnerable to guerrilla attacks; and until crops became harvestable the men would have to be fed from the diminishing stores. Some of the soldiers 'did once set themselves to plant some food, but of that little, what was not burnt up with the sun, was the most part spoiled for want of weeding'.[19] So many men went out to hunt cattle that to conserve the supply the authorities had to order that only selected piquets could leave camp, and it was soon clear that the bucolic charms that had lured some of Jackson's men to desert in 1643 were not so apparent after all.[20] By November 1655 the newly arrived English population was being ravaged not only by hunger but by its concomitant, disease, and a muster revealed the strength of the army as 2,194 men fit and 2,316 sick, most of whom died before the year was out. In addition there were 173 women and children. Although reinforcements of 800 troops had landed, some 3,700 men had died since the English arrived in May, and they were now dying at a rate of 140 per week, a figure that doubled by year's end. By 1 January 1656 after a regiment of 800 young soldiers was brought in under Colonel Humphrey together with eleven vital stores ships, the total was reduced to 2,600 with fifty now dying every week; on 3 January Fortescue himself died. Robert Sedgwick was shocked by what he saw:

> For the Army, I find them in as sad, and deplorable, and distracted a condition, as can be thought of; and indeed think, as ever poor Englishmen were in; the commanders some having left them, some dead, some sick, some in indifferent health; the soldiery many dead, their carcasses lying unburied in the high-ways, and among the bushes to and again; many of them that were alive, walked like ghosts or dead men, who as I went through the town, they lay groaning, and crying out, bread, for the Lord's sakes . . . It is strange to see young lusty men, in appearance well, and in three or four days in the grave, snatch'd away in a moment with fevers, agues, fluxes and dropsies, a confluence of many diseases, the truth is God is angry and the plague is begun, and we have none to stand in the gap.[21]

But after that with the coming of the dry season matters improved, and by March the population was stabilised at 2,500.[22]

Things were better with the fleet, whose sailors had little contact with the soldiers and did not succumb like them to malaria. When Goodson became head of the local naval station he decided that the best means of consolidation was a policy of aggression and he began issuing letters of marque. He soon turned the island into a den of privateers of all nationalities who thus gained a measure of legitimacy in return for handing over a portion of their gains to England, in the form at first of the republic and later of the crown. Simultaneously he promoted the settlement of smugglers and plantations to generate economic activity. Finally he took the decision to launch an attack against Tierra Firme, capturing Santa Marta and burning it to the ground; but, fearing he had insufficient forces to do the same to Cartagena, he had returned empty-handed to Jamaica in mid-November 1655.[23] Sedgwick and Goodson in their position as commissioners appointed Colonel Edward D'Oyley to command the army, effectively making him governor, and decreeing that every soldier was to be allocated thirty acres. But Sedgwick's view of the soldiers was uncomplimentary to say the least: 'I believe they are not to be paralled [sic] in the world; a people so lazy and idle, as it cannot enter the heart of any Englishman, that such blood should run in the veins of any born in England; so unworthy, so slothful, and basely secure: and have, out of a strange kind of spirit, desired rather to die than to live.'[24] But Sedgwick would not exercise authority for long; he too died on 24 May 1656.

Somewhat belatedly given the headway made by the Western Design, Spain declared war on England in March 1656, but her martial effort was derisory and her fleet remained in port. Yet at least one prisoner, Richard Hopp, claimed that the English could be easily dislodged from Jamaica if they were attacked from Port Morant in the south-east after cutting off their water supply. Hopp was a German from Düsseldorf who had previously served the King of Spain and been imprisoned on Jamaica after stabbing his captain in a dispute. He then escaped and went over to the Spanish. His plan was echoed by another prisoner who wrote to the king, the former governor of the island Jacinto Sedoño Alburuoz. But the only likely source of intervention was Cuba whose colonists, currently suffering from a serious plague, were concerned only with their own defence.[25] In April 1656 Goodson returned to Tierra Firme with the intention of capturing one of the Spanish fleet's vessels. He struck at Río de la Hacha without success and did not press home an attack against Cartagena's defences, so he returned at the end of June, pausing at Nevis to take on board 1,400 planters and workers to help populate Jamaica.[26]

Although Cromwell was bitterly disappointed with the failure of the Western Design, and regarded Jamaica as a poor reward for the effort involved, he realised the need for a larger population if it was to be held. Not only did he dispatch troops, but he encouraged settlers to go as planters, and arranged for numbers of Irish and Scots to be transported there. The ethnic cleansing of parts of Ireland where English 'plantations' were established might be said to have started on 24 August 1652 with the issuing of a proclamation that gave the commissioners of Ireland powers to seize and transport, either to Barbados or Virginia, anybody deemed dangerous to the Commonwealth. There was always a particular demand for young women, 'marriageable and not past breeding', because the planters, according to Henry Cromwell, 'had only Negresses and Maroon women [former slaves] to solace them'.[27] Irish slaves cost Bristol merchants £4 10 shillings and sold for £35 in Barbados, and as many as 50,000 were driven through Munster's ports in the next five years, many of them pitching up in Jamaica.

As the English consolidated their foothold on the island, the brethren of the coast were loosely integrated into the island's military forces and proved an immediate success. The buccaneers may have been well protected at Tortuga, but it offered neither the potential for revictualling or scope for sale of prizes offered by Caguaya, and the Spanish had evicted them once already. In 1657 D'Oyley invited 250 buccaneers from Española to Jamaica, men who expected to be 'protected in all those insolencies which they should commit', though D'Oyley did not intend to connive in 'such miscarriage among them as did tend to the prejudice of others'.[28] By luring them to this new base of operations, he was hoping both to obtain protection and to secure a valuable source of revenue; in return the buccaneers gained a superlative harbour that was increasingly well defended. To start with the buccaneers were mostly French, with a sprinkling of Dutch, English and Portuguese, but it appears that the army took well to the idea as the number of English privateers rose quickly.[29]

More significantly, Admiral Robert Blake blockaded Spain's coast throughout the winter of 1656–7, the first time such a feat was accomplished, and captured the flagship of the *galleones* carrying some 2 million pesos. This was far more serious a loss than merely the bullion's value, for within two years of losing Jamaica and finding herself at war with both England and France, Spain had lost the means to pay the interest on her enormous loans. And worse was to follow. The *flota*, which had been frightened into remaining at Veracruz by Goodson, made a dash for Spain, reaching the Canaries in February 1657. There news of Blake's presence near by prompted the Spaniards to unload its 10 million pesos of bullion and take it into the hills of Tenerife. The ships waited in the harbour, where Blake promptly arrived and sank all sixteen for the loss of just one vessel of his own. This brilliant action had far-reaching effects. Not only was the Spanish government effectively deprived of the bullion stored in the hills, but it was already so desperately short of shipping that it was having trouble assembling a fleet to recapture Jamaica. So Blake's attack effectively saved the island.[30]

On Jamaica itself there was little action. In January 1657 Goodson returned home to England and was replaced by his deputy, Christopher Myngs, who continued the strategy with considerable energy, though unfortunately few details of his service in the West Indies have survived.[31] Myngs organised defences and coastguard patrols and achieved much success against Dutch vessels. On 3 July two frigates left Cuba carrying 436 men including 206 Spanish Jamaican colonists who had arrived there after the English invasion. But Isasi was sceptical about these reinforcements and complained loudly about the lack of supplies. No sooner had they landed than he ordered their commander, Juan de los Reyes, to hand over his command to Isasi's eighteen-year-old nephew. To add insult to injury Reyes was expected to teach the youth the art of war, and he angrily retorted that he would not serve as a child's tutor.[32] As the column headed inland many men fell ill and were sent back to Cuba; in all five batches of reinforcements crossed from Santiago de Cuba to Jamaica between July and October, with only the last being intercepted. But no effective operations were launched beyond the usual raiding, and by the time a regiment departed Veracruz on 8 October it was too late. The Spanish on Jamaica had been defeated.

Six ships carrying the regiment of 806 men with food, ammunition and 25,000 pesos in silver first sailed to Santiago de Cuba, where they were integrated with other troops. Two captains were sent to Jamaica to confer with Isasi, who pleaded that food be sent for his men. Learning of this the English stationed a ship off Santiago, blocking any relief attempt despite there being three Spanish ships in port with 600 men. Eventually, on 19 May they sailed and, shadowed by the English, reached the Río Nuevo three days later only to find no sign of Isasi.

The Spanish charter captains were anxious to return to Cuba, but no word arrived from Isasi until the 26th. That day English ships tried to attack them, but were beaten back. A month later, having made no effort to attack anywhere, the Mexican force was still at Río Nuevo when the English suddenly appeared. On 25 June they landed 2,000 men from ten ships and D'Oyley sent a letter to Isasi demanding his surrender. After Isasi had refused, the English three days later launched a two-pronged assault against the now exhausted and starving Spanish, killing some 300 and scattering the remainder, most of whom then made their way as best they could back to Cuba.[33] In retaliation for this invasion attempt, Myngs sailed to Tierra Firme to attack Santa Marta and Tolú where he captured three merchantmen travelling between Cartagena and Portobelo, returning to Jamaica in triumph six weeks later. He then sold the captured ships to the buccaneers: the largest carrying eight guns was sold to Robert Searle, who renamed her *Cagway*; the second largest carrying four guns was sold to a Dutchman, Laurens Prins, who renamed her *Pearl*; and the third went to John Morris, who renamed her *Dolphin*.[34]

With the English now in control of the north coast and communications cut, Isasi – who had barely fifty followers left – demanded further aid early in 1658; but tension was strong between him and the governor of Cuba, Don Pedro de Bayana Villanueva, whose opinion of the general's military abilities was not high. 'Isasi has converted swords into pens, since he spends all his time exercising them' was his acid comment.[35] But it was Bayana whom the king decided to replace, and his successor Don Pedro de Morales arrived with explicit instructions to maintain cordial relations with Isasi and other island governors. But overall there remained a lack of understanding of Jamaica's significance to Spain, and a corresponding lack of aggressive action until in March Felipe IV called a council together at Cádiz to discuss the situation and plan Jamaica's recapture. Unfortunately, all such considerations were pointless without a fleet, and all that could be arranged was the dispatch of a military adviser to Isasi.

In 1659 Myngs set out on another expedition against the Main with the frigates *Marston Moor*, Hector and *Cagway* and supported by numerous buccaneers. In order to gain surprise he chose to tack hundreds of miles further east than he or Goodson had previously operated, and as a result gained the handsome advantage of surprise when his fleet burst on to a wholly unsuspecting Cumaná, ransacking the port. The English then sailed west before the wind to Puerto Caballo before an alarm could be carried overland, and repeated the tactic to attack Coro where at least twenty-two chests were taken from two Dutch merchant ships flying Spanish colours, each containing 400 pounds of silver ingots belonging to the King of Spain worth around £50,000. Myngs returned to Jamaica on 23 April with this fantastic haul, worth in total somewhere between £200,000 and £300,000. But when it came to be tallied it was discovered that the chests had been plundered during the voyage and a great deal of the treasure had been stolen. Before he could do anything to investigate, Myngs was accused by D'Oyley of appropriating 12,000 pesos 'without provision for the rights of the State'.[36] Myngs brushed this off by saying it was the common practice of privateersmen, but officials accused him of taking matters into his own hands and D'Oyley suspended him. Captain William Dalyson wrote home that he 'verily believed if the General [D'Oyley] were at home to answer for himself, Captain Myngs would be found no better than he is, a proud-speaking vain fool, and a knave in cheating the State and robbing merchants'.[37] Myngs was ordered to return to England to face trial.

By now the only effective resistance to English rule on Jamaica came from 300 or so maroons who had declined to follow their former owners to Cuba, having refused the general offer of freedom made by the English under Article XI of the terms of surrender, preferring their freedom in the mountains from where they could launch forays.[38] Although fiercely anti-English, they were also by now intensely hostile to the Spanish. On 6 February 1660 they attacked and killed thirteen Spaniards, and the English stepped in to offer those remaining terms for surrender and evacuation. Despite Isasi's repeated claims – made to impress his sovereign – that the maroons were under his control, it seems that fear of these former slaves rather than of the English led him two weeks later to decide to abandon the island, only to be attacked again on 22 February by maroons and English combined.[39] Finally on the morning of 9 May, seventy-six exhausted, starving Spaniards, plagued with lice, boarded two canoes and pulled away from Jamaica. Although thirty-six remained behind, all effective resistance to English rule was over.[40]

Jamaica proved to be an ideal base for raiding Spanish possessions and its conquest marked the beginning of the great age of buccaneering. The Lesser Antilles were too remote from the ordinary paths of Spanish commerce, and with sugar providing handsome profits there was little cause to tempt the inhabitants of those islands from more peaceful paths to fortune.[41] One privateer who took a commission from D'Oyley in 1660, and who would go on to earn great notoriety, was Captain Maurice Williams. He bought the Spanish prize *Rabba Bispa* and renamed her *Jamaica*, adding five guns from the state store. Being short of men D'Oyley agreed to a proclamation that 'such seamen aboard the *Marston Moor* frigott that will go along with the aforesaid captain Maurice Williams may have liberty to go on board the said *Jamaica* frigott at their pleasure'.[42] With this act D'Oyley was stretching his discretionary powers as governor to the limit, though he was not a man to worry unduly over legal niceties; the prize courts he established never received official approval from the Admiralty and were little more than an extension of the instructions issued for the initial expedition in 1655.[43]

In the meantime, upon the Restoration of Charles II in the summer of 1660, England and Spain concluded a peace treaty. On Barbados Modyford, the 'planter-governor', confidant and cousin of the newly appointed captain-general of the army, George Monck himself, proclaimed both his own commission and the king's accession in defiance of the Protectorate's appointment of Governor Searle, and Charles was pleased to confirm him in this position in November.[44] On Jamaica D'Oyley, knowing that he would have little chance of preferment under the new regime, had earlier sent dark warnings home about the chaotic situation that prevailed, with neither goods nor cash available and traders able neither to buy nor sell except at a loss; the government would have to reinforce and reconstruct the island, or abandon it. Mere 'expedients of dilatorice Propositions' would be useless, he wrote.[45] By this stage privateering had proved so popular and successful that both merchant ships and plantations went undermanned. For with the expansion of the sugar plantations, but before the full advent of large-scale African slavery, poor whites had left the land and, rather than return to Europe, had enthusiastically embraced buccaneering.

It was hardly surprising that they should; many were ex-soldiers tempted by the excellent business start-up that buccaneering presented, with a modest investment of a few hundred pounds offering the prospect of substantial early profits. The Caribbean had long been a refuge for those in debt or escaping the law; why stoop and labour like a slave when an hour's work with musket, pistol and cutlass might yield what a year's sweating toil never could? The most significant outlay would be a ship, but prizes were available at knock-down prices under D'Oyley's regime, and it would take until 1662 for a proper admiralty court to be established for their correct sale; even then a 200–ton ship would sell for a tenth of its value in England. Buccaneering was potentially a self-perpetuating business: it was worth keeping a good capture, for tropical waters were notoriously hard on hulls. Crews tended to be large for the size of the ship, partly to make the capture of prizes easier and partly to provide crews for any taken. Since men were employed on a 'no purchase, no pay' system, wages were not a problem, and crews were likely to be well motivated. But for all the apparent prospects and despite strict rules governing the distribution of booty, few dreams of great riches were ever realised given that whatever was seized was spread among so many hands. When nine ships were captured in Campeche in 1663, for example, yielding a total prize value of £1,341, once expenses had been factored in only £782 4s remained to be shared among some 1,500 men. A voyage might earn a man £30, or it might earn him nothing.[46]

In August 1660 D'Oyley finally received two frigates and in order to ensure that the buccaneers remained honest and were not tempted to take English vessels as prizes, he gave instructions to John Lloyd commanding *Diamond* to intercept 'divers rovers or private men of warre at sea, who daily commit insolencies on the bodies and goods of the allies and considerably of our nation', and to check that they carried commissions issued either by himself or by the high court of admiralty in England.[47] A typical commission would be to 'take, seize, apprehend and possess to otherwise destroy all [Spanish] ships and vessels together with their men, ladeing, goods, wars and merchandise'.[48] The Spanish would ignore these papers entirely, but they were essential for the occasional pirate-hunting missions that the Jamaican authorities launched, when those carrying papers would be free to pass. And on at least one occasion D'Oyley proved as good as his word, when on 23 January 1661 Captain Thomas Wilkes of *Convertine* received instructions to take on board five Englishmen in irons for robbery and piracy.[49] But there was no guarantee that the law would deal with them harshly. George Freeburne attempted to land a cargo secretly in 1661 and was arrested and sent to be tried for piracy in England, while his crew were distributed around the plantations to work as slaves. Freeburne was acquitted, however, and returned to the island where, in November the following year, he obtained a new commission.[50]

It was not until February 1661 that Charles II was pleased to confirm D'Oyley in his position, the same month in which the governor had to shoot two colonels for a republican insurrection, and the commission did not reach him until May, along with news of the peace treaty with Spain.[51] Immediately his policy underwent an important shift with orders to reverse that of the previous seven years and to 'obtain and preserve good correspondence and free commerce with the plantations belonging to the King of Spain'.[52] As long as Charles sought a profitable marriage with a Portuguese princess English policy towards Spain would remain cautious, for it was well known 'with what jealousie and offence' Spain viewed the settling of Jamaica, which was one of the critical colonial issues of the time.[53] Nobody could ignore its Spanish past nor guarantee that it would not have a Spanish future; and the recent sale of Dunkirk following repeated royal denials that this would happen both appalled and frightened Jamaica's current rulers. When in exile Charles had promised to return Jamaica to Spain, but now he began to see it in a new light as 'the navel of the West Indies' and 'a window on the power of Spain'.[54] Felipe IV was prepared to keep bidding up the price for its return, but he could not trump Portugal's offer of Bombay, Tangier and £300,000 as dowry for Catherine of Braganza, and her engagement to Charles was duly announced.

Myngs had arrived in England just as the Restoration crisis was in full swing, and his early declaration of support for King Charles II had seen him cleared of all charges by June 1660.[55] Now in an act of revenge he accused D'Oyley of receiving a greater share of plunder than he was entitled to, and as the governor was also keen to return to England his successor was appointed by the Committee of Foreign Plantations in August 1661. A convoy set out from England carrying his replacement, Thomas, seventh Baron Windsor, who travelled aboard the forty-six-gun frigate HMS *Centurion* commanded by Myngs, and arrived at Barbados in July 1662. From there he sent letters to the governors of Puerto Rico and Santo Domingo asking permission for English vessels to trade. But the Spanish still refused to recognise English settlements in the Indies for fear of endangering the trade monopoly of Sevilla. On 21 August Windsor and Myngs reached Cagway, now renamed Port Royal, and began the process of 'institutionalising' the colony.[56] D'Oyley, to whom Windsor was barely polite, left on 10 September aboard *Westergate*, which took eighteen months to return to England, yet Windsor himself remained in Jamaica barely ten weeks, performing a great many tasks in a tearing hurry.[57] He completed the fort that was being built to defend the port, naming it Fort Charles, raised the pay of the armed forces and disbanded the five regiments of soldiers distributed around the island, replacing them with 400 foot and 150 horse; he offered land for settlement and established a local assembly, a court and an admiralty court which would allow him to issue letters of reprisal and called in the commissions of the privateers, most of which were out of date if not entirely fictitious.

When he received final letters from the Spanish rejecting his requests for trade, he was in a position to implement secret orders that if the King of Spain refused to permit it he must 'endeavor to settle Such Trade by Force'.[58] To apply this order he issued new commissions 'to take Spanyards and bring them to Jamayca, there to come to Judicature, and pay their Publique dues, being the Tenths and fifteenths' of the admiralty court.[59] Spain's role, therefore, was to provide prizes for the needy, carrion to sustain the crows, all with official approval. This was a tremendous boon to the buccaneers, boosting their morale and increasing their numbers in short order, as they could now regard themselves as lawfully employed servants of the state. And although the state would shortly afterwards change its mind, it was too late: the damage was done, as was underlined when Windsor called on volunteers to join a great expedition against the Spanish under Myngs, now appointed commodore.[60] In three days the king's ships *Centurion* and *Griffin* were joined for the venture by ten privateering vessels and some 1,300 men had gathered, two-thirds of them buccaneers and many of them former soldiers, while among the officers was a young Welshman, Henry Morgan.[61] Born in 1635 in either Penkarne

(Monmouthshire) or more likely Llanrhymney (Glamorgan), and coming from a family with wide military connections, Morgan had arrived in Jamaica as part of Penn's and Venables' expedition. Once there he steadily learned his trade, having left school too young to be proficient in anything else and 'more used to the pike than the book'.[62]

With the excuse that it served as the point of departure for Spanish expeditions against Jamaica, Myngs selected Santiago de Cuba as his target as that port had been a major source of irritation to the English on Jamaica and the main base of Spanish operations aimed at its recovery.[63] The English fleet left Port Royal on 1 October 1662 and sailed west to Punta Negril at the western end of the island to avoid the Spanish watch, and met Sir Thomas Whetstone's vessel anchored and waiting to join the expedition. Whetstone was Cromwell's nephew and an extraordinary rogue who had remained loyal to the crown throughout the civil war and Protectorate. Having been thrown into Marshalsea Prison for debt and released on the Restoration, he emigrated and almost immediately turned pirate, commanding a seven-gun Spanish prize with a mostly Indian crew.[64] Myngs had already obtained intelligence about the layout of the Spanish defences and, following a council of war on board *Centurion*, he decided to launch a direct assault on the port in a bid to surprise the enemy. Reinforced by a further seven Jamaican buccaneer vessels he set off for Santiago and sighted the lights of the castle on the night of 5/6 October. But plans for a direct assault through the narrow entrance to the port were thwarted by unfavourable winds.[65]

Around noon next day the plan was altered, and making use of the offshore wind the fleet made instead for the town of Aguadores at the mouth of the River San Juan. At nightfall they landed a thousand men who began to advance, but 'the way [was] soe difficult and the night soe dark that they were forced to make stands and fires, and their guides with brands in their hands, to beat the path'.[66] At daybreak they reached a plantation three miles from Santiago where they paused to rest and replenish their water supplies. When they continued their march they succeeded in surprising the Spanish who, although they were aware of the English presence on Cuba, did not expect them to come up so quickly. Nevertheless, at the entrance to the city they were met by Governor Morales and 250 men with two guns; in reserve was the former governor of Jamaica, Isasi, who commanded 500 men.[67]

Myngs ordered an immediate assault and, with the aid of Isasi who now betrayed his own side, quickly overcame Morales. Some defenders took refuge in the castle while others fled into the mountains, and the English spent five days fruitlessly chasing the fugitives while the buccaneers sacked the city. But, apart from seven vessels anchored in the port, there was little booty. When some of his men proposed assaulting the castle, Myngs decided not to embark on a long siege but to blow up the walls instead. Five days later 700 barrels of gunpowder had been assembled for this purpose, as well as to destroy the cathedral, the governor's residence, the hospital and the main households. The ensuing explosions razed the city to the ground. This was followed by more ransacking before the English conducted a orderly retreat, carrying the guns and church bells with them, and returning to Port Royal on 1 November. It would take ten years for the citizens of Santiago to repair the damage inflicted on their city; losses to the English forces totaled twenty-six, of whom only six were killed in battle, the rest succumbing to sickness or accident. Three days after their return, on 28 October, Windsor departed for England claiming sickness, though the real reason was probably financial. He left Sir Charles Lyttelton as provisional governor with Myngs having been appointed to the Council of Jamaica. Windsor was taking advantage of permission granted in a royal letter of 3 May 1662 'to resort in person to our royal presence, either to informe us of the grounds and probabilities of our future designs ... or to solicite & procure such other supplyes and necessaries as occassion shall require'.[68] Richard Povey, Secretary of the Island, said that Windsor left because he was ill; Samuel Pepys, Secretary of the Navy, said that he was lazy, noting in his diary that Windsor arrived home 'unlooked for, [and] makes us think these young lords are not fit to do any service abroad'.[69]

In 1660 du Rausset's expedition had re-established French royal authority over Tortuga and Louis XIV duly appointed him governor, although he and his men were 'not to abuse their authority, which the Adventurers acknowledged of their own free will'.[70] Du Rausset was recalled three years later and forced to sell his 'rights' to the island to the French East India Company. And with the consolidation of Tortuga in the early 1660s as a safe haven for smuggling, the buccaneers threatened – not for the first or last time – to quit Jamaica.[71] What was needed was positive action to ensure the dissenters stayed to support the island's militia and this time it was decided to attack Campeche on the Yucután coast, supposedly to help the small community of logwood-cutters of many nations who had been operating along the isolated seaboard for many years.[72] Emboldened by his success at Santiago, Myngs persuaded Lyttelton and the Council that he should lead a squadron comprising his own frigate *Centurion* and *Griffin*, under Captain Smart with a crew of a hundred, joined by Edward Mansfield and his four-gun brig and other captains including William James,* giving a total of several dozen ships including four French vessels from Tortuga. They sailed on 12 January 1663 and on the night of 8 February Myngs landed a thousand men on a beach four miles west of Campeche. The Spanish raised the alarm at daybreak as a group of small vessels supported by two larger ones approached the city. Despite being taken completely by surprise and heavily outnumbered, the 150–strong Campeche militia offered stout resistance and, aided by the intricate defences, inflicted numerous casualties on the attackers, with Myngs being among the wounded – he was carried aboard *Centurion* and Mansfield took over command – but the joint assault was overwhelming and the city surrendered at 8 a.m. There were thirty dead among the invaders, and fifty among the brave defenders, 170 of whom were captured.[73]

Two days later the governor, Antonio Maldonado de Aldana, who had not been present at the battle, approached to offer surrender and ask that the city be spared. As the man he spoke to was Mansfield, the attack is known to the Spanish as the Mansfield attack, and the defenders, very naturally, complained bitterly about it to the English court.[74] Meanwhile the buccaneers remained in the city until 23 February, loading their spoils on to three 300–ton merchant vessels. But on departure they encountered foul winds and were dispersed; *Centurion* reached Port Royal on 26 April bringing booty of 150,000 pesos, and Myngs returned to England to convalesce and was knighted by the king.[75] But

---

* Legend has it that James was the privateer who discovered the value of logwood to the buccaneers having carried away a Spanish prize loaded with it, and being 'astonished upon reaching port at the high price his cargo fetched'. (D. F. Marley, *Pirates and Privateers of the Americas*, p. 203.)

his career as a buccaneer was over. Soon afterwards he was shot in the face and killed fighting the Dutch in the North Sea, aged only forty-one. He was accorded no great honours and Sir William Coventry was the only 'person of quality' to attend his funeral, according to Pepys who was also at the service at Whitechapel Church. That Myngs was highly regarded by those who served under him was demonstrated afterwards when a group of seamen attended Coventry's coach with tears in their eyes, telling him they wished to avenge their commander's death by taking a fireship against the enemy.

> We are here a Dozen of us that have long loved and served our dead commander, Sir Chr. Mings, and have now done the last office of laying him in the ground. We would be glad we had any other to offer after him, and in revenge of him – all we have is our lives. If you will please let his Royal Highness to give us a fireshipp among us all, here is a Dozen of us . . . that shall show our memory of our dead commander and our revenge.

Pepys believed Myngs was a shoemaker's son who had 'brought his family into way of being great'. The diarist thought that, by dying when he did, he would be 'quite forgot in a few months, as if he had never been, nor any of his name be the better by it'.[76]

In April 1663 Charles II assured the Duque de Medina Sidonia that he entirely disapproved of the raid on Santiago de Cuba, and when news arrived of the Campeche expedition he was quick to disavow that also. Orders from the king to halt all hostilities against Spain reached Jamaica in July but were contradicted by instructions from his brother, the Duke of York, who as lord high admiral was concerned about his income from the tenths that accrued to him, and who convinced Lyttelton that 'the war with privateers was not intended to be taken off by the King's instructions'.[77] But these orders made no specific mention of the buccaneers, who would in any case have been impossible to disarm. They took the apparent suppression of their trade with equanimity: when a Captain Sherdick captured St Thomas in the Virgin Islands in June 1663, his men did not return to Jamaica until the following May, having indulged very profitably in outright piracy in the meantime. During this period serious questions were raised both in

Jamaica and in England about the usefulness of privateering when it might provoke a Spanish backlash.[78]

Yet its usefulness was obvious, for as long as it continued to be profitable it was bound to thrive, and if England and Spain were not at war and it veered into piracy, nobody in Jamaica much cared. The island remained a hive of buccaneering activity with Port Royal reportedly having a fleet of fifteen private men-of-war in 1663, manned by 1,500 'desperate people, the greater part having been in men-of-war these twenty years'.[79] In addition to diverting Spanish attention from Tortuga, the Western Design had introduced two other important influences into the New World, where the practices of European mercenary troops blended easily with the thinking of the brethren of the coast and with the ideas embodied in the radical wing of the English revolution. Radicals rejected state religion and demanded tolerance, and many espoused democratic and proto-socialist ideas. With the Restoration many radicals emigrated to the West Indies, such as Captain William Righton, a former member of the Fifth Monarchists sect who became an active smuggler on Jamaica. J. S. Bromley has noted how the practices espoused by the buccaneers on the great raids that were to follow resembled those of mercenary forces operating in Europe, including marching in ranks, the use of the forlorn hope, the adoption of war names or *noms de guerre* instead of civil names, and the extraction of tribute from coastal settlements. The tradition of autonomy and of self-elected leaders, possibly arising out of radical sentiment connected to religious and political issues, is exemplified by Henry Morgan, whose two uncles had served as soldiers of fortune during the Thirty Years War and British civil wars. All of this helps to explain the rise of the buccaneers, for how else could the English defend their new colony in the absence of support from home.[80]

In June a captain named Barnard outfitted an expedition to San Tomé on the Orinoco and returned soon afterwards having sacked the town; as his crew spent the ill-gotten gains, he was pleased to tell everyone about it. In October another captain called Cooper brought into Port Royal a small Spanish barque and the galleon *María*, carrying a cargo of wine, olives, oil and, most significantly, 1,000 *quintales* (about 100,000 pounds) of quicksilver, or mercury. This was vital to the silver-processing *patios* of Nueva España, but in the debauched atmosphere of the time was useful for the treatment of syphilis and so was sent to England, raising loud protests from the Spanish ambassador, Don Patricio Moledi.[81] But Spanish protests were in vain; if Spain refused to recognise English possessions in the Caribbean, or even the presence of Englishmen there, how could she complain about phantoms? It was a nicely made point that exposed Spain's adherence to a legal fiction that would cost her dear. So the English shrugged off the *María* affair, with Lyttelton insisting that the peace treaty covered only land attacks, not those at sea.[82]

One factor that would lead to the eventual suppression of buccaneering was London's institution of the Royal African Company, specifically to provide slaves to the Spanish whose traders at Cartagena would pay 220 pesos per head. Joseph Williamson, secretary to the recently appointed secretary of state, Henry Bennet, wrote in his notebook:

> The King of Spaine hath a contract with Dominico Grillo for maintaining constantly in the West Indies tenn good shipps in lieu of the liberty he hath to import yearly thither 3500 slaves for the mines. The Spanish slave trade [in] 1663 brought in 43 shipps 7,998,000 pieces of eight besides as much more unregistered.[83]

Keen to get a slice of this action Parliament, given royal assent on 10 January 1663, established the long-mooted Company of Royal Adventurers Trading into Africa.[84] But Spanish slaves brought to Jamaica would prove to be highly unpopular, being the source of 'many mischiefs', although they could be bought cheaply and exported at a very considerable profit.[85]

The Dutch had long been involved in the trade but usually by dealing with slaves captured in foreign vessels, and it was not until the late 1650s that they became interested in importing them directly. The Treaty of Tordesillas had left Spain with no bases on the African coast and ever since 1518, when the Friar Las Casas and other settlers on Española had persuaded Carlos V to allow their importation, an *asiento de negros* had operated.[86] But because the *asiento* system was ineffective, most slaves were imported illegally, and from 1657–8 the WIC suddenly and dramatically increased its slaving activity, with as many as seven

ships landing 1,700 slaves throughout the Caribbean, not only at Curaçao but on the Guiana coast and on English and French islands. In 1661
D'Oyley noted that the company was the only consistent supplier of
slaves in the region, and when a Dutch ship arrived at Jamaica on 14
June carrying 180 slaves he ignored the law banning trade with the
Dutch and bought them, selling forty locally and the remainder 'at a
great price to a Spanish ship to which he also gave a safe conduct'.[87]

On Barbados Humphrey Walrond was keen to encourage Spanish
smugglers, for example in April 1662 when he countenanced the sale
of 400 slaves for 125–40 pesos per head, and then persuaded the Council
to impose an exorbitant tax of 220 pesos each. The Spanish later sold
the slaves at Cartagena, and Walrond extracted a £1,000 bribe from the
last Spanish traders he dealt with. (He then escaped from Barbados,
only to be imprisoned later in England.)[88] From 1662 the Dutch and
English got in on the *asiento* trade when the Spanish granted the
licence to supply 24,000 slaves over seven years to two wealthy Genoese
merchants, Domingo Grillo and Ambrosia Lomelin. But once they had
the *asiento* the Grillos also dealt in all sorts of contraband and were
accused of widespread smuggling, fraud and aiding foreigners to draw
up maps to plan attacks on Spanish forts.[89] It was also noted that they
had failed to build the ten ships they had promised the Spanish but
relied instead on north Europeans to do the actual dirty work, sub-
contracting both the WIC and the Royal African Company, with the
former gradually taking over until by 1667 it had a monopoly. The
volume of trade through Curaçao increased accordingly.[90]

Meanwhile Lyttelton had also tired of Jamaica, to be replaced on 4
June 1664 by Sir Thomas Modyford – now granted a baronetcy – whose
clan was beginning to find Barbados life oppressive, riven as it was
with factionalism. But Modyford's proven experience together with
the support of Monck, newly created Duke of Albemarle, secured his
appointment. When Colonel Edward Morgan, uncle to Henry and
appointed Modyford's lieutenant-governor, arrived in Barbados in April
he found the new governor already feverishly engaged in plans to move
some 1,700 Barbadians to help settle Jamaica and displaying a zeal for
the colony that until now had been conspicuously lacking. He took up
his post with specific orders forbidding the issuing of letters of marque,
but Morgan warned that suppression of privateering would only result

in indiscriminate piracy.[91] This was an important distinction made by the seamen themselves; the privateer might be a rough diamond but he was not an outlaw, and without these skilful, trained men in the service of the king, who then would defend honest planters, settlers and traders from the Spaniard? Nevertheless, on his arrival in Jamaica Modyford dutifully cancelled all existing commissions and made a public example by having a pirate called Munro publicly hanged. He hoped to tempt the buccaneers into planting, only to concede a mere two weeks later that he 'thought it more prudent to do by degrees and moderation what he had resolved to execute suddenly and severely'.[92]

Eventually however, instead of its suppression, buccaneering in Jamaica would reach its apogee under Modyford's stewardship. The physical distance between Jamaica and London ensured this, as it would take at least six weeks if not two months to inform London that Jamaica had been attacked, and at least the same again before effective help could be sent. Jamaica would therefore have to look to her own defence – and that meant the buccaneers.[93] Modyford was soon persuaded to accept existing commissions until they expired. As the president of the Council, Lieutenant-Colonel Thomas Lynch, observed shortly before Modyford's arrival, echoing Colonel Morgan, 'naked orders to restrain [the buccaneers] or call them in will teach them only to keep out of this port and force them (it may be) to prey on us as well as the Spaniards'.[94] Besides, if the buccaneers wanted for English commissions, they 'can have French and Portuguese papers, and if they take with them anything, they are sure of a good reception in the New Netherlands or Tortugas'.[95] In other words, it was simply too dangerous to get on the wrong side of them.

# 8

## FIRST ADMIRAL

Standing upon the margent of the Main,
Whilst the high boiling Tide came tumbling in,
I felt my fluctuating thoughts maintain
As great an Ocean, and as rude, within;
As full of Waves, of Depths, and broken Grounds,
As that which daily laves her chalky bounds.
Soon could my sad Imagination find
A Parallel to this half World of Floud,
An Ocean by my walls of Earth confin'd,
And Rivers in the Chanels of my Bloud:
Discovering man, unhappy man, to be
Of this great Frame Heaven's Epitome.

Charles Cotton, *The Tempest*

If it took until 1664 for effective English crown authority to be established over the Caribees – the Lesser Antilles – then watching developments with interest was Jean-Baptiste Colbert, the very capable minister of King Louis XIV of France. Colbert recognised that the root cause of French troubles in the Caribbean was the effective Dutch monopoly of trade. Commerce was still regarded in France as beneath the dignity of a gentleman, and on top of everything else the government imposed excessive duties on imports to the West Indies, a problem Colbert was determined to solve. The population of the French West Indies had risen from around 7,000 in 1642, mostly from Brittany and Normandy, to some 27,000 by 1655, of whom 15,000 were French and the rest slaves. Under proprietary rule between 1648 and 1664 trade increased steadily, mostly through the Dutch who controlled the bulk of the carrying trade of Europe and were able to undercut French merchants. The Dutch sent a hundred ships to the French West Indies alone at a time when all of France could muster barely 200 in total – and they were better, bigger, faster and cleaner than French vessels so that even Frenchmen took passage in them.[1]

On the eve of Colbert's ministry French owners controlled fourteen islands dominated by sugar plantations, but whose profit was largely controlled by the Dutch. It was time to bring them under the control of the French crown for the material benefit of France with a navigation system to exclude the pesky northerners. Colbert gathered twenty notables and procured 200,000 livres of capital with which to establish the Compagnie des Indes Occidentales (West India Company). He had selected Alexandre de Prouville, marquis de Tracy, as lieutenant-general of the archipelago when news that one thousand settlers had departed Martinique in disgust gave him an excuse to intervene. A small fleet was assembled at La Rochelle and departed on 26 February 1664. On arrival at Martinique it so impressed Thomas Willoughby at Barbados that he wrote, 'the dispute will be whether the King of England or of France shall be monarch of the West Indies, for the King of Spain cannot hold it long, and this is the first year's entrance of the King of France on his own account'.[2]

As Jamaica was strengthening its relationship with the buccaneers, so Tortuga and the French received a boost in February 1665 with the appointment as governor of Bertrand d'Ogeron, sieur de la Bouère, to the settlements at Léogâne, Petit-Goâve and Port-à-Margot, thus making him the founder of the colony of Saint-Domingue on the eastern part of Española. D'Ogeron arrived at Tortuga on 6 June and began a policy of attracting the buccaneers back to the island. But, to begin with at least, the colonists were few, and divided between *habitans* and *boucaniers*. Of the latter he wrote:

They live three or four or six or ten together, more or less separated one group from the other by distances of two or three or six or eight leagues wherever they find suitable places, and live like savages without recognising any authority, without a leader of their own, and they commit a thousand robberies. They have stolen several Dutch and English ships which has caused us much trouble; they live on the meat of wild boars and cattle and grow a little tobacco which they trade for arms munitions and supplies.[3]

Both planters and buccaneers made clear to d'Ogeron that they would not obey the company, only the king's authority was acceptable, and he had little choice but to agree. Thus the English conquest of Jamaica contributed indirectly to the re-establishment of the buccaneers on Tortuga and at Saint-Domingue.

On Tortuga, d'Ogeron, like other administrators, appealed for wives for his men and the authorities promptly dispatched fifty eligible girls, although their qualities were debatable. Morcau de Saint-Méry wrote that d'Ogeron obtained 'from France a supply of charming creatures, timid orphans, to bring to heel these arrogant men accustomed to rebellion'.[4] However, Alexandre-Stanislas, baron de Wimpffen, albeit writing more than a hundred years later, claimed that although France at the time 'abounded with poor, industrious and modest females, whose sweet and ingenuous dispositions would have softened, nay, purified the morals of men ... [the government] sent some prostitutes from the hospitals, abandoned wretches raked up from the mud of the capital, disgusting compounds of filth and impurity of the grossest kind'.[5] Whatever the truth, the women appear to have been a calming influence. But the company neglected to send more, and when a lull came in marauding expeditions, a number of young men drifted away to where women were more plentiful.[6]

In Jamaica Modyford had assumed that the state of affairs was one of emergency from the beginning, and with the shadow of Colbert growing daily over the region and the Dutch – marked out in court policy as 'the enemy' – still ubiquitous in the Caribbean, he might usefully turn the buccaneers from hunting the Spaniard to hunting the Dutchman. But changes of policy were slow to be implemented during the seventeenth century and it was not until January 1665 that the Duke of York authorised all English colonial governors to issue letters of marque against the Dutch.[7] Of the estimated 1,500 buccaneers on the island at the time, Modyford had fourteen in his gaol who 'were tried and condemned to death [for piracy] under the statute of Henry VIII', for he proved willing to act sometimes against those who disregarded his authority. But he proved even more willing to let them go when they accepted his terms, and on 6 February 1665, 'finding so moderate a sense touching privateers and the great occasions His Majesty might have for them, and having shown the law and force [I] changed my copy, pardoned all the pirates but three which I have reprieved, and declared publicly that commissions would be granted against the Dutch.'[8] Either way the Spanish were delighted to see the two northern sea powers at each other's throats, all the more so when they heard news of a French fleet bound for the Caribbean in April apparently to join the fray in support of the Dutch. But England could not spare ships from home waters, thereby making the buccaneers all the more vital for the defence of English Caribbean possessions.

In March Modyford painted a grim picture of a Jamaica abandoned by the buccaneers with defences reduced to a fifth, and merchants leaving Port Royal or withdrawing credit. The following month a Dutch fleet under the greatest naval commander of the age, Admiral Michel Adrianszoon de Ruyter, launched an attack on some forty English merchantmen escorted by a few warships at Barbados, right under Bridgetown's guns. According to his own report he caused considerable damage, but according to the English side he did so 'in the most confusedest manner possible'.[9] While still awaiting instructions from London and hearing rumours of war – and knowing that he could not rein in the buccaneers – Modyford quickly formed a partnership with them instead and issued letters of marque. Following de Ruyter's abortive attack, war was declared between England and Holland in May 1665, and Modyford commissioned the buccaneers to attack Dutch shipping, a move later extended to the French when they joined the Dutch side. English naval strategy during the Dutch wars hinged on massing the largest possible fleet in the North Sea: all other considerations, including defence of the West Indies, were secondary to this aim. Squadrons were withdrawn from overseas stations and merchants told explicitly 'that they [should] look to themselves'.[10] In due course Modyford would also wage a private war against Spain that the king could conveniently disavow if diplomacy demanded. But this proved to be personally advantageous too. Governors were expected to draw their salary from prizes, so they were more likely to grant commissions, and Modyford later admitted receiving £1,000 a year in fees and kickbacks from the buccaneers, though he probably got a great deal more.[11]

He claimed to charge £20 a time, while Windsor had charged £50, though the validity period of the letters of marque varied from six months to twenty-three. The court of admiralty also stipulated that two gentlemen should give bond that the privateer would 'observe, perform, fulfill' his commission and obey the instructions to enter all prizes in the court for the payment of tenths and fifteenths to admiralty and crown respectively, for which Windsor charged between £200 and £2,000.[12]

For now an expedition under Colonel Edward Morgan was organised with ten ships and some 600 men. The recently widowed and impecunious Morgan had arrived in Port Royal with his three daughters and two sons, his eldest daughter having died en route, and in due course the eldest surviving daughter, Mary Elizabeth, would marry his nephew Henry. Edward had spent many years in exile as a soldier of fortune on the continent of Europe and spoke excellent Dutch, and as England's relations with the United Provinces had long since deteriorated his appointment appears to have been made with a campaign against them in mind. He sailed in the *Speaker* (eighteen guns) and set out to gather more men at a rendezvous, being 'chiefly reformed privateers', according to Modyford, with:

> scarce a planter amongst them, being resolute fellows, and [they] are well armed with fusees and pistols. Their design is to fall upon the Dutch fleet trading [to] St Christopher's, capture St Eustatius, Saba, and Curaçao, and on their homeward voyage visit the French and English buccaneers at Hispaniola and Tortuga. All this is prepared by the honest privateer, at the rate of 'no purchase, no pay', and it will cost the King nothing considerable, some powder and mortar pieces.[13]

On 17 July they set out from Montserrat; the buccaneers were outnumbered and outgunned on St Eustatius, and Morgan died on landing, 'not with any wound, but being ancient and corpulent, by hard marching and extraordinary heat'.[14] The buccaneers carried on and the Dutch governor surrendered on 23 July without putting up a fight; nearby Saba fell equally easily. But these captures yielded little booty and the expedition, now thoroughly demoralised, fell to pieces as each man sought to secure his share. Morgan's successor, Thomas Cary, could not persuade the buccaneers to continue to Curaçao and they straggled back to Port Royal.[15]

In the meantime four towns in the Bay of Mexico had been pillaged by buccaneers carrying Lord Windsor's commission who had avoided hearing of Modyford's recall by staying out for twenty-two months and operating over 750 miles from Jamaica. Under the command of Edward Mansfield with Captain Henry Morgan as second-in-command, and including the latter's friends John Morris and Dutch-born David Martien, a group of vessels and some 200 men had departed in January and made a long and difficult voyage to land at Santa María de la Frontera on the coast of Tabasco. They then climbed towards the capital Villahermosa de Tabasco, fifty miles inland but entailing a 300–mile march following the Grijalva river which surpassed Drake's own march across the isthmus and which was driven by the need to get around the impassable swamps stretching either side of the river. They arrived at last on 24 February. This feat was made possible only by friendly Indian guides and by avoiding all settlements, so that their assault on the city took the inhabitants completely by surprise.[16]

On their return journey the buccaneers stopped at Santa Teresa where they demanded a ransom of 300 cattle in exchange for the 300 hostages they were holding, but as they were boarding their ships they spotted three Spanish frigates carrying 270 men under the command of José Aldana, nephew and lieutenant to Antonio Maldonado de Aldana, the governor of Campeche.[17] The buccaneer anchor-watches fled aboard a single vessel, abandoning the other ships and the booty. With their retreat cut off by Aldana, Morgan, Morris and Martien released their hostages and went west in two of the coasters, hoping to find another means of escaping to sea, only to be overtaken on the morning of 17 March by a second Spanish naval patrol in the buc-caneers' former boats opposite Santa Ana cay. Aldana called for their surrender but was ignored, and when he tried to attack the buccaneers the following morning he found them well dug in and was swiftly repulsed. Dawn the next day revealed that the Spanish had run aground, so the buccaneers made off north-eastwards, hugging the Yucután coast where they captured more seaworthy boats. These enabled them to continue their depredations at Trujillo on the coast of Honduras before making for Bluefields some 450 miles to the south.[18]

By now this epic voyage, a phenomenal piece of navigation and improvisation, had covered over 2,500 miles since Port Royal, more than half of it in canoes along the most dangerous coasts in the Caribbean. And it was by no means over yet. Withdrawing from Campeche to the uninhabited Roatán Island, the buccaneers stopped on the Mosquito Coast, probably at Cabo Gracias a Dios, to pick up some twenty Samba-Miskitas, a great asset to the buccaneers, 'as they are very good harpoonists, extremely skilful in spearing turtles, manatees and fish. In fact, an Indian is capable of keeping a whole ship's company of 100 men supplied with food, when he is at a place where there is something to catch.'[19] Meanwhile, although Nicaragua was the least wealthy and least accessible of Spain's American provinces, it inland port of Granada had become an important entrepôt whence precious metals and indigo were dispatched to Cartagena having previously been sent via Santo Tomás. All this was reported by Thomas Gage.[20] Now Granada seemed an excellent source of loot because, like the city of León to the northwest, it was previously untouched. It also appeared to be relatively accessible to the buccaneers despite being 300 miles inland and sheltered behind a wilderness inhabited by Caribs and as yet unpenetrated by friendly Samba-Miskitas. But the buccaneers could paddle up the 200–mile San Juan river with only a short portage to get around the Santa Cruz rapids, and then cross Lake Nicaragua: it seemed there was nowhere easier to attack. The combined force moved along the coast and up the San Juan, whose 111 miles took about three and a half days to negotiate, before they reached 'the entrance of a fair laguna, or lake . . . of sweet fresh water, full of excellent fish, with its banks full of brave pastures and savannahs, covered with horses and cattle, where they had as good beef and mutton as any in England'.[21]

Although the buccaneers crossed Lake Nicaragua slowly and carefully by night, hiding among the islands by day, apparently the citizens of Granada were expecting an attack. But the mayor, a nervous individual, exhausted them with his constant ringing of the bells day and night to practise their defensive drills. The citizens complained to the provincial governor in León who ordered that the bells should not be rung again without his express permission. When the buccaneers were sighted on 20 June a messenger was sent forthwith to León to seek leave to ring the bells, but before he could complete the 167-mile round trip the buccaneers ten days later fell upon the city.[22] In broad daylight they marched into the main plaza, fired a volley and overturned eighteen guns, then they herded 300 astonished and frightened militiamen into the main church before plundering the city for sixteen hours, ably assisted, as Morris reported to Modyford later, by more than a thousand local Indians who 'would have killed the prisoners, especially the churchmen, imagining the English would keep the place, but finding they would return home requested them to come again'.[23] And so, after sinking the lake boats to prevent pursuit, the buccaneers departed, taking 6,000 pesos and a number of African slaves with them, having bestowed on Granada a reputation as both rich and defenceless.

Towards the end of the year Modyford tried to rally the buccaneers once more against the Dutch but he and everybody else knew that it was only booty that spurred them and that the richest pickings came from the Spanish. Consequently, when the Council of Jamaica met on 22 February 1666 it passed a resolution listing no fewer than twelve good reasons why it was in the island's interests to issue letters of marque against the Spanish. This pointed out that the buccaneers helped replenish the island with coin and bullion, logwood, hides, tallow, cacao, indigo, cochineal and so on, thus stimulating trade; that they provided security for the island and that employing the buccaneers of Tortuga and Española prevented them from attacking Jamaica instead, while maintaining 'a high and military spirit among the inhabitants'; that it enabled them to intercept Spanish communications and therefore discover their intentions; and that it forced the Spanish to trade with them:

All ways of kindness producing nothing of good neighbourhood, for though all the old commissions have been called in, and no new ones granted, and many of the ships restored, yet they continue all acts of hostility, taking our ships and murdering our people, making them work at their fortifications and then sending them into Spain, and very lately they denied an English fleet heading for the Dutch colonies wood, water or provisions.[24]

As Modyford pointed out to his cousin Albemarle, the Spanish held the English responsible for attacks on Spanish possessions and the English received all the odium, so they might as well receive the profits and Jamaica gain the security that regular employment of the buccaneers granted.[25] In his answers Albemarle, as the Duke of York's deputy, told him to use his discretion when issuing letters of marque against Spain, doubtless considering his own position regarding prize money.[26] In London the pro-Spanish faction was led by Henry Bennet, now Lord Arlington, and in Jamaica by Colonel Thomas Lynch who as factor of the Royal African Company represented the merchants if not the traders of Port Royal, and who, despite being a devout Protestant and regarding popery as barely removed from witchcraft, was nevertheless determined to sell slaves to the Spanish. Imaginary profits allowed him to dream that a century and a half of 'no peace beyond the line' could be brushed aside, to say nothing of Spanish pride and hatred of heretics. Its corollary and throwback to the Elizabethan age, the all-pervading English hatred of the Spanish, should be neither forgotten nor underestimated, while it is hard to believe that the Duke of York's interests in the Royal African Company were not also considered, reinforcing Modyford's view that Spanish governors could be frightened into conniving with the slave trade.[27]

By now Louis XIV had finally and belatedly honoured his agreement of 1662 to aid the Dutch in the event of attack by the English, although he had managed to put off signing the declaration of war until 26 January 1666, and this news did not reach Jamaica until July that year; meanwhile on 22 February Modyford granted commissions against the Spanish.[28] It seemed the obvious step since Spanish prizes were the oil in the Jamaican machine, enabling the colony to buy commodities at easy rates and attracting New England men to barter their provisions; besides which, 'it is a matter of great security to the island that the men of war, cruising in all parts of the Spanish dominions, do often intercept their advices and thereby give seasonable intelligence to the Governor'.[29] It also persuaded the buccaneers of Tortuga, Española, the Bahamas and Caymans that there was no point in harassing Jamaica herself, and in all this the government quietly acquiesced.[30] Six days before the French declaration of war the colonists of St Christopher renewed their treaty, which was ratified immediately by the representative of the French WIC, but Governor William Watts prevaricated about sending it to Willoughby at Barbados for similar ratification. This raised well-founded suspicions among the French, for Willoughby had designs on French St Christopher, and Watts's force included seven boatloads of buccaneers, some 270 men under Thomas Morgan (no relation to Edward and Henry).[31]

When the French launched a surprise attack at dawn on 22 April, Watts, clad only in his gown and slippers, tried to instruct Morgan to lead the main body against the smaller French force at Pointe de Sable while he would take a company to loot the French plantations. Disgusted by this self-serving proposal, Morgan pointed a pistol at Watts's chest and told him they would go into battle together. Hastily dressed, Watts led the 1,400 English against the main French positions with the buccaneers in the van. Shortly before noon they crested a hill to gaze down on the 350 defenders of Pointe de Sable under Robert Lonvilliers de Poincy, then marched down through cane fields that were set alight by both sides, with the smoke adding to the confusion. As Morgan drove straight at the French centre French musketeers under Bernard Lafond de l'Espérance fired an effective volley from behind a brushwood hedge, halting the advance in its tracks. But the buccaneers pushed on once more and a brutal half-hour firefight ensued in which both sides suffered dreadfully, until the buccaneers were finally able to push through the hedge and gain contact with the French main body where de Poincy was killed. Yet when the Jamaicans advanced against Lafond's stronghold they were decimated by a gun firing grapeshot at short range, and their courage finally deserted them. They retreated, bearing away the badly wounded Morgan, only seventeen from 260 of them being as yet unharmed.[32]

When Watts then tried to find a way around the French he was ambushed and cut down. The now leaderless militia blazed away uselessly for a couple of hours, using up their precious ammunition and powder to no avail. They next retreated to a fort which they promptly abandoned having spiked the guns, before dissolving into a rabble that looted Watts' house as the French advanced to complete the conquest of the island. More than 8,000 English settlers were shipped away and their property seized by the victors.[33] Worse was to come for the English when Willoughby's relief attempt three months later was wiped out, with eighteen small vessels and a thousand men being sent to the bottom by a hurricane on 6 August somewhere between Guadeloupe and the Saintes. Only two ships escaped; one reached Montserrat with just the stump of her mizzen left standing, and a fireship made Antigua. Thus when a French naval squadron under Antoine-Lefebvre, sieur de la Barre reached Martinique on 1 October, followed by a Dutch one under Abraham Crijnssen in February 1667, the continental allies were assured of naval superiority in the Caribbean. It was not until London sent reinforcements under Captain John Berry and Rear-Admiral Sir John Harman that Franco-Dutch dominance could be challenged, by which time numerous English outposts had succumbed and pirates given free rein.

Meanwhile in mid-1666 Albemarle wrote to Modyford that, negotiations notwithstanding, he could continue to employ the privateers to pursue English interests in the West Indies. But in reissuing commissions, Modyford was effectively declaring war on Spain in his own name, so the king would have to disavow him if diplomatic exigencies should require it.[34] And when Modyford communicated the glad tidings to Tortuga he received a letter in return 'professing much zeal to his Majesty's service, and a firm resolution to attack Curaçao'.[35] At Tortuga d'Ogeron had been able to supply the buccaneers with letters of marque issued by Portugal against the Spanish, as the former was fighting for her independence, but Jamaica offered a better market for prizes than Tortuga, and Modyford hoped to persuade the buccaneers to accept commissions against the Dutch – who afforded poor takings – by sweetening them with commissions against the rich Spanish trade. In January the Dutch island of Tobago was taken by eighty men on two ships from Jamaica, and Modyford hoped to persuade the buccaneers to mount an expedition against Curaçao, to expel the Dutch once and for all from the Caribbean. Willoughby at Barbados was less sanguine about the chances of persuading them to make such a venture: 'they are all masters', he wrote, 'and reckon what they take to be their own, and themselves free princes to dispose of as they please'.[36] Nevertheless, almost immediately the buccaneers regrouped.

Although they were never formally constituted as a navy, in mid-January 1666 they appointed Edward Mansfield as 'admiral', to command a large buccaneer fleet with Henry Morgan as his second-in-command. Mansfield had himself sailed as second-in-command to Myngs in raids against the Spanish, and had then led a raid into the interior of Cuba where the buccaneers captured the town of Sancti Espíritus, taking 200 horses and numerous prisoners for whom they received a ransom of 300 fat cattle.[37] Mansfield would now lead the attack against Curaçao with fifteen ships and 500–600 men. But the men found little appeal in this, according to Exquemelin: 'there was more profit with less hazard to be gotten against the Spaniard, which was their only interest'.[38] Ignoring their orders to attack Curaçao the buccaneer fleet arrived at Portete in Costa Rica on 8 April 1666 and captured the nearby town of Matina, where they seized thirty-five prisoners. But an Indian named Esteban Yaperi ran to warn the governor of Costa Rica, Juan López de Flor, and by the middle of the month there were hundreds of militiamen in positions all around them. These militiamen were seriously short of arms, but Mansfield's men were suffering dreadful hardship in the jungle, so hungry that they fell to scrabbling over a few sacks of ground wheat; heartened by this report the Spanish advanced and the buccaneers retreated.[39] Thus the city of Cartago was saved and the faith of Cartagans in the patron saint of Ujarrás, to whom they had prayed fervently, was immeasurably deepened. Costa Rica, which until the 1780s Englishmen would falsely believe to be rich, was spared the fate of Nicaragua because the Reventazón river was far less accessible than the San Juan.[40] Two ships of the fleet departed for Tortuga and, desperate to vindicate himself after the failure in Costa Rica, Mansfield led the other four, joined by two French rovers, towards Santa Catalina, entirely contrary to Modyford's orders (although the governor did not seem to mind, despite receiving rumours that the buccaneers were considering setting up an independent state of their own).[41]

Five buccaneer vessels arrived at noon on 25 May and sailed along the coast to drop anchor at ten that night. As the moon rose around midnight some 180 buccaneers (including some women, according to Spanish reports), about half being English and the rest French, Dutch and Portuguese, marched across the island rounding up the inhabitants. The English force had caught the Spanish by surprise, and fighting began at 3 p.m. on the 26th. By 8 o'clock the following morning the buccaneers had taken the governor's house and the Spaniards surrendered. The buccaneers then stormed the citadel at first light on the 27th. There they found only eight soldiers, who were added to the sixty-two other prisoners, and all were granted quarter. The French meanwhile prevented the English from sacking the church. Ten days later Mansfield departed, taking 170 Spaniards whom he promised to restore to their countrymen, and leaving behind a garrison of thirty-five buccaneers and fifty black former slaves to hold the island until such time as he or another English authority returned.[42]

Mansfield dropped his prisoners off at Punta de Brujas in Panamá before setting off for Jamaica. He got there on 22 June and discovered, to his great good fortune, that in his absence Modyford and the Council had decided three and a half months earlier that it was in Jamaica's best interests to issue commissions against the Spanish. Thus, despite having been sent out specifically to attack the Dutch, his recapture of Providence enjoyed a *post facto* veneer of legality. 'I have yet only reproved him for doing it without order,' Modyford wrote to Arlington, four days later, 'which I should suppose would have been an acceptable service had he received command for it.'[43] In his turn Arlington claimed that the buccaneers had originally been intending to attack the 'Island of Curatoe' (Curaçao); he further claimed that Santa Catalina island had been captured because the expedition had been 'treated like barbarians' and denied common courtesies and needs. Because he could claim that the island had been taken by buccaneers without authority, he made no offer to restore it to Spain or of recompense.[44]

Modyford hastily arranged to send a garrison to Old Providence but could not afford to draw on the militia organised for the defence of Port Royal itself, so he called for volunteers. Meanwhile Mansfield set off for Tortuga to recruit more buccaneers; he either died on the way or was reported captured by the Spanish and taken to Havana, and 'suddenly after put to death'.[45] Either way, any plans for a buccaneer state died with him. Modyford was able to find an experienced soldier, Major Samuel Smith, to lead thirty-three other volunteers, and they were carried to Old Providence in a ship belonging to Sir Thomas Whetstone who had been speaker of the Jamaica Assembly for the previous two years. They sailed in July and Modyford made clear to Smith that he was to govern 'for His Majesty', thus making the island's seizure an official act. And having reported to Albemarle that Whetstone and Smith had sailed he described how his Lordship:

> cannot imagine what a change there is on the face of men and things, ships repairing, great resort of workmen and labourers in Port Royal, many returning, many debtors released out of prison, and the ships of the Curaçao voyage [previously] not daring to come in for fear of creditors, brought in and fitted out again . . . Had it not been for [the granting of commissions] I could not have kept this place against French buccaneers, who would have ruined all the seaside plantations, whereas now I draw from them mainly, and lately David Marteen, the best man of Tortuga, that has two frigates at sea, had promised to bring in both.[46]

But on arrival at Providence Smith found fewer men already there than he expected, just fifty-one. When by the end of September, by which time the Great Fire of London had finally burned itself out, Sir Thomas Whetstone had not returned to Jamaica it was feared that his ship had foundered. It would be another two years before the fate of the garrison became known in Jamaica.

Since their capture of Providence in 1641 the Spanish had made no effort to fortify it properly, but now its loss stung them into action. At first fearing that the affair heralded the start of a general conflict with England, they decided to concentrate on its recapture with an immediate expedition before it could be fortified, and with the possibility of extending operations to Jamaica. Madrid ordered a council of war to be held at Cartagena to consider the feasibility of both schemes, stating that if necessary a thousand men would be sent from home; the Spanish believed that the plague which had prostrated London in 1665, only to be followed by the Great Fire, would divert attention from the Caribbean. But the sailing of the *galeones*, the Tierra Firme fleet, was not to be delayed beyond 6 January 1667.[47] In preparation for the expedition the municipal authorities issued numerous orders; the Duque de Veragua was to take four ships to the Indies to join it. For once a council of war at Cartagena resulted in action; by summer 1667 an expeditionary force had been prepared by Don Juan Pérez de Guzmán, president of Panamá and captain-general of Tierra

Firme, although the plans to move on to Jamaica had been abandoned. Since pilots passing Santa Catalina reported that it was not heavily defended, a force of 230 men was deemed sufficient for its recapture. They landed on 12 August and the English garrison surrendered shortly afterwards despite putting up fierce resistance.[48]

In August 1668 two emaciated and severely scarred former prisoners reached Port Royal after being released from Havana, one being Major Samuel Smith. Two months later three more men with horrific stories arrived, and so the only four survivors of Providence were accounted for, and their testimony shows that the Spanish treatment of prisoners was little better than that meted out by the buccaneers to their captives. They had been:

> forced to work in the water from five in the morning till seven at night, and at such a rate that the Spanish confessed they made one of them do more work than three negroes, yet when weak with want of victuals and sleep, they were knocked down and beaten with cudgels, and four or five died. Having no clothes their backs were blistered by the sun, their hands raw with carrying stones and mortar, their feet chopped, and their legs bruised and battered with the irons.[49]

Smith swore that he surrendered on articles of good quarter 'which the Spanish did not in the least perform', as all but the three commanders were forced to work as slaves in irons on Spanish forts under the lash, while Smith himself, Whetstone and Smith's second-in-command, Captain Stanley, were sent to Panamá where they were imprisoned for seventeen months, before Smith, Stanley and the captain of a merchant ship were transferred to Cuba.[50] But despite his success Pérez was also soon in gaol: he met the newly arrived viceroy of Peru, the Conde de Lemos, and they argued about their respective jurisdictions; he would remain in confinement for two years while the wheels of Spanish justice turned slowly.

On Tortuga and at Saint-Domingue d'Ogeron's early success encouraged him in 1667 to achieve a measure of cohesion among the buccaneers under his jurisdiction, and he decided to attack one of Española's major cities, Santiago de los Caballeros. The city was taken on Good Friday and sacked by 400 men commanded by a man called Delisle. When the buccaneers were stopped on the way to the coast, in order to get away they had to threaten to kill their hostages, who included the governor.[51] Elsewhere other buccaneers were also active, notably the brutal Frenchman Jean-David Nau (called François by Exquemelin), known as 'L'Ollonais', or 'El Olonés' to the Spanish – 'the man from Ollone', so called after the district of Les Sables d'Olonne in the Vendée. Much of the information we have about him comes from Exquemelin and is based on hearsay. He apparently arrived in the Antilles as an *engagé* (indentured servant) around 1660, and later became a *boucanier* on Tortuga before throwing in his lot with the *flibustiers*. There he received command of a vessel with twenty men from the then governor, and was soon leader of eight vessels with 400 men. He led an attack on Campeche but was shipwrecked, though this did not stop him assaulting the city. But in doing so he lost most of his force and saved his own life only by playing dead and camouflaging himself with blood and sand. He then managed to escape and raise a few slaves in revolt, before stealing a canoe and returning to Tortuga.[52] Near Key Fragoso in Cuba he spotted a Spanish frigate that had been sent to hunt for him, and by setting an ambush succeeded in capturing it; he was especially brutal with the negro who was to have been his executioner.[53]

In April 1667 L'Ollonais left his base on Tortuga together with Michel Le Basque in eight small vessels with 650 men. Ignoring the war raging between England, France and Holland, he was delighted to hear three months later of a diplomatic rift between France and Spain. The buccaneers at once stood into the Mona Passage (which separates Española and Puerto Rico) where a Spanish vessel of sixteen guns was spotted and chased. After two or three hours' combat the Spaniard struck his colours to L'Olonnais' ten-gun sloop and turned out to be carrying cacao to Veracruz. Having sent this cargo to Tortuga and taken another prize, L'Ollonais adopted the first vessel as his flagship and decided he was now strong enough to attack Maracaibo on the Gulf of Venezuela. Sailing into the gulf the buccaneers quickly overran a feeble battery set up to defend the bar at its mouth, and passed on into the lagoon. The following morning they reached the town. Finding it abandoned, they occupied it for the next two weeks during which they sent out patrols to seek out hostages whom L'Ollonais would viciously torture in order to locate their treasure, but little of it was forthcoming. He therefore decided to cross the lagoon and attack the town of Gibraltar on the far side, although this was now reinforced by several hundred Spanish troops.[54] A fierce battle ensued with some forty buccaneers killed and thirty wounded, but the Spanish suffered much heavier casualties with hundreds of dead. Their bodies were loaded by the invaders on to two old boats, towed out into the lagoon and sunk. The town was then pillaged with the utmost brutality. 'Ollonais demanded a ransom of 10,000 pesos to leave the buildings standing, but dissatisfied by the response he razed the city anyway. He then returned to Maracaibo where he extracted a ransom of 20,000 pesos and 500 head of cattle to spare that place, and stole the bells and icons from the church.[55]

After two months in the lagoon he departed to divide the spoils at Île-à-Vache (Isla Vaca) and apparently visited Jamaica where he sold an eighty-ton twelve-gun Spanish brigantine to the Dutch buccaneers Roche Brasiliano and Jelles de Lecat, before returning to Tortuga in triumph a month later.[56] Some time afterwards he sortied once more with 700 men including 300 in his new flagship, the largest of his Spanish prizes. They cruised southern Cuba taking vessels for use in his next big project, an ascent of the San Juan river. It seems he hoped to emulate the feat of Morgan, Morris and Martien in sacking Granada; but on reaching Cabo Gracias a Dios his cumbersome new flagship struggled in the light winds and he found himself drifting westwards along the north Honduran coast while supplies dwindled. Foraging parties were sent up the Aguán river, but he continued drifting as far as Puerto Cabellos where he captured a Spanish merchantman of twenty-four guns and sixteen *pedreros* or swivel-guns and occupied the town. Two captives were terrified into leading the buccaneers inland to the nearest city, San Pedro Sula, while L'Ollonais' Dutch lieutenant Mozes van Klijn guarded the tiny port. En route they were waylaid by a Spanish party, and prisoners taken in the ensuing skirmish revealed that further ambushes were set along the road. Furious, L'Ollonais instructed his men to give no quarter; he believed in the practice of spreading terror seemingly for its own sake, but also for the efficacy of obtaining easy victory. The Spanish fought on nevertheless, and succeeded in repelling the initial assault on San Pedro Sula, enabling them to evacuate the city under a flag of truce. It was then pillaged by the buccaneers over the next few days before they returned to Puerto Cabellos. There L'Ollonais learned that a rich galleon was expected to arrive at the Guatemala river from Spain. After posting lookout boats, he took the rest of the squadron across the Bay of Honduras to careen their hulls. Three months of idleness followed before word came that the galleon had arrived. Recalling his men, L'Ollonais quickly launched an attack. But the booty taken proved to be mightily disappointing as most of the cargo had already been unloaded, leaving only some iron, paper and wine.[57]

Exquemelin described L'Ollonais as being spectacularly cruel and spiteful to his prisoners, apparently taking great delight in their anguish, though some of the more lurid tales such as the claim that he literally tore a man's beating heart from his body are surely exaggerated.[58] The Jesuit missionary and historian Charlevoix later observed of L'Ollonais: 'He could have made a great profit on indigo, but he wanted nothing but gold, silver or jewels.'[59] In other words, he did not understand that the future lay with the plantation economy or, if he did, he did not care – the psychopathic are seldom interested in business. And as quickly as his star had risen, so it set. Van Klijn and another lieutenant Pierre le Picard decided to seek other confederates and L'Ollonais was left with his Maracaibo prize, which was such a heavy sailer that she was entirely unsuited to the task of buccaneering. Soon afterwards she went aground among the Cayos de Perlas (near present-day Bluefields) and his men were forced to live ashore for six months while they constructed a longboat. When this proved inadequate to carry all the men L'Ollonais was forced to take a party to the mouth of the San Juan river in search of other craft, and here he was defeated by the Spanish and forced to flee even further away, sailing into the Gulf of Darién. His dwindling band was set upon by a group of angry natives and, according to the sole survivor, L'Ollonais was 'hacked to pieces and roasted limb by limb'.[60]

L'Ollonais was a man so heartily consumed with hatred for the Spanish that he ignored the war to pursue his vendetta against them. But early in 1667 the Dutch with French assistance retook St Eustatius and Saba, and also regained Tobago. In February Arlington sent instructions to restrain the buccaneers from further acts of violence against the Spanish, but by now Modyford was well used to drawing his own conclusions from his conflicting orders. On 31 July he wrote:

> Had my abilities suited so well with my wishes did your Lordship's, the privateers' attempts had been only practised on the Dutch and French, and the Spaniards free of them, but I had no money to pay them, nor frigates to force them; the former they could not get from our declared enemies, nothing could they expect but blows from them, and (as they have often repeated to me) will that pay for new sails and rigging?[61]

By May the situation in Europe had changed once again; with booty gained from the Dutch war nothing like as great as had been anticipated, the government decided to negotiate for peace before the campaign season of 1667 got under way. On the same day that Modyford was defending his actions, the Treaty of Breda was signed; it re-established the status quo of March that year, by which time the Royal Navy had recaptured a number of outposts. But peace did bring one substantial gain to England: the New Netherland and New Amsterdam (renamed New York) which closed the substantial gap in possessions between the Carolinas and New England, in return for which she gave up Surinam. France returned the English part of St Christopher, taking Acadia (Nova Scotia) as an equivalent, but she retained Tobago and St Eustatius. The Dutch would never recover their dominant position in West Indian trade, which at least mitigated Anglo-Dutch rivalry in the area. The Dutch war also greatly altered English relations with Spain; the unreliability of the buccaneers as a factor in naval warfare and the growing strength of France in the Caribbean now prompted English co-operation with Spain.[62]

Two months earlier, on 23 May, Spain and England had concluded a commercial treaty that was ratified four months later. The opening clause of the Treaty of Madrid declared that the subjects of the two kings should 'serve each other well by mutual aid, kindness, and all manner of friendship'.[63] It then guaranteed England the same rights that had been granted to the Dutch in 1648 by the Treaty of Münster, namely, right of possession of all territories held on the date of signing and of navigation and trade between them; but it continued to deny trade with Spanish colonies, and contained the usual provisions concerning letters of marque: that parties wronged by subjects of the other nation were to seek redress first through the law, and only if justice were refused, or if six months had passed, could letters of reprisal be issued. Modyford had first been made aware of the treaty in 1666 when Albemarle informed him that he could continue to use privateers if it served the king's interests. When he received a copy of the treaty it made the situation no clearer, as he was not aware of the terms of the Dutch treaty, and consequently he failed to recall the buccaneers but requested more specific orders, which the Privy Council failed to send.[64]

By December 1667 Modyford had news of all the developments in Europe and was alarmed to see that the treaty with Spain made no mention of Jamaica, which both countries continued to claim. In fact, there was only one oblique mention of the West Indies in the second clause which guaranteed the safety of subjects by land and sea, including those 'havens and ports where they have been previously accustomed to trade'.[65] This statement did not explicitly open Cartagena or Portobelo to English trade, and the merchants who were not part of Modyford's circle were deeply frustrated by these terms, as were the logwood-cutters of Campeche; such an ambiguous article could and would be interpreted by each government as desired. To make matters worse, Modyford had received reports from Cuba that preparations were in hand for a Spanish attack on Jamaica, and his only real defence remained the buccaneers, but he had no money to pay them: peace was, in fact, terrible news for the infant colony.[66] 'The Spanish look upon us as intruders wheresoever they find us in the Indies, and use us accordingly,' wrote Modyford to Arlington, pointing out the absurdity of the government's call for peaceful trade in the West Indies while failing to provide ships for defence or to exert diplomatic pressure on Spain. If they could, he continued, the Spanish 'would soon turn us out of our plantations; and is it reasonable that we should quietly let them grow upon us until they are able to do so? It must be force alone that can cut in sunder that unneighbourly maxim of their government to deny all access to strangers.'[67]

# 9

—◦◦◦—

# PORTOBELO

Nine armed sail from Port Royal Bay
Creep down to the Spanish main,
To loot and ravish and dearly reap
The spoils of the King of Spain.

The shores are steep and the towers are strong,
But little or naught are they;
The golden lure is a certain cure
For the dangers that bar the way.

Don C. Seitz, 'Porto Bello'

As 1667 drew to a close Modyford called a meeting of the Council of Jamaica, and it decided that as large a force of privateers as possible should be assembled at Port Royal and sent to Cuba to find out what was happening there, since it had long been recognised that cruising Spanish waters was as important for the business of gathering intelligence for the authorities as it was for gathering prizes for the buccaneers.[1] The first problem was one of command, and Modyford selected Henry Morgan, now married, wealthy and influential – he and Mary Elizabeth were frequent visitors at the Governor's residence. Morgan was given a commission 'to draw together the English privateers and take prisoners of the Spanish nation, whereby he might inform of the intention of that enemy to attack Jamaica, of which I have frequent and strong advice'.[2] For this he was given the local rank of admiral, although he was referred to by Colonel William Beeston in his journal at this time as 'General'.[3]

Certainly men wanted to follow him. Since he had taken command of the militia, now styled the Port Royal Volunteers, their strength had increased fourfold. Equally the brethren of the coast had no hesitation in accepting him as their admiral, and gathering assorted privateersmen and pirates was easier now that France was at peace with England and at war with Spain. Louis XIV's claims to the Spanish throne following the death of his father-in-law Felipe IV had led the War of Devolution to break out in May 1667, much to the delight of the *flibustiers* of Tortuga.[4]

Not only were the reports reaching Modyford about Spanish preparations in Cuba true, the reality was more alarming than he feared. The Council of the Indies had finally prised away five ships to reform the *armada de barlovento* under Captain-General Don Agustin de Diostegui. However, though the authorities in Spain thought them ideal for dealing with buccaneers, the ships chosen were too large and of too great a draught to chase the smaller and more manoeuvrable privateers around the shallows and shoals of the Caribbean Sea or the innumerable bays and cays of its islands. And before the summer was out the two most powerful of them were, in any case, recalled for duty in home waters, leaving the *almirante* (vice-admiral), Don Alonzo de Campos y Espinosa, to command the rump squadron.[5] So Morgan arranged a rendezvous at a good anchorage within the South Cays where he waited patiently, anchored to leeward for protection against the swell and clear of the land to avoid the mosquitoes that otherwise made the men's lives a misery. They would pass the time fishing and gambling, often using cards made from the leaves of a native tree which could be carved and dried like thin leather. By the appointed date of 28 March 1668 Morgan had a dozen vessels of various sizes and some 700 men, a mixture of English and French, escaped slaves and a few Dutch, all united by a passion for plunder and a consuming hatred of the Spanish and the Catholic church.

Despite his rank and references to the group of vessels as a fleet, the force was a small one. One of Morgan's larger ships was the *Dolphin* under John Morris the elder, now armed with eight guns and carrying a crew of sixty men. Although her dimensions are unknown, she was unlikely to exceed fifty feet on deck with a beam of about sixteen – no larger than a fishing smack or shrimper – and many privateers were smaller still: large open boats with a deck forward to provide some shelter for crew and provisions, with only a single mast but capable of being rowed among the shallows, and armed at best with a single gun in the bows. The men were seldom real seamen but often former soldiers. They would regularly sleep ashore, or on deck under just a blanket or more often a cow hide that served as a tent to protect against the frequent showers that might come before dawn. Modyford reported that the buccaneers 'never victual or careen in our harbours' but would find a spot amid the vast tracts of sparsely populated Spanish territory 'infinitely stored with cattle and hogs' and hunt there, often with the aid of dogs, soon supplying themselves with enough salted meat to sustain several months of cruising.[6] Meat was supplemented with turtle, fish and abundant fruit; a Port Royal sponsor would have only to provide bread (or biscuit) and liquor, plenty of which was also seized in raids.[7] The effective range of such vessels was limited by the amount of drinking water they could carry and how long the men could stand being soaking wet and short of sleep, and they preferred to outflank a Spanish town by a landward march rather than try to get to windward of a galleon.[8]

Morgan called a council where some were of the 'opinion 'twere convenient to assault the city of Havana under the obscurity of night', a task which might be made easier 'if they could but take a few of the ecclesiastics and make them prisoners'.[9] Several men present had been prisoners in Havana and they estimated that a force of 1,500 men would be needed to capture it, a doubling of their present strength, and the option was discarded. Several other targets were then discussed: Santiago, Trinidad, Sanctí Espiritus, Bayano and San Cristóbal on the south side of Cuba, and Santa Cruz on the north. Each was discounted until, according to Exquemelin, one man proposed the town of El Puerto del Princípe on the north of the island which he knew well. Being some way from the sea it 'never was sacked by any pirates, whereby the inhabitants were rich, as exercising their trade for ready money with those of Havana, who kept here an established commerce which consisted mostly in hides'.[10]

Although when founded 150 years earlier the town had been on the coast – one of seven administrative centres set up on the island – it had been moved to the centre of Camaguey province forty-five miles inland, and was no longer a port despite its name (since changed to Camaguey). Morgan and the others agreed and orders were duly given. They sailed for the Gulf of Ana María and anchored in a sheltered bay, planning to land next morning. But there had been a terrible breach of security. A Spanish prisoner on board Morgan's ship, a man they believed could not speak English and so had not bothered to send to another ship when the council meeting was held, jumped overboard and escaped to warn the townsfolk, who immediately began to hide their riches and carry away everything possible; they then raised every available man, some 800 in total, to form ambushes and defend their homes. But Morgan was by now experienced enough to know of the likelihood of betrayal on such an expedition, because any man could turn renegade and expect handsome reward for warning the Spanish; he also never made the mistake of assuming his enemy was stupid or unprepared, and he knew that his opponent was an experienced old soldier. Now expecting that the enemy had been warned, was prepared and had set ambushes, Morgan marched north-east off the road and over the rolling hills between the coast and the plain, sending advanced patrols to seize any locals lest they provide warning and, where possible, to be forced to act as guides.

'At last they came to a plain called by the Spaniards La Savana, or The Sheet,' recalled Exquemelin. The provincial governor sent forward a troop of cavalry, hoping to disperse the buccaneers. Undeterred, they advanced:

> at the sound of their drums and with flying colours. When they came nigh unto the horse they drew into the form of a semi-circle, and thus advanced towards the Spaniards, who charged them like valiant and courageous soldiers for some while. But seeing the pirates were very dextrous at their arms and their Governor with many of their companions killed, they began to retreat towards the forest . . . [11]

With the way now clear, Morgan's men took the city within an hour, locked all the inhabitants in the churches and set out to look for plunder, the whole justified by learning 'that 70 men had been pressed to go against Jamaica; that the like levy had been made all over the island, and that considerable forces were expected from Vera Cruz and Campeachy, with materials of war to rendezvous at the Havannah, and from Porto Bello'.[12] They then informed their prisoners that they must pay ransom or be transported to Jamaica, and the buccaneers would burn every house. Four prisoners were sent to fetch the ransom from those inhabitants who had earlier fled to the forest, but returned a few days later saying they could not find their people and asking for another fifteen days to raise the ransom, to which Morgan assented. But a few hours later several buccaneers reported finding 'considerable booty'; they had also seized an African carrying letters written by Don Bayona Villanueva, governor of the neighbouring province of Santiago, telling the negotiators to delay paying any ransom and to 'put off the pirates as well as they could with excuses and delays', to enable him to come to their aid.[13]

Morgan quickly convened his captains and explained how they were being deceived. He ordered all the booty taken to the ships and, without revealing his sources, told the Spanish that they had one day to pay the ransom or their homes would be reduced to ashes; he also demanded a thousand cattle and the salt to preserve them, to be carried to the ships by the Spanish themselves. Then he marched back to the coast taking six leading citizens as hostages. The Spanish arrived with the cattle and salt two days later, and the animals were swiftly slaughtered and stowed in casks whereupon Morgan released the hostages. During the process an Englishman slew a Frenchman in an argument over the cattle that almost provoked an insurrection among the French, but Morgan defused the trouble by putting the offender in chains with a promise that he would be dealt with at Jamaica.[14] The buccaneers left Cuba and divided their somewhat poor return totalling 50,000 pesos, a sum that caused resentment among the men as being insufficient to pay their debts. But the raid had achieved Modyford's aim of frightening the Spanish out of their plans to attack Jamaica, as Don Bayona wrote in a revealing report to Mariana, queen regent to King Carlos II in Madrid.[15]

The fleet now sailed to Cabo Gracias a Dios where a council of war was held to decide where to go next. Given that they had 'information' that practically the entire Spanish Indies were arming against Jamaica, this could mean almost anywhere. Morgan suggested Portobelo, where Drake had had died and was buried in a lead coffin in 1596, and which had been taken by William Parker in 1601. As the terminus of the Spanish treasure fleet and the key to the riches of Panamá and Peru, the very name had allure. But it was known to be well fortified, and there were scores of alternative unfortified towns, so the French 'wholly refused to join with us in that action as being too full of danger and difficulty', Morgan later reported.[16] Most of the French chose instead to try their luck with L'Ollonais on Tortuga, despite Morgan's best efforts to dissuade them; but they parted amicably enough. Left now with a tiny force, Morgan was fortunately soon reinforced by an unidentified 'pirate of Campeche', bringing his numbers up to 460 in twelve small ships.[17] Nevertheless, the French desertion was a blow, and it was probably apparent to Morgan that he had failed to extract the maximum profit from the expedition so far because he had not been ruthless enough. Having been schooled by the gallant Mansfield he had allowed the Cubans of Camaguey to string him along, and the French knew that L'Ollonais would extract the last possible ounce of silver from the hated Spanish, using whatever methods he deemed necessary no matter how vile.[18]

Most of the men remaining were English including captains John Morris, Edward Collier, Edward Dempster and Robert Delander (the latter would serve with Morgan for the rest of his career). The crews were mostly drawn from the settlers of Jamaica, ranging from gentlemen, impoverished planters and merchants to outright criminals, and included many men who were not English, even if they called Port Royal home; there were forty Dutchmen, several French, Italians, Portuguese, Africans and mulattos, and according to Spanish sources a citizen of Córdoba.[19] At the end of May this force sailed south with not a man among them except Morgan aware of their destination, a tribute to his persuasive tongue and a measure of his distrust of the men he led – rather than commanded, for despite their fraternal demeanour there was a constant risk of betrayal. After a few days they sighted the 1,700-foot sugar-loaf Pilón de Miguel de la Borda close to the Chagres river, then entered Naos Bay – now the northern end of the Panamá Canal – and anchored near Isla Largo Remo, then known as Longa de Mos. Morgan summoned a council and announced his intention of attacking Portobelo, the third strongest fortress in the Indies.[20] He knew from an Indian informant that it was in a very poor state of defence, and when several men objected that they had not the numbers to undertake such an operation, he supposedly replied by paraphrasing Shakespeare: 'If our numbers are small our hearts are great, and the fewer we are the better shares we shall have in the spoils.'[21]

So stirring was his speech, according to Exquemelin, who was no fan of the Welshman, that the others enthusiastically agreed to join in the design. For the crew of a privateer in the West Indies was one of the most democratic institutions of the seventeenth century: articles were drawn up between the captain and representatives of the crew to ensure fair distribution of spoils. Like all military ventures, discipline was necessary, but this too was covered by the articles. A man who, through drunkenness or neglect, slighted or denied 'the reasonable commands of his officer' would lose his share of any booty, or be punished by other means that the council of war 'thought most convenient'. But a captain who neglected his duty faced the same sanction. Booty was to be shared scrupulously 'man for man' according to strict rules that saw the captain gain a double share, craftsmen such as the carpenter and surgeon something more than a man's share, and boys only a half-share, while Morgan gained five shares 'for his care and expense over us'. Bonuses would be payable to those who showed particular courage so that if:

> we should meet with any strong opposition in any place . . . that we are intended and bound for, as castles, forts or other strongholds, the first man entering such place or places shall have £20, also he that first displays his colours in such a place . . . £20; as also to all those that carry ladders, for every ladder so carried and pitched up against the walls . . . £10.[22]

There were plenty of castles, forts and strongholds throughout the Caribbean and Spanish Main. Equally a measure of support was provided for those incapacitated in action. Therefore any man who 'shall lose a leg or an arm . . . in this term of voyage' and could prove the loss on the oaths of two surgeons would receive compensation to the tune of £120 or 'six able slaves'. Great care was taken to ensure that all booty was placed in the common pool with everybody made to swear on the Bible that 'he has not kept for himself so much as the value of a sixpence'.[23]

Morgan had commissions to take prizes at sea in order to gain information, but he did not strictly have permission to act against the Spanish on land. However, if he obtained information at sea indicating an attack on Jamaica, a landing might provide confirmation and serve to forestall such an attack. But what made action ashore particularly attractive was that the normal prize conditions no longer applied; he did not have to make a deduction from any loot taken for the king, the lord high admiral or the ships' owners, which in total came to nearly half. This point was made abundantly clear by the first two articles of association drawn up by Morgan with his captains and men: anything 'taken on shore shall be divided man for man as free plunder ... ships taken at sea within the term of this voyage, the tenths and fifteenths being deducted, the fourth part ... shall be for the respective ships of this fleet and their owners, and the other three fourths to be equally shared among such ships company generally ...'.[24] However, by the terms of Morgan's commission, prizes taken at sea could not be shared until they had been declared good at the court of admiralty in Jamaica, though this did not apply to booty taken onshore, which could be shared out immediately. So although action on land was more dangerous, it was commensurately more appealing as Modyford would later note, when clearing himself of accusations that royal takings from privateering were rather low. 'Of that from shore they pay nothing because not commissionated [sic] to it.'[25]

Soon Morgan gained further valuable information: he captured a small ship sent out to investigate his presence and learned thereby that the rumoured presence of *corsarios* had not alerted the Spanish defences. Soon afterwards the buccaneers met a canoe paddled by six emaciated men who hailed them in English and proved to be escaped prisoners who had been working on the fortifications at Portobelo. They also brought startling news that would provide the justification for his attack: levies were being made on towns in Panamá for an expedition against Jamaica.[26] Furthermore, they reported that 'Prince Maurice and divers Englishmen' were being kept in irons in dreadful conditions in the dungeon of one of its castles and Morgan wrote that he 'thought it our duty to attempt' the place. Indeed, nobody could rebuke Morgan for making such an attempt since nothing had been heard of the prince since his ship vanished near Puerto Rico five years before, and the tales of appalling brutality meted out against their fellow countrymen stirred the blood of Englishmen. Morgan noted simply that 'the enlargement of our countrymen' provided a secondary justification for his expedition whose principal purpose was to gain 'what further intelligence we could of ye enemies intention against Jamaica, and if possible to scatter those forces which might there have been brought together'.[27]

Portobelo certainly looked impressive with 150 handsome houses, two fine squares, two churches, a royal treasury, hospital, convent, warehouses and massive stables for the mules that carried the treasure over the isthmus of Panamá, and acres of shanty for its slaves. But for most of the time it was largely empty with a permanent population of just a few score Spaniards, including some friars and nuns in the hospital and convent, and a couple of hundred mulattos, free blacks and slaves. There were few women and children as it was no place to raise a family, and most merchants and artisans chose to live in the much larger and slightly healthier Panamá City. Portobelo was, according to Scottish barber-surgeon Lionel Wafer, who served on a later expedition, 'a very fair large and commodious harbour, affording good anchoring and good shelter for ships, having a narrow mouth and spreading wider within'. But it was extremely unhealthy and 'the sea at low water leaves the shore within the harbour bare a great way from the houses, which having a black filthy mud, it stinks very much and breeds noisome vapours, through the heat of the climate'.[28]

Portobelo was widely regarded among Spanish officials as the worst posting in the empire. Its solitary purpose was as a haven for the treasure fleet, and for the month or so when this was in port the town was a hive of activity as perhaps 10,000 people gathered for a great fair, forced to live in great tented shanties if they could not afford the exorbitant rents in town. The ships first unloaded their cargoes of European goods for sale to merchants who would take them to Panamá and Peru, then they loaded with the New World products they would take back to Spain: hides, dyes and drugs and other valuable local items. But far more important than any of these was the silver. Some 25 millions of pesos' worth – twice the annual revenue of King Charles II – might be stored in local warehouses, counting houses and in the public squares.[29] However, the decline in Spain's fortunes meant that the fleets came less and less often, perhaps every two or three years now, and it was over a year since the last one had arrived. Nevertheless, the town remained the third strongest city in the Spanish Indies, defended by probably as many soldiers as citizens.[30]

The town had no walls, its main defences being two large forts on either side of the harbour. On the west side, separated from the town by a small river, stood the castle of Triana Santiago with a paper garrison of 200 men and thirty-two guns; on the east, the fort of San Felipe de Todo Fierro (the Iron Fort) had 100 men and twelve guns. Between them the two strongholds created a crossfire that no ship could reasonably hope to weather. In addition a fort called San Gerónimo was being built just off the quay in the sea itself, by English prisoners captured in Santa Catalina in 1666 and chained every night in a prison near the royal treasury under armed guard. The forts were supported by blockhouses and lookout posts, but the soldiers had not been paid for at least eighteen months and morale was low, resulting in desertion, while others had obtained permission to make some money in trade, and in return for a percentage as a bribe to their officers had the privilege of living out. Consequently, the forts were seriously undermanned, with some eighty men at Santiago and barely fifty at San Felipe, with a serious shortage of gunners; and the guns themselves were not in good order – the humid climate did nothing to help, causing metal to corrode, material to rot and making powder damp. Such were the 'war materials' that had been reported to Morgan on Cuba. In addition the townsmen were supposed to muster in four militia companies organised according to race, but a muster of 1667 showed only 129 in total, and on the night of 10 July 1668 there were fewer even than this, with barely twenty Spaniards fit to bear arms.

Meanwhile Morgan's men, having left skeleton crews aboard all but one of their ships, transferred to the twenty-three canoes they had brought with them from Cuba. About forty feet long with a small sail as well as paddles, they were a common sight around the Caribbean and could each carry a score of buccaneers. Stealthily they could follow the coast escorted by their one large ship, paddling by night and laying up by day. With the coast largely deserted apart from the great fortress of San Lorenzo at the mouth of the Chagres river, the threat from Spanish warships was minimal, with the only guardship at Cartagena; and, buccaneering having effectively brought to a halt all commercial traffic, they were unlikely to be spotted from the sea, except perhaps by a fishing boat, as Morgan sought the benefit of surprise. The one boat they did encounter they captured, gaining a useful guide. This 'zambo' – half Indian, half African – knew the coast better than Morgan's Indian guide, and promised to put the buccaneers safely ashore near the town. Such men would often betray the Spanish for revenge or money, but this man was doubtless prompted by fear after seeing the bodies of his two black companions thrown into the sea for refusing to help.

It took four nights to cover the 150 miles to Orange Island where the wood-cutters on the evening of 10 July were not unduly alarmed by the sight of a solitary ship, the canoes being too far away to be seen. When they reported the ship to the mayor of Portobelo, Andres Fernandez Davila, he sent a canoe to check its identity; it might be pirates but a single ship posed little threat, and he resented having to pay the canoe's crew from his own pocket as money was always hard to recover from Spain. But night had fallen before the canoe set out, by which time interest in the strange ship had died in the town as the townsfolk prepared for bed at what was the beginning of the worst part of the wet season, suffocatingly hot and humid, surrounded as they were by mountains, without even the benefit of an evening breeze.[31] Morgan's gamble therefore paid off handsomely. He had achieved surprise as the buccaneers paddled their canoes quietly along the coast, when at about 2 a.m. they encountered the Spanish canoe sent to investigate the strange ship near Orange Island. They gave chase but could not prevent its escape and, now in some haste, landed some three miles from the town at 3 a.m. near the lookout post at Buenaventura. There they captured a sentry 'without firing a shot or making any noise', and Morgan questioned him closely.[32] Gagged and bound the unfortunate prisoner was forced to lead the buccaneers across country towards a blockhouse at La Rancheria, an old pearling station, which they reached without the alarm being raised and quickly surrounded. Once in position Morgan demanded its surrender, but the five-man garrison immediately opened fire, wounding two buccaneers and alarming the town. As startled residents began to dress and ask what was happening, the scout canoe returned and drums were beaten in alarm. But powder and shot for the muskets were held at Santiago castle to protect them from the humidity in the town. Some of the townsfolk took the

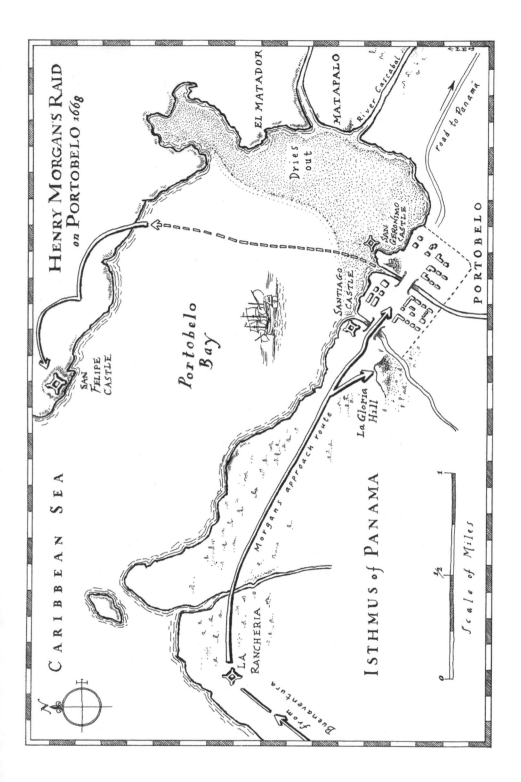

HENRY MORGAN'S RAID
on PORTOBELO 1668

CARIBBEAN SEA

N

EL MATADOR

MATAPALO

River Cascabal

road to Panamá

Dries out

SAN GERONIMO CASTLE

PORTOBELO

Portobelo Bay

SANTIAGO CASTLE

SAN FELIPE CASTLE

Morgans approach route

La Gloria Hill

LA RANCHERIA

from Buenaventura

ISTHMUS of PANAMA

Scale of Miles

0          ½          1

opportunity to hide their valuables or flee; others simply ignored the call and were still in bed when the buccaneers arrived.

The buccaneers had no artillery and their preferred weapons were swords, pikes and pistols; like true *boucaniers* they also carried French muskets – the finest available – although their heaviness made them unpopular, and their matchlock mechanisms were not very reliable. Besides, the humid atmosphere and heavy rainfall along this part of the Main meant that powder often became damp despite their best efforts to keep it dry, though they compensated for these shortfalls with what a contemporary described as 'an insatiable desire of riches, courage and disdain of risk'.[33] They quickly overwhelmed the defenders of the blockhouse and swept on towards the town. At Castello Santiago Sergeant Nicolas Trejo kept his head and ordered the gate left open until the enemy appeared, to allow those of the garrison who slept in town to get in; among the few who did was the Genoese constable of artillery, Manuel de Olivera, while Trejo went to summon the *castellan* (commandant) Juan de Somovilla Tejada. Trejo found him still in bed, and was drowsily told not to bother himself: it was probably only the six escaped English prisoners. Only when informed that several hundred well-armed men were approaching within musket range along Triana beach did Tejada finally stir.

As an engineer he was responsible for the imposing fortifications that greeted Morgan as he rounded the headland from La Rancheria. In a rare moment of panic Morgan grabbed the guide by the throat. 'We cannot go that way,' he shouted. 'This is a trick to slaughter us all.'[34] But Morgan's friends laughed and patted him on the back, saying the guns of Santiago were in complete disarray and he had nothing to fear. Reassured, he gave the order to charge, and with a piercing yell that was heard on the far side of the bay, the buccaneers split into two groups and raced across the open ground, one group of about seventy into a ravine leading up a hill that dominated the castle from the landward side, the remainder up to the castle walls and into the town itself, 'firing off their guns at everything alive, whites, blacks, even dogs, in order to spread terror'.[35] So far not a man had been killed. A few musket shots rang from the castle walls, but of its guns little was heard. Olivera was so incompetent that he loaded one with roundshot before the charge, and another sent its shot harmlessly over the heads of the attackers. None of the other guns were loaded with canister or grape shot that might have caused heavy casualties, and by the time the cumbersome pieces were reloaded the buccaneers were already picking off the gunners – many buccaneers had been sharpshooters in their earlier life – with skilfully aimed fire from behind cover within the town, their French muskets causing havoc from the first shot, which took a gunner in the head.[36]

The main body of the buccaneers soon had control of the town, killing or intimidating anybody who dared show resistance, and securing the convent, hospital and the royal treasury where they found eleven English prisoners chained in a stinking cell measuring ten feet by twelve. Only the apparently formidable fort of San Gerónimo offered resistance, and with the attackers unaware of the depth of the turbid water between the castle and the quay, the musketry duel continued. The buccaneers offered quarter which the *castellan* refused, but when some of the former prisoners emerged and, laughing, led their hesitant rescuers through the knee-deep water, the *castellan* quickly changed his mind and the garrison was shut up with the rest of the population in Portobelo church. The action had lasted half an hour, and as his men broke their fast Morgan turned his attention to Santiago. Without securing this castle and its sister San Felipe he would not be able to bring in his ships and secure his loot.

Contrary to Exquemelin's wilder claims about the buccaneers blowing up the entire castle with its occupants – it still stands to this day – Morgan left forty men to guard the prisoners and took the remainder of his force back to the west end of town where they engaged the garrison. 'Amidst the horror of this assault,' wrote Charles Leslie, historian of Jamaica, 'both parties behaved with equal courage and the pirates, observing the stout resistance they met with, prepared fire balls [heated shots] with which they designed to fire the gates'. This attempt failed when the defenders 'threw down great stones and flasks of powder [grenades] which killed a great many and compelled the rest to retire'. But the buccaneer marksmen continued to pick off the defenders.[37] Although Panamá was seventy miles away, Morgan had no time to waste, and in his impatience he returned to the church where the buccaneers selected a group of people who looked important enough or weak enough to suit his purpose – the mayor, two friars, several women including nuns and some old men. These unfortunates were then forced at gunpoint to walk across the bridge, wailing and screaming, as bent low behind them came buccaneers carrying axes and flaming torches to assault the gate.

Uncertain what to do, the Spanish hesitated, until somebody chose to put a match to a gun loaded with chainshot; two friars fell wounded and a buccaneer was killed, but the badly maintained gun was thrown from its carriage and the buccaneers forced the prisoners to continue the rest of the way and set to work on the gate.[38] Fortunately for Morgan, as he and practically the entire garrison watched the drama unfolding, another party of buccaneers had slipped around the seaward side of the castle with ladders they had found in the town. Their first assault was repulsed by the few defenders on that wall but the second succeeded, and they raised their red flag on the walls. Seeing this, the men on the hill in town rushed down to assist, and the final desperate assault by some 200 buccaneers with Morgan among them was too much for the Spanish to resist. Although many threw down their weapons, forty-five out of eighty in the garrison had been killed, including Tejada. Many others were wounded, including one man left for dead under bodies for four days until found to be still alive.[39] Thereafter the buccaneers, wrote Exquemelin, 'fell to eating and drinking after their usual manner – that is to say committing in both these things all manner of debauchery and excess . . .'.[40]

A mulatto shipowner from Cartagena who went to Jamaica hoping to gain compensation for an illegally taken prize since England and Spain were at peace at the time, claimed that the buccaneers killed the daughter of *castellan* Tejada as she wept beside her father's body, and that they tortured the leading lady of the town, Doña Agustina de Rojas. They stripped her, he said, and placed her in a barrel which they then filled with gunpowder; grinning, they held a lighted match to her face and asked if she still could not remember the location of her treasure.[41] The buccaneers were masters of coercion in collecting loot, and were accused by a disgruntled Jamaican, John Style, of appalling cruelty. He wrote to the secretary of state:

It is a common thing among the privateers . . . to cut a man in pieces, first some flesh, then a hand, an arm, a leg, sometimes tying a cord about his head, and with a stick twisting it until the eyes shoot out, which is called 'woolding'. Before taking Porto Bello ... a woman there was set bare upon a baking stone, and roasted, because she did not confess of money which she had only in their conceit.[42]

But the buccaneers were apparently assisted by two other, very friendly women who, according to Don Pedro Ladron de Guevara, were later punished by the Spanish by being 'burned in parts that for decency he will not refer to'.[43] And there were no accusations of rape in the subsequent Spanish inquiry. Morgan claimed that the women of Portobelo had been treated so well, at least those of quality, that when offered the chance to depart 'they refused, saying that they were sure now to be prisoners to a person of quality, who was more tender of their honours and reputation than they doubted to find' among Panamá's rude soldiers.[44]

More important than securing loot, there remained the castle of San Felipe to be captured before the fleet, which had come up from Boca del Toro, could enter the harbour to take it away. A canoe sent to demand a surrender was fired upon by the young *castellan*, Alexandro Manuel Pau y Rocaberti, although his forty-nine-man garrison, under half strength, had a total of just four pounds of bread to sustain them. When a dozen canoes carrying around 200 buccaneers were seen crossing the bay he ordered the gates reinforced, and despite a reported attempt by one of the guides, Sergeant Juan de Mallvegui, to draw the buccaneers unwittingly on to the castle guns, they already knew the ground too well to be deceived; Mallvegui was instead clubbed down and they took a trail that led to a flanking ravine. Although the Spanish repulsed three assaults it seems that after a couple of hours Rocaberti lost his nerve and surrendered, against the wishes of his officers. Although the garrison were allowed to march away to Panamá, the buccaneers reneged on the terms allowing the Spanish the honours of war and took their arms and colours. Rocaberti was mortified and, knowing he would be branded a coward, begged his captors for a flask of vitriol; he drank it, and died in agony two days later.[45]

In his report Morgan declared eighteen buccaneers dead and thirty-two wounded, and informed Modyford that he now had possession of the town and three forts; 'in the former were 900 men that bare arms', but the buccaneers were now free to search the surroundings for anything else of value, including slaves.[46] Meanwhile a Spanish horseman who had escaped the city reported to Panamá, where Don Agustin de Bracamonte had been appointed interim president. Unaware of the fall of San Felipe and faced with the alarming prospect of buccaneers besieging Portobelo, he immediately mobilised 200 men, leaving orders that another 600 were to be gathered, and marched to its relief. But the Spanish in their haste were hopelessly unprepared for a march and, besides, had few friends in the jungle, while various buccaneering expeditions had made allies of several groups of Indians who would warn Morgan of the enemy's approach. On Sunday Bracamonte encountered the dejected garrison of San Felipe and soon afterwards received a letter from Morgan in good Spanish demanding a ransom of 350,000 pesos to spare Portobelo. Bracamonte was outraged by the insolence of this pirate and refused out of hand. Morgan then sent another letter:

> Although your letter does not deserve a reply, since you call me a corsair, nevertheless I write you these few lines to ask you to come quickly. We are waiting for you with great pleasure and we have powder and ball with which to receive you. If you do not come very soon, we will, with the favour of God and our arms, come and visit you in Panamá. Now it is our intention to garrison the castles and keep them for the King of England, my master, who, since he had a mind to seize them, also has a mind to keep them.[47]

Morgan, despite carrying no commission to invade Spanish territory, hated being called a pirate, and insolently datelined his letter 'Portobelo, City of the King of England'.[48]

Bracamonte's force, bogged down outside the town, short of rations, sick with fever and hampered by damp powder, could do little. Morgan's men were, by contrast, comfortably ensconced and able to repel most of the patrols sent against them. After five days Morgan sent 200 men in a sortie that resulted in eight Spanish and one Englishman dead, with another captured. This prisoner and some escaped Spanish seamen were able to provide Bracamonte with a detailed description of the buccaneers' dispositions and intentions, but it was also suggested that the French were not present because they planned to attack Panamá while Bracamonte was distracted. On 23 July Bracamonte called a *junta* and, faced with apparent stalemate before Portobelo and an imminent threat to Panamá, the Spanish decided to retreat, sending an emissary to negotiate with Morgan.[49] Morgan again demanded 350,000 pesos, but the emissary, Captain Francisco de Aricaga, insisted that this was impossible. They could only offer 50,000 pesos up front with another 50,000 drawn on the Grillos, the Genoese bankers responsible for supplying slaves to the Spanish colonies.[50] Morgan laughed at being offered a bill of exchange, but his men were also beginning to suffer from fevers, and two days later he sent an envoy to the commander of the Spanish rearguard, Cristoval García Niño. The most he could extract was to drop the note of exchange, although 100,000 pesos remained a pitiful sum for a town of such importance, being barely enough to cover the value of the 300 captured slaves he would have to leave behind having no space aboard his ships to remove them.[51] But Morgan agreed, and García rushed to Panamá to report the terms on 29 July.

By now Bracamonte had learned that there was no French threat to Panamá and called another *junta* at which these excellent terms were agreed to. The money was raised in three days against the profit Portobelo could expect to make on the next treasure fleet – a clever move by the citizens of Panamá that would lead to lengthy legal wrangling – and on 3 August two mule trains delivered to the buccaneers twenty-seven bars of silver worth 43,000 pesos, plate worth 13,000, gold coin worth 4,000 and 40,000 in silver coin.[52] Morgan treated the messenger with great civility and gave him a pistol and a few bullets for the viceroy, with the message that he 'accept the slender pattern of the arms wherewith he had taken Portobelo, and keep them for a twelvemonth, after which he would come to Panamá and fetch them away'.[53] After thirty-one days in possession of the town and having loaded everything they could possibly could on to their ships, which had now arrived, including the best of the brass guns (they spiked the rest), Morgan and his little fleet set sail to end probably the most audacious and effective amphibious operation of the seventeenth century, one that firmly established him as a truly great – if ruthless – leader.

# 10

## MARACAIBO

Ho! Henry Morgan sails today
To harry the Spanish Main,
With a pretty bill for the Dons to pay
Ere he comes back again.

Him cheat him friend of his last guinea,
Him kill both friar and priest – Oh dear!
Him cut de t'roat of piccaninny,
Bloody, bloody buccaneer.

Anon., West Indian ballad

The buccaneers returned to Port Royal with flags flying and drums beating in a triumph not seen since the height of Myngs' operations. When the total booty came to be calculated it amounted to some 250,000 pieces of eight to be shared among the 300 participants according to their rank, a fantastic bounty that ensured Morgan would never be short of volunteers in the future.[1] From that point on the Spanish coins were used as legal currency in Jamaica, valued at five shillings. But for all Morgan's newfound fame in Jamaica, it would fall to Modyford to explain the saga to the king, whose own share of the proceeds came to a meagre £600, and that was held back to pay for repairs to the fortifications of Port Royal.[2] In fact, he addressed his reports to the Duke of Albemarle and in a letter written a month after Morgan's return, he noted that:

> It is almost certain that the Spanish had full intention to attempt this island but could not get the men, and they still hold the same minds, and therefore I cannot but presume to say that it is very unequal that we should in any measure be restrained while they are at liberty to act as they please upon us . . .[3]

This letter also contained bitter personal news about the fate of Mody-ford's eldest son Jack, missing for four years in the frigate *Griffin*. According to a Spanish captain's deposition, two English ships had been wrecked on the Florida coast in August 1664 and only five men survived, one of whom was a young man of 'very good face and light hair, somewhat curling' who said his name was John and he was son of the governor of Jamaica. He was 'questionless either murdered or sent into the South Seas by these, our cruel neighbours'.[4]

The sack of Portobelo was no less than an act of open war against Spain, and, presented with a *fait accompli*, Modyford decided that half-measures would serve no purpose. Before the end of October 1668 the entire buccaneers' fleet available to him of ten sail and 800 men set off once more under Morgan to cruise the coast of Venezuela, while Captain Edward Dempster and 300 men lay off Havana and the shores of Campeche.[5] The news of Portobelo reached London before it reached Madrid, but any notion that it would be greeted with dismay as a treacherous and potentially dangerous breach of a treaty barely signed would be false. England had just been through three calamitous years of disaster – plague, fire and humiliation at the hands of the Dutch – and in the heart of every good Protestant Englishman the name of the Welshman Morgan now stood alongside that of Drake as a scourge of popery. The Spanish ambassador, however, was never going to accept such an analysis, although the Conde de Molina's protests about the illegal seizure of Spanish shipping in the Indies had so far met with nothing more than polite dismissal, for beyond the line it was clear there was still no rule but that of force.[6]

The treaty of 1667 had never been proclaimed in Jamaica, and Molina was diplomat enough to understand Spain's weakness and need for friends in a hostile Europe where England represented a counterweight to France. When news of the outrage reached Spain she was, for once, at peace with everyone, and there were other ways to deal with the complaint of piracy in the faraway Indies than war. Nevertheless all Molina's efforts to gain recompense were ignored, coldly but cour-teously. In fact, the raid provided encouragement to those, notably the lord high admiral, the Duke of York, who supported a more active policy of imperial expansion.[7] Modyford had written repeatedly that if the king wished to exercise any measure of control over the buccaneers he would have to send two or three frigates to command their attention and to defend Jamaica. Prompted by the Duke of Albemarle the *Oxford* was finally dispatched and arrived on 14 October 1668, ostensibly for use in suppressing piracy, but carrying instructions countenancing the unofficial war and empowering Modyford to grant whatever commissions he deemed necessary. The instructions from the Privy Council to Albemarle had been to send a fifth-rate frigate but *Oxford* was a smaller sixth-rate, carrying twenty-six guns (she is sometimes referred to as carrying thirty-four). Built twelve years earlier at Deptford and measuring some seventy-two feet by twenty-four, she was no longer a Royal Navy ship and her costs were to be borne by Jamaica, so she was immediately fitted for a six-month cruise as a privateer with a crew of 160 men.[8]

When an unfortunate incident saw her captain, Samuel Hackett, kill her sailing master and run for his life, one of Morgan's lieutenants at Portobelo, Edward Collier, took over command of what was unquestionably the most powerful English ship in the Caribbean.[9] Collier's first action demonstrated his willingness to confront pirates, at least if it proved beneficial to his buccaneer comrades. He brought into Port Royal the captain and forty-five-man crew of *Le Cerf Volant* (fourteen guns) of La Rochelle, clapped in irons and accused of plundering a Virginia merchantman. Sir James Modyford, the governor's brother, had no difficulty in condemning the unfortunate French master, although he was later reprieved, and his ship was condemned as a lawful prize. Renamed *Satisfaction* she sailed to Morgan's rendezvous at Isla Vaca where the Jamaican buccaneers were gathering for a new cruise with several French buccaneers from Tortuga, a total of ten ships and some 900 men eager to follow the victor of Portobelo to gather fresh spoils from the Spaniard.[10]

On 2 January 1669 Morgan hoisted his flag on *Oxford* and called a council of war to discuss the next objective. Among the captains attending were two called John Morris (father and son), Captain Aylett of the *Lilly* (ten guns), and captains Thornbury, Bigford and Whiting, together with their mates and other attendants, some twenty-five officers in total. All sat down to hear what their admiral had to propose. Also in attendance was Surgeon Richard Browne at his first buccaneer council of war, and after numerous place names were bandied about he heard the council agree that although Cartagena was the best-defended harbour on the Main, with its great bay shaped like a clover leaf and several powerful castles including the enormous San Felipe, this would be the next target. Morgan was his usual cheerful and ebullient self, buoyed with confidence following Portobelo, and as the discussion ended he insisted that everyone stay for dinner. In the late afternoon they sat down together in the great cabin with Morgan seated at the centre of one side of the table and Collier on his right, the other captains arrayed around him at random. John Morris the elder sat on the same side as Morgan with his son opposite, and the other captains also opposite towards the foot of the table. Elsewhere on the ship the crew were eating and drinking and combining celebration of the successful council with another New Year's party. When it went dark, quickly as it does in the tropics, the ship's company were drinking, singing, dancing and joking on the foredeck, and toasts were being exchanged in the great cabin in anticipation of the glorious adventure they were about to commence. 'They drank the health of the King of England and toasted their good success and fired off salvoes.'[11]

The explosion was as sudden and devastating as it was unexpected. Morgan, Browne and Collier were thrown into the air and found themselves swimming amid shattered timbers and the broken bodies of the crew. A careless match or spark had ignited the magazine and the ship had detonated in a colossal blast that shook the very island itself. Browne splashed around until he managed to scramble on to part of the mizzen mast, and soon boats from the rest of the fleet were rowing through the vast circle of wreckage searching for survivors. By a quirk of fate all the captains sitting opposite Morgan had been killed, and apart from Collier and John Morris the elder, two seamen and four cabin boys, everybody else on board, some 250 men, perished. Although it was almost certainly an accident, rumours of a French act of revenge against Collier were mooted, but nobody among the citizens of Cartagena had any doubt about whom to thank for their deliverance. High above the city stood a monastery, the home of Cartagena's patron, Nuestra Señora de la Popa, and well known as the best possible defence against pirates. Many men claimed to have seen the patron return home wet and tired on the night the *Oxford* blew up.[12]

Certainly the citizens of Cartagena were spared, as the loss of *Oxford* and a fifth of his men convinced Morgan that a lesser target was necessary, especially as Collier then chose to set off on an independent cruise to Campeche in *Satisfaction*. Apparently unruffled by his close escape from death, Morgan made *Lilly* his new flagship – a much more cramped and far less salubrious proposition than *Oxford* – and set off with his greatly reduced and now decidedly sober squadron to cruise the south coast of Española, the plan being to head for Trinidad and then cruise westward along the coast of the Main. But the pattern of work was one of unremitting harshness with the men exposed to the elements in their small mostly undecked boats, only occasionally enlivened with raids ashore to find provisions and hunt wild pigs and cattle. Even these forays, normally so much fun for the buccaneers, proved hazardous in the face of the unusually vigilant soldiers and militia of Santo Domingo, who on more than one occasion chased the raiders back to their ships. The difficulty these operations imposed proved too much for some, and after a few weeks 'three of our best ships, pretending inability through distresse of weather not to beat to windward', departed.[13]

Morgan's squadron had now shrunk to just six ships, the diehard remnants of his Portobelo expedition, but these were men prepared to follow him wherever he chose to lead. Now at the favourite buccaneer haunt of Saona near the eastern end of Española, one of the Frenchmen suggested an alternative target that might yield richer rewards than Morgan's proposal of Venezuela and La Margarita, and which they could reach far sooner. This Frenchman had been with L'Ollonais at Maracaibo, and he reported that the defences were weak and the pickings to be had rich. The decision made, they sailed first for the Dutch island of Aruba to stock up with sheep and goats bought from Indian herdsmen. Two days later they set off, leaving at night to hide their destination, and sailing into the Gulf of Venezuela which leads to the Laguna de Maracaibo. The approach is a treacherous one of shallows and currents, but Morgan's pilots seem to have had no difficulty in bringing his little fleet up to a short distance from the breakers at the entrance of the twisting narrow neck of water connecting gulf and lagoon over the bar, the Barra de Maracaibo. Here they anchored on 9 March, a mere two months since the *Oxford* disaster.[14]

Daybreak, however, revealed a new problem. Since the raid by

L'Ollonais two years earlier the Spanish had increased the dangers of navigation by building a fort – Fuerte de la Barra – on the eastern extremity of San Carlos Island which completely dominated the channel. Fortunately this hazard would prove less formidable than it appeared. For despite being well stocked with food and ammunition and mounting eleven guns, it suffered from the perennial weakness of the Spanish Main, being chronically undermanned; the garrison comprised the *castellan* and just eight soldiers. Despite doing their utmost to convince the raiders that they were not so poorly represented by firing on Morgan's ships and men as they disembarked to assault the fort, and managing to hold out all day in a valiant if hopeless display of defiance, the garrison's nerve broke at nightfall and they slipped away in a boat, leaving a long fuse burning to the magazine.[15]

Alas for the Spanish, the luck that saved Morgan's life when the *Oxford* exploded was to save him once again. As they inched their way towards the fort in the darkness in readiness for an assault, the buccaneers were both amazed and delighted to find the place abandoned, but long experience had long taught them to temper such delight with caution. A rapid search for booby traps revealed a cellar full of powder with much more scattered about, and the spluttering fuse leading to it was snuffed out, according to the always dramatic Exquemelin, 'about an inch away from' detonation.[16] Morgan decided he could not afford to detach the fifty men necessary to garrison the fort and, unable to dismantle it, chose instead to spike the guns and throw them down from the walls where they were buried. The fort's stocks were then dispersed among the expedition and the fleet sailed over the bar into the lagoon, led by canoes to help them avoid the shoals and quicksands. Even so some ships ran aground and had to transfer their crews to others more fortunate as they approached Maracaibo itself.[17]

The city captain, Juan Sanchez Vorrego, had by now received warning of their approach and, determined to resist, ordered drummers to beat the call to arms. But the result was disappointing; only twelve men from the 400 families in the city were mustered, and the rest could be seen moving rapidly away towards the mountains in the west taking their families, slaves and as many of their possessions as they could manage. Cursing their cowardice, the good captain ordered the drummers to beat again and issued a proclamation that all citizens should muster 'on pain of their lives as traitors to the kingdom'.[18] But it was to no avail, and by the time Morgan arrived in the city it was deserted, even Captain Sanchez having realised the futility of trying to defend it alone. But some refugees did not flee far enough or fast enough. That evening a column of a hundred buccaneers set out into the countryside and returned with thirty prisoners and a mule train laden with plunder. The unfortunate Spaniards were tortured with the usual exquisite cruelty, and soon revealed more hiding places which in turn yielded more prisoners and more information. The buccaneers took up residence in houses around the market place and herded the wretched citizens into the main church. After a week of drunken carousing and extortion the buccaneers had collected a hundred prisoners and cleared the countryside of cattle – which were slaughtered and salted – as well as of slaves and anything else of value within a thirty-mile radius. Morgan decided it was time to move on and search the rest of the lagoon.[19]

Measuring eighty-six miles along and up to sixty miles wide, the lagoon offered plenty of scope for exploring, but it was unlikely that there would be much of value to find. Word had quickly spread of the buccaneers' presence and the entire west side where most riches might be located was now deserted. Morgan decided that his best chance of securing further booty was to sail to the end of the lagoon and take Gibraltar, which received the same treatment as Maracaibo when the town was also found deserted. Once again the surrounding area was scoured for those too slow, too old or too stubborn to get far enough away, and these unfortunates were rounded up and subjected to horrible interrogation. But Morgan agreed to take four hostages in return for a ransom of 5,000 pesos, and the prisoners were released once this had been collected.[20] The fleet then sailed north once more towards the mouth of the lagoon, taking with them not only everything of value that could be carted away, but numerous other hostages for ransom carried in vessels that had been found en route – a large Cuban merchantman and five *plantaneros* (banana boats). They returned to the still deserted Maracaibo on 17 April and prepared to sail home.[21]

Morgan had divested the local inhabitants of almost £50,000 worth of silver, jewels, silks, slaves and other commodities, but getting it home was going to prove much more troublesome. In early February word had reached Havana of the gathering at Isla Vaca and the plan to raid Cartagena. And so it came to the ears of the one man in a position to do something decisive about these accursed marauders that were driving the governors of Spanish territories throughout the region to absolute distraction: Don Alonzo de Campos y Espinosa, commanding the *armada de barlovento*. Morgan was thus in serious trouble as the Spanish fleet was now out to get him. Campos had three powerful warships: the 412-ton *Nuestra Señora de la Magdalena* (thirty-eight guns), the 218-ton *San Luis* (twenty-six guns) under Mateo Alonzo Huidobro and the fifty-ton tender *Nuestra Señora de la Soledad* alias *Marquesa* (fourteen guns).[22]

Campos had orders to be in Veracruz by May 1669 in order to escort the *flota* to Havana and out through the Florida Channel, so he had plenty of time to investigate the reports of the buccaneer fleet at Isla Vaca and possibly destroy it. He planned to go north of the Greater Antilles and gain the wind on them, and he duly arrived at Puerto Rico on 19 March. But there was no news, so he returned on the 25th to Santo Domingo where he gained positive word from a French prisoner of the plan to sail to Trinidad and back along the Main. Sailing again on 30 March he heard from a Dutch sloop out of Curaçao that the buccaneers had bought meat before setting off to sack Maracaibo. The trail was rapidly hotting up and Campos set off under all the sail he could raise. When the *armada* arrived at the Gulf of Venezuela he learned from the shore that the buccaneers had sacked Gibraltar but were still in the lagoon. It seemed all his prayers were being answered, for here was the main body of the Jamaican buccaneers seemingly trapped in an enclosed body of water with no prospect of escape. These insolent heretical foreign pirates who had been the scourge of the Spanish Indies for years were about to get their just deserts; it must have seemed that the glory of bringing them to justice, to say nothing of the fame and wealth that would attend it, were his for the taking.[23]

Letters were hastily sent to summon help from Coro and La Guaira and from the governors of Maracaibo and Mérida. As soon as pilots were to hand he sailed to the bar where he was delighted to find no garrison in the Fuerte de la Barra, and he quickly landed forty musketeers. When they managed to restore six guns to the fort he drank a toast to the pirates' destruction and sent letters to the surrounding villages requesting further assistance, but he was still not altogether happy about his position. His large flagship drew too much water to cross the bar and her anchorage beyond it was an uncomfortable one, as every afternoon and evening a strong north-easterly whipped up the shallow waters of the gulf and threatened to push her on to a coast inhabited by fierce and reputedly cannibalistic Caribs. He decided that she would have to cross the bar, and had all the ship's ballast and water thrown overboard. On 15 April, after some nervous manoeuvring, *Magdalena* took up a position near the island of Zapara in the middle of the channel within range of Fuerte de la Barra and with the other ships anchored to the west. For the buccaneers there was absolutely no way out of the Laguna de Maracaibo without a fight.[24]

The Spanish sealed the bottle on the same day that Morgan reached Maracaibo, where he learned of the trap from a man so poor that he could afford to remain in the town. Morgan defiantly demanded a war tribute, but two days later Campos insisted that he surrender, offering clemency and free passage should the buccaneer yield up his booty, but also promising absolute destruction if the offer was refused. 'This is my final resolution: take heed, and be not ungrateful for my kindness, I have with me valiant soldiers, yearning to be allowed to revenge the unrighteous acts you have committed against the Spanish nation in America.'[25] Decisively outgunned and outnumbered, Morgan was unperturbed. He called his men together in the market place and read out the letter, first in English, then in French, before asking his men what they wanted to do: surrender and take their chances on Spanish mercy, or fight their way out? With one voice these democratic scoundrels announced that they had fought for their booty once and were ready to fight for it again. Morgan was to prepare to lead his thirteen vessels out of the gulf. As the buccaneers cheered their leader, Morgan called for his clerk and dictated a reply:

> Sir, I have seen your summons, and since I understand you are soe neare, I shall save you ye labour with your nimble frigotts to come here, being resolved to visit you with all expedition, and there wee will putt to hazard of Battle in whose power it shall be

to use clemency (yours wee are acquainted with nor doe wee expect any).

In a repetition of his insolence at Portobelo he dated the letter 'from His Majesty of England's citty of Marracaia' and added as a final flourish: 'Farewell'.[26]

For a week the buccaneers worked unceasingly to prepare for the forthcoming battle. Knowing there were spies to report this activity to Campos they converted the big Cuban merchantman into a flagship, putting five extra guns into her and reinforcing her for battle. They also prepared one of the sloops as a fireship, an obvious yet terrifying tactic to employ against an anchored line of wooden ships. Consequently Campos took appropriate precautions, sending work parties ashore to cut long booms in order to fend off any such attack and ensuring that great water tubs were placed along the decks of the ships in readiness should matters get to the stage of firefighting. On 25 April the buccaneers came forward in their thirteen ships, the big Cuban to the fore, before anchoring out of range of Spanish guns. Clearly the reports from Maracaibo had been accurate. Now they would wait until wind and tide favoured them before launching their attack. Two days later conditions were perfect and at 9 a.m. the buccaneer fleet sailed directly toward the *armada de barlovento*, led by the big Cuban with Morgan's former flagship *Lilly* to one side and another smaller sloop on the other. But even together these three appeared puny to the 280 men aboard *Magdalena*, especially when the guns opened fire and the buccaneers clearly got the worst of the exchange. Still they came on, directly towards the Spanish flagship. Then they divided, one heading for the stern of the big Spaniard, one for her bow, and the big Cuban with her guns firing and her flags streaming, going straight for her amidships. Campos let her approach and was preparing to send a powerful boarding party as sailors on the Cuban threw grappling irons to bind them together. But when the Spanish leaped on deck they found the Cuban suddenly deserted; the only men they could see were a dozen desperately pulling away by canoe as fast as they could paddle, as were the other buccaneer frigates to port and starboard.[27]

They had not expected to capture the buccaneer flagship with such ease, when all at once she exploded, flames rising up with astonishing

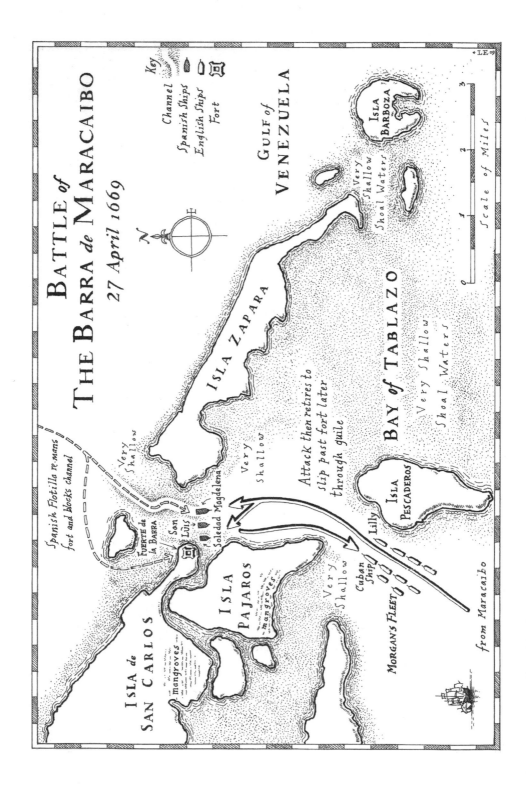

BATTLE of
THE BARRA de MARACAIBO
27 April 1669

*Key*

Channel

Spanish Ships

English Ships

Fort

GULF of
VENEZUELA

N

ISLA
BARBOZA

Scale of Miles

Very
Shallow
Shoal Waters

ISLA ZAPARA

Spanish Flotilla re-mans
fort and blocks channel

Very
Shallow

Very
Shallow

Attack then retires to
slip past fort later
through guile

BAY of TABLAZO

Very Shallow
Shoal Waters

Soledad Magdalena

FUERTE de
la BARRA

San
Luis

ISLA
PESCADEROS

Lilly

ISLA PAJAROS

Very
Shallow

mangroves

mangroves

Cuban
Ship

MORGAN'S FLEET

ISLA de
SAN CARLOS

from Maracaibo

speed to engulf her, igniting sails and spars and consuming her within a matter of seconds that would have seemed impossible to the burned survivors had they not seen it with their own eyes. The strong southerly wind spread the fire rapidly to *Magdalena* so that the water tubs remained useless on her decks. The big Cuban had been skilfully disguised as a flagship to conceal her true identity, as the fireship she really was. Although Morgan later claimed this as his own idea, it was, according to Exquemelin, a suggestion made by one of the men who also described in detail how it should be done.[28] Campos remained on board to the last moment, throwing spars and other jetsam to the struggling sailors in the water before finally leaping in himself, probably wondering how on earth he was going to explain this complete and utter disaster back home. Flagships were not supposed to be used as fireships, but the Cuban had been manned with just twelve volunteers and the rest of the 'crew' were dummies made of logs 'with caps on top, to look like the crew'.[29] Extra gun ports had been cut in her hull but the extra guns were logs, stuffed with powder, and she had been packed with every last drop of tar, pitch, brimstone and other combustible material that the buccaneers had been able to lay their hands on, while the decks and spars had been suitably treated to ensure they went the same way as the hull. All the real crew had to do was lash the two ships together, light the touch papers and run.[30]

At first *San Luis* tried to come to the aid of her flagship but seeing that *Magdalena* was beyond all assistance she instead turned towards the protection of the fort, pursued by three buccaneer ships. Once under the guns of the fort the buccaneers drew off and left the Spaniard to beach herself on a sandbank as the tide dropped, after which her captain ordered the crew to cut holes in the hull and hack away the rigging, then put everything they could manage ashore and join the garrison of the fort while he and a small party fired her to prevent her capture. Aboard the *Marquesa* Captain Diego de Varrio was not to be so successful. On seeing the fate of *Magdalena* he ordered the anchor cables severed and planned to set off for the fort, but a rope got stuck in a pulley and she drifted helplessly towards land out of range of the fort's guns, pursued by eight buccaneer vessels and a fleet of canoes, all desperate to be the first to reach the one possible prize on offer that morning. As the ship went aground near a mangrove swamp most of the crew jumped overboard, and Varrio had no time to fire her before the leading buccaneers scrambled aboard, forcing him to leap over the far gunwale. He reached the fort naked and soaking wet as the triumphant buccaneers sailed their prize back to join their mates.[31] Thus in two hours ended the career of the *armada de barlovento* designed to protect the coasts of the Indies from the pirates that infested them.

The jubilant buccaneers were keen to add the fort to their tally of success, but this would prove somewhat more difficult. They spent the rest of the day sniping at the garrison with their muskets and at dusk tried to creep up to the walls and throw fireballs over them, but they were driven back by intense fire, and in the meantime the fort barred their exit from the lagoon.[32] Until it was reduced or otherwise bypassed, they could not get home to enjoy the fruits of their latest brilliant victory. And the garrison had now been reinforced by seventy militiamen from Maracaibo who had come out of the hills, as well as some 140 men from *San Luis* plus numerous others from the other two ships. The one man who had failed to make it back was Campos who, having been picked up by *Magdalena*'s long-boat, was chased by buccaneer canoes and forced ashore a very long way to the south, then spent three days hiding in the mountains before making his way somewhat sheepishly to Fuerte de la Barra. But the *castellan*, Antonio Camarillo, would prove a redoubtable deputy, and he was able to repel Morgan's initial attempts to take the fort with heavy losses the following day. A stalemate had been reached in which the buccaneers, despite their astonishing success, remained trapped in the lagoon with the prospect of more Spanish frigates arriving from La Guaira and other ports to challenge them once again.[33]

While Morgan thought the problem over, the charred wreck of *Magdalena* was salvaged, with divers managing to recover 20,000 pesos worth of coin and bullion, much of it melted by the fire into great lumps. One of the prisoners explained that the Spanish had been warned that the buccaneers were preparing a fireship but had dismissed the news, saying they did not have the intelligence or materials to do so. He also said the Spanish were told they could expect no quarter which was why so many had drowned, fearing to cry out for assistance from the English. The prisoners were informed that if they could persuade Campos to allow them passage they would be released and set ashore at Maracaibo without a ransom demand. But following his humiliation afloat Campos was now defiant ashore. 'The fort was his, he himself had wrested it from the enemy, and therefore could do with it whatever he thought good for the advantage of his King and the maintenance of his own honour.'[34] In all likelihood this was the response Morgan had expected, and his fertile imagination had already conceived a plan to overcome this stubborn resistance. The Spanish watched as canoes packed with armed buccaneers sped across the lagoon to a mangrove swamp some distance away, then returned to the fleet to collect more men. It seemed clear that the buccaneers were planning a night assault on a large scale, and Campos repositioned some of his guns to cover his exposed landward flank.[35]

That night after dark, as soon as the current of the ebb tide was flowing at more than a knot, the buccaneer squadron slipped its anchors and drifted northwards along the channel out towards the Gulf of Venezuela. In the castle the Spaniards heard a distant report to seaward, then another and another until in total seven shots were heard. As each of the ships the buccaneers retained had passed the castle they had let out their sails, completing a passage that was difficult and dangerous enough in daylight, and had fired a single passing shot. By the time Campos had repositioned his guns it was too late to engage them. Another Morgan ruse had worked for there was no night assault; the canoes that apparently carried hundreds of men had returned to the ships with the men lying flat on their bellies and on top of each other, and had then gone back to the mangrove carrying 'more' men as they sat up.[36] Next morning Morgan set most of his prisoners ashore on Zapara Island in the middle of the channel, there being no reason to hold them longer apart from some hostages from Gibraltar who had yet to pay their ransom, and the buccaneers fired a farewell salute as he and his men sailed for home. They arrived triumphant on 27 May, exactly a month after the battle of the bar, led by Morgan's new flagship *Marquesa*.[37]

Once again they were greeted by cheering crowds lining the quays as Port Royal enjoyed another boost to the taverns and brothels of supposedly the most sinful city in the world. Their success was made all the sweeter by the news that the ships which had deserted the expedition off the coast of Española had been seriously defeated, while at the same time as Morgan's Maracaibo campaign another group of buccaneers under Roche Brasiliano, Joseph Bradley and Jelles de Lecat had tried their luck in the Gulf of Mexico. Brasiliano, so called because he had lived in Brazil when it was under Dutch control, was one of the most notorious buccaneer leaders. According to Exquemelin, he had:

> no self control at all, but possessed of a sullen fury . . . He perpetrated the greatest atrocities possible against the Spaniards. Some of them he tied or spitted on wooden stakes and roasted them alive between two fires, like killing a pig – and all because they refused to show him the road to the hog-yards he wanted to plunder.[38]

Having assembled in the spring of 1669, these thirty-four Dutch and six English buccaneers blockaded Campeche but managed not a single capture. Then by torturing some fishermen Brasiliano learned of the approach of a merchant vessel carrying a new governor. However, before he could attack it the pirates were scattered when the Spanish sent three ships after them. Lecat stayed behind and, together with Jan Erasmus Reyning, managed to capture a Spanish merchant ship which they renamed the *Seviliaen*.[39]

However, it was Morgan who was proving himself the man of the moment and a commander of immense resolution and ingenuity, although his self-justificatory claim that the Spanish had been preparing another descent on Jamaica was false, and times were changing in London and Jamaica. Morgan's destruction of the *armada de barlovento* was just as well, because Spanish anger at the Portobelo raid had scuttled any chance of peace; queen regent Mariana was demanding full reparations and Modyford's dismissal. Arlington had written to Modyford on 21 May insisting on an end to all hostilities, and on 24 June the drummers marched through Port Royal as the town crier made an important announcement in the name of the governor:

> Inasmuch as the forces under the command of Admiral Morgan, with the blessing of God, have happily destroyed the fleet which the Spaniards intended against this island and since Our Sovereign Lord the King through his Ministers of State instructed me that the subjects of His Catholic Majesty be from now until further order treated

and used as good neighbours and friends . . . I, by this present proc-lamation, make null and void all commissions which I have pre-viously conceded to privateers and from now on prohibit any acts of hostility against the vassals of His Catholic Majesty by whatsoever person or persons . . .⁴⁰

The following day Modyford wrote to offer the services of the buc-caneers to the Spanish against the French, but in such insolent tones that when both proclamation and letter came under scrutiny at the Council of the Indies in November they were dismissed out of hand. For years Morgan and Modyford had justified their actions on the basis of Spanish hostility towards Jamaica, but now their hands were tied by peaceful instructions just as that threat finally became very real and as Morgan was preparing to enjoy his marriage and invest the benefits of his ill-gotten wealth in his plantation. And as gloom settled over Port Royal at the news that the buccaneers' chief source of income had dried up, Spanish colonial officials began sending out the queen regent's declaration of war against Jamaica.⁴¹

In 1666 proposals had been made to the Council of the Indies by Flemish and Biscayan *armadores* to send privateers to America in order to fight English fire with fire, but they had been rejected due to their requirement that they be accompanied by two supply ships laden with duty-free merchandise. Now the Spanish decided to authorise colonial governors to issue *potentes de corso* (letters of marque) against the English, except there were no suitable ships available to commission apart from that of a strange bombastic Portuguese captain called Manoel Rivera Pardal. Somewhat conveniently this would provide Modyford with the necessary excuse to abandon Jamaica's newly declared peace and recommence the private war against the Spanish, when one of the most popular captains among the buccaneers was killed.⁴²

Captain Bernard Claesen Speirdijke, a Dutchman also known as Bart Nicholas, commanded the *Mary and Jane*, a small six-gun vessel with an eighteen-man crew. In January 1670 he was sent on a conciliatory mission to Cuba and anchored in Manzanillo Bay where he soon convinced the locals of his honest trading intentions and sold his cargo of much-wanted European goods. As he was leaving he was approached by a vessel flying English colours, and sent two men in a boat to welcome the newcomers. But this was Rivera in the *San Pedro y La Fama*. The Portuguese, being in possession of a letter of marque against the English, had just been raiding the Jamaican dependency of Grand Cayman where he had burned half the fishermen's huts, and sailed away with a ketch, a canoe and four children.[43] Rivera immediately captured the two men then hoisted Spanish colours and attacked, declaring, 'I come as a punishment for heretics.' Rivera had a crew of seventy and fourteen guns and in the subsequent uneven fight, despite a desperate resistance, the 'good old captain' Nicholas and four of his men were killed and the rest were forced to surrender.[44] Rivera had a great sense of his own importance and wrote an extraordinary poem about his exploits in which 'the mob all trembled at my name'. But success was so rare among the Spanish that when he reached Cartagena with four prisoners, having sent the rest home to Jamaica in their boat to tell of his glory, the city held a great fiesta in his honour. Two more ships were fitted out to support him and he was granted the distinction of flying the royal standard in his own ship, which became the *capitana* of this new squadron.[45]

Modyford and Morgan agreed that they could not deal with Rivera until they had evidence; they needed to capture one of these Spanish privateers with a commission on board. Meanwhile Modyford had to deal with the delicate matter of Robert Searle (or Searles, alias John Davis), who had been at New Providence in the Bahamas shortly after Morgan's Maracaibo raid when Spanish ships coming down from Florida sacked it. In retaliation, Searle and several other privateer captains attacked San Agustin (St Augustine) on the north-east coast of Florida. Searle and a number of fellow Jamaicans captured some Spanish supply vessels bound for San Agustin and, by holding their Spanish crew at pistol point with most of the privateers safely hidden below deck, they slipped unnoticed into Florida's capital in their floating Trojan horses. Taken completely by surprise the inhabitants – men, women and children – were killed indiscriminately, and although Searle lacked the heavy artillery necessary to reduce the fort, the houses, churches and public storehouses were looted; even sails were stripped from vessels in the harbour. At last, though vowing to return, the unwanted guests departed.[46] Modyford felt that in the light of his instructions from Arlington he would have to make an example of Searle. But the buccaneer, suspecting that he was out of favour after hearing that Modyford 'was much incensed against him for that action of St Augustine, went to Macary Bay, and there rides out of command'.[47] Eventually he ventured into town only to be immediately arrested and held until word should come from England about his punishment for the raid.[48] However, confirmation soon arrived of the Spanish commissions when a Spanish privateer, *San Nicolas de Tolentino*, encountered two small Jamaican vessels off Yucután, en route to collect logwood at Campeche. Instead of returning with them as prizes to Cuba as the Spaniards had expected to do, they discovered that their crews were unemployed buccaneers and were instead themselves captured, along with numerous papers including commissions, the queen regent's *cédula* of war against Jamaica, and news that warships were to be sent from Spain. Modyford quickly informed Arlington that the buccaneers were incensed and the planters and merchants frightened.[49] Soon afterwards Captain Thomas Rogers brought a Spanish prize into Port Royal saying the Spaniard had attacked him first, with news that Cartagena was planning 'war against Jamaica'. An Englishman from Curaçao next reported a similar proclamation had been made at Portobelo, and in early March the *Amity* of Bristol was taken off Grenada. These actions caused consternation in Jamaica where there was a great desire to avenge Nicholas, and Modyford wrote home once more asking for latitude in dealing with these Spanish depredations.[50]

In May Rivera sailed on his second cruise and attacked William Harris' sloop off the coast of Jamaica, chasing the crew inland before sailing off towards Cuba. A week later he raided Montego Bay, destroying the settlements, and on 3 July he was sighted again, this time on the south side of the island, and was shadowed along the coast by the militia. He landed to burn some houses and two days later posted an extraordinary, boastful challenge.[51] 'I am arrived to this coast and have burnt it, and I come to seeke Generall Morgan with two shippes of twenty gunns and, haveing seene this, I crave hee would come out uppon ye coast to seeke mee, that he might see ye valour of ye Spaniards.'[52] When the Council of Jamaica met to discuss the situation it was soon agreed to commission Morgan as admiral and commander-in-chief of all the buccaneers in order to attack and destroy the enemy wherever he could be located. The Spanish were going to regret that they had ever given a commission to Manoel Rivera Pardal, and his ludicrous boasting would come back to haunt them badly for, as Richard Browne, Morgan's surgeon-general, would later say, 'we doe the Spaniards more mischiefe in one hour than they can doe to us in seven yeares'.[53]

By 1670 Port Royal had twenty private men-of-war manned by around 2,000 buccaneers.[54] The prospects for privateering appeared so good that Modyford declared in July that no course could be 'more frugall, more prudentiall, more hopeful in laying a good foundation ... for the great increase of His Majesty's dominions in these parts'.[55] Indeed, at one time it may have been, certainly before large-scale planting got into full swing, yet Modyford remained concerned about how his return to the private war between Jamaica and the Spanish would be received at home. And despite Morgan's success thus far, there were already signs that the opportunities for plunder had peaked due to 'overfishing' as the privateers faced increased costs for greater risks and diminishing returns.[56] By 1671 Sir William Beeston remarked that lately the more sparsely populated Spanish territories, 'having been so infested in the dayly alarum of the privateers are kept much in armes by which planting is neg-lected'.[57] For although the 'dead carcass' of Spanish power could still occasionally provide rich pickings, it was no strategy for long-term colonial development. Consequently privateering would peak within a year before entering a steady decline, although it would linger on for another quarter of a century.[58]

Despite Rivera's desire to go after Morgan, instead he ran into John Morris and his sixty-man crew aboard Dolphin (now carrying ten guns) as they were heading out to join Morgan at Isla Vaca in October. As a terrible storm hurled both ships towards the Cuban coast, Rivera decided to take shelter in a bay, only to find Morris there ahead of him. Rivera manoeuvred to try and block the Englishman's exit but Morris foresaw the move and boarded San Pedro. Rivera was killed with a shot to the neck, and seeing their captain fall the Spanish and Indian crew panicked and jumped into the sea, where they drowned or were fin-ished off by the buccaneers. A few were later found hidden below deck and were made prisoner, including Rivera's Indian cook who joined the buccaneers in the same capacity. So ended the 'vapouring captain that so much amazed Jamaica, in burning the houses, robbing some people upon the shore and sent that insolent challenge to Admiral Morgan'.[59]

# 11

—⟨⟨⟩⟩—

# PANAMÁ

> This is the ballad of Henry Morgan
> Who troubled the sleep of the King of Spain
> With a frowsy, blowsy, lousy pack
> Of the water rats of the Spanish Main,
> Rakes and rogues and mad rapscallions
> Broken gentlemen, tatterdemallions
> Scum and scourge of the hemisphere,
> Who looted the loot of the stately galleons,
> Led by Morgan, the Buccaneer.
>
> Berton Braley, 'The Ballad of Henry Morgan'

It was not until January 1669 that Don Juan Pérez de Guzmán was cleared of the charges laid against him by the viceroy of Peru, the Conde de Lemos, and restored to his roles of president of Panamá and captain-general of Tierra Firme, with his lost salary and expenses to be repaid to him by Lemos. But a residual and lasting bitterness would blight relations between these two key figures in Spanish America, and once returned to his presidency Pérez found his requests for modest military support from the viceroy rebuffed. Nor were reinforcements forthcoming when the *galeones* arrived at Portobelo to collect two years' worth of silver and other goods for shipment to Spain; most of the men were ravaged by disease and a great many already dead. But Pérez badly needed support for, on 6 June 1670, he reported to the queen regent that he had learned from spies and prisoners that the English planned to descend on Panamá with 1,500 men via the River Chagres.[1]

This news was 'confirmed' to the pious Pérez by a Franciscan monk who preached to a horror-stricken congregation in the great cathedral of Panamá that a fellow Franciscan, Brother Gonzalo, had seen a vision in which a Jamaican man invaded the kingdom and the streets ran with fire and blood. Brother Gonzalo's vision was so vivid that he

202

commissioned an artist to recreate it, and the result was terrifying: English buccaneers ran through the streets brandishing cutlasses and pistols as grinning black demons on the rooftops set fire to the city.[2] Faced with the prospect of imminent attack Pérez took all possible steps to strengthen the defences, including the approach from the River Chagres guarded by the inadequate Fuerte San Lorenzo. But with Morgan's destruction of the *armada de barlovento* there was nothing to prevent the buccaneers from landing wherever they might choose, and his efforts were hampered by lack of resources. The city of Panamá had ossified through lack of trade, although like all Spanish colonial cities it maintained a façade of respectability – a carefully constructed replica of Spanish society, with the cathedral of San Anastasius and its tower that was the highest point in the city, seven monasteries, a convent, several churches and a hospital. But apart from a dozen stone structures including the cathedral, the supreme court, the royal stables and several houses belonging to rich merchants, most of it was built of wood and the castle of Santiago in the city was in an appalling state, having been extremely badly designed in the first place.[3]

With the preposterous Rivera having jammed his stick into the hornet's nest of Jamaica, Pérez was right to be nervous. On 1 August, three weeks after the meeting of the Council, Morgan received his commission. Modyford probably wanted fresh instructions from home, having requested them six months earlier, but in the interval there was plenty for Morgan to do in anticipation of his orders. Since the proclamation of peace, although a few buccaneers had drifted away to Tortuga, many more were away raiding, trading or otherwise engaged around the Caribbean and the Main, and it would take time for word to spread summoning them to seek fresh glories, and a general rendezvous was appointed at the old meeting place, Isla Vaca off the south coast of Española.[4] For example, Dr George Holmes had sent Humphrey Thurston to load logwood in the Bay of Campeche in his thirty-ton ship *Port Royal*. But now, and without breathing a word to Holmes, Thurston made 'of the said shipp a man of warr' by putting extra guns aboard (for a total of twelve) and signing fifty-five of the toughest buccaneers he could find; he then seized a Spanish vessel of fifty tons carrying silk, wine, new Spanish cloth and other goods. Finding that she was quicker and handier than *Port Royal* he fitted her out of the latter which he signed over to James Delliatt, despite her being 'really worth £300', and the pair of them took off to join Morgan – if it was any consolation to Holmes, he retained rights as owner.[5] Word was also sent to Tortuga whence several hundred Frenchmen were expected to join the fleet, and it was hoped the Protestants among them might be tempted to remain in Jamaica afterwards. On Jamaica itself many buccaneers had already retired and would have to seek credit in order to fit out new ships, and while this was easily obtainable it would still take time.[6]

By 24 August Morgan was ready to set off himself in *Satisfaction* (twenty-two guns), at 120 tons the largest privateer on the island, and at the last moment Modyford released Robert Searle to join him. Richard Norman commanded *Lilly*, Morgan's old flagship at Maracaibo, and Joseph Bradley the seventy-ton *Mayflower*, while Richard Dobson was aboard *Fortune* – just twenty-five tons with only six guns, but carrying a crew of thirty-five experienced buccaneers rounded up from the taverns and bordellos of Port Royal. In all Morgan led eleven ships carrying 600 men, numbers that he hoped would treble at the rendezvous.[7] Shortly after his departure a sloop caught up with the fleet summoning Morgan back to a conference with Modyford, who had finally received a letter from Arlington, dated 22 June, but was obviously uninformed of recent developments. In it Arlington dismissed Rivera's attack on Bart Nicholas as 'not at all to be wondered at after such hostilities as [Modyford's] men have acted upon their territories', and warning the governor that this private warfare was 'neither honourable nor profitable to his Majesty'. The king wished to put an end to it, and was expecting news at any moment from Sir William Godolphin in Madrid of a treaty 'as might make them and us live like good neighbours together'. This was all well and good, but what Modyford wanted were clear instructions, and Arlington had drafted the letter either very carelessly or very cunningly. He went on:

> His Majesty bids me let you know his pleasure is, that in whatever state the privateers are, at the receipt of this letter, you keepe them soe till we have a final answer from Spaine (which shall be immediately signified to you) with this condition only, that you oblige them to forebear all hostilities at land.

This probably came as a relief; the privateers being now at sea, then at sea they must stay, and Morgan agreed to follow these orders as far as possible notwithstanding the need to land on Spanish shores in order to revictual, and knowing that should he then discover enemy war preparations the king would not want him to 'spare such a place'. Modyford noted in his reply that Spain had declared war on Jamaica but was doing so on the cheap, by hiring corsairs, insufficient to do any real damage but intensely annoying all the same. He thought a 'little more suffering' would be enough to convince the Council of the Indies of 'their condition and force them to capitulations more suitable to the sociableness of man's nature'.[8] Alas, poor Spain, just a little more suffering!

At this point the correspondence with London suddenly ceased, and with negotiations poised at a delicate stage, as Peter Earle notes in his excellent account of Jamaica's private war, one can only assume that this was how London wanted things. Since Albemarle's death in early December, this way nobody could be accused of making a wrong decision except the governor of Jamaica – for, as Modyford, Morgan and the planters feared, they no longer had any friends on the Privy Council. Apart from sending the *Oxford*, the king had spent not a penny on Jamaica for years, yet he continued giving land grants to his favourites, the latest being 3,000 acres to the Earl of Clarendon, though that worthy soul had never even visited the island.[9] And plans were already afoot to replace Modyford, the buccaneers' friend, with the Spanish-speaking hispanophile representative of the merchant class, and former Cromwellian soldier, Thomas Lynch.* Arlington accepted Lynch's vision of the island as a major supplier of slaves and manufactures to the Spanish, and trade was increasingly seen as the way to prosperity.[10] Modyford was therefore condemned *in absentia* and long before Morgan embarked on the expedition that finally damned him, while Lynch's appointment on 15 January 1671 ensured that Jamaica's authorities would no longer be allowed to connive in buccaneering as Modyford had done. The king specifically required of Lynch that 'as

* The Earl of Carlisle would be appointed governor but remain in England with Lynch as lieutenant-governor, a common way of increasing the income of the nobility at public expense. As was customary on his appointment, Lynch received a knighthood.

soon as he has taken possession of that government and [Fort Charles] so as not to apprehend any ill consequences thereupon, he cause the person of Sir Thomas Modyford to be made prisoner and sent home under strong guard'.[11]

Meanwhile Morgan set off westward along the south coast of Jamaica then east along the south coast of Cuba to check for Spanish activity, and show the fleet to deter any further attacks out of Santiago de Cuba. When a storm scattered his ships he led eight of them to Tortuga where he recruited some French buccaneers, before rounding the great white cliff of Cap-Tiburón at the western end of Española into the sheltered waters between the main island and Isla Vaca on 12 September. Already some buccaneers were waiting but many more were expected, and while Morgan was gathering his fleet he sent his vice-admiral, Edward Collier, with six ships to the Main to secure provisions for 'the whole fleet' and obtain intelligence. Collier with his 400 men and their additional supplies were vital to success, and he had been away eleven weeks before returning on 8 December having sacked Río de la Hacha, where he missed 200,000 pesos hidden in the fort. But he had taken a ship from Cartagena full of maize and ransomed the town for another 5,000 bushels. He also brought thirty-eight prisoners taken from a Spanish privateer, *La Galliardena*, a former French privateer of Tortuga that had been in consort with Rivera, and whose captain made a statement that Cartagena was 'in arms offensive to the English people'.[12] By the time Collier returned, Morgan's numbers had swelled considerably as men arrived in small open boats and canoes, all desperate to take part in what promised to be the biggest and most lucrative of Morgan's expeditions so far, and they included many *boucaniers* from Tortuga and Española with their own muskets – crack shots if indifferent seamen. So many men arrived, in fact, including John Morris and *Dolphin*, that Morgan had not enough ship space to carry them all, a problem exacerbated by a storm on 7 October that drove all the ships apart from *Satisfaction* on to the coast, though fortunately all but three were successfully refloated.[13] Nevertheless, it meant he could not expect to sail before early December, and he sent to Jamaica for additional shipping of whatever type was available.[14]

Among his reinforcements were three French ships from Tortuga and eight vessels carrying 400 men from Jamaica, including a group just returned from an unauthorised expedition of their own. To protect Granada the governor of Nicaragua had built a fort some forty miles upriver of the mouth of the River San Juan manned by seventy musketeers and four light guns. Completed in 1667 the fort was named San Carlos in honour of the new king, Carlos II, and like him it suffered from severe congenital defects. Wood soon rots in the jungle, but far worse was the fort's situation: it was not only poorly chosen but it had been assumed that the garrison would be able to hold out until relief came from Granada.[15] Three years later Laurens Prins entered the estuary with 200 men after they had failed in an attempt to sack Mompos, 150 miles inland along the River Magdalena in modern Colombia.[16] With the palisades already rotten, the fort's commander, Gonzalo Naguera y Robboledo, had only thirty-seven effectives left, who nevertheless put up a stout resistance killing six of the attackers and wounding another eight. But despite sending a messenger upriver he was forced to surrender, and the buccaneers double-manned a canoe and set off in pursuit of the messenger, who was run down three days later. Granada was sacked once again with great brutality, Prins sending a priest's head in a basket to demand 70,000 pesos' ransom for his remaining prisoners, and although the booty eventually taken was not great, it was enough to hold out the promise of more in the future.[17] When these desperadoes returned to Jamaica they were reproved by Modyford for attacking the Spanish without a commission, but he thought it best 'not to press the matter' and instead sent them to join Morgan, who was so impressed with his new recruit, a genuine fighting captain, that he made him third in command after himself and Collier.[18]

As the buccaneers' preparations went forward Modyford was beset by rumours that Prince Rupert was due in the region with a large fleet and that Jamaica might be sold back to Spain. In such a state of uncertainty it is unsurprising that he was prepared to turn a blind eye to the transgressions of the buccaneers, the only defence Jamaica had.[19] But among their faults was a complete inability to keep quiet about their future plans. When Collier's men raided Río de la Hacha they loudly blabbed about the growing numbers of their mates at Isla Vaca, and how they planned to descend on either Cartagena or Panamá by way of the River Chagres. But the Caribbean was always as awash with rumours of impending raids as it was with buccaneers themselves, and preparations were made at the most likely target, Cartagena, as best they could – which thanks to a chronic lack of resources was not very well.[20] As 1670 drew to a close news arrived of a fresh 'American' treaty signed between England and Spain which went most of the way to regularising the English position in the Indies and which granted most English demands. The Treaty of Madrid, signed by Godolphin on 21 July, was ratified in London on 28 November and a further eight months were allowed for its publication in the Indies; but although unofficial news reached Cartagena at the end of December nobody believed it and official news from Spain, including a copy of the treaty, did not arrive until 12 February 1671.[21]

Meanwhile at Panamá Pérez learned of the gathering at Isla Vaca only on 15 December 1670, just three days before Morgan sailed out from Cap Tiburón. Pérez was convinced that Panamá was the buccaneers' target and set to work to prepare his defences based on the coast, the isthmus of Darién, and the city itself. Although it was possible to land at numerous places along the Caribbean littoral of Panamá, such a large force would probably do so at Portobelo, or travel up the River Chagres to Venta de Cruces and then march overland. Portobelo was already a much tougher proposition than the city Morgan had raided two years earlier: the castles had been improved and the garrison was close to full strength as Pérez sent supplies and 200 men to reinforce it, including nearly all the regular troops in Panamá.[22] He also did everything possible to reinforce the Chagres position, more than doubling the garrison of Castello San Lorenzo to 360 men by sending his fifty remaining regular soldiers of the Panamá garrison and seventy Spanish and eighty mulatto and free black militia. He also sent supplies and specialists, including a 'very skilled gunner'. The *castellan*, Don Pedro de Elizalde, reported that even 'if all England were to come, they would not capture' it.[23] In addition Pérez made a former *castellan* of San Lorenzo, Francisco Gonzalez Salado, captain of the river itself with some 400 militiamen, mostly local Indians, blacks and mulattos, based on Venta de Cruces with four stockaded strongpoints prepared downriver, the largest being where the river narrowed at Barro Colorado. Finally Pérez considered the defence of the city itself, and although its mostly slave population could not be trusted with arms, he could muster about a thousand men. But having deployed his best troops forwards, he could have little confidence in their martial abilities.[24]

Aware that peace threatened to break out at any moment Morgan could not afford to wait at Isla Vaca for ever. With Collier's return the buccaneers set about their prisoners to obtain evidence of Spanish belligerent intent against Jamaica, and the captain of La Galliardena was hanged when he refused to say what the buccaneers wanted to hear. But two 'pityfull spirited Spaniards' were prepared to do so, and Morgan's secretary John Peake carefully noted their depositions to provide the necessary excuse for the planned invasion of Spanish territory.[25] Morgan's fleet now comprised some thirty-six vessels of varying sizes with Morgan's own Satisfaction the largest, but only thirteen of the others carried more than ten guns and seventy-five men, and five of the Jamaica vessels carried no guns at all. Some 1,800 men had gathered – approximately one-third of them Frenchmen, representing about 80 per cent of the available manpower of Saint-Domingue and Tortuga, and it represented a tremendous concentration of pirate power to the frightened prisoners.[26] There was also a woman, who according to Juan de Lao, the Indian cook captured on Rivera's ship, was 'small and old and English and it was publicly said that she was a witch whom the English had brought along to prophesy for them and through her diabolical arts to advise them what to do'.[27]

On 12 December Morgan gathered his captains for a council of war where he issued commissions to those without them and articles of association were drawn up, which, besides offering more generous than usual compensation for injury, included additional payment for acts of courage such as five pesos per grenade thrown into a fort.[28] Morgan anticipated that grenades would be an important factor in this campaign and considerable numbers were carried, along with other bombs and incendiaries. Then with administrative arrangements concluded came the discussion of likely targets, of which there were only four realistic candidates: Santiago de Cuba promised too little gain for too much danger, while Veracruz (like Portobelo) was too much of a ghost town without a flota in port, and besides, the buccaneers had no nicely signed evidence of its hostile intent towards Jamaica; this left only Cartagena and Panamá. After lengthy discussion a unanimous decision was made in favour of the latter, despite its position seventy miles across the isthmus.[29] None of the buccaneers had ever been there but its legendary aura as flowing with gold and silver made it irresistible to men inspired by dreams of untold riches, and the captains duly signed a declaration that:

> having seriously considered of what place may prove most advantageous for the safety of the English and more especially for the security of his Majesty's island of Jamaica to prevent the invasions of the Spanish ... [they had decided] to take Panama, the President thereof having granted severall commissions against the English to the great annoyance of the island of Jamaica and our merchantmen – as by the oath of two Spaniards hath been made most evidently appeare.[30]

The declaration along with depositions of the prisoners were then filed, thus providing legal cover for an attack to be launched in the pursuit of profit on the basis of trumped-up intelligence of a non-existent threat. The council then got down to discussing the precise details of how to achieve their aim.

On 18 December the fleet sailed and made rapid progress southwestward, arriving six days later at Santa Catalina. The island had reverted to lethargy since its recapture from the English, and having blocked the exit from the port, Morgan landed more than a thousand buccaneers. At first inclement weather aided the Spanish and they were able to defend themselves on the smaller island. According to Exquemelin, although he is unsupported by any Spanish accounts, Morgan then entered a curious negotiation with the Spanish commander, Don Joseph Ramírez de Layva, seemingly designed to save the latter's reputation. The buccaneers were to make a great show of fury and the garrison an equally pretentious one of resistance, then the latter would surrender. Morgan agreed with the proviso that if any of his men were killed the garrison would be slaughtered to the last man. In the ensuing battle much powder was burned and nobody died, and all proceeded satisfactorily.[31] Morgan was now free to pursue the main objective of the campaign. Realising the importance of the castle guarding the River Chagres, on 30 December he sent 470 men in three ships under Lieutenant-Colonel Joseph Bradley to secure it. It appears he did not want to reveal his strength and trusted Bradley's skill enough to send him against the fortress with scarcely more men than garrisoned it.[32] Morgan, meanwhile, rounded up all the slaves and plunder to be found on Santa Catalina, amounting to some £500 worth, and thoroughly destroyed the fortifications after deciding he could not afford to garrison it. Among the prisoners he sought guides to lead him to Panamá, and offered them freedom and a share of the loot in return. Unsurprisingly there were several volunteers, including an Indian called Antonillo who knew the river well, and Morgan set sail a few days after Bradley.[33]

When lookouts reported that 300–400 pirates had landed and three ships were anchored in El Portete de Naranjos (The Port of Oranges) four miles from San Lorenzo, the Spanish remained confident that they could see them off, particularly as they had been expecting anything up to 3,000. Better still, scouts' reports suggested that the pirates would use the same approach route as their last attempt in 1656, and Don Pedro de Elizalde had ordered an ambush. But Bradley was an experienced soldier: he had been standing offshore for two days in order to get a good look at his objective, and he had made a sound appreciation. He landed further down the coast and marching his men quickly despite having to hack through dense undergrowth, he covered four miles in two hours and avoided the ambush to arrive behind the castle. But an assault would still be extremely hazardous as the buccaneers would have to cross a wide stretch of open ground and a gully before reaching the palisades of the castle itself. Although he had no artillery, Bradley decided on an immediate assault. But in the teeth of fierce fire from artillery, muskets and Indian bows, the buccaneers were driven back with heavy losses.[34]

Determined not to be beaten by mere Spaniards the buccaneers returned to the assault an hour later, but once more the fire through which they advanced proved too heavy for them. The defenders danced and sang 'Victoria! Victoria!' as it seemed they had prevailed, but Bradley's leadership would prove its worth: the fort might contain little of value but the buccaneers, too, had their pride. As evening fell they rushed once more across the open ground and this time reached the gully. The attackers' fire forced the defenders, now silhouetted against the afterglow of the sunset, to keep their heads down, and their

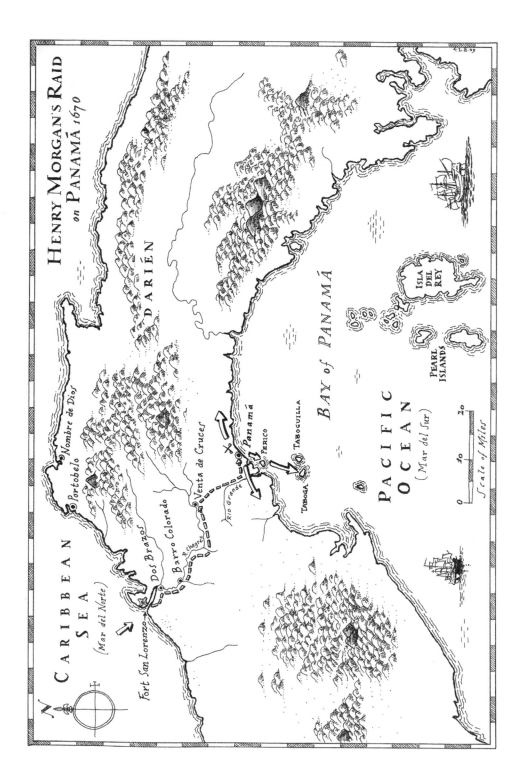

HENRY MORGAN'S RAID
on PANAMÁ 1670

E.L.E. '09

CARIBBEAN
SEA
(Mar del Norte)

N

Nombre de Dios

Portobelo

Fort San Lorenzo

Dos Brazos

Barro Colorado

R. chagres

Venta de Cruces

Rio Grande

D A R I É N

Panamá

Perico

Taboguilla

Taboga

BAY of PANAMÁ

PACIFIC
OCEAN
(Mar del Sur)

ISLA
DEL
REY

PEARL
ISLANDS

Scale of Miles

0          10          20

grenades managed to ignite the reed and palm thatch that provided a roof above the palisade. While Pérez had been lingering in gaol Bracamonte had criticised the earth, wood and thatch construction of San Lorenzo, for what might have been fine in the wet season was now, at the height of the dry season, desiccated and horribly vulnerable to incendiaries.[35] The grenadiers were assisted by the musketeers when one of them demonstrated an effective means of fire-starting.

> One of the buccaneers was pierced through the shoulder by an arrow; in a fury he wrenched it out, took a wad of cotton from his pouch, tied it to the arrowhead and set fire to it. When it was well alight, he stuck the arrow in his musket and shot it into the palm-leaf thatch of some houses within the fortress walls. The other buccaneers, seeing his idea, began to do the same. At last, they succeeded in setting the roofs of two or three houses on fire.[36]

Once they took hold the fires spread swiftly causing consternation but not yet panic among the garrison, as Elizalde quickly organised a bucket chain to fight the flames. But a large bronze gun that had inflicted considerable damage on the attackers then blew up, ripping a large breach in the main curtain wall, and as the buccaneers slowly worked their way forward, hurling grenades as they went, another huge explosion took the garrison's reserves of arms and ammunition up into the night air.

The morale of the garrison was now severely weakened. Fire and death at the hands of savages seemed unavoidable, and by midnight many defenders had begun to slip away towards the river to escape in canoes moored at the water's edge. But at least half of them remained alongside the *castellan* as dawn approached and the final assault seemed inevitable. The Spanish might have no powder or ammunition, but swords and lances were in any case better suited to such close-quarter fighting, and when the buccaneers attacked at first light they were twice thrown back with appalling losses. But they regrouped with the Frenchmen of Tortuga and Española given the place of honour in the van. This time they broke through, and those fleeing upriver could now hear the French singing 'Victoire! victoire!' Yet still the fight was not over. Elizalde gathered some seventy survivors around him, and refusing all quarter they fought to the last, taking many heretic dogs with them, until Elizalde himself gave the buccaneers no choice but to shoot him down. The buccaneers had never been in so desperate an action: Bradley lay dying of wounds received, and, apart from thirty men killed in action, another seventy-six buccaneers would die of their wounds, while many more were badly injured. Such appalling casualties in their first action boded ill for the rest of the expedition as they still had to fight their way to Panamá.

News of the disaster at San Lorenzo reached Pérez the day after at Panamá, where he lay sick in bed. The surgeons were worried and there was talk of calling a priest, but the sixty-two-year-old did not despair at the loss of his best men or at the knowledge that the road to the city lay open. He still had many men left and faith in divine providence, and he rose from his sickbed to rally his citizens and appeal for support from Cartagena. At San Lorenzo the surviving buccaneers under Captain (now styled Major) Richard Norman set to work to rebuild the defences and await the main fleet. This proceeded to sail into the mouth of the river amid wild cheering from both sides, and straight on to the Leja reef. *Satisfaction* struck with an almighty crash which brought down her masts and rigging and threw several men overboard, and was followed by four other ships before the remainder put up their helms and steered clear. The fleet had already lost two ships on Santa Catalina, but the buccaneers seem always to have been so confident of their ability to find other ships that they did not much care about the ones they had. They saved most of the men – ten drowned – and important stores, and ultimately their carelessness had no adverse effect on the operation. Morgan spent a week at San Lorenzo, then, leaving Norman and some 300 men as a garrison, he set off upstream on 19 January 1671 with some 1,400 men in seven of the smaller ships towing thirty-six boats and canoes.[37]

Waiting to halt his progress across the isthmus was Gonzalez Solado and his 400 militiamen, who between them mustered only 210 firearms, 114 lances and 69 bows. Solado was at Barro Colorado, the strongest of his stockades, when news reached him of the fall of San Lorenzo, and leaving Captain Luis de Castillo in command he retired upstream to Barbacoas, the last stockade, sending forward to Castillo every man he could muster in the hope that they could be replaced by men from

Panamá. He then remained at Barbacoas which was, he said, a convenient place for distributing men and orders. Pérez was inclined to take his whole army forward to Venta de Cruces and meet the English there, as his predecessor had done, but was persuaded against this as the buccaneers would probably have good guides and could bypass the main river via its tributary the Gatun. Instead he sent just two companies forward, and as at this stage he knew of only 300–400 buccaneers who had already lost a lot of men, it seemed a strong relief force might retake San Lorenzo. Three captains then in gaol in Panamá on an unknown charge offered to lead such a force, and Pérez accepted. They took 150 men with orders to collect another 150 from Solado and attempt to regain San Lorenzo. Meanwhile Morgan advanced upriver through the verdant country, scattering the frightened population before him, until on the morning of 12 January their guide warned that Barro Colorado was close by. Morgan sent a strong party to creep through the undergrowth and assault it, which they did with a great cheer, only to discover that the enemy had fled. Castillo had lost his nerve and called a *junta* of the officers who decided to burn the post and all its provisions.[38]

This was more of a blow to the buccaneers than might be expected, as they had planned to gain food on the march from the places they passed through. They still had another fifty or sixty miles to go and the ships could go no further with the river level being very low. Now the men would have to march, hacking their way painfully slowly through dense undergrowth of bramble and thorn, crossing endless rivers and streams. Seen from the river, the forest of mahogany, palm and bamboo was vividly illuminated by the bright red passion-flowers now in full bloom and by brilliantly coloured parrots and humming birds, while the chattering of monkeys could be heard. But as the men crashed through the jungle they found no sign of the game that had seemed so abundant; the noise they made drove it away. Yet there were innumerable biting things to contend with – snakes, mosquitoes, sandflies, centipedes, tarantulas, scorpions, wood ticks, jiggers and enormous black and red ants. As they reached each stockade the buccaneers raced forward to seize what they hoped would be a feast, only to find that Solado had now ordered them all to be abandoned and destroyed. Not a morsel was to be found. Solado also abandoned Barbacoas and retired on Venta de Cruces, hoping to make a final stand there. Meanwhile the buccaneers became increasingly desperate. At one stage they found a small barn with some maize still in it and this was devoured on the spot. After three days' march they arrived at Venta de Cruces. They were now reduced to a straggling rabble, but were prepared to fight all the same, driven by the promise of food at last.[39]

Yet their hopes were dashed once more as plumes of smoke were seen rising from the buildings. Pérez had struggled there from his sickbed only to see his army disintegrate as the buccaneers approached, and finding 'myself with two-thirds less men through the fear which infested them I *had* to retreat to Panamá'.[40] All had been torched at Venta de Cruces apart from the royal stable and customs house, where sixteen jars of Peruvian wine were found, which made desperately hungry men sick. The only food to be found was a few stray dogs which were shot and eaten, but Morgan urged his men on: this was no time to turn back. As the terrain became hillier, so they found themselves subject to ambushes, although these proved ineffective. By the morning of the fifth day the buccaneers had crossed the watershed and were marching now across savannah, when to their joy they breasted a hill and saw cattle and horses that the Spanish had carelessly failed to drive off. 'I commanded a general halt to bee made,' reported Morgan, 'and our men did kill horses and beefe enough to serve them all.'[41] Fed and rested during the midday heat, the buccaneers were now ready to march again and to fight. Having defeated the rivers and jungle, as the tiled roofs of the city finally hove into view they 'gave three cheers and threw their caps into the air for joy, as if they had already gained the victory. It was decided to sleep there, and march down on Panamá in the morning. They pitched camp on the plain, and began to beat the drums and blow the trumpets and wave their flags, as if at a celebration.'[42]

On the morning of Saturday 25 January Pérez went to mass in the cathedral and read a proclamation calling on the citizens to defend their city, then he distributed his worldly wealth among its religious institutions. On the Monday morning the city began to empty of women, children and the elderly, and most of the men followed Pérez to Mata Asnillos, his chosen site for battle. He had 400 cavalry, which was his only advantage; the rest of his troops were hopelessly ill equipped or ill prepared to stand against experienced and hardened fighters like the buccaneers. And although one Spaniard was heard to declare in a loud voice, when Morgan's advance guard first appeared on Tuesday evening, that the pirates were 'no more than six hundred drunkards', his comrades' hearts began to waver as the rest of the buccaneers arrived, and another officer was heard to proclaim that he had two good horses ready for flight and everyone else should get their mules ready for the same purpose. Despite the immediate arrest of the officer the damage was done; too many among the Spaniards heartily agreed.[43]

At about 7 o'clock next morning the buccaneers advanced towards them in a column of four battalions of about 300 men each. The van was commanded by Laurens Prins and John Morris, followed by Morgan with what would become the right wing when they deployed into line, then Edward Collier with the left wing, and the reserve led by Colonel Bledry Morgan (no relation), a newcomer and 'good old soldier' who had arrived from Jamaica with a message for his namesake which at least 'gave no countermand' to their purpose.[44] Facing them were some 1,200 poorly armed Spanish militiamen, only about half of them carrying firearms, together with some 400 horse who might be expected to cause more trouble as the buccaneers carried no pikes. As Morgan approached he was better able to appreciate the situation, and saw that instead of assaulting this large body frontally there was a small hill to the right of the Spanish from which he could attack their flank. He ordered his vanguard with the *boucaniers* to the fore to wheel left where they disappeared into a gully and swiftly secured the high ground. The Spanish horse on that flank charged but were just as swiftly repulsed by accurate fire from the French sharpshooters, the survivors immediately departing in the direction of Panamá. But at about the same time the Spanish foot on the opposite flank started to rush forward, thinking that the buccaneer main body was retreating as it followed the vanguard into the gully, and there was nothing their officers could do to control them.[45]

This rush was stopped in its tracks by a single well-aimed volley, and the charge immediately became a rout as the ill-trained Spanish turned to flee. Pérez found himself alone, but nevertheless went forward towards the enemy to comply with my word to the Virgin, which was to die in her defence. I held my staff high, like a mast, beside my face, and they struck it with a bullet. God permitted them to kill many that were sheltering themselves behind my horse but, although no person ever passed through such a great number of bullets, God our Lord let me stay alive to endure the torment of giving Your Majesty the account of so great a disaster.[46]

With the army of Panamá no more, the president had no choice but to ride away from the field, a broken man incapable of doing any more to protect his city or the surrounding district. His final desperate plan to have two herds of oxen stampeded at the buccaneer line had come to nought, and now one of the richest prizes in Spanish America lay helpless before the attackers.[47] But as they hurried to cover the remaining distance to Panamá they heard a resounding detonation as the city's magazines were blown, followed by more explosions as another 200 barrels of powder that had been placed in houses throughout the city went up, while more fires were started by militiamen applying flaming torches to the wooden houses. The buccaneers rushed forward against limited and sporadic resistance and tried desperately to prevent these acts of destruction and to stop the citizens escaping with their portable valuables, only to quench their thirst on broached wine barrels as the situation dissolved into chaos. At four in the afternoon the last ships in the harbour at Perico set sail carrying the remaining nuns and other fugitives away, leaving a scene of complete devastation with huge columns of smoke obscuring the sun as it settled in the west.[48]

The buccaneers struggled to save what they could from the flames before giving up the struggle at around midnight. 'Thus was consumed the famous and antyent city of Panama,' wrote Morgan nonchalantly in his report.[49] It would prove to be the city's epitaph, for the Spanish never rebuilt it, allowing the jungle to reclaim the site when they later erected a new city along the coast at Perico. Only a few public buildings of stone were spared as the ruins of what should have been the richest prize in all Spanish America, one that had eluded Drake himself, lay smouldering at Morgan's feet.

Now the buccaneers set about the task of unearthing the silver that had lured them here in the first place. If perishables such as cloth and silk had been consumed in the flames, the most valuable treasure had been evacuated on three large ships to Ecuador while much portable silver had been carried away by the fugitives. Nevertheless hiding places in cisterns and other places had also been revealed where large items of gold and silver plate were still to be found, and the poor return was improved beyond the city. A barque was seized at La Tasca down the coast, and this enabled others to be taken. Once waterborne, the buccaneers under the command of Robert Searle swept quickly through the defenceless islands of the bay, but Exquemelin says that as they were searching for refugees on the island of Taboga they found a store of wine, and the galleon *Santissima Trinidada* 'loaded with the King of Spain's silver, together with all the jewels and treasure of the foremost merchants of Panamá', was missed only because Searle could not persuade his men to stop 'drinking and sporting with a group of Spanish women'.[50]

At the same time prisoners were being rounded up on the mainland and their hiding places easily located. Every day, wrote William Frogg, 'our men marched out in parties, sometimes 100, sometimes 40, sometimes 10 in a party, and took prisoners every day, but never saw an enemy to face them'.[51] The threat of torture would usually be enough to reveal others and their often pitiful stock of treasure, a bag of coins, a few jewels or holy items. In due course Morgan claimed that 3,000 prisoners were collected, mostly people of little consequence, although those with smooth hands or fancy clothes could expect closer scrutiny and more severe treatment, for the buccaneers were experts at persuading Spaniards to yield up their valuables. Yet surgeon Richard Browne later insisted that reports of atrocities were greatly exaggerated.

What was in fight and heat of blood in pursuit of a flying enemy I presume pardonable. As to their women, I know or never heard of any thing offered beyond their wills. Something I know was cruely executed by Capt. Collier in killing a friar in the field after quarter was given, but for the Admiral he was noble enough to the vanquished enemy.[52]

In fact the Spanish were quite used to torture and brutality themselves, but what shocked them in the aftermath of the capture of Panamá was that so many of the victims should die as a result of it, apparently a consequence of frustration on the part of the buccaneers at the paltry spoils they were gathering. One way they might have increased their spoils would have been to sail south and attack Peru, but though some apparently planned to do so, Morgan was impatient to get back to Jamaica.[53]

Meanwhile Pérez had retreated seventy miles to Nata where, a week after the fall of Panamá, he finally issued a proclamation calling for a relief army to clear away the heretics – not that he could do much by now – and fewer than 300 men were mustered. In defeat he was lethargic, and only sent envoys to the Conde de Lemos and to Porto-belo about two weeks after his defeat at the battle of Mata Asnillos, by which time news had arrived by other means, and it was three weeks before he got around to reporting the disaster to the queen regent in which he sought to put the best possible gloss on affairs. From Porto-belo Governor Pedro de Ulloa wrote to Morgan demonstrating a remarkably accurate and detailed knowledge of events, and thanks to the testimony of Juan de Lao, who had since escaped the buccaneers, accused Morgan of knowingly acting in contravention of the Treaty of Madrid. But this feeble remonstrance was the only counter the Spanish could muster, and we do not even know if Morgan received the letter.[54] At the end of February, following an occupation of some four weeks, he decided it was time to leave, and the buccaneers set off past the battlefield towards Venta de Cruces, trailed by 175 mules loaded with booty and by over 500 prisoners, mostly slaves. From Venta de Cruces the journey was made easier by the rains that had now swollen the River Chagres, enabling them to return to their ships by boat. They found that the garrison at San Lorenzo had been busy scouring the surrounding countryside. 'There was not a man on the coast whom they did not take prisoner, nor a horse, a mule or a cow or any other kind of animal, grain or fruit which they did not kill or collect for their sustenance as a result of their great hunger and lack of provisions.'[55]

After a few days San Lorenzo was destroyed and the expedition prepared to disperse homewards. The treasure was divided after a thorough search, at least according to Exquemelin, to make sure nobody was concealing anything, an unusual step that seems to have caused some murmuring among the French as it was customary simply to swear an oath to that effect. The spoils proved disappointing, amounting to some £30,000 among twice as many men as at Portobelo two years earlier, and causing further disquiet as many buccaneers refused to believe that everything had been declared and others thought an unfair value had been put on gems and bullion, 'for which Morgan was publicly accused'.[56] Whether Morgan had swindled them or not, the fraternal spirit that once united the brotherhood of the coast had by now dissolved as Peter Earle notes; here was 'an ugly crowd of bitter, disappointed men, grumbling at the smallness of their pay'.[57] Morgan did not hang around and departed without even signalling the other vessels in the fleet, and in due course the rest of the expedition followed. But while Morgan made straight for Jamaica, many others went looking for more plunder elsewhere and most, perhaps four-fifths, never returned to Jamaica. In Port Royal the grumbling grew louder.[58]

At a council meeting in June 1671 Morgan's report was read out and he received public thanks for having cowed the Spanish. Sir James Modyford agreed that 'we are prettie well revenged for their burning our houses on ye north and south side of this island and threatening more when we intended and proclaimed peace'.[59] Governor Modyford was now trying to implement that peace and in May wrote to his counterpart in Puerto Rico thanking him for receipt of copies of the treaty between their respective crowns, stating that he had yet to receive copies from home. A similar correspondence was carried on with Española. It seems London deliberately kept Modyford and Morgan in the dark to allow for one last great coup, knowing that blame could be diverted on to the principals; and despite receiving his commission in early January, Lynch did not relieve Modyford until 1 July. He arrived with two royal ships, *Assistance* and *Welcome* – the first to be sent since *Oxford* blew up – and was greeted with full honours by Modyford and Morgan. Then, following a formal dinner of welcome, the revocation of Modyford's commission was read out, at which the people 'seemed not much pleased', commented Lynch.[60]

Lynch also carried orders for Modyford's arrest, an event which he was to manage as circumspectly as possible. He waited six weeks, during which time Modyford gave him every assistance and even accommodated him in his own home, while Lynch assiduously built up his own party with the distribution of honours and became spokesman for the planters. But he remained wary of antagonising the buccaneers and made his move only when news arrived from London that Modyford's son had been detained as hostage to his father's good behaviour. Modyford was lured aboard *Assistance* on a pretext and then arrested; he behaved with considerable dignity, protesting only the manner of his apprehension. Lynch appears to have been considerably embarrassed by his behaviour in the matter and sought to reassure the former governor that his life and estate were not in danger. He also had instructions to issue a general amnesty to the buccaneers, including Morgan, if they agreed to return to Jamaica and submit within a certain period. Modyford, it seemed, was to be London's sole scapegoat not only for earlier buccaneer depredations, also for the sack of Panamá.[61]

# 12

## FRENCH SERVICE

Where'er thy navy spreads her canvas wings,
Homage to thee, and peace to all she brings;
The French and Spaniard, when thy flags appear,
Forget their hatred, and consent to fear.
So Jove from Ida did both hosts survey,
And when he pleased to thunder, part the fray.
Ships heretofore in seas like fishes sped,
The mighty still upon the smaller fed;
Thou on the deep imposest nobler laws,
And by that justice hast removed the cause
Of those rude tempests, which for rapine sent,
Too oft, alas, involved the innocent.

Edmund Waller, 'To the King, On his Navy'

Since its arrival in the 1640s sugar had quickly become England's leading colonial import. Sugar, not plunder, as Morgan now realised, was the way to sustained riches. When the English first landed, Jamaica had only seven sugar works producing negligible amounts. The real planting of the island had begun in 1664 when Modyford brought 700 experienced planters from Barbados and himself set out a fine plantation. But by 1671, having concentrated his energies on privateering, and despite the presence of some 9,000 African slaves, there were fewer whites on the island than there had been seven years earlier, with only fifty-seven plantations and exports running at around 1,000 hogsheads (each 1,000 pounds) per annum.[1]

Sir Thomas Lynch found Jamaica in a rough state; the population was scattered and demoralised with many settlements in need of attention. Lynch, being strong-minded and purposeful, was determined to drive the buccaneers away and expand agriculture by encouraging settlers to take up land where buccaneers had been squatting. However, the capital generated by buccaneering was being steadily reinvested in planting, and this would expand rapidly: by 1684 there were 246 plantations, and by the end of the decade production was fast approaching that of Barbados.[2] Lynch also promised the islanders that peaceful trade would be not only more honourable, but infinitely more profitable than buccaneering, and he sent messages of peace to Spanish ports in the Indies hoping to open trade links. When he was rebuffed he complained bitterly that the Spanish were 'the most ungrateful, senseless people in the world'.[3] But the prospect of trade with the Spanish attracted merchants to Port Royal all the same. Colonists could buy goods more cheaply, and dispose of their own produce more quickly – very important where perishable agricultural produce was concerned – and thereby created an economic logic too strong to be denied, however much the Spanish authorities might frown upon it.[4] This trade was normally carried out in bays and creeks away from the main towns, but the trade in slaves, for which the Spanish continued to rely on middlemen, helped open the doors of the large towns and provide cover for the smuggling of manufactures.[5]

In August Lynch issued a proclamation that promised pardon not only to those who had followed Morgan but to all who had followed 'the Course' as privateering was known since 1660. Those who came in would receive thirty-five acres of uncleared land, although this was hardly likely to appeal to seamen, a great many of whom already had experience of trying to scrape a living from a smallholding and were well aware of the fate such ventures faced in a sugar economy where they could never hope to afford slaves. But there was an alternative: logwood.[6] Logwood found a ready market in Europe that had yet to be fully exploited. The cutters lived rough and free, much as the original *boucaniers* had done, labouring thigh-high in water with their arms stained red from the dye and reeking of the sweet, cloying yellow logwood flowers. Many of them, being former buccaneers, would enjoy drinking binges lasting for days, and all liked to keep well clear of authority.[7] By the autumn of 1670 there were a dozen ships at Campeche, Cabo Gracias a Dios, along the Mosquito Coast and in other 'deserted' (Spanish-free) places. Lynch soon realised that logwood-cutting was resented by the Spanish and might neutralise his efforts to effect a peace. He begged repeatedly for directions from England regarding it and in the meantime decided to connive at the business, although he compelled all who brought the wood into Port Royal to swear that they had not stolen it or done violence to the Spanish.[8] The English authorities were happy to turn a blind eye to this enterprise, logwood was fetching £20–£35 per ton, and by July 1671 there were said to be forty vessels on the logwood coasts with some 2,000 tons cut that year worth over £40,000, which made it four times more valuable than sugar exports.[9]

A year later there were 900 men working on Beef Island and Triste in the Bay of Campeche, a great many of them former buccaneers. The Spanish, however, were outraged, and they sought to capture any English ships they could; they sent their own privateers, including Mateo Guarín, Juan Corso, Arturo Brea, Francisco Ugáz, Manoel Antonio Maldonado and the Sagonazos brothers, who together would account for at least 150 'pirate' craft between 1672 and the end of 1675.[10] But the Spanish were not above employing English and Dutch buccaneers to harass the cutters. Following the sack of Panamá, Reyning and Lecat had continued their patrolling of the Gulf of Mexico and were harrying a Spanish coastguard vessel when they ran into HMS *Assistance*. She forced them to flee to Campeche where they were arrested and severely punished, and threatened with death if they did not submit. These renegade buccaneers accepted the role of coastguards and even came to embrace Catholicism, and on their first patrol in the Laguna de Téminos captured four English vessels. On 28 April 1672 Reyning sailed from Campeche aboard the *Seviliaen* to carry the retired governor Fernando Francisco de Escobedo to Tabasco, arriving on 18 July with a hold full of cacao and brazilwood. But in August Reyning learned of the renewed war between England, France and Holland and set off out to sea for an unknown destination. When Lecat returned he sailed off to search for his friend, but neither was ever heard of again.[11] In the same month Morgan was taken aboard HMS *Welcome* as a prisoner, although Lynch wrote beseeching Lord Arlington to favour him 'in all you may with Honour and Justice'.[12] Despite initial hopes that Spanish anger would be soothed over the sack of Panamá by blaming Modyford, it seemed the Spanish would not be satisfied until the perpetrator of this most heinous act of piracy was also seen to be punished.

Meanwhile, of all the privateers hired by the Spanish to harass the logwood-cutters, the most notorious was the Irishman Captain Philip FitzGerald, operating under the name Felipe Geraldino. He was first issued with a local *guardacosta* (coastguard) commission from Havana in late 1672 and soon captured Matthew Fox's *Humility* out of London, and Timothy Stamp and other crew members were so ill treated that they died at his hands.[13] Lynch complained that this Spanish counter-action cost Jamaica greater losses than seven years of Modyford's wars and that the Treaty of Madrid allowed free English navigation; but the Spanish riposted that the treaty made no mention of trade and that logwood was therefore contraband and the Englishmen who cut it were thieves. On 22 June 1672 the queen regent issued a *cédula* declaring logwood-cutters to be 'pirates', and in May 1673 another of FitzGerald's captures caused diplomatic ructions.[14] The 130-ton merchantman *Virgin* under Edmond Cooke, bound for London from Jamaica, was condemned at Havana for carrying logwood. Cooke sought redress in Madrid which was offered only grudgingly, and he would later turn pirate and raid the Spanish.[15] Meanwhile Lynch reported in July that forty English ships had been lost as a result of Spanish counter-measures against the logwood-cutters.[16] Legal argument and counter-argument ensued during which time Lynch was replaced in January 1674 by John, second Lord Vaughan, an inexperienced outsider, and the logwood-cutters were told that they continued the business at their own risk. But with Vaughan's arrival in Jamaica returned the redoubtable duo, Modyford and Morgan. Morgan, the scourge of the Indies, spent little time as a prisoner, for Spanish desire for revenge soon withered, even towards Modyford. And after a sojourn in London where he was knighted Morgan now returned to Jamaica as lieutenant-governor, judge of the court of vice-admiralty and a member of Council. Morgan's intentions of defending the buccaneers' interests greatly alarmed the Spanish, and nobody, Lynch tartly informed Arlington, 'ever thought it possible that his Majesty should send the Admirall of the privateers to govern this Island!'[17] Despite being in no position actually to employ buccaneers after he returned to Jamaica, Morgan nevertheless soon proved a good friend to his old drinking chums, and recommended the best of them to d'Ogeron at Saint-Domingue, so that a steady stream of experienced Englishmen strengthened the hand of the French there and at Tortuga. He received a commission for this service and as a consequence those tenths and fifteenths were lost by the crown of England to the crown of France.[18] Modyford was also rehabilitated, two years languishing in the Tower without trial being deemed sufficient penance for his seven-year tenure as Jamaica's governor, and he was now appointed chief justice.[19]

For Spain had been able to take a strong line against logwood-cutters and other intruders only because England, France and Holland were at each other's throats. In 1672 the Dutch had suffered a double dose of trouble: England declared war on 17 March and France joined in the following month, in which contest Spain ranged herself with the Dutch, a war that led to the crash of the Amsterdam exchange and marked the beginning of the end of Dutch commercial dominance.[20] Being weak at sea France was liberal in dispensing licences, and when the governor-general of the Windward Islands, Jean-Charles de Baas Castelmore, learned of his country's declaration of war on Holland, he quickly began to organise an expedition against Curaçao. For this he detached the fifty-gun *Ecueil* and the smaller *Petite Enfant* to Saint-Domingue with orders for d'Ogeron to organise volunteers from among the *boucaniers* to join him off Saint-Croix. They arrived at Tortuga on 16 February 1673 having raised some 400 volunteers, but on the night of 25 February *Ecueil* was wrecked near Arecibo on the north-west of Puerto Rico, with the loss of many lives, and the 500 or so survivors who managed to struggle ashore were quickly interned by the Spanish.[21] D'Ogeron sent his nephew, Jacques Nepveu de Pouançay, to take word to the local Spanish authorities. But the French had for so long been Spain's mortal enemies that, in spite of official neutrality in the war with Holland, the survivors found themselves under attack from the local militia, and another forty or fifty of d'Ogeron's men were killed for the loss of ten Spaniards dead and a dozen wounded. Nor was any effort made to prevent local people plundering the wreck and murdering a number of other Frenchmen, and the hard-nosed governor, Gaspar de Arteaga y Aunavidao, ordered the remainder detained. They were taken to the middle of the island and given cattle to sustain themselves, loosely watched over by sixty Spanish soldiers.

Eventually d'Ogeron managed to escape and stole a fishing boat in which he and a companion reached the French settlement at Samaná

Bay. D'Ogeron was determined to free the rest of his force and raised another 500 buccaneers at Tortuga for the task, sailing on 7 October and pausing at Samaná for reinforcements. He reached Puerto Rico in the middle of the month and blundered ashore, only to be ambushed on the third day barely six miles inland where he lost seventeen men and hastily fled, leaving his wounded to be butchered by the Spanish. His temerity only prompted the Spanish to take reprisals against the captives at Hato de Arriba, as Arteaga ordered forty of them to be executed and the rest placed in strict confinement. D'Ogeron cruised uselessly off the coast for a couple of months until news of war between France and Spain dashed any hopes of gaining release for the captives, and he returned empty-handed to Tortuga on 29 December where he requested permission to visit France. He never saw any of his men again. By the spring of 1674 scarcely 130 remained alive, slaving on fortifications, and now in failing health d'Ogeron left Saint-Domingue to be replaced by his nephew, de Pouançay.[22]

Busy at first in the English Channel, the Dutch could do little in the West Indies, but Anglo-French rivalry in the Caribbean in no way diminished and relations could not improve as long as the buccaneers of Saint-Domingue and Tortuga took a steady toll of English shipping. In 1673 the Dutch sent Admiral de Ruyter to shore up their Caribbean empire, but his attack on Martinique failed, and after the English had been beaten at the battle of Texel in August 1673 England signed a separate peace with Holland in February 1674 under the Treaty of Westminster. But France would continue the war for another four years, whereupon peace with England unwittingly paved the way for the French to secure the services of the remaining buccaneers, and as a consequence English buccaneers continued to be active under French commissions. Even though they were fighting wars against the Dutch these 'shopkeepers' continued to smuggle goods into French possessions, just as they did into English and Spanish ones. Here sugar took a gradual hold despite tobacco making a last stand on Saint-Domingue, and by 1674 in these same French possession, buccaneers turned planters with their assorted bands of forced labour produced 3 million pounds of it annually, after which output rapidly tailed off.[23] In July the Spanish frigate *San Antonio y las Ánimas* was captured by a brigantine captained by an Englishman called 'Juan de Emprená' or

'Juan de Prensas', according to a twenty-eight-year-old witness, Simón Rodríguez, who describe a multi-national crew of buccaneers sailing under a French commission from Tortuga. In recounting the incident, in which the Spanish were robbed of 6,000 pesos and put ashore as the buccaneers sailed away in the frigate, Rodríguez reported that the English captain was awaiting the dispatch of an English fleet to be led by Morgan 'with 4,000 men to join and incorporate with pirates of the island of Jamaica and other places and islands where they reside', their purpose being to seize Cartagena or 'go up the Magdalena River to sack the Villa of Mompóx'.[24]

In truth there was no English fleet on its way; instead the war continued. In early 1674 Jurraein Aernouts had been commissioned by Governor Jan Dancker of Curaçao to attack the English and French. After an expedition to North America where he learned of the peace with England following the Treaty of Westminster, Aernouts returned to the Caribbean in summer 1675 and, along with Jan Erasmus Reyning and around a hundred men, descended upon the French island of Grenada. They succeeded in occupying the main fort but then found themselves besieged and starved into submission, and were sent to a plantation on Martinique. Aernouts, Reyning and five others contrived to escape after drugging the guards' wine and stealing a *piragua* – a flat-bottomed two-masted vessel – in which, desperate and starving, they reached Maracaibo where they were briefly incarcerated. Despite being common foes of the French, Dutchmen remained deeply suspicious to the Spanish, but the seven were eventually restored to Curaçao the following year.[25] Meanwhile the Dutch dispatched a fleet to the Caribbean under Vice-Admiral Jacob Binckes with three ships-of-the-line, six frigates and supporting vessels with the aim of evicting the French from their Caribbean colonies.

By now Morgan's trafficking had become too blatant to be concealed, and matters came to a head early in 1676 with the case of Captain John Deane, who was accused of carrying stolen goods and operating under various national colours, none of which were English. Deane was accused of intercepting the merchant ship *John Adventure* and Vaughan ordered Morgan 'to imprison the offenders' on a charge of piracy.[26] Morgan supported Deane as Vaughan led the prosecution, and the case would lead to a significant change in attitude by the home government, which granted the first standing commission to an overseas colonial court of 'oyer and terminer', the right to issue death sentences without the option of appeal to higher courts in England. While criminals had always been executed in Jamaica, only after 1677 could pirates be executed simply for being pirates, an important innovation.[27] The problem of English buccaneers operating under foreign commissions was also addressed by a law of April 1677 forbidding the practice, and a number of English buccaneers relinquished French commissions as a result. Others, such as the Scottish captain James Browne, active during the late 1670s, continued to plunder Spanish and Dutch shipping under commissions from Tortuga. And when Browne was captured with a cargo of stolen slaves in a Jamaican bay he was quickly tried and hanged for piracy.[28] But plenty of English buccaneers continued to operate alongside their French brethren, among them William Barnes who in June 1677, along with John Coxon and a French captain called La Garde, captured Santa Marta on the Main and took numerous prisoners including the governor and local bishop, and held them to ransom until three warships of the *armada de barlovento* arrived to drive the buccaneers off. On 28 July Lynch noted the arrival of the expedition in Jamaica complete with hostages, and the French were ordered to leave while the English were curtly informed that such operations would no longer be tolerated. Vaughan took good care of the bishop and hired a vessel to send him to Cartagena, at which 'the good old man was exceedingly pleased'. He also endeavoured to obtain the custody of the Spanish governor and other prisoners, but without success, 'the French being obstinate and damnably enraged the English had left them'.[29] As a result of his shenanigans Morgan once more faced charges instigated by Lynch and Vaughan, but the latter remained a figure of suspicion in London and the authorities there eventually sided with the wily Welsh scoundrel.[30]

In May 1676 Binckes occupied Cayena and Marie Galante and retook St Eustatius, then began to look for new objectives. On 16 June he sighted Guadeloupe, but decided not to attack. Instead the Dutch landed on San Martín, where they killed the governor and seized a hundred slaves. Then in mid-July Binckes reached Tobago, which according to his instructions was the ideal place to set up a fortified base. Having landed and evicted the French population he left his

Henry Morgan, perhaps the most notorious buccaneer of all, was a master politician and an inspiring leader in battle. Born into a Welsh farming family, he was knighted and made Governor of Jamaica in 1674.

When Morgan and his men sacked the town of Puerto del Principe in Cuba, its riches proved disappointing. A Spanish prisoner aboard his ship overheard the plan and sent word to warn the townsfolk, who immediately began to hide their possessions.

Henry Morgan's battle with the Spanish at Lake Maracaibo in Venezuela became the stuff of legend after he turned his vessel into a fire-ship and successfully sailed it into the Spaniards' galleon.

The local population often bore the brunt of the buccaneers' brutality, as the treatment of the citizens of Maracaibo at the hands of Morgan and his pirates shows.

The notoriously brutal French
filibuster Jean-David Nau,
known as 'L'Ollonais', or
*El Olonés*, was by all accounts the
most bloodthirsty of the pirates.
Here he is shown *(right)* cutting
out the heart of a Spanish prisoner in the Honduran jungle
and pushing it into the mouth
of another victim.

*(Above)* In London, Henry Bennet, 1st Earl of Arlington, spearheaded the pro-Spanish, Catholic faction, and did his best to thwart the buccaneers of Jamaica as they waged war against the Spaniards in Cuba and on the main.

*(Above right)* While in exile Charles II had promised to return Jamaica to the Spanish, and his accession to the throne in 1660 threw the island into turmoil. But he came to see the colony in a new light as 'the navel of the West Indies' and 'a window on the power of Spain'.

*(Right)* As Captain-General of the Army, George Monck, later Duke of Albemarle, played a crucial role in the peace treaty concluded between England and Spain upon the Restoration of Charles II.

Howard Pyle vividly imagined the experiences of the buccaneers in his illustrations:

*(Opposite page)* A group of French buccaneers extorting ransom from a Spanish prisoner in Cartagena in 1697

*(Right)* A gang of pirates attacking a Spanish galleon.

The English buccaneer and scientist William Dampier published three books describing his adventures, and is a crucial source for much of our knowledge of the buccaneers.

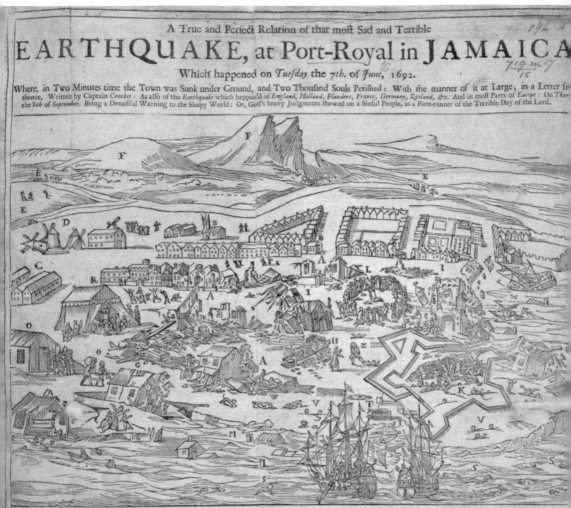

The earthquake in 1692 that destroyed the pirates' lair of Port Royal was believed by many to be the judgement of God.

second-in-command, Pieter Constant, as governor and headed for Española where he planned to incite the buccaneers to switch sides.[31] Vaughan, like Lynch before him, issued a proclamation calling in all privateers and forbidding them to take commissions from foreign princes. Although this was unpopular in Jamaica, no Englishman fully trusted French intentions, and having to rely on the buccaneers for the island's protection while the government in London still did nothing to defend it aroused anger. The attitude thereby created was 'let His Matie send what Orders he will about Privateering, there are almost none to execute them but who are interested in one way or another'.[32] In fact, both buccaneers and planters regarded Vaughan as an intruder and the leading planters took charge of the Assembly.

In response to Binckes the French assembled a major fleet of twelve ships-of-the-line under Admiral Jean Conde d'Estrées which approached the Leeward Islands in the autumn and by December was operating in the Caribbean. Every English and Spanish eye in America was fastened on the fleet's progress as d'Estrées first recovered Cayena, then put in to Martinique where he gathered volunteers and in February 1677 anchored off Tobago. On the 21st he landed a thousand men and blockaded the port with fourteen light vessels, but Dutch numerical superiority proved too much and he was forced to retire with heavy losses, but not before irreparably damaging ten of thirteen Dutch vessels in the harbour. He then recrossed the Atlantic before returning to attack Tobago again in November. By now de Pouançay on Tortuga had received instructions to furnish a buccaneer squadron of around a thousand men in a dozen ships who were placed under the command of 'chevalier' Michel de Grammont, whose legend has him born in Paris the son of an officer in about 1650, and running away to sea after killing a man in a duel aged just fourteen. He was small and active and had quickly risen among the brethren of the coast who appreciated his bravery, liberality, hard-drinking ways and ready wit.[33]

The Dutch were now desperately short of men on Tobago, partly as a result of battle casualties, but mainly from disease. On 6 December the French landed and in the subsequent assault killed 250 Dutchmen, about half the total number, including Binckes. The French were now in a position to assume the offensive and it was clear that if Spanish power in the Caribbean succumbed to France then nothing would save the English. But when the fleet sailed west towards Curaçao, having rendezvoused with a thousand buccaneers at St Christopher, the threat was eased considerably after d'Estrées had run his ships aground at Las Aviès at 9 o'clock on the evening of 11 May 1678.[34] No fewer than seven ships-of-the-line were lost, together with three transports, at least three buccaneer vessels and around 500 lives. The remnants of the fleet were forced to return to France, but the remaining buccaneers, under de Grammont, apparently made the best of a bad situation by camping out on the island and salvaging the wrecks. The English buccaneer chronicler William Dampier later claimed that they lived quite well like this as the waves brought in the flotsam, and one of the men:

> told me that if they had gone to Jamaica with £30 a man in their Pockets, they could not have enjoyed themselves more. For they kept in a Gang by themselves, and watched when the Ships broke, to get the Goods that came from them; and though much was staved against the Rocks, yet abundance of Wine and Brandy floated over the Riff, where the Privateers waited to take it up. They lived here about three Weeks, waiting an Opportunity to transport themselves back again to Hispaniola; in all which Time they were never without two or three Hogsheads of Wine and Brandy in their Tents, and Barrels of Beef and Pork.[35]

Eventually they were forced to seek refuge at Saint-Domingue and from this point the buccaneers were determined to have little to do with regular navies and to seek their own adventures.

Under de Grammont who had, according to a contemporary, 'a particular secret for winning [buccaneers] hearts, and insinuating himself into their spirits', the buccaneers would take effective control of the Caribbean, but they would always be more of a problem for Spain than for England.[36] These French buccaneers occupied a curious and anomalous position; they were not ordinary privateers nor were they quite pirates, for they had never been declared outlaws, and they confined their attentions to the Spanish. They served under conditions which they themselves imposed, or deigned to accept, and were always ready to turn against the representatives of authority if they believed they had aught to complain about.[37] When in August 1678 a treaty was signed between France and Holland at Nijmegen that significantly made no reference to the Caribbean, the buccaneers, pleased with their new status as friends and agents of France, widened the scope of their operations. On 12 June the governor of Santo Domingo had written to the crown.

> The finances of the community are in ruins. The closing of the sea routes for fear of French attack not only has left the island without trade, but also the payroll, munitions, and supplies for our garrisons have not been delivered for a year. Only loans from loyal citizens save us. The threat of attack has forced us to stand at arms for over five months and all businesses are idle.[38]

That month de Grammont decided to sail across the Gulf of Venezuela to attack Maracaibo with no fewer than 2,000 men in six large and thirteen smaller vessels. Having landed half his men, who marched over the San Carlos peninsula towards the fort guarding the city, he entered the lagoon with his thirteen smaller vessels. Governor Jorge Madureira Ferreira had been in post only a week and did not inspire the support of the locals, who fled in panic, the governor himself retreating to the inland town of Maicao with his handful of regular troops. The city fell on 14 June and those inhabitants unfortunate enough to be captured were tortured to death if they did not reveal where their treasure was, and even if they did, which provoked great horror in people inured to it, 'something which not even a Turk or a Moor would do'.[39] The city was occupied for fifteen days, during which time de Grammont sent out mounted patrols to scatter the Spanish still further, before the buccaneers sailed across the lagoon to Gibraltar whose garrison of just twenty-two men quickly surrendered. De Grammont then marched fifty miles inland to Trujillo, whose inhabitants had also been evacuated another twenty-five miles away to Mérida de la Grita. This place was more solidly defended, with a fort manned by 250 men with four guns and supported from surrounding hilltops. Following an ineffectual bombardment the buccaneers withdrew on 1 September, and after razing Gibraltar in reprisal for his failure, de Grammont sailed away on 3 December taking many captives and a substantial booty estimated at 150,000 pesos. They reached Petit-Goâve on Christmas Eve to be received as heroes.[40]

Meanwhile King Charles II created a new colonial council, the Lords of Trade and Plantations, who replaced Vaughan with Charles Howard, Earl of Carlisle, on 1 March 1678. Carlisle arrived on 18 July to find that Vaughan had already left for home due to ill-health, leaving Morgan in charge. The earl immediately invited the privateers to come in, hoping perhaps to use them in the threatened war with France, for the island had 'not above 4000 whites able to bear arms, a secret not fit to be made public'.[41] The result was disappointing; some buccaneers came in, but even these abused the pardon they received. Elsewhere Spanish privateers and coastguards were making numerous captures, and the largest ports remained free of attack while contrabandists were busiest in remote areas.[42] But the buccaneers' efforts were proving counter-productive, for by now King Carlos II had agreed to provide five frigates ranging from 140 to 450 tons to form a new *armada de barlovento*, and he promised to send another three ships then under construction in the Spanish Netherlands together with two confiscated 300–ton merchant vessels.[43] Many of the buccaneers taken were Englishmen carrying French commissions, such as George Spurre who was prowling off the north coast of Cuba in April 1678, accompanied by Edward Neville's sloop with 105 men between them. They took a Spanish dispatch vessel, *Toro* ('Bull'), and having deposited the crew on shore Spurre took it for his own after burning his old ship. They then crossed to the Laguna de Terminos in Nueva España where they captured a ketch and learned enough to plan a raid on Campeche, for which they raised their numbers to 180. Once ready the expedition sailed north in the two ships towing eight *piraguas*, and after a reconnaissance on the night of 6/7 July they landed 160 men with instructions to signal the anchor watches of their ships should they succeed.

Having made a roundabout approach march they appeared before the city an hour before dawn on Sunday 10 July. There a captive Indian seized en route gave the password. In the gloom they then rushed the gate and headed directly for the main plaza, ignoring startled churchgoers. The garrison was caught completely by surprise and quickly surrendered, and the two buccaneer ships came in when signalled. Over the next two days the city was thoroughly ransacked before the buccaneers withdrew, taking with them a ship, *San Antonio*, a barque and another boat plus 250 blacks, mulattos and Indians to sell as slaves. The number of such hit-and-run raids was staggering: over the next four years, a Cartagena resident would lament,

> Trinidad has been robbed once; Margarita and Guyana robbed once and sacked twice; La Guaira sacked once and its inhabitants sold ... [Pirates also] entered Puerto Cabello and sacked Valencia, which is more than twenty leagues inland. Maracaibo has been robbed many times ... the city of Río de la Hacha abandoned, the city and garrison sacked more than three times and burned once ...[44]

Meanwhile Spurre's raid would lead to reprisal, if somewhat late, when in October 1678 the Spanish descended in strength on the logwood camps along the coast of Campeche, taking the ships that they found there and dispersing the settlements.

With the demise of the WIC in 1675 a new company had been instituted along similar lines with a board of ten directors – the Heren X.[45] But its success was always unlikely and with its rapid demise, followed by the Treaty of Nijmegen on 10 August 1678, the cumulative effect of the three Anglo-Dutch wars was that the Dutch had lost the battle for commercial supremacy in the Caribbean. Although they maintained a strong commercial position in Curaçao, later reinforced by the astonishing success of St Eustatius in the Leewards group, with Jamaica increasingly taking over as a slave centre the Dutch were effectively reduced to the role of impotent bystander.[46] But if the Dutch no longer ruled the waves, fear of commercial competition remained, as Sir Thomas Lynch was only too well aware, noting that 'the Dutch can sell European goods 30 per cent cheaper than we and will pay dearer for American goods'.[47] The continued struggle for the West Indies demonstrated the unique importance to trade of the buccaneers who, for all their violent proclivities, were essential in the peacetime role of suppliers of cheap slaves and all sorts of other commodities, both trade and luxury; and though these goods were often taken from prizes, they supplied the needs of Spanish, English and French colonists alike. Little wonder, therefore, that continued efforts devoted by the

English and French to their suppression were half hearted, as they continued to play all off against each other.[48]

In the autumn of 1679, several buccaneer vessels under Captains John Coxon, Bartholomew Sharp and others made a raid in the Gulf of Honduras plundering the storehouses there; they carried off 500 chests of indigo, besides quantities of cocoa, cochineal, tortoiseshell, money and plate, then returned to Jamaica.[49] Unsure how they would be received, one vessel landed her cargo in a quiet spot on the coast and sent word that she would sail to Rhode Island or a Dutch plantation if prevented from bringing the booty into Port Royal. Despite Carlisle having taken security for good behaviour from some of the captains before they left Jamaica, they were allowed to enter the indigo at the custom house. But the sudden glut of indigo disturbed Jamaican trade considerably, and for some time it took the place of native sugar and tobacco as a means of exchange. Manufacture on the island was hindered, prices fell, and only the king's customs saw any real benefit. In reply to Spanish complaints Carlisle feigned ignorance of the source of the indigo, claiming that it was brought 'in lawful ships by lawful men'.[50]

Although they held commissions only to cut logwood in the Bay of Honduras, Coxon held an illegal assembly at Port Morant where he recruited four other captains – Sharp, Essex, Allison (or Alliston) and Margott (or Mackete) – for a descent on Portobelo. They departed for this act of outright piracy on 17 January 1680, and rendezvoused offshore with a French brigantine commanded by Jean Rose who brought commissions from Saint-Domingue. The buccaneers made their way to the San Bernardo (or Friends) Islands near Cartagena where they stole four *piraguas* and six large canoes for use as landing craft, then moved to Isla de Pinos (Isle of Pines) where 250 buccaneers transferred to the boats and began to row ashore. On the approach they encountered a large ship at anchor which proved to be a French buccaneer, Captain Lessone, who added another eighty men to the assault party, and soon afterwards they slipped into the Gulf of San Blas from which they proceeded on foot to avoid curious Spanish eyes.[51]

Following Morgan's raid on Panamá, the paths across the isthmus had become steadily overgrown, although two unsuccessful attempts to traverse it had been made by French buccaneers in 1675 and 1678.

But a consequence of these efforts and constant patrolling of the north coast garnered friendly relations with the local Indians, who hated the Spanish and were prepared to show Coxon's raiders the way, although 'many of them were weak, being three days without any food, and their feet cut with the rocks for want of shoes'.[52] They attacked Portobelo on 7 February 1680:

> A boy came running into the town ... at ten in the morning, and shouting: 'To arms Christians, the English are coming.' Those who heard him were confused and refused to believe him, but then they saw some five or six Englishmen coming towards them at a quick pace pointing their guns, which was sufficient to send them fleeing to Santiago castle to shut themselves in.[53]

As the inhabitants had had little time to remove their belongings, the place was open to plunder, and for the loss of thirty men (according to Spanish account) the buccaneers gained booty of 50,000 pesos of silver and 20,000 pesos' worth of cloth, and inflicted another 25,000 pesos' worth of damage.[54] In the evening of the following day the buccaneers took their prisoners and booty to a cay half a mile from the town of Bastimentos whence a boat was sent to summon their ships. They left just in time to avoid a force of 700 Spanish troops sent from Panamá who fired at them from the beach but did no damage.[55]

After capturing two Spanish vessels bound for Portobelo with provisions from Cartagena, the buccaneers divided their plunder and departed for Boca del Toro, some fifty leagues northwards, where they careened and provisioned, and were joined by two more Jamaican privateers commanded by John Sawkins and Peter Harris. They then sailed for Golden Island, where Coxon announced his intention to emulate Morgan once more, and travel overland to Panamá and attack the Spanish Pacific flank. William Dampier, who sailed with Sharp, wrote of this planned first irruption of the buccaneers into the Pacific:

> Before my first going over into the South Seas with Captain Sharp ... about 4 leagues to the East of Portobel, we took the Pacquets bound thither from Cartagena. We open'd a great quantity of the Merchants Letters, and found ... a certain Prophecy that went about

Spain that year, the Tenour of which was, That there would be English Privateers that Year in the West Indies, who would ... open a Door into the South Seas ... This Door they spake of we all concluded must be the Passage over Land through the Country of the Indians of Darien, who were a little before this become our Friends, and had lately fallen out with the Spaniards ... and upon calling to mind the frequent Invitations we had from these Indians a little before this time, to pass through their Country, and fall upon the Spaniards in the South Seas, we from henceforward began to entertain such thoughts in earnest, and soon came to a Resolution to make those Attempts which we afterwards did.[56]

The French among them, however, chose to remain in the Caribbean, where they spent the next four months operating on the isthmus, in the Gulf of Panamá and off Nueva España. But on 5 April 1680 the English party of 334 men began marching, in companies each with their own colours, overland across the Isthmus of Darién to the coasts of Panamá and the South Seas.[57]

Aided by Kuna Indians whose chief they called the 'Emperor of Darién', they soon had 250 auxiliaries determined to avenge the Spanish rape of the emperor's daughter which 'had hugely incensed him against the Spaniards'.[58] Their first target on 15 April was Santa María at the eastern end of the isthmus, but there was little plunder as they had missed out by just three days on 300 pounds of gold sent to Panamá. 'This was not so good a place as we did expect,' wrote Sharp, disappointedly. 'It was a small pitiful place all thatched houses and but one church.'[59] However, encouraged by José Gabriel, who had ravished the emperor's daughter (she was found safe but pregnant), and who grovellingly promised to lead them to the governor's bedchamber door to avoid the cruel revenge of the Indians, the combined force confirmed Coxon as leader and decided to attack the city. Thereafter they crossed the isthmus to continue their adventures in the Pacific, where they captured *La Santissima Trinidada*, in which battle Harris was mortally wounded. Although Coxon, piqued at charges of cowardice in that battle, returned to the Caribbean with seventy men, the rest now led by Sawkins set out to cruise the Pacific coast of South America.[60] For eighteen months these pirates, which they undoubtedly were despite sailing under 'Jamaica discipline' (the buccaneers' code), burned and plundered and kept the Spanish provinces of Equador, Peru and Chile in a fever of apprehension; and, although two groups departed to return to the Caribbean – including Dampier, his friend Lionel Wafer and forty-two others in April 1681 – they created no settlements and left no lasting impression on the region before sailing for home towards the end of that year, rounding Cape Horn and returning to the Windward Islands in January 1682.[61]

Meanwhile in the spring of 1681 d'Estrées reappeared in the Caribbean and made a leisurely cruise blatantly inventorying the Spanish islands for his master. Both Spanish and English were nervous at this openly aggressive reconnaissance.[62] Meanwhile the Spanish raided and dispersed the English logwood camp at Triste and went on to capture New Providence in the Bahamas, while de Grammont led a daring raid on La Guaira, into which forty-seven buccaneers stole on 26 June as the inhabitants slept. When the latter awoke they found the stronghold already occupied and its 150 defenders helpless. Captain Juan de Laya Mijica managed to escape to warn Caracas, and the royal treasury was evacuated inland before the buccaneers could arrive to surprise that city too, as Governor Francisco de Alberto prepared the defences. When de Grammont arrived, he was held up by the militia as Mijica led a sortie that killed a number of buccaneers and wounded others including de Grammont himself, who took a sword blow to the neck. But after a bitter fight the attackers prevailed and made off with substantial booty, taking with them the reputation of Caracas as an impregnable city, and raising de Grammont's reputation still higher.[63]

By now Port Royal was the most heavily fortified place in English America. Four forts mounted ninety-four guns guarding the sea approaches, with sixteen guns covering the landward side, and manned by two regular companies. In addition Morgan's militia regiment mustered 1,181 all ranks, although around 400 of these were 'Sea-Faring Men', not 'Residents', and might be expected to be away fishing, turtle-hunting in the Cayman Islands or buccaneering.[64] The city had out-stripped Bridgetown in Barbados, and only Boston, Massachusetts, exceeded it in size and importance in English America, while a far greater proportion of the island's white population lived in the town, suggesting a much higher ratio of non-agricultural workers.[65] John

Taylor noted in his diary that the merchants and gentry lived 'in the height of splendour', served by black slaves in livery.[66] But the craftsmen also lived far better than in England, as the wages were three times those at home and work was easily obtained. Food was abundant and cheap with three markets a day stocked with fruit, fish and meat, and luxuries were also freely available. Although food prices in Port Royal were higher than in London, they were lower in real terms because of the much higher wages.[67] Turtles were plentiful and, at half the price of beef, formed the chief staple of the 'lower sorts' and of ships' provisions.[68] Cocoa, made into chocolate, was also very popular, but bread was generally of poor quality. All in all, observed Taylor, the people lived 'with full food tables, not wanting anything requisite to satisfy, delight and please their curious appetites'.[69]

There was also a wealth of entertainment: a bear-garden, cock-fighting, billiards, music houses and shooting at targets, to say nothing of 'all manners of debauchery', which the prudish blamed on 'the privateers and wild blades which come hither'. Eyebrows were raised by many at the large number of ale houses and the 'crue of vile strumpets and common prostratures' who seemed in no way deterred by frequent imprisonment in a cage by the harbour. For, as Taylor put it, 'with the help of the Spaniard's purse', the inhabitants 'have advanced their fortune' and were now rich.[70]

Among Port Royal's prostitutes none was more famous than Mary Carleton, a fiddler's daughter from Canterbury. Born Mary Moders in 1642 she went to London in 1663 determined not to remain a low-born nobody for the rest of her life, and by becoming 'Maria von Wolway', a German princess down on her luck, she managed to bag a man who thought he was getting a catch – until he discovered the scam. Her trial at the Old Bailey was a notable real-life Restoration drama, and Sam Pepys even visited her in gaol. Although she was acquitted she was eventually caught out in another scam, and in 1671 was sentenced to penal transportation to Jamaica. There she joined the denizens of the waterfront in relieving buccaneers of their hard-won silver. She called them 'Bully-Ruffins' and said her only danger was drowning in rum or being killed by their kindness. But despite painting the buccaneers as gentlemen-rogues she must have worked hard for her money – roaring-drunk pirates would not have been easy customers. Nor did she stay for long; after two years she returned to her old ways in London, marrying an apothecary and absconding with his money, and for returning from transportation without permission Mary was hanged.[71]

With all the boozing in Port Royal it was hardly surprising that alcoholic excess generated 'disorder, poverty and disease'.[72] But, for all the wild excesses of its inhabitants, far more significant was its situation, as the city was 'in the Spaniard's bowels and the heart of his trade'.[73] Contraband was carried out in Jamaica sloops of which there were around eighty by 1680. They were usually under fifty tons and 'not like those of England' but of a particular build; they were heavily armed, carrying up to eight guns, and were well manned by up to twenty-five men, since Port Royal had 'an abundance of seamen'.[74] And because the one commodity that could gain entrance to Portobelo or Veracruz was slaves, Jamaica was an ideal base as transport costs were 20 per cent lower than at Curaçao. The Royal African Company had by 1680 developed a substantial trade in slaves, with between a quarter and a half of the annual supply being sold to the Spanish, for which convenience they paid 35 per cent extra. It was, according to planter John Helyar, 'a much easier way of making money than sugar'.[75] The successful exploitation of Jamaica's strategic position by the buccaneers through plunder and contraband had fuelled the growth of Port Royal, and provided the capital that was needed to kick-start the plantation culture.[76] And so, ironically, by enabling the island's economy to thrive the buccaneers helped to reduce the desire for and reliance on plunder, thus hastening the demise of buccaneering.

# 13

## SUPPRESSION

Dime Lorençillo ai
te tentó el demonio
pues con nueve velas, Marita
diste vista al Morro

el caso que hicimos ai
de tus nueve velas
fue poner cuidado, Marita
En las zentinelas*

Anon, Spanish song

The irruption of buccaneers into the Pacific may not have produced any lasting effects in that ocean, but it had repercussions in the Caribbean. The Earl of Carlisle as governor of Jamaica cannot escape the charge of culpable negligence in relation to Coxon's raid on Panamá, having permitted buccaneer vessels to leave Jamaica in the first place. All the expedition leaders were notorious for repeated involvement in piratical outrages against the Dutch and Spanish; the buccaneers themselves claimed they had Carlisle's permission to cut logwood, which was probably true, yet they had used the very same ruse when they went to Honduras, so the governor must surely have suspected their real intentions. But in truth he had little practical power to suppress buccaneering. 'The governor', wrote the Council of Jamaica to the Lords of Trade and Plantations in May 1680, 'can do little from want of ships to reduce the privateers, and of plain laws to punish them'; and it urged the ratification of the Act passed by the Assembly two years before, making it a felony for any British subject in the West Indies to serve under a foreign prince without leave from the governor.[1]

---

* Tell me, Lorençillo, / Were you tempted by the Devil? / For you came with nine ships, Marita / in sight of Morro Castle. / And what we did / On seeing your nine ships / Was to alert, Marita / All of our sentries.

In April 1681 Carlisle suddenly departed for England on the frigate HMS *Hunter*, leaving the old rogue Morgan in charge as lieutenant-governor. On his passage home Carlisle encountered Coxon, who, following the quarrel with his companions in the Pacific, was again hanging about off Jamaican shores. *Hunter* gave chase for twenty-four hours, but being outsailed was content to take two small vessels accompanying Coxon which had been deserted by their crews.[2] Morgan issued a warrant on 1 July for Sharp's arrest in which he referred to Portobelo – one wonders whether he saw the irony.[3] Three men who had taken part in the expedition were captured and thrown into prison until the next meeting of the court of vice-admiralty. But Coxon's friends, including apparently almost all the members of the Council, offered £2,000 security if he was allowed to come into Port Royal, and promised he would never take another commission except from the King of England; Morgan wrote to Carlisle seeking his approbation.[4]

From 1681 a new phase in English policy was initiated which continued the change in attitude to the buccaneers. By now, under pressure from both the home government and local planters, Morgan had developed into a true pirate-hater, and he had repeatedly written to urge the dispatch of small shallow-draught frigates to coast the island, and had begged for orders to command them himself, for 'then I shall not much question to reduce them [the buccaneers] in some time to leave them shipless'.[5] At the end of January he received word that the armed sloop of a notorious Dutch privateer, Jacob Everson, was anchored on the coast with a brigantine he had lately captured. Morgan manned a small vessel with fifty picked men and sent it secretly to seize the pirate. Everson's sloop was boarded and twenty-six men captured, but Everson himself and several others jumped overboard and swam ashore. The prisoners, most of whom were English, were tried six weeks later, convicted of piracy and sentenced to death; but Morgan suspended the execution and wrote to the king for instructions. On 16 June the king in council ordered the execution of the condemned men.[6]

Sharp and his men remained unaware of this as they returned to the Caribbean, but at Barbados they learned that the frigate HMS *Richmond* was lying in the road, and fearing seizure they sailed to Antigua where the governor, Colonel Christopher Codrington, refused them permission to enter the harbour. Impatient and determined to go their separate ways, some of the party landed on Antigua nevertheless, while Sharp and sixteen others went to Nevis where they obtained passage to England, arriving at Dartmouth on 26 March 1682. Of four more who went to Jamaica, Morgan himself related that they were found guilty and condemned: 'he that surrendered himself is like as informer to obtain ye favour of the courts, one of the condemned is proved a bloody and notorious villain and fitt to make an example of, the other two being represented to me fitt objects of mercy by the court I will not proceed until his Majesty further commands'.[7] The king duly approved the execution of the one prisoner deemed worthy of it, while Sharp, Coxon and three others were tried at the high court of admiralty on 19 May 1682. When all five were acquitted it drew howls of protest from the Spanish, but though his subsequent career is obscure, it seems that Sharp followed Morgan as something of poacher turned gamekeeper, and he served briefly as governor of Anguilla in 1688.[8]

The passage of Jamaican anti-pirate legislation and the subsequent Jamaica Act of 1683 cemented England's new anti-buccaneer policies. Sir Thomas Lynch returned as governor in May 1682, but this time with troops, sloops and a frigate, and he immediately sacked Morgan as lieutenant-governor and lieutenant-general of Jamaica. Astonished and perturbed by his peremptory dismissal, Morgan took once more to drinking heavily and from that point onwards his health rapidly deteriorated.[9] To demonstrate the new hard line, one of Lynch's first acts following his return was to chase a buccaneer vessel known as *La Trompeuse* (The Trickster), a French vessel hired out to English logwood-cutters and stolen by a French renegade buccaneer, Jean Hamlin, who took sixteen to eighteen Jamaican trading vessels before being chased away by a frigate sent out by Lynch and taking refuge on Danish St Thomas. A year later following depredations along the coast of Africa, his ship was destroyed in the harbour at St Thomas by HMS *Francis*, which had ignored Danish protests; but he was soon operating again in *La Nouvelle Trompeuse*, illustrating the difficulty in suppressing piracy.[10] Nevertheless, further additions were made to royal forces as Jamaicans began to clamour for the punishment of buccaneers and conniving officials, because buccaneer activities were hurting trade. The slave trade in particular was beginning to thrive as the Royal

African Company provided slaves legally for the official price at Port Royal Market, while interloping traders, many of them ex-buccaneers, brought them from wherever they could lay hands on them and sold them for whatever they could get.[11]

Under increasing pressure in Jamaica buccaneers went to Saint-Domingue and sought commissions from the French, or began to look elsewhere for bases such as the lagoons and islands of Central America, where a few turned to outright piracy. Or they went to New Providence in the Bahamas where Governor Robert Clarke had issued letters of marque against the Spanish in retaliation for local disputes in the Straits of Florida, despite this being technically illegal. In fact, many former buccaneers then made a good living out of salvaging the numerous wrecks in the notorious reef-filled archipelago, and when Clarke was replaced by Robert Lilburne in July 1682, the latter was powerless to prevent their activities.[12] Large groups were gathering once more at Saint-Domingue under de Grammont and Laurens Cornelis Boudewijn de Graaf. That month de Graaf in his ship *Tigre* surprised the Spanish frigate *Princesa*, part of the reformed *armada de barlovento* under Captain Manuel Delgado, as she was seeking provisions at Puerto Rico and carrying 120,000 silver pesos. A fifth of Delgado's crew were killed and the rest captured and later put down at Cuba. De Graaf's crew earned themselves 700 pesos each, and de Graaf took the ship as his own.[13]

De Graaf – or Lorençillo (Little Lawrence) as he was known to the Spanish – became a remarkably popular figure among Spanish sailors, and inspired a number of songs that celebrated his later exploits at Veracruz and Campeche; they mentioned his Lutheran religion, and that he had betrayed his own prince and had once served on Spanish vessels.[14] As a young man he left Holland and married a Spanish woman on the Canary Islands where he was recruited for a fleet bound for the Americas, as he was considered a skilled seaman and a crack shot with any weapon. The Spanish would come to regret this when he turned against them and soon became an inspirational leader of the brethren of the coast. Tall and blond, he wore a spiked moustache *à l'espagnole* 'which suited him very well', according to a contemporary chronicler.

> He always carries violins and trumpets aboard which entertain himself and amuse others, who derive pleasure from this. He is

further distinguished amongst filibusters by his courtesy and good taste. Overall he has won such fame that when it is known he has arrived at some place, many come from all around to see whether 'Lorenzo' is like other men.[15]

His chief flaw was a vicious temper while his greatest strength was his cunning which, combined with his knowledge of the Spanish and their ways, enabled him to surprise them constantly. Able to secure for his men easy and profitable victories, he was a natural leader in the world of the buccaneers.

News of this latest development reached Santo Domingo in early 1683, just as Nikolaas van Hoorn was arriving with a shipment of 300 slaves from Cádiz. Although legally contracted to supply slaves, van Hoorn was a known smuggler and friend of the buccaneers, and was arrested by Governor Francisco de Segura when artefacts from Cádiz were discovered on board. He assured the governor that he had no part in de Graaf's action and accused him of acting in reprisal; but when he saw he would get no change from the Spaniard he managed to escape with twenty men and a quarter of his cargo. In March a group of Bahamian buccaneer–salvagers under Thomas Pain attempted once again to attack the fortress of San Agustin under French colours, but succeeded only in raiding a few neighbouring villages. After they had retired to New Providence the Spanish retaliated and, by sacking the little town twice in 1684, forced its temporary abandonment.[16] Meanwhile the rest of the buccaneer fleet, some 2,000–3,000 men under de Grammont, spent two months loitering unproductively in the vicinity of Punta Icacos before returning to Saint-Domingue and then proceeding to the Bahamas, where they made a number of captures.

On arrival at Petit-Goâve van Hoorn obtained a letter of reprisal from de Pouançay and, stealing a fifty-gun ship, *St Nicholas* (a former English slaver named *Mary and Martha*), sailed to join de Grammont, de Graaf and his lieutenant Michiel Adrieszoon who were blockading Cuba. But after failing to take any great prizes they had turned their attention to Cartagena, where they encountered two large Spanish merchant ships anchored off the Honduran coast which were duly captured.[17] Frustrated by the lack of prizes off Cuba, the buccaneers decided to take the fight to the very harbour where the Nueva España fleet was anchored and to seize the silver before it was loaded on board. To plan this coup in detail and gather reinforcements they retired to Roatán, where they met van Hoorn and learned of his mission. On 7 April there was a huge gathering of buccaneers on the beach where they roared their approval when asked to assist with his mission against Santo Domingo. But de Graaf went one better: why waste time on impoverished Santo Domingo when there were greater riches to be had at Veracruz? It had remained untouched since the time of Hawkins more than a century earlier; its defences were neglected and its vigilance lax, especially as European relations were good at the time and former English prisoners there could attest that it would be an easy prize. The buccaneers signed up for this scheme enthusiastically, but reinforcements would be needed, and to gather them they transferred to Guanaja Island. Before their departure, one of the Honduran prizes, the *Nuestra Señora de la Consolación*, was burned, while the other, *Nuestra Señora de Regla*, was incorporated into the buccaneer fleet.[18]

On 17 May 1683, as Governor Don Luis Bartolomé de Córdova y Zúñiga and other city dignitaries were enjoying a banquet, two ships were sighted from the shore which proceeded to anchor despite the wind being favourable for them to enter the port. This aroused the suspicion of John Murphy, an Irish Catholic former buccaneer who had settled and prospered among the Spanish. Smelling danger he alerted Don Mateo Alonso de Huidobro, the *sargento mayor* (second-in-command) of the town garrison, who requested that he be allowed to take 400 men of the *armada de barlovento* to investigate. But the governor insisted there was no danger.[19] That night a forlorn hope of 200 buccaneers under de Graaf landed and stole quietly towards the city. At 4 a.m. they and other parties of buccaneers launched simultaneous assaults on different key points and took both the garrison and the city's inhabitants completely by surprise. De Grammont had deliberately panicked the garrison with a noisy show of force by deploying small groups of men all around to create an impression of overwhelming strength, and although no more than two dozen Spaniards were killed during the assault, the swiftness of the attack combined with the defenders' lack of gunpowder ensured success for the buccaneers. Soon the governor's palace remained the only point of resistance, and that not for long.[20]

Huidobro was among those killed, and once the fighting was over the city was systematically ransacked for four days. English logwood-cutters sought out and murdered Don Pedro Estrada, the *alguacil mayor* (chief constable) of the Holy Inquisition who had been so severe to them during their incarceration in the city, and many other Spaniards died in the confusion, as the first that many inhabitants knew of the city's fall was the sound of their houses being broken into by rampaging buccaneers carrying French flags.[21] By the following morning over 4,000 inhabitants had been herded into the church of La Merced where they suffered appallingly in the cramped conditions without food or water. Daylight revealed a large body of irregular horsemen under the *alcade* (mayor) of Antigua Veracruz, Don José de Esquivel, who had come to relieve the town, but they were quickly dispersed by the wily de Grammont, who mounted a troop of his own men and rode out to confront them. Among those tortured to reveal their riches was Murphy, who was hoisted up in the main square with his hands tied behind his back, then slashed and beaten by Lorençillo himself.[22] As news of the raid finally reached the viceregal capital at Mexico City on the morning of 21 May, the raiders withdrew to the island of Sacrificios, carefully avoiding the fort at San Juan de Ulúa which still held out, and taking more than 4,000 hostages with them, including the governor and Murphy, for whom they posted an astronomical ransom. Meanwhile they started to divide spoils that Spanish officials later estimated at 800,000 pesos in coin, 400,000 pesos in silver and a further 200,000 pesos in precious stones and other items.[23] But, impatient to gain the ransom, van Hoorn sent word to his Spanish contacts that unless it was paid shortly he would forward to them a dozen captives' heads. De Graaf arrived just in time to put a stop to this particularly barbaric scheme, and the two men argued, de Graaf insisting it would be wrong to behead men who had surrendered and been given quarter. In his anger at being thwarted van Hoorn made the fatal error of drawing his blade, and de Graaf quickly slashed his wrist and kicked him down on to the sand. His men then hauled van Hoorn off to the *Francesa* and clapped him in irons.[24]

Ironically van Hoorn's threats worked, and soon after on 29 May Spaniards appeared at Los Hornos beach carrying money chests. The buccaneers duly released their Spanish prisoners but took some 1,500 blacks and mulattos with them aboard their thirteen ships. Just as they were preparing to leave, the Nueva España fleet of two warships and nine merchantmen arrived under Admiral Don Diego Fernández de Zaldívar, Knight of the Order of Calatrava, who was in an excellent position to attack the raiders. But when a council of war was convened his captains proved reluctant to risk their own precious cargoes for the sake of the city, and he decided against taking action. Consequently the buccaneers 'sailed off mocking us', a broken-hearted Spaniard observed, 'triumphant and powerful, having lost all respect for Catholic arms'.[25] Able to make their way to sea unmolested, the buccaneers were now free to concentrate on the next task of smuggling their ill-gotten booty past the Jamaican authorities' none-too-close scrutiny, while the instigator of the scheme, van Hoorn, died some three weeks later as a result of an infection to his wound.[26]

Perhaps unsurprisingly the sack of Veracruz helped provoke a new round of war between France and Spain, despite the raid being entirely unauthorised by Versailles. However Spain was by now so enfeebled that France was practically able to ignore these hostilities. Following the death of Colbert in September 1683 Louis XIV initiated a policy of 'direct force' in the Caribbean, the main approach of which was the establishment of royal control over Saint-Domingue and the subjugation of the buccaneers to his direct instructions. This meant the application of European treaties to the Americas, the seizure of Spanish territory there and open confrontation with Spain should better treatment of French merchants not be forthcoming. But when the new governor of Saint-Domingue, Pierre-Paul Tarin de Cussy, arrived at Petit-Goâve in April 1684 supported by royal forces, he found the buccaneers on the point of open revolt because of the efforts made by François Depardieu de Franquesnay, the temporary governor, to enforce the strict orders from France for their suppression. De Cussy tried to implement the king's orders by building forts, both to strengthen the defences and to gain the support of the populace. Furthermore, by encouraging immigration and the development of plantations, he hoped to pacify the colony and wean it off the debauched ways of the buccaneers. But as long as he was surrounded by jealous neighbours, and as long as peace in Europe remained precarious, the safety of Saint-Domingue, like Jamaica before it, depended upon them.

Two commissioners were sent to aid de Cussy in reforming this dissolute society, but they soon drew the same conclusions as the governor, and sent a memoir to King Louis advising less severe measures. The king did not agree with their suggestion of compromise and de Cussy, compelled to deal harshly with the buccaneers, found his task by no means easy. When de Grammont and several other captains demanded commissions against the Spanish, he finally consented on condition that they persuade all the buccaneers driven away by de Franquesnay to return to the colony.[27] Indeed, so bad had things become during de Franquesnay's short tenure that de Graaf let it be known that he desired to enter the service of the governor of Jamaica. The Privy Council empowered Lynch to treat with him, offering pardon and permission to settle on the island on receiving security for his future good behaviour. But when de Cussy reversed de Franquesnay's policy he also received de Graaf with all the honour due to a military hero, and in spite of his instructions endeavoured to engage him in government service.[28]

In any case, before the new policies could become effective Andrieszoon organised another expedition to Tierra Firme with Cartagena as his target. News of this reached Governor Juan Pando Estrada, who took the precaution of seizing three powerful merchant ships then at anchor in the port – *San Francisco* (forty guns), *Nuestra Señora de la Paz* (thirty-four guns) and a galliot of twenty-eight guns. With these he sent out Andrés del Pez on Christmas Eve to intercept and disrupt the buccaneers. But things went badly for the Spanish from the outset. The smaller buccaneer vessels swarmed about the larger Spanish ships, and in the confused fighting that followed *San Francisco* ran aground, and was captured after a further four hours of fighting. De Graaf's Dutch-born lieutenant, Jan Willems, then captured *Nuestra Señora de la Paz* after a fierce and disorderly action in which some ninety Spaniards and twenty buccaneers lost their lives. Once refloated *San Francisco* was given to de Graaf, who renamed her *Fortune* (later *Neptune*) and passed *Francesa* on to Willems, while Andrieszoon received *Nuestra Señora de la Paz*, which he renamed *Mutine* (Rascal). With all effective resistance at sea now eliminated, the buccaneers were free to block the port with an old ship on Christmas Day 1683 and bide their time. When an English slaving party arrived in the middle of January 1684, the buccaneers, respecting English neutrality, allowed it through, and a few days later they lifted their blockade and made for Saint-Domingue.[29]

In the spring they tried once more to blockade Cuba. On 18 May near Havana two Dutch ships were intercepted belonging to the VOC, *Stad Rotterdam* and *Elisabeth*. Since the French and English had reached a secret agreement to hinder the passage of Dutch shipping, Andrieszoon, ignoring official Dutch neutrality, ordered an inspection of the cargo and boarded the ships with ninety men. This revealed that substantial merchandise and numerous important people had been taken on board at Cartagena in the hope of evading the blockade under the Dutch flag, and Andrieszoon demanded that half the value of the cargo worth 200,000 pesos and the Spanish passengers be surrendered. After loud protests the conditions were met and the ships were allowed to proceed; the ships' captains later insisted they would never have allowed Andrieszoon to board had they known his intentions. They also alleged that the buccaneers had taken all the cargo, thus profiting in no small amount themselves. Having lifted the blockade in spring 1684 de Graaf encountered a Spanish ship of fourteen guns accompanied by another unidentified vessel. During the night he took the ship's cargo of quinine and forty-seven pounds of gold, then discovered in the morning that the second vessel was an English merchantman captured by the Spanish near Cuba. This he returned to Jamaica with a letter bearing his respects to the governor, which Lynch repaid when he later interceded on de Graaf's behalf, so that the Dutchman was pardoned for his attacks on English shipping and naturalised as an Englishman; Lynch even provided the necessary credentials and safe conducts to the Spanish authorities so that his wife might join him.[30]

Meanwhile, in Guatemala, the fort of San Felipe de Lara had languished in idleness since its completion in 1655, its guns unfired and its men mired in indolence. Thus it came as a profound shock for the garrison to find itself suddenly under attack in 1679, so much so that the fort fell without a shot being fired, although five Spaniards were killed, apparently at close quarters.[31] The buccaneers then made off with a thousand bottles of wine and 800 chests of indigo from the nearby warehouses and were not seen again until 27 April 1684, when around 400 buccaneers and Samba-Miskitas again stormed the fort, killing another five Spaniards including the *castellan*. In Europe the

Treaty of Ratisbon signed between France and Spain on 15 August 1684 was intended, among other things, to make it increasingly hard for buccaneers to practise their trade, especially in the Caribbean, but it did not prevent English and French buccaneers from making further major incursions into the Pacific, and almost exactly a year later French buccaneers took Granada from the Pacific side. Eight months after that another force of 400 buccaneers, including John Strong and William Dampier, landed at Realejo before marching on the capital, León, with its splendid cathedral, convents and churches. Again they easily overwhelmed the startled militia before ransacking the town. Perhaps the most unexpected aspect of this episode was the Spanish capture of an English architect from among the buccaneers, who helped to rebuild the cathedral.[32] Like the foray of 1681–2 this second Pacific wave of buccaneers had no lasting results; nor did they leave any permanent traces of their depredations along the coast of the viceroyalty of Peru. But in truth the failure to establish trading posts or settlements is unsurprising considering how little territory Spain had lost to foreigners up to this point, and given the difficulty of challenging and dislodging her in the far more accessible waters of the Caribbean.[33]

In January 1685 buccaneers under de Graaf made their way to Curaçao where the governor refused their requests to carry out repairs having not forgotten the assault on the Dutch Indiamen in Cuban waters. De Graaf continued towards Honduras to plan more attacks on the mainland reinforced by Andrieszoon, who then returned to Saint-Domingue and by May was back off Cuba.[34] Here he was joined by more buccaneers, including de Grammont, Willems and as many as twenty other captains, a gathering so impressive that it even intimidated Captain David Mitchell RN of the most powerful English warship in the West Indies, HMS *Ruby* (forty-eight guns). Mitchell went aboard de Grammont's ship to inquire after a Jamaican renegade called George Bannister whose *Golden Fleece* (thirty-six guns) was among the fleet, suspected of illegally operating under a foreign commission. When de Grammont insisted that Bannister had not actually entered French service, Mitchell thought it wise not to pursue the matter.[35] One of the boldest ventures by the buccaneers followed soon afterwards, when in June de Graaf, with de Grammont as his second-in-command, led some 700 men in six large ships and four smaller ones together with six sloops and seventeen *piraguas* to lurk in the vicinity of Cabo Catoche for about a month. Lookouts at Yucután had observed these movements and provided warning to the deputy governor of Campeche, Don Felipe de la Barrera y Villegas, who prepared the city's defences.

When Barrera received news at the end of June that an attack was imminent he closed the port, and on the afternoon of 6 July the buccaneers approached within six miles of the coast. A landing party took to boats and began heading for Campeche, but the Spanish were ready, and seeing four companies of militia waiting on the beach to oppose them the buccaneers retired to concoct a new plan.[36] They sat in their boats bobbing on the swell all night before retreating next morning towards their ships; but this was a feint to draw the defenders away, and before the Spanish could react the buccaneers managed to effect a landing close by the city. They then divided into four columns with the main body moving directly towards the city and de Grammont leading an encircling movement, forcing the Spanish to withdraw. In desperation Captain Cristóbal Martínez de Acevedo decided to sink the *Nuestra Señora de la Soledad*, a coastguard frigate that had been prepared to defend against a direct attack on the port. At first he planned to bore holes through her hull for this, but the buccaneers' rapid advance instead caused him to instruct the boatswain to lay a powder trail to the magazine. Unfortunately for the Spanish the effect of the explosion was a disastrous collapse of the defenders' morale; they took refuge in the citadel and left the city to the tender mercies of the raiders, who devoted the next few days to plundering and subduing the remaining points of resistance.[37]

On the morning of 12 July a bombardment of the citadel commenced but was interrupted by the arrival of two relief columns of militia that hurried over from Mérida de Yucután. They engaged the invaders in a desperate and prolonged battle but were finally defeated when de Grammont skilfully got behind them and caught them in a crossfire, forcing them to withdraw in confusion. With all hope of external relief gone and mistrusting the French, the garrison quietly slipped away that night, leaving a couple of English prisoners to shout out to the buccaneers, who in return called for the guns to be discharged. As soon as this was done they swarmed over the ramparts.

For the next two months the buccaneers held undisputed sway over the city but found little by way of plunder as it had long been evacuated. On 25 August the buccaneers celebrated the festival of St Louis by lighting a huge bonfire in honour of the French king, on which they burned logwood to the value of 200,000 pesos, representing the greater part of their booty.[38] Mounted patrols were sent out but, despite torturing those unfortunate enough to fall into their hands, the buccaneers were forced to leave empty handed when Governor Don Juan Bruno de Téllez de Guzmán refused to pay their ransom demand of 80,000 pesos and 400 head of cattle, saying contemptuously that Spain had ample means to rebuild Campeche and people to repopulate it. Deeply irritated by this offhand reply and knowing that the Spanish were gathering to retake the city, de Grammont organised a mass execution in the main square. But when the first few victims had been hanged de Graaf intervened to halt the proceedings after being pressed by Barrera and other leading citizens. Much bickering ensued, for the Spaniards rightly perceived the Dutchman as being more humane than the 'chevalier'.[39]

In early September, after torching the city, the raiders left Campeche and began to disperse. But on the 11th a strong contingent of the *armada de barlovento* under the elderly Admiral Andrés de Ochoa y Zárate intercepted them. The *Nuestra Señora de Regla* under Pierre Bot and a sloop were taken as the remainder of the buccaneer fleet escaped, but the latter soon fell foul of the *armada* when they spotted the frigate *Nuestra Señora de Honhón* and the eight-gun tender *Jesûs María y José*, alias *El Sevillano*, which looked to be easy prey. But these two vessels been sent to lure the buccaneers on to Ochoa's main squadron, and at four in the afternoon of 13 September his flagship *Santo Cristo de Burgos* and the vice-admiral's *Nuestra Señora de la Concepción* appeared. Quickly appreciating the danger de Graaf tried to flee as the Spanish ships bore down on him, but in due course they overhauled him on either flank. With great skill and good fortune he managed to escape this trap as both sides manoeuvred and fired repeatedly, with de Graaf's lighter ship proving more manageable. He somehow succeeded in not getting blown out of the water despite the expenditure of vast amounts of ammunition by the Spanish.

As daylight faded so did Ochoa's resolve. He had started the day in a deckchair on his quarter deck but by nightfall was so weak he had to be given the last rites. In the darkness he informed Vice-Admiral Antonio de Astina Barrera that he was now in command, just as de Graaf was jettisoning his guns and everything else he could offload to try and gain the wind. By morning he was upwind of the Spanish and they began half-heartedly beating towards him as he clawed his way slowly through the Yucután Channel. When a south-easterly picked up, *Santo Cristo's* weakened superstructure collapsed and fell overboard, forcing the Spanish to heave to and leaving de Graaf to make good his escape. It was a humiliating failure for the *armada de barlovento*, for so long being unable to get to grips with buccaneers that had plagued Spanish America, to see such elephantine strength now rendered worthless. Ochoa died a few days later, at least spared the disgrace of a court-martial, while de Graaf carried on as before, seemingly unfazed by his narrow escape.[40]

In a 1685 report colonial authorities in Martinique recorded that pirates still 'go to buy their weapons, nautical equipment and munitions in Jamaica, where they bring absolutely all the money they make, which considerably prejudices the colony'.[41] And in spite of the efforts being made to suppress them the combined buccaneer force available to France was by now very impressive. The Council of the Indies compiled an intelligence report which concluded that buccaneer strength in 1685 was sixteen ships totalling 3,650 tons and 350 guns (with ten ships carrying more than eighteen guns each), carrying 3,097 men, including some 2,000 who had crossed into the Pacific from Central America.[42] But from this point onwards their very strength and numbers would speed their decline; they had by now plundered all the places their force enabled them to, and most of the smaller towns could not provide enough booty to make an attack worth while. Nearly all the colonies that were once friendly were now hostile to them, and small island havens such as Danish St Thomas and English New Providence were regularly visited by English and Dutch naval ships. Even the French king had cancelled the old commissions and was doing his best to bring them under control, while the Spanish were finally taking effective steps against them with the *armada de barlovento*, local privateers and eventually a privateering squadron sent from Spain. It became increasingly tempting for buccaneers to accept legal employment, to look for plunder in African or Asian waters or to seek refuge in North America.

Their reputation was also highlighted by the case of two English booksellers, Thomas Malthus and William Crooke, who in 1684 produced translations of a book first published in 1678 by a Fleming seaman, Johan Esquemeling, called *De Americaenische Zee Roovers*. In the intervening years this had been a phenomenal success and had been translated into French and Spanish, from which latter edition the English version, *The Buccaneers of America*, was produced. In Jamaica Sir Henry Morgan read a copy and immediately instructed his London lawyer, John Greene, to force the publishers to retract certain claims made in it about his past. While Crooke complied instantly with an insert to the second edition and a grovelling pamphlet, Malthus not only resisted but seems to have spread more malicious propaganda to generate publicity for his edition. At first Morgan ignored the matter, hoping it would die down, as his political position was uncertain and he could not afford litigation. But when in February 1685 the Catholic hispanophile King James II succeeded to the throne, Morgan's reputation as an alleged murderer and torturer prompted him to sue in the first ever case of libel in English law for having been called a 'pirate'. He was not a pirate, he said; he was a privateer, and therefore respectable. He does not appear to have objected to some of the other often lurid claims about him, but insisted that 'there are such thieves and pirates called buccaneers who subsist by piracy, depredations and evil deeds of all kinds without lawful authority, that of these people Henry Morgan always had and still has hatred'. The suit was settled and Morgan won £200 and £10 costs.[43]

Certainly the remaining buccaneers were now a constant source of trouble to Jamaica. They attacked English merchant ships and fishing sloops, and when pursued took refuge in Petit-Goâve where they paid scant respect to the royal authority of the governor; in turn, the governor, although he refused to give his support, also feared to disavow them.[44] Lynch sent repeated complaints to de Pouançay and his successor, and also wrote to England begging the Lords of Trade and Plantations to ascertain from the French ambassador whether these governors had authority to issue commissions of war, so that his frigates might be able to distinguish between the pirate and the lawful privateer.[45] Apart from at Petit-Goâve, however, the French wanted peace with Jamaica, and did what they could to satisfy the English demands without irritating the buccaneers. But they were in a similar position to that of Lynch in 1671, when he had been anxious for peaceful relations with the Spanish but had dared not alienate the buccaneers lest they turn against him.

Since 1671 it had officially been the task of the Royal Navy to intercept pirates, but in reality little was done to suppress them for many years, although after 1680 the North American colonies increasingly became the resort of those driven from West Indian waters by the stern measures of the island governors.[46] In the Caribbean some renegades, like Sawkins, continued to elude the authorities, but others were taken. A notable case was Captain Joseph Bannister who in early January 1684 'ran away with a ship ... of thirty or forty guns, picked up over a hundred men from sloops and from leeward, and has got a French commission'.[47] Unfortunately for Bannister, his privateering expedition would not prove successful as three Royal Navy ships tracked him down on 27 July, and captured his vessel while he was stocking up on turtle in the Cayman Islands. Lynch exulted that the buccaneers would be 'found guilty of pyracy', and that might well have seemed likely when it turned out that Bannister actually held no French commission but had taken two Spanish prizes. It was one thing to capture a renegade buccaneer or pirate, however, and quite another to gain a conviction in a Port Royal court, and much to the Spaniards' disgust Bannister gained a formal discharge when the grand jury threw out the bill of piracy. Then in August 1684 Lynch died and Colonel Hender Molesworth, by virtue of his commission as lieutenant-governor, assumed his authority.[48]

By April 1685 Bannister had fallen in with French buccaneers and by November was cruising alone somewhere to leeward of Jamaica. Eventually he was hunted down once more, discovered while careening his vessel, the *Golden Fleece*, at Samaná in April 1686, by HMS *Falcon* and HMS *Drake*. A regular battle ensued, although the navy ships could not get close enough inshore to fire the *Golden Fleece* and when they ran short of ammunition had to withdraw to restock at Port Royal. On their return they found that Bannister had himself set fire to *Golden Fleece* and was trying to escape in a smaller vessel which they eventually tracked down early in 1687. Bannister was brought back and finally hanged with several others on 28 January.[49]

In 1685 a group of shipowners in Guipûzcoa offered terms for a Spanish privateer squadron that interested the Council of the Indies, something it had previously resisted as such an entity would be beyond its direct control. An agreement was signed on 6 November and the following August eight ships forming the Escuadrón Vizcaíno or Guipûzcoano (Biscayan or Guipûzcoan Squadron) sailed for the Caribbean, making the naval defences of the Spanish Caribbean considerably more robust than at any previous point in the century.[50] Ironically, however, this competition would contribute to a mutiny within the *armada de barlovento*, and the squadron's first encounter with foreign vessels at the Cape Verde Islands was less than auspicious when its commander, Commodore Francisco García Galán, was killed in an action with an English East Indiaman. The ships were old and of poor quality, 'more intended for carrying cloths and trading with the Indies than to doing harm to the enemy', according to one observer.[51]

On arriving in the West Indies one ship under Fermín Salaverri took dispatches to Nueva España while the remainder went to cruise off Trinidad and La Margarita, where they plundered the hundred-ton *Relief* of London and a Bermuda sloop *Speedwell*, then shortly afterwards the Jamaican sloop *Phoenix* belonging to John Jennings, causing outrage among the English authorities. Soon the Biscayers were making hay by attacking every English vessel they could find, down to the humblest fishing boat, and Morgan complained of 'the most unchristianlike conduct and unneighbourliness of the Spaniard, who takes all our ships at sea or in port. They have this year captured twenty-two sail and absolutely ruined our Bay trade.'[52] In April 1686 a serious incident occurred when Captain George St Loe of HMS *Dartmouth* went after a Spanish privateer cruising the Virgin Islands and stealing slaves. It was reported to have taken refuge in Puerto Rico and St Loe followed him to San Juan where, following an initially friendly reception from the governor, the Spanish tried to intern the Royal Navy's finest; they made it out only after enduring a two-hour bombardment from the shore batteries.[53]

In the same month news reached the governor of Yucután of a buccaneer raid on Valladolid; de Graaf with 500 men on seven ships had landed in the Bay of Ascención and marched inland, apparently seeking revenge for the Spanish seizure of a hundred of his slaves from Tortuga. The first town they came to was Tihosuco which they found abandoned, and the thirty-six militiamen at Valladolid quickly vanished when the buccaneers approached. But before the governor could mount a counter-attack the buccaneers returned whence they came.[54] A legend grew up in Yucután that this inexplicable retreat was thanks to a clever mulatto called Núñez who, seeing that the buccaneers were eager to collect personal items abandoned by refugees, added a set of fake instructions purportedly from the local military commander, Luis de Briaga, that the buccaneers were to be lured into a trap.[55] But, whatever the truth, that same month de Grammont formed a new squadron when de Cuss appointed him lieutenant of the coast of Saint-Domingue. On the last day of the April a Spanish ship was spotted near Matanzas, and de Grammont set out to give chase only to discover the remains of a wrecked vessel three days later. He then headed north into the Bahamas and no word came of him for the next eighteen months, until the buccaneer Captain du Marc returned from Santo Domingo having escaped from a Spanish prison: he reported that de Grammont and his crew of 180 men had all perished in a storm.[56]

In March 1687 Salaverri arrived at Havana, continuing to Veracruz in April. On his way to Nueva España he had his first encounter with de Graaf, fleeing with the Dutchman in hot pursuit; but luck was on his side and a passing Cuban coastguard chased de Graaf away.[57] During this action the brother of the corsair Blas de Miguel was killed, and the Spaniard swore he would seek vengeance. On 9 August Miguel led a buccaneer-style canoe-borne raid on Petit-Goâve in an attempt to surprise the Dutchman. But having taken the town he stayed too long to plunder it, blinded by rage and greed, and the French were able to assemble 500 men to confront him. When his ammunition ran out Miguel was forced to flee, but was captured along with his surviving companions. After a summary trial he and two of his lieutenants were sentenced to be 'torn alive on the rack', and the rest were hanged.[58]

In September de Cussy sent de Graaf with 250 men to occupy Isla Vaca and wrote to the governor of Jamaica to explain his intentions. In fact, he wanted to keep the English away from Saint-Domingue and to prevent the Spanish coastguards from using it as a base.[59] In 1685 the governorship of Jamaica was assigned to Sir Philip Howard, but he died soon afterwards, and the second Duke of Albemarle was appointed in his stead. But Albemarle did not reach Port Royal until December 1687, whereupon he promptly reversed the policy of Lynch and Molesworth and immediately set about trying to increase his fortune. Although only thirty-four years old his health was poor following a life of excess, and he soon fell in with a group of men known for their debauchery in a city renowned for impropriety. In July 1688 Sir Henry Morgan was readmitted to the Council chamber, though he did not have long to enjoy his newly restored dignity.[60] About a month later he succumbed to a sharp illness, effectively having drunk himself to death. His plantation was valued at £5,236 and included 122 slaves, and he was buried in St Catherine's Church in Port Royal on 26 August, following a state funeral with a horse-drawn cortège and a salute of twenty-two guns.[61] Harry Morgan's death was symbolic of the death of buccaneering in Jamaica, a gradual process that had started with the Treaty of Madrid in 1670 and saw the transfer of Jamaican enthusiasm from buccaneering to smuggling. Port Royal was now a commercial hub where English, French, Dutch and Spanish interests overlapped; not only were French privateers and Dutch smugglers to be found aplenty but so were Spanish merchants and *asientos* looking for slaves.[62]

The value of empire was seen to derive from maritime commerce rather than territory and dominion, as a report to the Lords of Trade explained in 1686.

> It being no more a secret of state now that he that hath the greatest force by sea (how little soever his dominions be) hath the greatest opportunity to give law to the rest of the world ... [and he that] hath the greatest and most constant employment for seamen must be in the hopefullest way of raising the greatest force by sea ... it seems not to be anywhere avoided [but] we must apply ourselves closely to the same concern ...[63]

Once the merchant class of Jamaica reached ascendancy in the mid-1680s, the volume of smuggling between the island and Central America increased dramatically, just as the Atlantic trade also increased – the English merchant fleet had almost doubled by 1688 from some 90,000 tons in 1663, and would reach 262,222 tons enhanced by technological improvements by 1701.[64] Puerto Rico was one very important market, which William Dampier noted was the most popular source of indigo and ottar for Jamaicans.[65] Indeed, Puerto Rico's close proximity to the Lesser Antilles made it a natural hub for illicit trade with both English and French smugglers, which had the effect of weakening Spanish royal authority. This increase in trade put further pressure on the buccaneers in Jamaica, because raiding damages the mutual trust necessary to smooth commercial trans-actions, including smuggling. Eventually, smuggling became the more popular enterprise, reinforced with the establishment of English logwood-cutting settlements along the Central American coast.[66]

Those involved in smuggling included merchants, shopkeepers, petty traders, factors and agents, governors, customs officials, naval captains and foreigners of every stripe; effectively everyone in the Caribbean was involved in some form or other with very few excep-tions. Because no nation in the Caribbean sanctioned trade with any other, smuggling, which had originally been centred on Cuba, Española, Puerto Rico, Portobelo, Cartagena and Central America came to encompass the Dutch and French islands, despite the 1686 Act of Neutrality that was supposed to prevent it. Thus buccaneering evolved into smuggling, usually with the connivance of the Spanish authorities, until by 1688 even the French were seizing English ships off Spanish Caribbean coasts: that year, Leonard Godfrey, William Chapman and other smugglers complained that the French authorities had appre-hended their vessel with 8,000 pesos off Portobelo.[67] Yet old buc-caneering habits died hard: on 22 May 1687 King James II renewed a proclamation against it and dispatched a squadron under Sir Robert Holmes to clean up the Caribbean. Holmes sent Stephen Lynch as his agent to Jamaica. Lynch arrived the following year and immediately arrested fifty-six 'pirates or privateers' with French commissions who were enjoying themselves in Port Royal taverns. But, rather than allow-ing them to apply for pardon and offering security against future good behaviour, as envisaged under the proclamation, Lynch chained them heavily and threw them into gaol, claiming they 'intended off on their wanted depredations'. Their surprised petitions at being treated 'little differing from slaves under the Turks' instead of receiving the 'mercy and protection they expected here' provided the Duke of Albemarle with the excuse needed to order their swift release. They immediately sued Lynch, who 'stole privately away' having learned that, almost twenty years after the Treaty of Madrid, privateering still played an important role in Port Royal life.[68]

In early 1688 another of the Biscayan captains, José de Leoz y Echalar, intercepted *Dragon* commanded by Roger Whitfield as she sailed from Jamaica for New York and left her at Santiago de Cuba. He then sailed to Santo Domingo where most of his crew settled as local coastguards and began to harass English shipping. On 21 March that same year the governor of Barbados complained about a sloop that had fallen 'into the hands of the Biscayers about Porto Rico, who are taken into the King of Spain's service to take pirates, and who interrupt English traders more than the pirates ever did. They not only confiscate the ship and goods, but put all men to death, so they are never heard of again.'[69] In November a petition was sent to the king by Jamaica's planters and merchants protesting against Albemarle's regime. Fortunately Albemarle had already rendered his greatest service to the colony by dying, and Molesworth was immediately commanded to return to Jamaica as governor with authority to use the Royal Navy to protect English shipping and put an end to the Biscayers' depredations. Eventually the Biscayers split up and went their separate ways, the squadron being officially disbanded in 1692.[70] But more significantly Molesworth was another big planter and an agent for the Royal African Company, so that the slave trade was also given another major boost.

# 14

———∂∕∂∕∂∕———

## THE END OF THE BUCCANEERS

Then learn, my honest Country-men
To take yourselves the Pence;
Wisely prevent the Courtier's gain,
And save us the Expence.

Ye gallants all, take heed how you
Come to untimely Ends;
Justice has bid the World adieu;
And dead Men have no friends.

Sir Charles Sedley, 'A Ballad to the Tune of Bateman'

For some thirty years the Spanish had acquired most of their slaves from the Dutch out of Curaçao, and by 1689 Jamaica was close to paralysis having suffered three major slave revolts between 1675 and 1686. But from 1689 onwards, with Spain and England allies in a new war with France, there was a sudden upsurge in trade with Jamaica, in both slaves and other commodities.[1] Before that, however, the 'Glorious Revolution' created an effective union between England and Holland when King James II fled the throne and Prince William of Orange was proclaimed King William III to secure the Protestant succession. This marked not only the end of the Stuart autocracy but a final repudiation of the buccaneers and their ways, for by now the small farming interest on Jamaica and in the Lesser Antilles had almost completely given way to that of the large planters. Finally excluded from power, the remaining buccaneers drifted away to Saint-Domingue and the Bahamas.[2]

In November 1688, the same month that William of Orange landed at Torbay in the last successful invasion of England, a forty-two-year-old slaver and French royal navy officer, Jean-Baptiste Ducasse, led an unsuccessful attack against the Dutch colony of Surinam on the wild coast of South America. However, full-scale war did not erupt until the following year when King Louis XIV aligned himself with the now

263

exiled former Stuart king of England, and found himself at war with England, Holland and Spain, as well as various lesser European powers. The War of the League of Augsburg (known in America as King William's War, and later as the Nine Years War) that began in May 1689 therefore derived, as all the wars of the period did, from European frictions. A broad coalition had for some time been slowly coalescing against Louis' overarching ambition, and being initially unprepared for war and absorbed with trying to support James II's restoration, the French king sent little support to his Caribbean colonies. The Lesser Antilles – always the first to gain news of European developments – witnessed the first hostilities. Most of Saint-Domingue's colonists were destitute, and the loss of some 1,400 buccaneers during the late 1680s had substantially weakened the colony, so that de Cussy could scarcely count on a thousand good men.[3] But the French governor-general and governor of Martinique, Charles de Roche-Courbon, comte de Blénac, having already seized the Dutch island of St Eustatius, mustered around two dozen vessels including six warships and attacked St Christopher on 27 July. Some 120 buccaneers went ashore and laid siege to Fort Charles, which surrendered two weeks later.[4]

The loss of these islands to the Protestant cause was aggravated by other buccaneers in French service attacking English and Dutch shipping, with one writer estimating English losses alone at sixty-two ships worth over £300,000.[5] The declaration of war had soon drawn English reinforcements to the Caribbean, however. One of the first to respond was Captain Thomas Hewetson, who set off from England in 1688 with an expedition to set up a settlement in Chile. But unable to beat through the Magellan Straits he retired to Tobago, where he learned that the change of regime at home had rendered his commission invalid. Worse, when he reached Barbados one of his three ships had blown up, and with most of his men having deserted he was planning to sail homeward as escort to a merchant convoy when Governor Robert Robinson issued him with a commission on 19 October. With this he was able to raise a crew of 350 for his flagship *Lion* (fifty guns), and he went to Antigua to offer his services to Christopher Codrington. As governor-general of the Leeward Islands, Codrington immediately appointed Hewetson as 'commander-in-chief of all vessels fitted out' in those waters, which included the *Blessed William* with some ninety men commanded by a forty-year-old native of Greenock in Scotland who had endeared himself to the English authorities, Captain William Kidd. Hewetson first led his squadron of three ships and two sloops against the French island of Marie Galante on 30 December, and after ransacking it for five days departed with considerable booty.[6]

In early 1690 Ducasse took command of three warships, a sloop and a brigantine to escort 700 reinforcements that were to be sent to San Martín, which was under attack by English forces under Sir Timothy Thornhill, who had earlier recaptured St Christopher and St Eustatius. They arrived in time to relieve the defenders and take the English by surprise, cutting them off in their turn. On arriving at Nevis, Hewetson was immediately sent to assist Thornhill, arriving in late January. The two squadrons confronted each other offshore and exchanged broad-sides throughout the day until Ducasse retired, and the following day Hewetson was able to bring Thornhill's men away, returning to Nevis in triumph. However, not everyone enjoyed the sense of elation over a military operation smartly carried out: the unpaid buccaneers among the crews were not best pleased at being involved in a full-scale line-of-battle engagement with heavily armed men-of-war rather than taking weakly defended booty-rich prizes. When Kidd went ashore on 12 February his crew, who had been muttering about his 'ill-behaviour', mutinied and made off with the *Blessed William*, taking with them the captain's £2,000 share of the Marie Galante loot. Codrington presented Kidd with a French prize renamed *Antigua* and he set off in angry pursuit, eventually reaching New York where he married and settled down for a while.[7]

Hewetson transferred to Barbados in April where he received another commission, then decided to seek better commercial oppor-tunities elsewhere and chartered *Lion* to the factor of the Spanish *asiento*, before departing the Caribbean to carry slaves. West Indian freebooters were proving a distinctly unreliable military force.[8] De Graaf himself began engaging Jamaican shipping and touched at Montego Bay on the north coast with 200 men in October; he threat-ened to return and plunder the whole north side of the island. The people were so frightened that they sent their wives and children to Port Royal and the Council armed several vessels to go in pursuit of the Dutch 'Frenchman'.[9] For Jamaicans it was a new experience to feel the threat of invasion by a fearsome foreign foe, giving them an insight into the terror their Spanish neighbours had felt for the buccaneers, whom they had always been so ready to fit out or to shield from the law. And de Graaf was as good as his word; he returned to Jamaica at the beginning of December with several vessels, seized eight or ten English trading sloops, then landed on the north shore and plundered a plantation.[10]

A counter was made by Captain Edward Spragge of HMS *Drake*, but he failed to deter the buccaneer. Between March and May 1690 de Graaf consolidated his blockade of Jamaica so that no ship could arrive or depart without running the gauntlet of buccaneers. But when they encountered HMS *Drake* off the Cayman Islands as she escorted a convoy to break the blockade, the buccaneers got the worst of the action and in June de Graaf was forced to withdraw to Saint-Domingue, where rumours were rife of an imminent English attack.[11] But de Cussy discounted them and instead took the offensive; on 6 July he attacked Santiago de los Caballeros with 900 buccaneers and 200 former slaves and sacked and razed the town, until a Spanish counter-attack from Santo Domingo forced the French to retreat. And he also issued so many new licences that English shipping would suffer severely as a result. Six months later in January 1691 the expected attack on Saint-Domingue took place. The *armada de barlovento*, supported by an English detachment, carrying 200 soldiers, 300 militiamen from Santiago and another hundred from Montecristi, attacked Guarico. De Cussy led his few royal troops, supported by around 300 ex-buccaneers whom he had trained and equipped partly at his own expense, to Sabana Real; but the latter proved fickle allies, and fled the field leaving him to be killed by the Spanish on the mountain battlefield above Limonade. De Cussy and another 300 Frenchmen perished, and Port-de-Paix, Cap-François (or Cabo Francés, the modern Cap-Haïtien) and Port-au-Prince were all razed to the ground.[12]

When Ducasse arrived later that month he found the place devastated and a disgusting battlefield strewn with corpses not yet buried, being rotted and half desiccated'. By the time he returned to Martinique after reporting to La Rochelle, he discovered that a large English force under Captain Lawrence Wright RN had arrived in the Antilles and together with Codrington had laid siege to Guadeloupe. With two infantry companies and 600 buccaneers he sailed to relieve this island but avoided direct confrontation with the English. Having freed Marie Galante from English occupation when he finally disembarked at Grosier on 23 May, he was able to force the English to withdraw once again two days later, as by now they had been ravaged by disease after enduring unending torrential rain. But despite returning to Martinique in triumph the crews of his own ships were suffering from yellow fever and 250 of his men succumbed. On 1 October a letter from Paris arrived informing Ducasse of his promotion to governor of Saint-Domingue, where his first task was to rebuild and restore morale to the ravaged colony.[13]

One of his first moves was to relocate the government to Cap-François, causing a mass exodus from Tortuga. In February 1692 came news that a fresh Spanish assault was being planned although the timely dispatch of reinforcements to de Graaf ensured that this never took place, and as soon as the buccaneers were aware of this they departed. Despite his long association with these free-spirited men Ducasse found their self-centred behaviour galling in the current climate of crisis. 'They are very bad subjects,' he wrote,

who believe they have not been put in the world except to practise brigandage and piracy. Enemies of subordination and authority, their example ruins the colonies, all the young people having no other wish than to embrace this profession for its libertinage and ability to gain booty.[14]

The English authorities had long held similar views, and given the alliance with Holland and Spain the only prizes available to English privateers were French ships which soon disappeared from the seas or were corralled into tightly guarded convoys. Consequently English buccaneers began to turn their attentions to the Far East which offered tempting prizes without military escort, and when word spread of sanctuary athwart the tracks of the fabled East Indiamen on Madagascar they forsook the Caribbean and north Atlantic in large numbers for this new pirate refuge, an exodus given greater impetus when disaster struck Port Royal.

On Wednesday 7 June 1692 the Anglican rector Dr Emmanuel Heath went after morning service to drink a glass of 'wormwood wine' with the president of the Council, John White, 'as a whet before dinner'.[15] But these distinguished gentlemen would get no dinner that day as their pre-prandial was interrupted by a geological calamity.

> The sand in the street rose like the waves in the sea, lifting up all persons that stood upon it, and immediately dropping down into pits; and at the same instant a flood of water rushed in, throwing down all who were in its way; some were seen catching hold of beams and rafters of houses, others were found in the sand that appeared when the water was drained away, with their legs and arms out.[16]

Dr Heath watched in horror as many were trapped in the ground which seemed to close up again after bursting open in this way; he ran and managed to reach his own house which he found intact, standing on the coralline mass. 'The ground opened,' reported a Quaker merchant, 'and the sea gushed up a wonderful height that in a moment almost the whole place was under water.'[17] To the north the wharves fell thirty or forty feet into the water and some two-thirds of the town disappeared. The church, the wharves, the exchange, two of the four forts and the three main streets were all submerged; hundreds of people drowned and their corpses soon floated on the water's surface. 'Great men who were so swallowed up with pride, that a man could not be admitted to speak to them, and women whose top knots seem to reach the clouds, now lie stinking upon the water and are made meat for fish or fowles of the air.'[18] In all around 2,000 people perished including the attorney-general, the provost-marshal and other notables. Unsurprisingly the earthquake was widely regarded as evidence of God's judgement on the wicked city of Port Royal, and sermons soon followed suggesting that it had got what it deserved.[19] Undoubtedly the damage was worse than it might have been because of the nature of the buildings, which were facsimiles of their English equivalents. Three- or four-storey houses of brick had been erected eschewing the Spanish style of low-slung houses constructed around poles driven deep into the ground. Stone piled upon stone had been the preferred look despite being built on a layer of sand thirty to sixty feet deep, lying in turn on gravel and coralline limestone in an area notoriously prone to earthquake and tsunamis.[20]

By the time the earthquake had destroyed the buccaneers' former playground, nobody was in any doubt that sugar was the new king of Jamaica.[21] Besides, the buccaneers were no longer the free-spirited 'brethren' of old, but had been more or less absorbed into the colonial systems of the maritime powers, having tended to coalesce into national groups, and with captains increasingly likely to exempt ships of their own nations from attack.[22] The French in Saint-Domingue took advantage of the distress caused by the earthquake to attack the island, and nearly every week hostile bands landed and plundered the coast of slaves and other property.[23] Worried by French actions in the Caribbean the government in London came under severe pressure from merchants to do something about the situation there, and in 1693 an expedition under Admiral Sir Charles Wheler was mounted with fifteen warships, several fireships, numerous transports and some 2,000 troops. They arrived in the West Indies in March with orders to attack Martinique, and at Barbados another thousand men were raised. They made a landing and easily devastated large areas before reinforcements arrived under Codrington, but this powerful combined force did little apart from carry off some 3,000 slaves valued at £60,000 before Wheler departed for New England.[24]

Ducasse decided to keep the few hundred buccaneers he could muster occupied by sending them against Jamaica, and in December 1693 a party of 170 swooped down in the night upon St David's, only twenty miles from Port Royal, plundered the entire parish and escaped with 370 slaves in the first instance. Thus encouraged Ducasse gathered 400–500 buccaneers in six ships under Charles-François Le Vasseur, sieur de Beauregard, to plunder the parishes of St Thomas and, for a second time, St David's. But they were deterred by the presence of the patrolling frigate HMS *Falcon*, and deciding 'that they would only get broken bones and spoil their men for any other design', they turned tail and ran, with one being captured and brought in.[25] On returning to Petit-Goâve, Beauregard found that the French naval ships *Téméraire* (fifty-four guns), *Envieux* and *Solide* had just arrived with a merchant convoy from France, and Ducasse sent them to patrol *Falcon*'s patch where they succeeded in taking her despite stout resistance. Governor

Sir William Beeston was not about to take this on the chin, but could not persuade the Assembly to cough up the money necessary to patrol against 'the daily depredations of French privateers on our coasts', and minor raids continued.[26] Then in June 1694 came startling news from an escaped prisoner, Stephen Elliott, an intrepid smuggler who had been brought to Saint-Domingue after being captured on the Spanish Main by two French buccaneers. While being held there he discovered French plans, then managed to escape in a stolen canoe with two companions, putting out to sea on 5 June. He arrived at Jamaica five days later and stumbled into Beeston's house where the governor was entertaining guests; if he was surprised by the sight of Elliott, 'in a very mean habit and with a meager weather-beaten countenance', he was astounded by the news that the French would soon descend on the island with twenty ships and 3,000 men, and worse, that they were expecting 500 Jacobites to join them upon landing.[27]

Indeed, Ducasse had assembled twenty-two ships mounting 378 guns and carrying 3,164 men, but by the time the major part of this fleet anchored in Cow Bay east of Port Royal on 27 June, the island was prepared, and Beeston quickly adjourned the Assembly, gathered the Council and proclaimed martial law. He then barricaded the streets and hurried to Fort Charles, which along with its thirty-eight guns remained in good condition, put the merchantmen in harbour into line and prepared a fireship. The population in the parishes east of town and at Port Morant were evacuated, while the shot and powder at Fort William were brought in and the guns there were spiked. Next morning the French fleet appeared with Ducasse anxious to attack immediately, but his naval commander, the chevalier du Rollon, vetoed this as being too risky. Instead he landed 800 men and rampaged through the eastern part of the island, killing people and livestock and setting up headquarters at Port Morant.[28] The expedition remained on the island for a month sending out raiding parties, then returned to Cow Bay intending to take on Port Royal, which Ducasse planned to assault overland with a force marching from Carlisle Bay, under the command of his old friend de Graaf.

After landing some 1,500 men the previous night, on 29 July de Graaf attacked the town and succeeded in throwing the defenders out of a prepared position at heavy cost, although the figures were disputed;

the French claimed to have inflicted 360 casualties but the English admitted to only twenty-two.[29] Next morning de Graaf sent 500 men to round up prisoners and cattle and ravage the neighbourhood. But every house the buccaneers came to was strongly fortified with stout walls, behind which the planters had gathered their valuables and as many men as needed for protection; the buccaneers got as good as they gave and had to content themselves with plundering as best they could. When Ducasse arrived a few days later he was sorely disappointed with the booty collected and had to settle for about 1,500 slaves, some indigo and a few pieces of sugar machinery. He sailed back to Petit-Goâve on 3 August, arriving home on the 14th.[30] The harm done to Jamaica by the invasion, however, was considerable; the French wholly destroyed fifty sugar works and many plantations, burned and plundered about 200 houses, and killed every living thing they found. The Jamaicans lost about a hundred killed and wounded, although French losses appear to have been several times that number. Once home Ducasse reserved all the slaves for himself, and, exasperated by the division of spoils which further underscored the notion that large expeditions did not pay, many men deserted the governor and resorted to raiding on their own account.[31]

A retaliatory English attack mounted on Saint-Domingue with three warships, a fireship and two barques in October achieved little, and de Graaf was involved in organising the defence against a joint Anglo-Spanish attack in 1695. But despite a warning many of the buccaneers were now away on cruises and could not be recalled, and it was the turn of the French to suffer.[32] However, on Jamaica Beeston was in despair, for as well as the losses suffered the previous year there was a general exodus of fighting men. From a total of 2,440 effectives his numbers were reduced to 1,390 by August, and from 1,200 seamen to 300 after various Royal Navy captains ignored his express orders and pressed many men, causing many others to flee to Petit-Goâve and join the buccaneers.[33] That spring saw an English expedition arrive in the Antilles with some two dozen vessels and almost a thousand troops under Colonel Luke Lillingston and Commodore Robert Wilmot RN. They joined forces with the Spanish at Santo Domingo and the *armada de barlovento* and on 15 May descended on Cap-François where they easily swept aside the outnumbered defenders under de Graaf, who offered no resistance apparently for fear of falling into the hands of his old enemies. After the departure of the allies de Graaf was deprived of his post and made captain of a light corvette.[34] A month later the squadron captured Port-de-Paix which was razed, followed by Port-à-Margot, Planemon and other strongholds, with Ducasse being forced to retreat to Léogâne. By the end of the campaign 600 Frenchmen had been killed and another 900 taken prisoner, including de Graaf's wife, Anne Dieu-le-Veut,* and two daughters, together with 150 guns and some 200,000 pesos' worth of booty.[35] But disagreements over the division of these spoils saw the disintegration of Anglo-Spanish co-operation, and the two sides withdrew to their respective bases. Ducasse then sent de Graaf and his French counterpart, La Boulaye, to France to stand trial for desertion, and although de Graaf was eventually acquitted he did not return until after the war's end when he was finally reunited with his family.[36]

No major campaigns could be mounted by either side in 1696 because of the shortage of available manpower. Many English buccaneers had long since either quit to take up other pursuits or decamped to New England, the Bahamas or Madagascar. In Jamaica Beeston was moved to lament the dearth of seamen,

> for besides the losses through death, the press for the King's ships frightens away many, and many go to the Northern Plantations [that is, North America], where the Red Sea pirates take their plunder, are pardoned and fitted out for a fresh voyage, which makes all kinds of rogues flock to them.[37]

Since 1687 the Moguls who dominated India had been at war with the English East India Company, providing ample opportunities for plunder, and when the likes of Rhode Islander Thomas Tew and Englishman Henry Avery made massive hauls in the Arabian (Red) Sea from spectacular single captures, they provided a new model for

---

* Anne, or Marie-Anne, was probably a *fille du roi*, one of those women deported to Tortuga or Saint-Domingue to help civilise the buccaneers. Legend has it that de Graaf killed or insulted her former husband, and when she challenged him he refused to fight a woman but proposed on the spot which she accepted. In fact, they were never formally married, and she certainly accompanied him on some of his voyages.

gaining vast riches – one seemingly much less risky than attacking Spanish towns as Morgan had done – and sapping the buccaneers' military resolve yet further. Many English adventurers duly set sail for the Indian Ocean, for although the Moguls remained dominant on land they had practically no navy to speak of, and native accounts speak of 'Roberts' (probably 'robbers') and his crew making over 400 seizures.[38] But although they had faded from English service the buccaneers still had time for one swansong.

The French assault on Cartagena in 1697 ranks among the greatest raids mounted against the Spanish Main, a bloody and largely pointless success made at a time when the long war was drawing to a close, with peace feelers already put out by both sides. The possibility of a Caribbean expedition was raised in France in early 1696, and was intended to furnish King Louis with the money needed to continue the war, his astute diplomacy having already separated Lombardy from the alliance ranged against him. Both Ducasse and Admiral Jean-Bernard-Louis Desjeans, baron de Pointis, were urging action, with the latter's plan accepted by the king in May. Born in 1645, de Pointis had risen to command a line-of-battle ship at Beachy Head in 1690, and served at the battle of La Hogue two years later, at which the French navy suffered a severe defeat that saw the beginning of its demise while France's opponents rapidly expanded their forces. From then on King Louis began to stress privateering over regular naval warfare, and after 1694 the French navy rarely showed itself, forcing de Pointis to rely, for one last time, on the buccaneers.[39] For although the proposed design involved the loan of twenty ships and soldiers (but not seamen) paid for by the crown, in return for the usual one-fifth *prêts de vaisseaux*, de Pointis would have to raise the balance of the money to furnish the expedition himself, which would take the rest of the year. Eventually the remaining costs fell on 666 private subscribers – courtiers, financiers, naval contractors and officers of both pen and sword, and in the meantime orders were sent to Ducasse to be ready to provide 1,000–1,200 men in locally armed frigates and sloops.[40]

According to de Pointis, rumours of impending peace restricted interest, because from the beginning of 1697 negotiations for a treaty were under way at Rijswijk, and when the expedition sailed from Brest it was weaker than expected. De Pointis eventually reached Petit-Goâve on 16 March aboard the *Esceptre* (eight-four guns), with ten ships-of-the-line carrying between fifty and ninety-eight guns, four frigates and several troop transports carrying some 2,800 men. On arrival he was furious to learn that instead of the 1,200 men he had expected, Ducasse had mustered only some 200 buccaneers, the rest having set off on their own adventures due to his late arrival. Relations between the two contingents worsened a day later when a French naval officer arrested an unruly buccaneer ashore and sparked a riot in which two or three others were killed, a revolt that ended only when Ducasse intervened.[41] The buccaneers resented the secondary role they had been allotted and refused to take part in the venture without the lure of booty, a problem that was not solved until Ducasse was appointed commander of local forces. Some 170 of these were garrison troops with another 110 militiamen or settlers, plus about 180 blacks – some slaves, some free – but the majority amounting to around 650 buccaneers.[42] They would have done nothing but skulk in the woods had Ducasse not attended and negotiated a prior agreement to share the plunder. Furthermore, there were serious differences between the two commanders over objectives; de Pointis was concerned only with booty and glory, while Ducasse was concerned primarily with his colony and the wider interests of France, and he wanted the expedition to clear the Spanish from Santo Domingo which he regarded as being worth a thousand Canadas. Eventually it was agreed to attack Cartagena, although Ducasse remained deeply sceptical about the entire venture.[43]

According to the careful historian Charlevoix, who had access to government records as well as the papers of Father Jean-Baptiste Le Pers, a fellow Jesuit who was serving on the coast of Saint-Domingue at the time, Ducasse's contingent conducted themselves with the resourcefulness and audacity that might be expected of them.[44] But while de Pointis in his *Account* praised the blacks, he considered the buccaneers nothing but a 'troop of *banditti* . . . idle Speculators of a great Action . . . this Rabble that base Kind of Life', gifted only with 'a particular talent for discovering hidden Treasures'. He deeply resented having 'to court them in the most flattering Terms'.[45] Having assembled at Cap-Tiburon on 8 April the expedition set out for Cartagena, arriving a week later. De Pointis' initial plan was crude; he proposed to disembark the buccaneers immediately on the city outskirts under

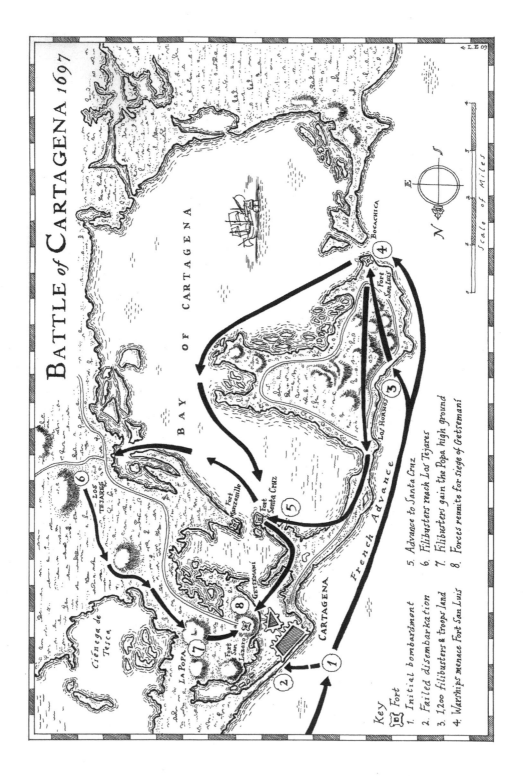

# BATTLE of CARTAGENA 1697

BAY OF CARTAGENA

Botachica

Fort San Luis

Los Hornos

French Advance

Fort Santa Cruz

Fort Manzanillo

Los Tejares

Ciénega de Teca

LA POPA

Fort San Lazaro

Getsemani

CARTAGENA

Key

⊞ Fort

1. Initial bombardment
2. Failed disembarkation
3. 1200 filibusters & troops land
4. Warships menace Fort San Luis
5. Advance to Santa Cruz
6. Filibusters reach Los Tejares
7. Filibusters gain the Popa high ground
8. Forces reunite for siege of Getsemani

N S
E
Scale of Miles

← L.E 09

covering fire of his warships' guns. But when he and Ducasse conducted a reconnaissance, their boat was overturned on the dangerous reefs and they barely avoided drowning, so they decided to force the harbour entrance to the south instead. They disembarked with 1,200 men at Bocachica five days later near the hamlet of Los Hornos, and as they were preparing their positions the buccaneers captured a coastguard patrol boat carrying reinforcements from Portobelo. They used this to escort a number of vessels towards Cartagena, but the defenders sniffed the ruse and opened fire from the fort, forcing the buccaneers to scatter, much to the disgust of de Pointis. During the night a Spanish sortie killed seven buccaneers and six soldiers and wounded twenty-two others including Ducasse, leaving Joseph d'Honon de Gallifet, a new-comer to Saint-Domingue and unknown to most of the buccaneers, to assume command.[46]

De Pointis ordered the buccaneers to assault the hill of Nuestra Señora de la Popa to the east of the city while his main body attacked across the plain, but the buccaneers held back until de Gallifet seized one by the arm and tried to force him towards the boats. When he was thrown off de Pointis intervened, and had the offender tied to a tree in anticipation of a firing squad. But in a contrived gesture de Gallifet publicly intervened on the buccaneer's behalf, and to help the new commander ingratiate himself with his unruly charges, de Pointis agreed to release the man. The buccaneers then proceeded somewhat grudgingly to pursue their mission, and were relieved to find that the Spanish had abandoned the heights. Following this the French took higher positions where they emplaced artillery, during which operations de Pointis received a leg wound from a Spanish sharpshooter, and was forced to direct proceedings from a litter.[47] The French began a bombardment on 28 April, and when Ducasse returned to duty on 1 May he met a Spanish officer outside the city to negotiate surrender terms, arguing that the French had opened a breach in the defences. When the Spanish refused to concede, de Pointis ordered a final assault for 4 o'clock that afternoon, and in a bloody hand-to-hand battle the French grenadiers and buccaneers fought their way through the gap to the very edge of the city itself. A white flag was hoisted there the following day.[48]

While the surrender terms were being negotiated de Pointis heard that a Spanish relief column of over a thousand men was approaching, and ordered Ducasse to oppose them with his buccaneers and several hundred regular troops. But it proved to be a false report and by the time Ducasse returned on 4 May he found the city gates closed to him, and his men were forced to billet themselves in the impoverished and devastated suburb of Getsemaní. The buccaneers were alarmed to see de Pointis stowing the best of the loot and insisting that they should receive only a modest wage for their efforts, instead of the one-quarter share they had expected. A notice had been posted at Petit-Goâve announcing that the buccaneers would be participating *homme par homme* with royal personnel. Ducasse assumed that this meant his men would receive the same proportion of booty as the regulars, and de Pointis was careful not to disabuse him of this until ready to embark; besides, the buccaneers had no concept of the joint-stock operation that had funded the expedition in the first place.[49] Ducasse faced a dilemma, as he watched the booty being loaded on to the naval ships with his men growing ever more restless and unruly. Aware that he had been duped, he risked losing all control over them – control that relied as much on his own force of character as on his royal commission. But as a commissioned officer and royal governor he could not countenance rebellion and had no choice but to accept de Pointis' assurances. Ducasse estimated his side's share of the booty at 2 million livres tournois, but by the end of May everything of value had been purloined, including guns and church bells. De Pointis was in the process of blowing up several forts when the buccaneers learned they were entitled to only one-tenth of the first million livres, and one-thirtieth of any subsequent millions which were variously estimated at between eight and forty.[50]

In extreme anger the buccaneers promptly returned to the city on 30 May and sacked it again, rounding up every inhabitant they could lay hands on and herding them all into the principal church where they sprinkled them with gunpowder and threatened to blow them all up unless another 5 million pesos were produced. This was plainly impossible, though brutal torture succeeded in bringing enough precious metal to give each man one thousand pesos instead of the measly twenty-five each that they would have made, and they finally weighed anchor on 3 June. Four days later de Pointis was intercepted by the

Royal Navy, which had sent a squadron after him under Vice-Admiral John Neville. For two days a running fight ensued until de Pointis, his crews severely laid low by sickness, managed to slip away at sunrise on 10 June, and after an extremely eventful voyage he returned to France – although not as a conquering hero, as he had probably anticipated, because adverse reports had arrived ahead of him.[51] The chase had brought Neville very close to Cartagena which he briefly visited before setting off north-eastwards in pursuit of the buccaneers. On 25 June he sighted Ducasse at anchor with eight of his laggardly vessels off Sambay. Having been cheated by their own side, the buccaneers now found themselves being chased by the Royal Navy, which quickly overtook *Gracieuse* (eighteen guns) and the fifty-gun *Christe* (possibly a prize, originally named *Santo Cristo*), as well as driving *Saint Louis* (eighteen guns) aground. The crew managed to escape ashore but were soon hunted down by the locals, and forced to work on the reconstruction of Cartagena. Ducasse himself managed to escape as the other vessels scattered, and made it back to Saint-Domingue, but the *Cerf Volant* (eighteen guns) was also driven on to rocks off that coast and its cargo later sold at Jamaica for £100,000. Thus the buccaneers ended up with very little to show for their efforts, and their morale suffered a fatal blow, while the quarrel among the French factions would persist for years afterwards.[52]

On 30 September 1697 the Treaty of Rijswijk finally ended the war as the assault on Cartagena marked its end in the Caribbean, save for an inconsequential and unsuccessful attack by English buccaneers against Martinique in October.[53] Indeed, it effectively marked the end of the age of the buccaneers, who also suffered a revolt on Madagascar, forcing them to flee their base at St Mary's because of the numbers of local blacks they had sold into bondage. Since 1671 English government policy had consistently sought to suppress them and, with a few exceptions, the governors sent to Jamaica had done their best to carry out these wishes. Increasingly the buccaneers had degenerated into mere pirates, or had quit their libertine life altogether for more civilised pursuits. Although it was ten years or more before the French court saw the situation in a similar light, the exigencies of war and defence in French Saint-Domingue then prevented their governors from instituting effective measures towards suppression. For the buccaneers, whatever their origin, were intrepid men, not without a sense of honour among themselves, and inured to a life of constant danger which bred tremendous hardiness. When an expedition was projected against their traditional foes, the Spaniards, they took little notice what flag they sailed under. English, French and Dutch alike became brothers under a chief whose courage they recognised, and as long as they confined themselves to His Catholic Majesty's ships and settlements, they enjoyed immunity arising from the traditional hostility existing between the English and Spanish of the era.[54]

For the Spanish their record in the Caribbean was a terrible one. From 1655 to 1671 buccaneers sacked eighteen cities, four towns and more than thirty-five villages – Cumaná once, Cumanagote twice, Maracaibo and Gibraltar twice, Río de la Hacha five times, Santa Marta three times, Tolu eight times, Portobelo once, Chagre twice, Panamá once, Santa Catalina twice, Granada in Nicaragua twice, Campeche three times, Santiago de Cuba once, and many other settlements in Cuba and Española innumerable times. The Marqués de Barinas in 1685 estimated the losses of the Spaniards at the hands of the buccaneers since the accession of King Charles II to be 60 million crowns (or ducats), and this merely covers the destruction of towns and treasure, on top of which may be added more than 250 merchant ships and frigates.[55] But the trail of woe was by no means one sided; the advantages accruing to the marauders and the colonies that supported them hardly covered their costs.

By diverting manpower, resources and energy elsewhere buccaneering impeded the essential development of Jamaica. It was later estimated that some 2,600 men were lost during expeditions mounted between 1668 and 1671, a very significant number for an isolated and struggling young colony with enemies on all sides. As a contemporary noted:

People have not married, built or settled as they would in time of peace – some for fear of being destroyed, others have got much suddenly by privateers bargains and are gone. War carries away all freemen, labourers and planters of provisions, which makes work and victuals dear and scarce. Privateering encourages all manner of disorder and dissoluteness; and if it succeed, does but enrich the worst sort of people and provoke and alarm the Spaniards.[56]

In relentlessly attacking Spanish property the buccaneers hampered the development of English trade, since the Spanish of the colonies if not of Castile would probably have permitted trade with the English islands, as indeed they increasingly did, albeit illicitly. At home the attitude of the government was to encourage trade, but as long as it remained incapable of providing defence for the colonies they, not unnaturally, took matters into their own hands. The Spanish could hardly be blamed, therefore, for regarding English protestations of goodwill as being hollow and worthless. But buccaneer depredations in the Caribbean also hampered trade much further afield, since it was English, French and Dutch ships that serviced Cádiz and the Spanish-American fleets, and when a treasure fleet returned it was, in fact, they who carried away most of the silver and other valuables. It was a realisation that the way to appropriating the wealth of the Americas was through trade rather than war that changed the attitude of governments, first in London then in Paris. They went from encouragement or connivance of buccaneering to disapproval and outright antagonism. And as the century drew to a close so control was strengthened by a now greatly expanded Royal Navy, that could provide defence for English colonies, and chase the pirates away.[57]

Now the Treaty of Rijswijk recognised French rights in the Caribbean, effectively ending two centuries of Spanish dominion over the sea, although it would continue to be a scene of international rivalry for another two centuries to come. Although a few minor privateering actions took place in the War of the Spanish Succession during the early part of the eighteenth century (1702–13) and privateering would remain a legitimate mode of war until well into the nineteenth century, these were strictly individual commercial ventures aimed at making money, and were no longer instruments of government policy operating in fleets on specific instructions. With both France and Britain – truly a United Kingdom after 1707 – making the defence of their West Indian possessions the responsibility of their navies, the buccaneers were dispersed. The English Act of Piracy in 1699 allowed more colonial courts to execute sea robbers, and the Royal Navy – which had only twenty-five ships in pay in 1685 – had expanded dramatically during the long war-years to 234 ships with more than 45,000 men. By the time William Kidd – having once more been bitten by the adventure bug and placed in charge of a supposed pirate-hunting vessel called *Adventure Galley* before turning pirate himself – was left swinging from the gallows at Wapping on 23 May 1701 (as much a political as a judicial act), buccaneers were quite clearly unwelcome.[58]

As luck would have it, Kidd's death occurred just as the peace of 1697 was fraying, and by 1702 the Royal Navy would be expanding rapidly once more, this time absorbing the most recalcitrant pirates. With the return of peace in 1713 some pirates remained active in Madagascar or, unwanted, in the Caribbean, as their remnants drifted north to New Providence and the mid-Atlantic coast – Charleston among other towns had long been a notorious pirate base. The period following the War of the Spanish Succession then witnessed the so-called Golden Age of piracy – though by 1730 even this had been suppressed – involving the likes of Stede Bonnett, 'Black Bart' Roberts, 'Calico Jack' Rackham, Anne Bonny and Mary Read, and Edward Teach – the notorious 'Blackbeard'. But Blackbeard and the others had no legitimacy, nor did they seek it. They were regarded and treated by authority everywhere as what the Spanish had always said they and their predecessors were: pirates.

# NOTES

## Abbreviations
AGI – Archivo General des Indias, Sevilla
BL – British Library, London
*CSP – Calendar of State Papers, Colonial Series, America and the West Indies*
*CSP D – Calendar of State Papers, Domestic*
*CSP V – Calendar of State Papers, Venetian*
*HAHR – Hispanic American Historical Review*
HMC – Historical Manuscripts Commission
TNA – The National Archives, Kew
*WMQ – William and Mary Quarterly*

## Introduction
1 Arciniegas, *Caribbean: Sea of the New World*, p. 3; Goslinga, *Dutch in the Carribean and on the Wild Coast*, p. 41.
2 Pope, *Harry Morgan's Way*, p. 15.
3 'Portobelo' is the current common spelling. See Dominic Salandra, 'Porto Bello, Puerto Bello, or Portobelo?', *HAHR*, 14 (1934), pp. 93–5.
4 Lane, *Pillaging the Empire*, p. 96.
5 Elliott, *Count-Duke Olivares*, pp. 677–80.
6 Williams, *Capitalism and Slavery*, p. 52.
7 Smith, *The Wealth of Nations*, 2, p. 187; H. McD. Beckles, 'The "Hub of Empire": The Caribbean and Britain in the Seventeenth Century', in Canny, *Oxford History of the British Empire*, 1, p. 218.
8 Lynch, *Spain under the Habsburgs*, 2, pp. 1–13.
9 J. C. Appleby, 'English Settlements in the Lesser Antilles, 1603–1660', in Paquette and Engerman, *Lesser Antilles in the Age of European Expansion*, pp. 86–7.

## Chapter 1: A New World
1 Lloyd, *British Empire*, p. 4.
2 Savelle, *Origins of American Diplomacy*, p. 15.
3 For studies of Sevilla, see Huguette and Pierre Chaunu, *Séville et l'Atlantique*; Clarence H. Haring, *Trade and Navigation between Spain and the Indies in the Time of the Habsburgs*; J. H. Parry, *Spanish Seaborne Empire*.
4 Andrews, *Spanish Caribbean*, pp. 1–11.
5 See Hugh Thomas, *Conquest: Cortés, Montezuma, and the Fall of Old Mexico*.
6 Andrews, *Spanish Caribbean*, p. 13.

7 Pope, *Harry Morgan's Way*, pp. 12–13.

8 Lane, *Pillaging the Empire*, p. 21.

9 Rodger, *Safeguard of the Sea*, pp. 176–8; Wernham, *Before the Armada*, pp. 112–41; Andrews, *Spanish Caribbean*, p. 83.

10 Rodger, *Safeguard of the Sea*, pp. 181–2; Wernham, *Before the Armada*, pp. 157–9; Connell-Smith, *Forerunners of Drake*, pp. 133–47; Loades, *Tudor Navy*, pp. 143–8.

11 Quinn and Ryan, *England's Sea Empire*, pp. 79–81.

12 Lloyd, *British Empire*, p. 4.

13 Wernham, *Before the Armada*, pp. 162–90.

14 Rodger, *Safeguard of the Sea*, p. 196.

15 Wernham, *Before the Armada*, p. 279; Sir Nicholas Throckmorton quoted in Monson, *Naval Tracts*, 1, p. 7.

16 Andrews, *Elizabethan Privateering*, pp. 160–2.

17 Phillips, *Six Galleons for the King of Spain*, pp. 9–15.

18 Hoffman, *Spanish Crown and the Defense of the Caribbean*, pp. 1–5, 224–5, 236; Rodger, *Safeguard of the Sea*, p. 242.

19 Loades, *Tudor Navy*, p. 215.

20 J. C. Appleby, 'Devon Privateering from Early Times to 1688', in Duffy et al. (eds), *New Maritime History of Devon*, 1, pp. 90–7; Michael J. G. Stanford, 'The Raleghs Take to the Sea', *Mariner's Mirror*, 48 (1962), 18–35; M. J. French, 'Privateering and the Revolt of the Netherlands: The *Watergeuzen* or Sea Beggars in Portsmouth, Gosport and the Isle of Wight, 1570–71', *Proceedings of the Hampshire Field Club & Archaeological Society*, 47 (1991), 171–80.

21 Kendall, *Private Men-of-War*, pp. 3–4; René de Mas Latrie, 'Du droit de marque ou droit de représailles au moyen âge', *Bibliothèque de l'Ecole Chartres*, 27 (1866), 529–77; 29 (1868), 294–347, 612–35.

22 Rodger, *Safeguard of the Sea*, pp. 199–200.

23 National Archives of Scotland, AC1/1 'Acts of the Admiralty Court of Scotland [*Acta Curiae Admirallatus Scotiae*] 1557–1562', pp. 194–203; MacDougall, *James IV*, p. 239.

24 Rodger, *Safeguard of the Sea*, pp. 201–3.

25 Andrews, *Spanish Caribbean*, p.108; Wright, *Spanish Documents Concerning English Voyages to the Caribbean*, pp. 28–59; F. A. Kirkpatrick, 'The First Recorded English Voyage to the West Indies', *English Historical Review*, 20 (1905), 115–24.

26 Cook and Borah, *Essays in Population History*, 1, pp. 376–460.

27 Andrews, *Trade, Plunder and Settlement*, pp. 117–18.

28 Lloyd, *British Empire*, pp. 8–9. See also Andrews, *Spanish Caribbean*, chs 5 and 6. For a recent biography of Drake see Kelsey, *Sir Francis Drake*.

29 Roland D. Hussey, 'Spanish Reaction to Foreign Aggression in the Caribbean to about 1680', *HAHR*, 9 (1929), 287.

30 Cadoux, *Philip of Spain and the Netherlands*, p. 133.

31 For a study of the development of Dutch maritime influence see C. R. Boxer, *Dutch Seaborne Empire*; Lane, *Pillaging the Empire*, pp. 64–5.

32 See Parker, *Dutch Revolt*, passim.

33 See Engel Sluiter, 'The Word Pechelingue: Its Derivation and Meaning', *HAHR*, 24 (1944), 683–98.

34 Goslinga, *Dutch in the Caribbean and on the Wild Coast*, pp. 6–8, 26.

35 Andrews, *Trade, Plunder and Settlement*, pp. 129–34.

36 Corbett, *Drake and the Tudor Navy*, 1, pp. 144–89.

37 Andrews, *Drake's Voyages*, pp. 58–83; Corbett, *Drake and the Tudor Navy*, pp. 216–310.

38 Richard Boulind, 'The Strength and Weakness of Spanish Control of the Caribbean, 1520–1650: The Case for the *Armada de Barlovento*', PhD dissertation, University of Cambridge, 1965, pp. 234, 242, 247; Scammell, *World Encompassed*, p. 438; Elizabeth Bonner, 'The Recovery of St Andrews Castle in 1547: French Naval Policy and Diplomacy in the British Isles', *English Historical Review*, 61 (1996), 578–85; Rotz, *Idrography*, pp. 3–7.

39 John Hooker quoted in Andrews, *Elizabethan Privateering*, p. 4; Richard Boulind, 'Drake's Navigational Skills', *Mariner's Mirror*, 54 (1968), 349–71; Waters, *Art of Navigation*, pp. 79–80, 101.

40 Parker, *Dutch Revolt*, pp. 213–19; Andrews, *Spanish Caribbean*, pp. 147–52; Andrews, *Drake's Voyages*, pp. 92–4; Corbett, *Drake and the Tudor Navy*, 2, pp. 1–59; Keeler, *Drake's West Indian Voyage*, pp. 9–23.

41 Rodger, *Safeguard of the Sea*, pp. 251–3.

42 M. J. Rodríguez-Salgado, 'The Anglo-Spanish War: The Final Episode in the "Wars of the Roses"?', in Rodríguez-Salgado and Adams, *England, Spain and the Gran Armada*, pp. 2–8; Wernham, 'Elizabethan War Aims and Strategy', in Bindoff et al., (eds), *Elizabethan Government and Society*, pp. 340–68.

43 See Martin and Parker, *Spanish Armada*; Parker, *Dutch Revolt*, pp. 221–2.

44 Wernham, *After the Armada*, pp. 239–45.

45 See Andrews, *Last Voyage of Drake and Hawkins*; Corbett, *Drake and the Tudor Navy*, 2, pp. 402–37; Rodger, *Safeguard of the Sea*, pp. 282–4.

46 Torres Ramírez, *Armada de Barlovento*, pp. 3–5, 19–46.

47 Paul E. J. Hammer, 'Myth-making: Politics, Propaganda and the Capture of Cadiz in 1596', *Historical Journal*, 40 (1997), 621–42.

48 Wernham, *Return of the Armadas*, pp. 55–112, 132–40, 184–90; Corbett, *Successors of Drake*, pp. 56–116, 139–51, 212–27.

49 Williamson, *Maritime Enterprise*, p. 122; K. R. Andrews, 'The English in the Caribbean, 1560–1620', in Andrews, Canny and Hair (eds), *Westward Enterprise*, pp. 103–18.

50 Apestegui, *Pirates*, p. 109.

51 Wernham, *After the Armada*, pp. 246–59.

52 Andrews, *Spanish Caribbean*, pp. 156–92: Andrews, *Elizabethan Privateering*, pp. 182–4: K. R. Andrews, 'Caribbean Rivalry and the Anglo-Spanish Peace of 1604', *History*, 54 (1974), 1–17; K. R. Andrews; 'English Voyages to the Caribbean, 1596–1604: An Annotated List', *WMQ*, 3rd Ser., 31 (1974), 243–54; Engel Sluiter, 'Dutch–Spanish Rivalry in the Caribbean Area, 1594–1609', *HAHR*, 28 (1948), 165–96.

53 Andrews, 'English Voyages to the Caribbean', pp. 243–54.

54 Boxer, *Dutch Seaborne Empire*, pp. 3–5; Israel, *Dutch Primacy in World Trade*, p. 17.

55 Lane, *Pillaging the Empire*, p. 65.

56 Dieve, *Tangomangos*, pp. 82, 99–100, 112, 175.

57 Tenenti, *Piracy and the Decline of Venice*, pp. 56–71.

58 Andrews, *Elizabethan Seamen*, p. 260; Waters, *Art of Navigation*, pp. 203–32; Thomas R. Adams, 'The Beginnings of Maritime Publishing in England, 1528–1640', *Library*, 6th Ser., 14 (1992), 207–20; Rodger, *Safeguard of the Sea*, pp. 294–6, 305.

59 MacCaffrey, *Elizabeth I, War and Politics*, p. 6.

60 See Bréard and Bréard, *Documents rélatifs à la marine normande*, pp. 148–78.

## Chapter 2: Tobacco and Salt

1 Wallerstein, *Modern World System*, p. 165.

2 Stein and Stein, *Silver, Trade and War*, pp. 54, 86.

3 Pope, *Harry Morgan's Way*, p. 28.

4 Chaunu and Chaunu, *Séville et l'Atlantique*, 2, pp. 258, 434–5.

5 Andrews, *Spanish Caribbean*, p. 79.

6 Spellings of place names varied considerably at the time. See Dominic Salandra, 'Porto Bello, Puerto Bello, or Portobelo?', *HAHR*, 14 (1934), 93–5.

7 Ives (ed.), *Rich Papers*, pp. 179–80; Pennell, *Bandits at Sea*, p. 45.

8 AGI Santo Domingo 177, Melgarejo to crown, 21 June 1604.

9 Andrews, *Spanish Caribbean*, pp. 55–64, 70–2, 74; Irene A. Wright, 'Rescates, with Special Reference to Cuba', *HAHR*, 3 (1920), 333–61.

10 *CSP V* 1603–7, No. 307.

11 Erwin Walter Plam and C. Engel Sluiter, 'Letters on the Dutch in the Caribbean', *HAHR*, 28 (1948), 626–8.

12 Apestegui, *Pirates*, pp. 112–15.

13 Goslinga, *Dutch in the Caribbean and on the Wild Coast*, p. 65.

14 Avermaete, *Gueux de mer et la naissance d'une nation*, p. 144.

15 Goslinga, *Dutch in the Caribbean and on the Wild Coast*, pp. 20–2.

16 Irene A. Wright, 'The Dutch and Cuba, 1609–1643', *HAHR*, 4 (1921), 599.

17 Lucena Samoral, *Piratas*, p. 127; Apestegui, *Pirates*, p. 109; Israel, *Dutch Republic and the Hispanic World*, pp. 5–11. For an excellent overview of Dutch–Iberian rivalry in this period, see Engel Sluiter, 'Dutch Maritime Power and the Colonial Status Quo, 1558–1641', *Pacific Historical Review*, 11 (1942), 29–41.

18 Goodman, *Spanish Naval Power*, p. 15.

19 Boxer, *Dutch in Brazil*, p. 1.

20 Israel, *Dutch Republic and the Hispanic World*, pp. 44–5.

21 Haring, *Spanish Empire*, p. 332.

22 K. R. Andrews, 'Caribbean Rivalry and the Anglo-Spanish Peace of 1604', *History*, 54 (1974), 1–17.

23 Apestegui, *Pirates*, pp. 109–10.

24 AGI Indiferente General 1667, Spanish war council to crown, 10 April 1606.

25 Smith, *True Travels*, p. 15.

26 Rodger, *Safeguard of the Sea*, pp. 347–51.

27 Wesley Frank Craven, 'The Earl of Warwick, a Speculator in Piracy', *HAHR*, 10 (1930), 459.

28 Wright, 'Rescates, with Special Reference to Cuba', pp. 337, 352, 354.

29 AGI Santo Domingo 100, r. 4, Gaspar de Pereda to crown, 1 April, 23 November 1609; Santo Domingo 54, *Información* before Diego Gómez de Sandoval, 23

November 1609; Santo Domingo 84, r. 3, *Testimonio de un peublo* ... In fact, the deposition, taken in Cumaná, makes clear the settlement was on Española.

30 W. Frank Craven, 'An Introduction to the History of Bermuda', *WMQ*, 2nd Ser., 17 (1939), 449.

31 BL Lansdowne Mss, 84, ff. 16–20, 44; MacInnes, *Early English Tobacco Trade*, p. 35.

32 James I, *Counter-Blaste to Tobacco*, p. 34.

33 Willan (ed.), *Tudor Book of Rates*, p. xli; Harris (ed.), *Relation of a Voyage*, p. 105.

34 BL Add. Mss 36319, f. 149, Pedro Suárez Caronel to the crown, 18 December 1607.

35 BL Add. Mss 36319, ff. 294 et seq., Deposition of Thomas 'Icurri' [Hickory/Curry?] made in Santo Domingo, 26 June 1611.

36 Harris (ed.), *Relation of a Voyage*, p. 105.

37 BL Add. Mss 36319, ff. 268–71, *Información* from London, 28 March 1611.

38 BL Add. Mss 36320, f. 4, *Consulta* of the Junta de Guerra, 11 March 1612.

39 AGI Santo Domingo 100, Gaspar de Pereda to crown, 18 December 1612; Wright, *Historia documentada*, p. 103.

40 I. A. Wright, 'Spanish Policy towards Virginia', *American Historical Review*, 25 (1920), 448–79; I. A. Wright, 'Spanish Intentions for Bermuda, 1603–1615', *Bermuda Historical Quarterly*, 7 (1950), 65–6.

41 BL Add. Mss 36319, ff. 281–2, Diego Gómez de Sandoval to the crown, 30 March 1615; AGI Indiferente General 1868, *Consulta* of Consejo de Indias, 19 November 1615; Wright, *Santiago de Cuba*, p. 44.

42 Daher, *Singularités de la France équinoxiale*, p. 286.

43 Haring, *Buccaneers*, p. 303.

44 Apestegui, *Pirates*, p. 124.

45 Andrews, *Spanish Caribbean*, pp. 230–4.

46 A. M. Millard, 'The Import Trade of London, 1600–1640', PhD dissertation, University of London, 1956.

47 Joyce Lorimer, 'The English Contraband Tobacco Trade in Trinidad and Guiana 1590–1617', in Andrews, Canny and Hair (eds), *Westward Enterprise*, p. 135; Davies, *North Atlantic World*, pp. 145–6.

48 Pares, *Merchants and Planters*, p. 5 et seq.; Davies, *North Atlantic World*, pp. 147–50.

49 Israel, *Dutch Primacy in World Trade*, p. 63; Goslinga, *Dutch in the Caribbean and on the Wild Coast*, pp. 116–17, 119; Davies, *North Atlantic World*, p. 30.

50 Andrews, *Spanish Caribbean*, p. 202; Israel, *Dutch Primacy in World Trade*, pp. 87–9.

51 Velius, *Chronyk van Hoorn*, pp. 524–5.

52 AGI Santo Domingo 187, Pedro Suárez Caronel's letters to the crown, August 1606 to June 1608.

53 Marley, *Pirates and Engineers*, pp. 9–10.

54 Engel Sluiter, 'Dutch–Spanish Rivalry in the Caribbean Area, 1594–1609', *HAHR*, 28 (1948), pp. 166–7.

55 Lane, *Pillaging the Empire*, pp. 66–7.

56 Irene A. Wright, 'The Dutch and Cuba, 1609–1643', *HAHR*, 4 (1921), 601.

57 AGI Santa Fé 38, Cartagena Petition, 28 July 1618; Indiferente General 1868, 23 August 1618; Santo Domingo 100, Rodrigo de Velasco to crown, 25 June 1619, 6 July 1620.

58 AGI Santo Domingo 100, Francisco Bonegas to crown, 20 August 1620, 18 February and 3 August 1621; Santo Domingo 156, Juan de Vargas to crown, two undated letters, received 22 August 1622; Vila Vilar, *Historia de Puerto Rico*, p. 133.

59 Elliot, *Count-Duke of Olivares*, pp. 82–3, 196–200.

60 Wright and van Dam (eds), *Nederlandsche Zeevaarders*, 1, pp. 13–20.

61 Lucena Samoral, *Piratas*, p. 133.

62 Goslinga, *Dutch in the Caribbean and on the Wild Coast*, pp. 127–8.

63 AGI Indiferente General 1868, Juan Rodrigo de Las Varillas, 25 September 1618; Santo Domingo 180, Memorial concerning the responsibility of Barlomé de Vargas Machuca, Andreas Rodrigo de Villegas to crown, 5 June 1620; Wright and van Dam (eds), *Nederlandsche Zeevaarders* 1, pp. 14–36; Apestegui, *Pirates*, p. 129.

64 Marx, *Pirates and Privateers*, p. 104.

65 Wright and van Dam (eds), *Nederlandsche Zeevaarders*, 1, pp. 23–6.

**Chapter 3: Piet Hein**

1 For biographies, see J. F. Jameson, *Willem Usselinx*, and C. Ligtenberg, *Willem Usselinx*.

2 Blok, *History of the People of the Netherlands*, pp. 296–7.

3 Boxer, *Dutch in Brazil*, pp. 2–5; Goslinga, *Dutch in the Caribbean and on the Wild Coast*, p. 38.

4 I. A. Wright, 'The Dutch and Cuba, 1609–1643', *HAHR*, 4 (1921), 604–9.

5 Winter, *Westindische Compagnie ter kamer Stad en lande*, pp. 8, 12–13, 18; Boxer, *Dutch Seaborne Empire*, pp. 24–5.

6 Thompson, *War and Government in Habsburg Spain*, pp. 147–9.

7 Elliott, *Richelieu and Olivares*, pp. 63–4.

8 Goslinga, *Dutch in the Caribbean and on the Wild Coast*, pp. 90–3, 112–13.

9 Boxer, *Dutch in Brazil*, pp. 14–16.

10 Ibid., pp. 19–25.

11 Laet, *Iaelyck Verhael*, 1, pp. 30–1, 50–74; Boxer, *Salvador de Sá and the Struggle for Brazil and Angola*, pp. 57–60.

12 Picó, *Historia general de Puerto Rico*, p. 90.

13 Sáiz Cidoncha, *Historia de la piratería en América española*, p. 150; Zapatero, *Guerra del Caribe en el siglo XVIII*, pp. 301–7.

14 Apestegui, *Pirates*, p. 135.

15 Lucena Samoral, *Piratas*, p. 138.

16 Goslinga, *Dutch in the Caribbean and on the Wild Coast*, pp. 161–2.

17 Wright, 'Dutch and Cuba', pp. 611–12.

18 Laet, *Iaelyck Verhael*, 1, pp. 87–104.

19 Naber and Wright, *Piet Heyn en de zilverfloot*, p. lxxvii; Duro, *Armada Española*, 4, p. 96.

20 Wright, 'Dutch and Cuba', p. 613.

21 Laet, *Iaelyck Verhael*, 2, pp. 1–16, 41.

22 Wright, 'Dutch and Cuba', p. 614.

23 Goslinga, *Dutch in the Caribbean and on the Wild Coast*, pp. 178–9.

24 Apestegui, *Pirates*, p. 137.

25 Laet, *Iaelyck Verhael*, 2, pp. 42–6; Wright and van Dam *Nederlandsche Zeevaarders*, 1, pp. 103–9.

26 Naber and Wright, *Piet Hein en de zilvervloot*, pp. 37–45; Guerra y Sánchez, *Manual de historia de Cuba*, p. 100.

27 Apestegui, *Pirates*, p. 138.

28 Lucena Samoral, *Piratas*, p. 141.

29 Goslinga, *Dutch in the Caribbean and on the Wild Coast*, pp. 186–90.

30 Pope, *Harry Morgan's Way*, p. 40.

31 Apestegui, *Pirates*, p. 138.

32 Wright, 'Dutch and Cuba', p. 616.

33 Phillips, *Six Galleons for the King of Spain*, pp. 21–4.

34 Naber and Wright, *Piet Hein en de zilvervloot*, pp. 52, 89.

35 Boxer, *Dutch Seaborne Empire*, p. 77.

36 Naber and Wright, *Piet Hein en de zilvervloot*, p. 33.

37 Boxer, *Dutch in Brazil*, pp. 29–31.

38 Wright and van Dam, *Nederlandsche Zeevaarders*, 1, pp. 114–15; Lucena Samoral, *Piratas*, p. 147.

39 Apestegui, *Pirates*, pp. 138–9.

40 Goslinga, *Dutch in the Caribbean and on the Wild Coast*, pp. 217–21.

41 Ibid., p. 108.

42 Gage, *Travels in the New World*, p. 315.

43 Lane, *Pillaging the Empire*, p. 71.

44 AGI Indiferente General 1873.

45 Laet, *Iaelyck Verhael*, 3, pp. 187–95, 203.

46 Goslinga, *Dutch in the Caribbean and on the Wild Coast*, pp. 230–1.

47 Wright and van Dam, *Nederlandsche Zeevaarders*, 1, pp. 140–6.

48 Ibid., pp. 129–32, 229–30; Boxer, *Dutch in Brazil*, pp. 51–2.

49 Wright and van Dam, *Nederlandsche Zeevaarders*, 1, pp. 163–6.

50 AGI Indiferente General, leg. 3568, Paper by Olivares, 23 March 1633.

51 Vila Vilar, *Historia de Puerto Rico*, pp. 152, 159–64; Thomas G. Matthews, 'The Spanish Dominon of St Martin, 1633–1648', *Caribbean Studies*, 9 (1969), 2–23; Wright and van Dam, *Nederlandsche Zeevaarders*, 1, pp. 286–91.

52 Goslinga, *Dutch in the Caribbean and on the Wild Coast*, p. 134.

53 Wright and van Dam, *Nederlandsche Zeevaarders*, 1, pp. 136–40, 166–9, 203–4.

54 Biblioteca Nacional de Espagna, Mss 18719, p. 146.

55 Apestegui, *Pirates*, p. 132.

56 Goslinga, *Dutch in the Caribbean and on the Wild Coast*, pp. 265–9, 271–4, 279–83.

57 Torres Ramírez, *Armada de Barlovento*, pp. 35–6; Alvarado Morales, *Ciudad de México ante la fundación de la Armada de Barlovento*, pp. 37–44; Vila Vilar, *Historia de Puerto Rico*, pp. 164–8.

58 Elliot, *Count-Duke of Olivares*, pp. 172–3.

59 Serrano Mangas, *Segura travesía del Agnus Dei*, p. 245.

60 Wright, 'Dutch and Cuba', pp. 625–7.

61 Haring, *Buccaneers*, p. 303.

62 Postma, *Dutch in the Atlantic Slave Trade*, pp. 11–16; Goslinga, *Dutch in the Caribbean and on the Wild Coast*, p. 105.

63 Wright, 'Dutch and Cuba', pp. 628–30.

64 Lucena Samoral, *Piratas*, p. 144.

65 Israel, *Dutch Primacy in World Trade*, pp. 243–4.

66 Phillips, *Six Galleons for the King of Spain*, pp. 192–4; Lynch, *Spain under the Habsburgs*, 2, p. 163.

67 BL Sloane Mss 3663, f. 59.

68 Israel, *Dutch Primacy in World Trade*, pp. 240–1.

69 Goslinga, *Dutch in the Caribbean and on the Wild Coast*, chs 12, 13 and 14.

70 Lane, *Pillaging the Empire*, p. 91.

## Chapter 4: Brethren of the Coast

1 John C. Appleby, 'War, Politics and Colonization', in Canny (ed.), *Oxford History of the British Empire*, 1, p. 62.

2 Rodger, *Safeguard of the Sea*, p. 159.

3 Canny (ed.), *Oxford History of the British Empire*, 1, pp. 1–3, 17–18.

4 Alastair MacFadyen, 'Anglo-Spanish Relations, 1625–1660', PhD dissertation, University of Liverpool, 1967, pp. 171–2.

5 Williamson, *Caribee Islands*, pp. 13–18.

6 For a recent biography of Raleigh, see Raleigh Trevelyan, *Sir Walter Raleigh*. On Jamestown see R. Appelbaum and J. W. Sweet (eds), *Envisioning an English Empire*.

7 AGI Santo Domingo 156, Gabriel de Rojas Paramo to crown, 25 August 1613.

8 BL Sloane Mss 3662, f. 53.

9 Andrews, *Spanish Caribbean*, pp. 235–6; Lloyd, *British Empire*, pp. 19–20. The classic account of the early American colonies is Charles M. Andrews, *The Colonial Period of American History*, but Perry Miller, *Errand in the Wilderness* is useful for redressing the imbalance in Andrews' lack of enthusiasm for religious factors in colonisation.

10 Andrews, *Colonial Period in American History*, 1, pp. 46–7.

11 Ruigh, *Parliament of 1624*, p. 220.

12 Boucher, *Cannibal Encounters*, p. 31.

13 Bernard Schnapper, 'À propos de la doctrine et de la politique coloniale au temps de Richelieu', *Revue d'Histoire des Colonies*, 41 (1954), 314–28.

14 For a biography of Warner see Aucher Warner, *Sir Thomas Warner*.

15 Smith, *True Travels*, 2, p. 190.

16 Boucher, *Cannibal Encounters*, pp. 38–9.

17 Burns, *History of the British West Indies*, pp. 188–90.

18 See Petitjean Roget, *Société d'habitation à la Martinique*, 1, pp. 43–4, 178–80.

19 Crouse, *French Pioneers in the West Indies*, pp. 10–12.

20 Smith, *True Travels*, 2, p. 191.

21 D'Esnambuc was fortunate to present his proposals just as Richelieu was embarking on a far-reaching naval programme. For an overview see Lucas Alexandre Boiteux, *Richelieu*.

22 Crouse, *French Pioneers in the West Indies*, pp. 16–18; Du Tertre, *Histoire générale des Antilles habitées par les Français*, 1, pp. 8–15. It was Du Tertre who created the myth

of the 'noble savage' where he placed 'the virtuousness of the heathen Caribs above the immoral life of the Europeans'.

23 *CSP* 1574–1660, p. 281; Burns, *History of the British West Indies*, pp. 191–2.

24 Gragg, *Englishmen Transplanted*, pp. 29–31. On Courteen, see *DNB*; Andrew, *Ships, Money and Politics*, pp. 51–2. On Hay, see Roy E. Schreiber, *The First Carlisle*.

25 BL Egerton Ms 2395, 'A true State of the case between the Heires and Assignes of Sir William Courten Knight, Deceased, and the Earl of Carlisle, and Planters of the Island of Barbadoes, annexed to the Petition of William Courten, Esquire, and others, exhibited in Parliament'.

26 Du Tertre, *Histoire générale des Antilles habitées par les Français*, i, pp. 3–4. In *La Société d'habitation à la Martinique* Petitjean Roget wonders if the Caribs were taken by surprise and if, indeed, they were planning an attack: i, p. 55; Boucher, *Cannibal Encounters*, p. 41.

27 Crouse, *French Pioneers in the West Indies*, pp. 19–20.

28 Du Tertre, *Histoire générale des Antilles habitées par les Français*, i, pp. 17–20.

29 Cayetana, *Politics and Reform in Spain and Viceregal Mexico*, pp. 17–18; Israel, *Empires and Entrepots*, pp. 265–83.

30 Elliot, *Count-Duke of Olivares*, pp. 144–5.

31 Ibid., pp. 49–50, 244–8.

32 Boucher, *Cannibal Encounters*, p. 40.

33 Du Tertre, *Histoire générale des Antilles habitées par les Français*, i, p. 28; Harlow (ed.), *Colonizing Expeditions*, p. xix.

34 Burns, *History of the British West Indies*, pp. 195, 200.

35 See Ann Kossmaul, *Servants in Husbandry in Early Modern England*, and Hilary McD. Beckles, 'Plantation Production and White "Proto-Slavery": White Indentured Servants and the Colonisation of the English West Indies, 1624–1645', *Americas*, 41 (1984–5), 21–45.

36 Smith, *Colonists in Bondage*, p. 5.

37 On the transformation of servitude see Warren M. Billings, 'The Law of Servants and Slaves in Seventeenth-Century Virginia', *Virginia Magazine of Biography and History*, 99 (1991), 45–62, and Beckles, 'Plantation Production and White "Proto-Slavery"'.

38 Goslinga, *Dutch in the Caribbean and on the Wild Coast*, p. 206.

39 Peña Battlé, *Isla de la Tortuga*, pp. 118–19.

40 If the original was occasionally tendentious, the translations were blatantly so, and magnified the role of one country's heroes over another. Pennell (ed.), *Bandits at Sea*, p. 4.

41 For the tragic story of this people, see Irving Rouse, *Taínos*.

42 P. P. Boucher, 'The "Frontier Era" of the French Caribbean, 1620–1690', in Daniels and Kennedy (eds), *Negotiated Empires*, p. 218.

43 Du Tertre, *Histoire générale des Antilles habitées par les Français*, i, p. 415.

44 Pope, *Harry Morgan's Way*, p. 60.

45 Talty, *Empire of Blue Water*, pp. 53–5. For details see Stephen Grancsay, *Master French Gunsmiths' Designs of the XVII–XIX Centuries*.

46 Pope, *Harry Morgan's Way*, pp. 58–9.

47 Labat, quoted in Haring, *Buccaneers*, p. 68.

48 Exquemelin, *Buccaneers of America*, p. 36.

49 Lane, *Pillaging the Empire*, pp. 97–8.

50 Senior, *Nation of Pirates*, p. 26.

51 Bromley, *Corsairs and Navies*, pp. 4–6.

52 Charlevoix, *Histoire de l'isle Espagnole*, 3, pp. 11–12.

53 M. Rediker, 'Libertalia: The Pirate's Utopia', in Cordingly, *Pirates*, p. 122.

54 AGI IG 2541, Viceroy of New Spain to queen, 14 June 1669.

55 Bromley, *Corsairs and Navies*, pp. 9–10.

56 Snelders, *Devil's Anarchy*, p. 102.

57 Crouse, *French Pioneers in the West Indies*, pp. 24–6, 28, 80–1.

58 Eleanor B. Adams, 'An English Library at Trinidad, 1633', *Americas*, 6 (1955), 26.

59 See Philip P. Boucher, 'Reflections on the "Crime" of Nicholas Fouquet: The Fouquets and the French Colonial Empire, 1626–1661', *Revue Française d'Histoire d'Outre-mer*, 73 (1986), 5–19.

60 Maurice de Lavigne Sainte-Suzanne, *Martinique au premier siècle de la colonisation*, p. 205; Petitjean Roget, *Société d'habitation à la Martinique*, 1, p. 179.

61 Boucher, 'The "Frontier Era" of the French Caribbean, 1620–1690', in Daniels and Kennedy (eds), *Negotiated Empires*, pp. 213–14.

62 Boucher, *Cannibal Encounters*, pp. 45–7.

63 Crouse, *French Pioneers in the West Indies*, pp. 84–6.

64 Moya Pons, *Manual de historia Dominicana*, p. 78.

65 Peña Battlé, *Isla de la Tortuga*, pp. 140–1.

66 Crouse, *French Pioneers in the West Indies*, pp. 88–9.

## Chapter 5: Sugar and Slaves

1 Quoted in Herrero García, *Ideas de los españoles del siglo XVII*, pp. 484–5.

2 Kupperman, *Providence Island*, p. 24.

3 Ligon, *True & Exact History of the Island of Barbados*, p. 28.

4 Williamson, *Caribee Islands*, pp. 219–25; Gragg, *Englishmen Transplanted*, pp. 32–4.

5 Gragg, *Englishmen Transplanted*, pp. 36–9.

6 Andrews, *Ships, Money and Politics*, p. 100.

7 Dunn, *Sugar and Slaves*, pp. 49–56; Bridenbaugh and Bridenbaugh, *No Peace beyond the Line*, pp. 53–5.

8 Wesley Frank Craven, 'The Earl of Warwick, a Speculator in Piracy', *HAHR*, 10 (1930), 457–79; John C. Appleby, 'English Privateering during the Early Stuart Wars with Spain and France, 1625–1630', PhD dissertation, University of Hull, 1983, p. 206.

9 Strangeways, *Sketch of the Mosquito Shore*, pp. 131–3.

10 Floyd, *Anglo-Spanish Struggle for Mosquitia*, pp. 21–2.

11 See John A. Holm, 'The Creole English of Nicaragua's Moskito Coast', PhD dissertation, University of London, 1978, pp. 179, 315.

12 Ives (ed.), *Rich Papers*, pp. 319–21.

13 TNA CO 124/1, pp. 1–10.

14 Kupperman, *Providence Island*, pp. 25–8, 194–6. See also Stanley Pargellis and Ruth

Lapham Butler (eds), 'Daniell Ellffryth's Guide to the Caribbean, 1631', *WMQ*, 3rd Ser., 1 (1994), 273–316.

15 Newton, *Colonising Activities of the English Puritans*, pp. 52–3.

16 Kupperman, *Providence Island*, pp. 1–5.

17 See Craven, 'Warwick'.

18 Russell, *Parliaments and English Politics*, pp. 76–81, 323–6.

19 Kupperman, *Providence Island*, pp. 190–2.

20 Ibid., pp. 35–44, 85–6, 91–2.

21 See Sir Walter Raleigh to Bess Throckmorton, 14 November 1617, *The Works of Sir Walter Ralegh, Kt*, Oxford, 1829, VIII, pp. 620–2; Harris (ed.), *Relation of a Voyage*, pp. 11–13.

22 Kupperman, *Providence Island*, pp. 93–5, 97, 100. For a study of the relationship between the English and Moskito Indians, see J. Preston, *The Mosquito Indians and Anglo-Spanish Rivalry in Central America, 1630–1821*.

23 Kupperman, *Providence Island*, pp. 75, 105.

24 Crouse, *French Pioneers in the West Indies*, pp. 82–3; Peña Battlé, *Isla de la Tortuga*, p. 137.

25 TNA CO 124/2, p. 279.

26 Gage, *Travels in the New World*, p. 451.

27 TNA SP 94/42.

28 TNA HCA 3/102, p. 9.

29 TNA CO 124/2, Providence Island Company to Samuel Axe, 26 March 1636.

30 TNA CO 1/8, 'A Declaration made the 21st of December 1635 To the Right Honourable the Earl of Holland'.

31 Kupperman, *Providence Island*, pp. 197–8.

32 R. M. Smuts, 'The Puritan Followers of Henrietta Maria in the 1630s', *English Historical Review*, 43 (1978) 26–45; Barbara Donagan, 'A Courtier's Progress: Greed and Consistency in the Life of the Earl of Holland', *Historical Journal*, 19 (1976), 317–53.

33 BL Add. Mss 36323, Venezuela Papers, 'The Council of State to crown, on the settlement made by the English on Santa Catalina with suggestions for dislodging them', etc. Madrid, 11 December 1636, f. 294.

34 Kupperman, *Providence Island*, pp. 201–8.

35 Ibid., pp. 267–71.

36 On Butler's life see Perrin (ed.), *Boteler's Dialogues*, pp. vii–xxix. On his governorship of Bermuda see Craven, *Introduction to the History of Bermuda*, pp. 20–40, 131–40, and Wilkinson, *Adventurers of Bermuda*, pp. 130–45.

37 BL Sloane Mss 758, Butler Diary, 2, 5 July and 14 August 1639; Kupperman, *Providence Island*, pp. 210–11, 213–14.

38 BL Sloane Mss 758, Butler Diary, 31 May and 6–20 June 1639. A. P. Newton asserts that Butler gained 16,000 pesos from this expedition but appears to have confused Butler's failure with Jackson's success. (*Colonising Activities of the English Puritans*, p. 257.)

39 Kupperman, *Providence Island*, pp. 278–80.

40 For respective Spanish and English accounts of the battle see AGI, Santa Fe 223:

'Account of the journey and battle of Santa Catalina Island written by father friar Mateo de San Francisco, Chaplain major and administrator of the Armada of Portugal, under the command of Don Gerónimo Gomes de Sandoval, Royal Admiral of the Ocean and Captain General of Galleons and fleet in the city of Cartagena de indias, the 29th of November of 1640'; Leicestershire County Record Office, Finch Mss, Halhead, Lane, Sherrard and Leverton to the Providence Island Company, 17 June 1640; calendared in HMC, 17th Report (1913), I, pp. 51–8.

41 Kupperman, *Providence Island*, pp. 288–92.

42 On seventeenth-century 'etiquette of belligerence', see Barbara Donagan, 'Codes and Conduct in the English Civil War', *Past and Present*, 118 (1988), 78–81.

43 Kupperman, *Providence Island*, pp. 293–4, 322–5, 336.

44 TNA SP 94/42.

45 Craven, 'Warwick', p. 473.

46 AGI Santa Fe 223, Francisco Díaz Pimienta to crown, 11 September 1641.

47 Kupperman, *Providence Island*, pp. 336–8.

48 Burns, *History of the British West Indies*, p. 210.

49 Donald Rowland, 'Spanish Occupation of the Island of Old Providence, or Santa Catalina, 1641–1670', *HAHR*, 15 (1935), 300.

50 Ibid., pp. 301–2. Events were reported from the English point of view in an anonymous newsletter in 1642. BL Thomason Tracts E.141.10, 'A Letter from the Low Countries', pp. 5–6.

51 Vincent T. Harlow (ed.), 'The Voyages of Captain William Jackson, 1642–1645', *Camden Miscellany*, 13 (1923), 1.

52 Ibid., pp. 1–2; BL Sloane Mss 793 or 864, p. 4.

53 AGI Santo Domingo 215, 'Declarations of the prisoners captured in 1642'.

54 Chaunu and Chaunu, *Séville et l'Atlantique*, 8(I), p. 57.

55 Haring, *Buccaneers*, p. 50.

56 Floyd, *Anglo-Spanish Struggle for Mosquitia*, p. 24.

57 Harlow, 'Voyages of Jackson', pp. 32–3.

58 Alastair MacFadyen, 'Anglo-Spanish Relations, 1625–1660', PhD dissertation, University of Liverpool, 1967, pp. 185–6.

59 Cundall and Pietersz, *Jamaica under the Spaniards*, p. 40.

60 Harlow, 'Voyages of Jackson', pp. 34–5.

61 TNA CO 1/11, p. 7.

62 Craven, 'Warwick', p. 475.

63 Davies, *North Atlantic World*, pp. 72–96.

64 For studies of this transformation, see R. S. Dunn, *Sugar and Slaves*, and R. B. Sheridan, *Sugar and Slavery*.

65 Dunn, *Sugar and Slaves*, pp. 117–260; Hilary McD. Beckles, 'The Economic Origins of Black Slavery in the British West Indies, 1640–1680: A Tentative Analysis of the Barbados Model', *Journal of Caribbean History*, 16 (1982), 52–3; Hilary McD. Beckles and Andrew Davies, 'The Economic Transition to the Black Labor System in Barbados', *Journal of Interdisciplinary History*, 18 (1987), 225–47.

66 See Hilary McD. Beckles, 'A "Riotous and Unruly Lot": Irish Indentured Servants and Freemen in the English West Indies, 1644–1713', *WMQ*, 3rd Ser., 47 (1990), 503–22.

67 Williams, *From Columbus to Castro*, p. 100.

68 Dampier, *Travels*, II, p. 240.

69 Williamson, *Caribee Islands*, pp. 113–14, 121–3, 125–9.

70 Ligon, *True & Exact History of the Island of Barbadoes*, p. 57.

71 Campbell, *Some Early Barbadian History*, pp. 165–74.

72 Foster, *Briefe Relation*, pp. 1–4.

73 Cundall, *Governors of Jamaica in the Seventeenth Century*, p. 21.

74 TNA CO 1/11/23; *CSP* 1574–1660, pp. 349–40.

75 Harlow, *Colonizing Expeditions*, p. 75; Davis, *Cavaliers & Roundheads*, pp. 229, 232–8.

76 Davis, *Cavaliers & Roundheads*, pp. 241–4; Foster, *Briefe Relation*, pp. 9–10; BL Add Mss 11411: 'Articles agreed on the 11th day of January 1651: by and between Lord Willoughby of Parham on one part, and Sr. George Ayscue Knt. Daniell Searle Esqr. And Capt. Michaell Packe on the other parte . . .'.

77 Pope, *Harry Morgan's Way*, p. 53.

78 AGI Indiferente General 1871, *Consultas* of the Junta de Guerra de Indias, 27 April 1634; 1873, 29 April 1638.

79 TNA SP 94/41 (I), Hopton to Coke, 29 April 1639, p. 84.

80 MacFadyen, 'Anglo-Spanish Relations', p. 212.

81 Fortune, *Merchants and Jews*, pp. 99, 101, 105.

82 Sheridan, *Sugar and Slavery*, pp. 38–9; Israel, *Dutch Primacy in World Trade*, p. 239.

83 Quoted in Egerton, *Short History of British Colonial Policy*, p. 76.

## Chapter 6: The Western Design

1 Padrón, *Spanish Jamaica*, p. 179.

2 Pope, *Harry Morgan's Way*, p. 55.

3 John Donoghue, 'Radical Republicanism in England, America, and the Imperial Atlantic, 1624–1661', PhD dissertation, University of Pittsburgh, 2006, pp. 263–4.

4 Clarke, *Clarke Papers*, 3, pp. 203–6.

5 *CSP* V 1655–6, pp. 128–9; Venning, *Cromwellian Foreign Policy*, p. 72.

6 See Frank Strong, 'The Causes of Cromwell's West Indian Expedition', *American Historical Review*, 4 (1898–9), 228–45; Hill, *God's Englishman*, p. 161.

7 For a study of this phenomenon see William S. Maltby, *Black Legend in England*.

8 Perrin, *British Flags*, pp. 63–4.

9 Michael Baumber, 'The Navy during the Civil Wars and Commonwealth', MA dissertation, University of Manchester, 1967, p. 255.

10 Venning, *Cromwellian Foreign Policy*, p. 74.

11 See Pincus, *Protestantism and Patriotism*, pp. 1–3, 6–7, 184–5, 189; Venning, *Cromwellian Foreign Policy*, pp. xii–xiii, 11–12, 71–90. For the earlier debate on Cromwell's foreign policy, see Roger Crabtree, 'The Idea of a Protestant Foreign Policy', in Roots (ed.), *Cromwell: A Profile*, pp. 160–89, and Charles P. Korr, *Cromwell and the New Model Foreign Policy*.

12 John F. Battick, 'A New Interpretation of Cromwell's Western Design', *Journal of the Barbados Museum and Historical Society*, 34 (1972), 76–84.

13 Hamilton, *American Treasure and the Price Revolution in Spain*, pp. 32–8; D. A. Brading and Harry E. Cross, 'Colonial Silver Mining: Mexico and Peru', *HAHR*, 52 (1972), 569.

14 Cromwell to Cotton, 2 October 1651 in Hutchinson (comp.), *Collection of Original Papers Relative to the History of the Colony of Massachusetts-Bay*, 1, p. 266; 'Diary of Samuel Sewall, 1674–1729', Massachusetts Historical Society, *Collections*, 5th Ser., 6 (Boston, 1879), 437.

15 See William S. Maltby, *Black Legend in England*, and Benjamin Keen, 'The Black Legend Revisited', *HAHR*, 49 (1969), 703–19.

16 Bulstrode Whitelock reported that Cromwell had acted 'by the advice of one Gage, a minister, who had been long in the West Indies': *Memorials of the English Affairs from the Beginning of the Reign of Charles the First to the Happy Restoration of Charles the Second*, 4, p. 189; Venables, *Narrative*, p. 125; Laurence, *Parliamentary Army Chaplains*, pp. 7–8.

17 Birch (ed.), *Thurloe State Papers*, 3, pp. 62–3; Taylor, *Western Design*, p. 6.

18 Armitage, *Ideological Origins of the British Empire*, pp. 60–125; Linebaugh and Rediker, *Many-Headed Hydra*, pp. 145–7; Strong, 'Causes', p. 236.

19 BL Add. Mss 11410, 'A Copie of the Original Design upon which Cromwell sett out the fleet for the taking of the island of Hispaniola', ff. 61–80.

20 Canny, *Oxford History of the British Empire*, 1, p. 21.

21 Clarke, *Clarke Papers*, 3, pp. 207–8.

22 Birch (ed.), *Thurloe State Papers*, 1, pp. 759–61.

23 Davies, *Early Stuarts*, p. 231; Newton, *European Nations*, pp. 211–14.

24 On Venables see Lee Porcher Townshend (ed.), *Some Account of General Robert Venables*.

25 Venables, *Narrative*, pp. x, 136.

26 BL Add. Mss 11410, 'A copy of y$^e$ Commission$^{rs}$ Commission 1654'.

27 *CSP D* 1649–50, 22 June 1649, p. 202.

28 Venables, *Narrative*, p. 5; Paige, *Letters of John Paige, London merchant*, p. 107.

29 Donoghue, 'Radical Republicanism', pp. 285–7.

30 Davies, *Early Stuarts*, p. 232.

31 I.S., *Brief and Perfect Journal*, p. 8.

32 Venables, *Narrative*, pp. xxxiii, 5, 40–4, 91–3, 100.

33 Taylor, *Western Design*, pp. 10–12.

34 On participants see Venables, *Narrative*, pp. xxi, xxvi, 20. On Kempo Sabada, see Jameson (ed.), *Privateering and Piracy in the Colonial Period*, p. 14n.

35 Cromwell to Major-General Richard Fortescue, October 1655, in Cromwell, *Writings and Speeches*, p. 858.

36 HMC, 7th Report, p. 572; Matthew Craig Harrington, ' "The Worke Wee May Doe in the World": The Western Design and the Anglo-Spanish Struggle for the Caribbean, 1654–1655', MA dissertation, Florida State University, 2004, pp. 55–7. This excellent account is available online, and much of what follows is based upon it.

37 BL Sloane Mss 3926, 'Journal by H. Whistler of Admiral Penn's voyage from England to the W. Indies 1654, 1655'.

38 Edward Winslow to Thurloe, 16 March 1655, in Birch (ed.), *Thurloe State Papers*, 3, p. 250.

39 Venables, *Narrative*, p. 30.

40 Thomas, *Religion and the Decline of Magic*, p. 18.

41 Venables, *Narrative*, pp. 50, 60.

42 Taylor, *Western Design*, pp. 16–18.

43 O'Callaghan, *To Hell or Barbados*, p. 137.

44 Venables, *Narrative*, pp. xiv, xxx–xxxii, 11.

45 John F. Battick (ed.), 'Richard Rooth's Sea Journal of the Western Design, 1654–55', *Jamaica Journal*, 5 (1971), 8–9.

46 Harrington, ' "The Worke Wee May Doe in the World" ', pp. 51–3.

47 Wright (ed.), *Spanish Narratives*, pp. 47–8, 51–2, 60, 63.

48 Taylor, *Western Design*, pp. 23–9.

49 Venables, *Narrative*, p. 130.

50 Penn, *Memorials of the Professional Life and Times of Sir William Penn*, pp. 74, 82; Venables, *Narrative*, pp. 151–2; HMC, 7th Report, p. 572.

51 Venables, *Narrative*, pp. 154–5; Wright (ed.), *Spanish Narratives*, pp. 8–14.

52 BL Sloane Mss 3926; Venables, *Narrative*, pp. 155–6.

53 Taylor, *Western Design*, pp. 30–1.

54 Venables, *Narrative*, pp. 133, 158; HMC, 7th Report, p. 573.

55 Taylor, *Western Design*, pp. 32–3; Wright (ed.), *Spanish Narratives*, pp. 21–5.

56 I.S., *Brief and Perfect Journal*, pp. 17–18.

57 Cundall and Pietersz, *Jamaica under the Spaniards*, p. 50.

58 Venables, *Narrative*, pp. 18–19.

59 Wright (ed.), *Spanish Narratives*, p. 34.

60 Battick, 'Rooth's Journal', p. 15; Venables, *Narrative*, p. 161; Birch (ed.), *Thurloe State Papers*, 3, pp. 511, 689. The latter is unsigned, but from the complaints made Gregory Butler is the most probable author.

61 Harrington, ' "The Worke Wee May Doe in the World" ', pp. 90–1; Taylor, *Western Design*, pp. 49–50, 52.

62 Clarke, *Clarke Papers*, pp. 3, 59.

63 HMC, 7th Report, p. 573.

64 Wright (ed.), *English Conquest*, p. 3; Venables, *Narrative*, p. 163; HMC, 7th Report, p. 574.

65 AGI Santo Domingo 178B, Don Juan Ramírez de Arellano to crown, 24 May 1655.

66 Padrón, *Spanish Jamaica*, pp. 187–8.

67 AGI Santo Domingo 178B, 'Account of events in the island from May 20 of the year 55 when the English besieged it until July 3, of the year 56', by Captain Julián de Castilla'; Taylor, *Western Design*, pp. 57–61.

68 Harrington, ' "The Worke Wee May Doe in the World" ', pp. 95–6; Taylor, *Western Design*, pp. 71–2.

69 Wright (ed.), *English Conquest*, p. 11; Clarke, *Clarke Papers*, 3, p. 59; Firth, *Cromwell's Army*, pp. 400, 404.

70 Birch (ed.), *Thurloe State Papers*, 3, pp. 508, 511.

71 HMC, 7th Report, p. 571.

72 Long, *History of Jamaica*, 1, pp. 240–1; HMC, 7th Report, p. 575; Birch (ed.), *Thurloe State Papers*, 3, p. 510.

73 *CSP D* 1655, p. 204.

74 Battick, 'Rooth's Journal', pp. 18, 20; Birch (ed.), *Thurloe State Papers*, 3, pp. 752–3; Taylor, *Western Design*, p. 73.

75 *CSP D* 1655, pp. 396, 402–3; *Publick Intelligencer*, No. 4, October 22–October 29, 1655, p. 64; No. 5, October 29–November 5, 1655, p. 78.

76 Harrington, ' "The Worke Wee May Doe in the World" ', pp. 103–4; Long, *History of Jamaica*, 1, p. 241.

77 Hume, *The Court of Philip IV*, p. 439.

78 David Armitage, 'The Cromwellian Protectorate and the Languages of Empire', *Historical Journal*, 35 (1992), 540–2.

79 Sedgwick to Winthrop, 6 November 1655, in 'The Winthrop Papers', Massachusetts Historical Society *Collections*, 5th Ser., 1 (Boston, 1871), 381.

80 See Blair Worden, 'Oliver Cromwell and the Sin of Achan', in Beales and Best (eds), *History, Society and the Churches*, pp. 127, 135–41. Barry Coward saw the failure of the Western Design as prompting Cromwell to self-pity and fear of God's personal judgement leading to a thorough attempt at religious reform in England, and the institution of the rule of major generals to enforce that reform (*Oliver Cromwell*, pp. 133–5), while J. C. Davis saw Cromwell's attempt to discover and atone for the reason that providence deserted him over the debacle on Española as proving the genuineness of his religious beliefs (*Oliver Cromwell*, pp. 129–30).

81 Kupperman, *Providence Island*, p. 354.

82 Armitage, 'The Cromwellian Protectorate and the Languages of Empire', 532–7, 553–4.

83 Strong, 'Causes', p. 245.

## Chapter 7: Buccaneer Islands

1 John Masefield, *On the Spanish Main*, London: Methuen, 1906.

2 P. P. Boucher, 'The "Frontier Era" of the French Caribbean, 1620–1690', in Daniels and Kennedy (eds), *Negotiated Empires*, pp. 213–14.

3 For continuing warfare with the Caribs, see Boucher, *Cannibal Encounters*, pp. 49–60.

4 Peña Battlé, *Isla de la Tortuga*, pp. 145–6, 148–9.

5 Crouse, *French Pioneers in the West Indies*, pp. 84–6; Apestegui, *Pirates*, p. 147.

6 Peña Battlé, *Isla de la Tortuga*, p. 150.

7 Haring, *Buccaneers*, p. 82.

8 Lane, *Pillaging the Empire*, pp. 100–1.

9 Apestegui, *Pirates*, p. 147.

10 Haring, *Buccaneers*, pp. 114–15; Crouse, *French Struggle for the West Indies*, pp. 122–5.

11 Du Tertre, *Histoire générale des Antilles habitées par les Français*, 3, pp. 130–4.

12 Crouse, *French Struggle for the West Indies*, pp. 125–8.

13 Kennedy, *Rise and Fall of the Great Powers*, p. 41.

14 See Worth, *Timucuan Chiefdoms of Spanish Florida*, 2, pp. 45–50, 66–7, 86–7.

15 Birch (ed.), *Thurloe State Papers*, 4, pp. 633–4.

16 Cromwell, *Letters and Speeches*, p. 134.

17 Padrón, *Spanish Jamaica*, pp. 193–4.

18 Birch (ed.), *Thurloe State Papers*, 3, pp. 507–8, 622.

19  Ibid., 4, p. 435; Taylor, *Western Design*, pp. 41, 87–90.

20  Venables, *Narrative*, p. 39; Haring, *Buccaneers*, p. 91.

21  Birch (ed.), *Thurloe State Papers*, 4, pp. 153–4.

22  Taylor, *Western Design*, pp. 91–2.

23  Apestegui, *Pirates*, p. 153.

24  Long, *History of Jamaica*, 1, p. 254.

25  AGI Santo Domingo 178A, Declaration of the prisoner Richard Hopp, Cartagena, 7 August 1656; Jacinto Sedeño Alburuoz to crown, 25 February 1656; Long, *History of Jamaica*, 1, p. 260.

26  Capp, *Cromwell's Navy*, p. 98.

27  O'Callaghan, *To Hell or Barbados*, pp. 77–9, 85–6.

28  BL Egerton Mss 2395, Letter from Col. D'Oyley upon the death of Col. Brayne, 1657, f. 145; Add. Mss 11140, Mr Worley's Discourse of the Privateers of Jamaica, f. 636.

29  Violet Barbour, 'Privateers and Pirates of the West Indies', *American Historical Review*, 16 (1911), 541.

30  Rodgers, *Safeguard of the Sea*, pp. 292–4; Pope, *Harry Morgan's Way*, pp. 75–6.

31  C. H. Firth, 'The Capture of Santiago, in Cuba, by Captain Myngs, 1662', *English Historical Review*, 14 (1899), 536. See also Florence E. Dyer, 'Captain Christopher Myngs in the West Indies', *Mariner's Mirror*, 18 (1932), 168–87.

32  AGI Santo Domingo, 178B: Letter of Don Cristóbal de Isasi, 16 September 1657.

33  Padrón, *Spanish Jamaica*, pp. 202–4, 208–10.

34  Marley, *Pirates and Privateers*, p. 278.

35  AGI Santo Domingo 178B, Don Pedro de Bayana to crown, 23 January 1658.

36  Marley, *Pirates and Privateers*, p. 279.

37  *CSP* 1675–6, Addenda, No. 328.

38  AGI Santo Domingo 178B, Terms of Surrender signed between the English and Spanish, May 1655.

39  Campbell, *Maroons of Jamaica*, pp. 18–19, 21.

40  Padrón, *Spanish Jamaica*, pp. 213–15.

41  Barbour, 'Privateers and Pirates of the West Indies', p. 540.

42  BL Add. Mss 12423, f. 63.

43  Pavison and Buisseret, *Port Royal*, p. 21.

44  BL Egerton Mss 2395, Commission from the Keepers of the Liberties of England to Colonel Thomas Muddiford [Modyford] as Governor of Barbadoes, [24 Apr. 1660], f. 245.

45  BL Egerton Mss 2395, Report of the Committee of the Council, 'The State of affaires of the English in Jamaica', 27 March 1660, f. 241.

46  Nuala Zahedieh, 'A Frugal, Prudential and Hopeful Trade: Privateering in Jamaica, 1665–1689', *Journal of Imperial and Commonwealth History*, 18 (1990), 148, 150–1.

47  BL Add. Mss 12423, f. 67.

48  TNA HCA 49/59, ff. 836–926.

49  BL Add. Mss 12423, f. 101.

50  TNA HCA 49/59, pp. 21–5b.

51  Thornton, *West India Policy under the Restoration*, pp. 39, 45.

52 *CSP* 1661–8, D'Oyley to all governors etc, 5 February, March 1661, pp. 17, 61.

53 TNA CO 1/17, Charles II to Lyttelton, 28 April 1663, p. 23.

54 Talty, *Empire of Blue Water*, p. 48.

55 Haring, *Buccaneers*, pp. 98–9.

56 Lucena Samoral, *Piratas*, pp. 176–7.

57 BL Add. Mss 12408, The Journal of Sir William Beeston, 1678–1702, f. 1.

58 TNA CO 389/5, Additional Instructions, 8 April 1662, pp. 58–9.

59 TNA CO 324/1, 'The condition of Jamaica at Lord Windsor's departure on 20th October, 1662', pp. 258–9.

60 Thornton, *West India Policy under the Restoration*, pp. 56–7.

61 Marley, *Pirates: Adventurers of the High Seas*, p. 28.

62 *CSP* 1661–8, No. 1304; Pope, *Harry Morgan's Way*, pp. 62–5; Breverton, *Admiral Sir Henry Morgan*.

63 Firth, 'Capture of Santiago', p. 538; Lucena Samoral, *Piratas*, p. 177.

64 Marley, *Pirates: Adventurers of the High Seas*, p. 29.

65 Pope, *Harry Morgan's Way*, pp. 93–5.

66 HMC, Calendar of the Heathcote Mss, p. 34.

67 Firth, 'Capture of Santiago', pp. 539–40.

68 TNA CO 138/1, p. 20.

69 Pepys diary, III, p. 41; Thornton, *West India Policy under the Restoration*, p. 58.

70 Charlevoix, *Histoire de l'isle Espagnole*, 1, p. 41.

71 BL Add. Mss 11410, 'An Account of the Private Ships of War belonging to Jamaica and Tortudos, 1663'.

72 Pope, *Harry Morgan's Way*, p. 97.

73 Apestegui, *Pirates*, p. 158.

74 *CSP* 1661–8, No. 443.

75 Haring, *Buccaneers*, p. 108; Peña Battlé, *Isla de la Tortuga*, p. 185.

76 Pepys diary, VII, pp. 165–6.

77 *CSP* 1661–8, 11 August 1663, p. 152; 15 October 1663, p. 164.

78 Thornton, *West India Policy under the Restoration*, pp. 78–9.

79 TNA 1/17, No. 112; Haring, *Buccaneers*, p. 273.

80 Snelders, *Devil's Anarchy*, pp. 86–90.

81 TNA SP Spain, vol. 46, f. 280.

82 Haring, *Buccaneers*, pp. 109–11; Lane, *Pillaging the Empire*, pp. 109–10.

83 TNA SP 9/28, p. 277.

84 When this company went bankrupt the Commons supported another in 1672 which became the Royal African Company. See Davies, *Royal African Company*, passim.

85 TNA CO 140/1, Minutes of the Council of Jamaica, 26 November 1667, November 1668, ff. 170, 261.

86 Rout, *African Experience in Spanish America*, pp. 23–4, 37.

87 *CSP* 1661–8, No. 106; Harlow, *History of Barbados*, p. 62.

88 Fortune, *Merchants and Jews*, p. 111.

89 AGI Indiferente General 2830–3 – a veritable mountain of papers.

90 Postma, *Dutch in the Atlantic Slave Trade*, pp. 26–7, 31–2.

91 TNA CO 1/18, E. Morgan to H. Bennet, No. 82; Thornton, *West India Policy under the Restoration*, pp. 60–4; Pope, *Harry Morgan's Way*, pp. 106–7.

92 *CSP 1661–8*, No. 762 of 26 June 1664.

93 Pope, *Harry Morgan's Way*, pp. 87–8.

94 *CSP 1661–8*, No. 744 of 25 May 1664.

95 Ibid., No. 664 of 18 February 1664.

## Chapter 8: First Admiral

1 Mims, *Colbert's West India Policy*, pp. 5–6, 30, 44–8.

2 *CSP 1661–8*, No. 823.

3 D'Ogeron to Colbert, 20 July 1665, quoted in Vassière, *Saint Domingue*, p. 13.

4 Vassière, *Saint Domingue*, pp. 21–2.

5 Wimpffen, *Voyage to Saint Domingo*, pp. 81–2.

6 Crouse, *French Struggle for the West Indies*, p. 133.

7 *CSP 1661–8*, 9 January 1665, p. 910.

8 Ibid., No. 942.

9 Ibid., No. 980.

10 David Davies, 'The Birth of the Imperial Navy? Aspects of English Naval Strategy c. 1650–90', in Duffy (ed.), *Parameters of British Naval Power*, pp. 19–20.

11 His charging policy towards the buccaneers can be traced in his dispatches home. *CSP 1661–8*, Nos 629–35, 664, 739, 767, 942, 979, 1264, 1276, 1383. A contemporary critique of his policy can be found in William Beeston's journal published in *Interesting Tracts*, pp. 281–7.

12 TNA HCA 49/59, ff. 83b–92b, 120b, CO 1/20 Modyford to Arlington, 5 June 1665, f. 49b.

13 *CSP 1661–8*, No. 979.

14 Ibid., No. 1081.

15 Violet Barbour, 'Privateers and Pirates of the West Indies', *American Historical Review*, 16 (1910–11), 547; Haring, *Buccaneers*, p. 130.

16 *CSP 1661–8*, No. 1264; Pope, *Harry Morgan's Way*, pp. 111–12.

17 Apestegui, *Pirates*, pp. 165–6.

18 Marley, *Pirates: Adventurers of the High Seas*, pp. 33–5.

19 Exquemelin, *Buccaneers of America*, p. 220.

20 Floyd, *Anglo-Spanish Struggle for Mosquitia*, p. 29.

21 *CSP 1661–8*, No. 1264.

22 Gámez, *Historia de Nicaragua*, p. 184.

23 *CSP 1661–8*, No. 1264.

24 Ibid., No. 1138.

25 Barbour, 'Privateers and Pirates of the West Indies', p. 548.

26 TNA CO 1/20, Modyford to Albemarle, 1 March 1666, No. 24. Albemarle's letter of 30 May 1665 does not appear to have survived.

27 Pope, *Harry Morgan's Way*, pp. 109–10, 124.

28 TNA CO 140/1, Minutes of the Council of Jamaica, 22 February 1666, pp. 143–7; *CSP V 1666–8*, p. 11; *CSP 1661–68*, Nos 1130, 1132–7.

29 TNA CO 1/20 No. 24(I), 22 February 1665/6.

30 Thornton, *West India Policy under the Restoration*, pp. 98–100.

31 The best account of the action is Du Tertre, *Histoire générale des Antilles habitées par les Français*, 4, pp. 21–40: See also *CSP 1661–8*, Nos 1204, 1212, 1214, 1220, although these give little detail and are vague and contradictory.

32 Marley, *Pirates: Adventurers of the High Seas*, pp. 38–9.

33 Clark, *Later Stuarts*, p. 327.

34 *CSP 1661–8*, Nos 1264, 1276.

35 Ibid., 8 March 1666, p. 363.

36 Ibid., 29 January 1666, p. 354.

37 Marley, *Pirates and Privateers of the Americas*, pp. 271–2.

38 *CSP 1661–8*, No. 1213.

39 Marley, *Pirates and Privateers of the Americas*, p. 242.

40 Bancroft, *History of Central America*, 2, pp. 461–3; Floyd, *Anglo-Spanish Struggle for Mosquitia*, p. 31.

41 Pavison and Buisseret, *Port Royal*, p. 27.

42 Earle, *Sack of Panamá*, pp. 16–24.

43 Marley, *Pirates and Privateers of the Americas*, pp. 242–3.

44 Donald Rowland, 'Spanish Occupation of the Island of Old Providence, or Santa Catalina, 1641–1670', *HAHR*, 15 (1935), pp. 305, 309.

45 TNA CO 1/23 No. 43, Deposition of Henry Wasey, 19 August 1668. There are other accounts of Mansfield's death but this seems the most likely. The date remains uncertain.

46 *CSP 1661–8*, No. 1264.

47 Rowland, 'Spanish Occupation of Providence', pp. 306–8.

48 Earle, *Sack of Panamá*, pp. 29–35.

49 *CSP 1661–8*, No. 1851.

50 Pope, *Harry Morgan's Way*, pp. 130–2.

51 Moya Pons, *Manual de historia Dominicana*, p. 89.

52 Marley, *Pirates and Privateers of the Americas*, pp. 286–7.

53 Lucena Samoral, *Piratas*, p. 186.

54 Marley, *Pirates and Privateers of the Americas*, pp. 287–8.

55 Apestegui, *Pirates*, pp. 161–2; Exquemelin, *Buccaneers of America*, pp. 76 et seq.

56 Marley, *Pirates and Privateers of the Americas*, p. 219.

57 Marley, *Pirates: Adventurers of the High Seas*, pp. 41–4.

58 Exquemelin, *Buccaneers of America*, p. 107.

59 Charlevoix, *Histoire de l'isle Espagnole*, 2, p. 73.

60 Exquemelin, *Buccaneers of America*, p. 117.

61 *CSP 1661–8*, No. 1264.

62 Clark, *Later Stuarts*, pp. 63–8, 325–8.

63 Davenport, *European Treaties*, 2, p. 106.

64 Barbour, 'Privateers and Pirates of the West Indies', pp. 553–4.

65 Ibid., p. 554.

66 Pope, *Harry Morgan's Way*, pp. 134–5; Earle, *Sack of Panama*, p. 55.

67 *CSP 1661–1668*, Modyford to Arlington, 30 July 1667.

## Chapter 9: Portobelo

1 TNA CO 1/20 No. 24(I), 22 February 1665/6.

2 TNA CO 1/23 No. 43, Deposition of Henry Wasey, 19 August 1668; *CSP* 1661–8, Information of Admiral Henry Morgan and officers, 7 September 1668.

3 BL Add. Mss 12424, Journal of Sir William Beeston, 1671–1702.

4 Pope, *Harry Morgan's Way*, p. 136.

5 For information on the *armada* see AGI Indiferente General 2516, 2541, 2696, Contratación 3161 and 5102.

6 TNA 138/1, Modyford to Privy Council, f. 38.

7 Nuala Zahedieh, 'A Frugal, Prudential and Hopeful Trade: Privateering in Jamaica, 1665–1689', *Journal of Imperial and Commonwealth History*, 18 (1990), 149.

8 Pope, *Harry Morgan's Way*, pp. 138–40.

9 Exquemelin, *Buccaneers of America*, p. 128.

10 Ibid., p. 129.

11 Ibid., p. 130.

12 TNA *CSP/*WI 1838.

13 Exquemelin, *Buccaneers of America*, p. 131; Pope, *Harry Morgan's Way*, pp. 142–4.

14 TNA *CSP/*WI 1838.

15 Pezuela, *Historia de la Isla de Cuba*, 2, pp. 165–6.

16 TNA *CSP/*WI 1838.

17 Exquemelin, *Buccaneers of America*, pp. 133–4.

18 Talty, *Empire of Blue Water*, pp. 91, 96–7.

19 AGI EC 462A, I, Residencia a Don Agustin de Bracamonte, 320v–327.

20 Leslie, *New History of Jamaica*, p. 114.

21 Exquemelin, *Buccaneers of America*, p. 136.

22 AGI IG 1600, Morgan's Articles of Association; Haring, *Buccaneers*, pp. 70–8.

23 Exquemelin, *Buccaneers of America*, p. 76.

24 AGI IG 1600, Expendiente de la Junta de Guerra y represaliás de Franceses e Ingleses, 1671–6.

25 TNA CO 1/24, Narrative of Sir Thomas Modyford, 23 August 1669. This sentence does not appear in the Calendar, which has led many historians to underestimate the real takings of privateers by basing their calculations on official figures of tenths and fifteenths.

26 TNA *CSP/*WI 1851, 'Depositions of Robert Rawlinson' etc, 5 October 1668.

27 TNA *CSP/*WI 1838; Earle, *Sack of Panamá*, pp. 62–3; Pope, *Harry Morgan's Way*, p. 147.

28 Wafer, *New Voyage*, pp. 41–3. For other accounts see Vásquez de Espinosa, *Compendium*, pp. 303–4; Gonzalez Carranza, *Geographical Description*, pp. 81, 130–2; and Gage, *English-American*, pp. 62–7.

29 See Allyn C. Loosley, 'The Puerto Bello Fairs', *Hispanic American Historical Review*, 13 (1933), 314–35; Ward, *Imperial Panama*, pp. 67–88.

30 Earle, *Sack of Panamá*, pp. 55–7.

31 Ibid., pp. 64–5.

32 The following account is mostly based on TNA CO 1/23, Morgan's relation, 7 September 1668; CO 1/24, Account of Jean Dogler (John Douglas), 7–17 January

1669; AGI EC 462A; EC 577A, Cartagena Pleitos 1688, pza 3, 'Informaciones *hechas* en la forma que el enimigo coxio la ciudad de San Felipe de Puerto Bello', pza 4, 'Autos y acuerdos . . . sobre la recuperación de Puertovelo'; Panamá 81, 'Expeditentes sobre el emprestito de 100 mil pesos de los vecinos de Panamá para rescatar Portobelo a las piratas, 1669–78'. Exquemelin is very inaccurate and has been largely discounted.

33 AGI IG 1877, Sir Richard White in a paper discussed at a *junta*, 4 December 1671.

34 Many Spanish prisoners heard this story from their guards. See AGI EC 462A I, 138v (Evidence of Rodriguez), I, 127v (Arredondo) etc.

35 AGI Panamá 81, Evidence of Alonzo Sanchez Randoli.

36 Earle, *Sack of Panamá*, pp. 69–71.

37 Leslie, *New History of Jamaica*, pp. 119–20.

38 This infamous incident is reported with considerable embellishment by Exquemelin, *Buccaneers of America*, pp. 136–7, but is well covered in the evidence taken at the *averiguación*. AGI EC 462A i, 249v (Evidence of Astudillo); i, 258v (De la Parra) etc.

39 Earle, *Sack of Panamá*, pp. 73–4.

40 Exquemelin, *Buccaneers of America*, p. 137.

41 BL 1342 c.3 (21), 'Memorial del Captain Sebastian Crespo', p. 18.

42 TNA *CSP/WI* 1669, 74, No. 138.

43 AGI EC 462A i, 149; TNA *CSP/WI* 1669–74, No. 138, John Style to the principal secretary of state, 4 January 1670.

44 TNA CO 1/23: Morgan's 'Relation', 7 September 1668.

45 Earle, *Sack of Panamá*, pp. 75–8.

46 TNA *CSP/WI* 1838, Report of Admiral Henry Morgan and his officers, Port Royal, 7 September 1668.

47 AGI Panamá 81, 1669 (III), ff. 33v–9v.

48 Earle, *Sack of Panamá*, pp. 80–4.

49 AGI EC 462A i, 318–49, Papers relating to *junta* of 23 July 1668.

50 Ibid., ii, 291v–9v, Evidence of Aricaga.

51 Ibid., 161v–80, Evidence of Cristoval García Niño.

52 TNA *CSP/WI* 1838; Earle, *Sack of Panamá*, pp. 86–9.

53 Exquemelin, *Buccaneers of America*, p. 139.

## Chapter 10: Maracaibo

1 Westminster Abbey Muniments, 11920, Sir James Modyford to Sir Andrew King, 4 October 1668; TNA CO 1/25, 'Narrative of Sir Thomas Modyford, 23 August 1669', p. 145; CO 1/24, 'Memorial of Spanish Ambassador, 7 January 1669', p. 1.

2 Pope, *Harry Morgan's Way*, pp. 154–5.

3 *CSP* 1661–8, No. 1850.

4 Ibid., No. 1859.

5 Ibid., Nos 1863, 1867, 1892.

6 *CSP V* 1667–8, Piero Mocenigo to Doge, 31 August 1668, p. 253.

7 Earle, *Sack of Panamá*, pp. 92–6.

8 Pope, *Harry Morgan's Way*, pp. 155–6. On *Oxford*, see Anderson, *List of English Men-of-War*.

9 Most of the information on the *Oxford* comes from four letters written by Surgeon Richard Browne in *CSP* 1661–8, Nos 1867, 1892; ibid., 1669–74, No. 21; ibid., 1674–6, No. 1207. See also Beeston's Journal in *Interesting Tracts*, p. 287.

10 Pope, *Harry Morgan's Way*, pp. 164–5.

11 Exquemelin, *Buccaneers of America*, p. 142.

12 Dampier, *Travels*, 1, p. 72.

13 A. P. Thornton, 'The Modyfords and Morgan', *Jamaican Historical Review*, 11 (1952), 54.

14 Earle, *Sack of Panamá*, pp. 109–11.

15 AGI EC 699A, pza 1, ff. 39v–40; Thornton, 'Modyfords and Morgan', pp. 55–6.

16 Exquemelin, *Buccaneers of America*, p. 146.

17 Pope, *Harry Morgan's Way*, p. 172.

18 AGI Escribana de Cámara 699A, pza 1, f. 45v.

19 Earle, *Sack of Panamá*, pp. 112–13.

20 Pope, *Harry Morgan's Way*, pp. 174–6.

21 Earle, *Sack of Panamá*, pp. 114–15.

22 AGI Contratación 3161; Indiferente General 2541, viceroy to queen, 5 April 1669; Escribanía de Cámara 660A, Evidence of Varrio, ff. 2–3.

23 AGI Contratación 3164, 'Información fecha por partte de D. Alonço de Campos . . .', ff. 1–4.

24 Earle, *Sack of Panamá*, pp. 120–3.

25 Exquemelin, *Buccaneers of America*, p. 154.

26 Morgan's report in Thornton, 'Modyfords and Morgan', p. 55.

27 Earle, *Sack of Panamá*, p. 124.

28 Pope, *Harry Morgan's Way*, p. 178.

29 Exquemelin, *Buccaneers of America*, pp. 155–6.

30 Earle, *Sack of Panamá*, pp. 125–6.

31 AGI Escribana de Cámara 660A, Evidence of the *castellan*, Antonio Camarillo, ff. 35v–6.

32 Pope, *Harry Morgan's Way*, p. 181.

33 Earle, *Sack of Panamá*, p. 127.

34 Exquemelin, *Buccaneers of America*, pp. 159–61.

35 Earle, *Sack of Panamá*, p. 128.

36 Pope, *Harry Morgan's Way*, pp. 185–6.

37 Morgan's report in Thornton, 'Modyfords and Morgan', p. 55.

38 Exquemelin, *Buccaneers of America*.

39 Apestegui, *Pirates*, p. 171. On Reyning see Snelders, *Devil's Anarchy*, pp. 108 ff.

40 AGI Indiferente General 1877, Translation of English proclamation discussed at the Council of the Indies, 23 November 1669, quoted in Earle, *Sack of Panamá*, p. 144.

41 TNA CO 1/25, p. 125; *CSP* 1669–74, No. 172(i).

42 TNA CO 138/1, Modyford to Arlington, 6 July 1670, 'Copy of a Commission of War by the Spaniard against the English in the West Indies being a translation of the original in Spanish'; 'Consideration from Sir Thomas Modyford which moved him to give his consent for fitting the privateers of Jamaica against the Spaniards', p. 136.

43 TNA CO 1/27, Depositions of Boys and Cobino, pp. 65–6.

44 Pope, *Harry Morgan's Way*, pp. 193–4.

45 TNA CO 1/25, Deposition of Cornelius Carsetens, p. 51; Rivera's Commission and Poem, pp. 128–9, 157–8; *CSP* 1669–74, No. 161.

46 US Library of Congress, J. T. Conner Collection; AGI 54-5-18, Francisco de la Guerra y de la Vega to Charles II, St Augustine, 8 August 1668.

47 www.searlesbuccaneers.org/searle_bio.htm. For a detailed account of the raid go to www.sealesbuccaneers.org/Searles_History.htm.

48 Pope, *Harry Morgan's Way*, p. 200.

49 *CSP* 1669–74, No. 162.

50 Ibid., No. 214.

51 Earle, *Sack of Panamá*, pp. 149–51; Nuala Zahedieh, 'A Frugal, Prudential and Hopeful Trade: Privateering in Jamaica, 1665–1689', *Journal of Imperial and Commonwealth History*, 18 (1990), 155.

52 *CSP* 1669–74, No. 310(ii).

53 TNA CO 1/27, Browne to Williamson, 21 August 1671, p. 69.

54 TNA CO 1/25, Charles Modyford's Report on Jamaica, 1670, p. 5.

55 TNA CO 138/1, Modyford to Lord Ashley, 6 July 1670, p. 50.

56 Nuala Zahedieh, ' "The Wickedest City in the World": Port Royal, Commercial Hub of the Seventeenth century Caribbean', in Sheperd (ed.), *Working Slavery, Pricing Freedom*, p. 7.

57 BL Add. Mss 12424, Journal of Sir William Beeston, 1671–1702, f. 6.

58 Institute of Jamaica, MS 390, letter to Nottingham, March 1689; Zahedieh, 'Frugal, Prudential and Hopeful Trade', pp. 153–4.

59 *CSP* 1669–74, No. 293; TNA CO 1/25, p. 159.

**Chapter 11: Panamá**

1 Earle, *Sack of Panamá*, pp. 132–3.

2 BL Add. Mss 11268, Papers relative to affairs at Carthagena and Jamaica, 1670–1, f. 57v.

3 Earle, *Sack of Panamá*, pp. 141–3; Pope, *Harry Morgan's Way*, pp. 231–2.

4 Pope, *Harry Morgan's Way*, pp. 201–2.

5 TNA CO 140/1, Minutes of Council of Jamaica, 21 September 1671, pp. 233–5; Pope, *Harry Morgan's Way*, p. 200.

6 Earle, *Sack of Panamá*, pp. 155–6.

7 BL Add. Mss 11268, f. 73.

8 TNA CO 1/25, Modyford to Arlington, 30 August 1670, p. 116.

9 Pope, *Harry Morgan's Way*, pp. 201–2, 204.

10 Earle, *Sack of Panamá*, pp. 159–60.

11 *CSP* 1669–74, No. 405.

12 BL Add. Mss 11140, Morgan's 'Relation', pp. 332–3.

13 Southey, *Chronological History of the West Indies*, 2, pp. 99–100.

14 Earle, *Sack of Panamá*, pp. 162–3.

15 It was apparently the last one to leave. Donald Rowland, 'Spanish Occupation of the Island of Old Providence, or Santa Catalina, 1641–1670', *HAHR*, 15 (1935), pp. 307–8.

16  AGI Panamá 93, Ulloa to crown, 16 November 1670; Marley, *Pirates and Privateers of the Americas*, pp. 333–5.

17  Floyd, *Anglo-Spanish Struggle for Mosquitia*, pp. 32–3.

18  *CSP* 1669–74, No. 310; AGI Panamá 93, Ulloa to crown, 16 November 1670.

19  Pope, *Harry Morgan's Way*, pp. 207–9.

20  Earle, *Sack of Panamá*, pp. 168–71.

21  For details see Davenport, *European Treaties*, 2, pp. 183–96.

22  AGI Panamá 93, Report on the defences of Portobelo, 1 February 1671.

23  AGI EC 461B, pza x, f. 222v.

24  Earle, *Sack of Panamá*, pp. 172–5.

25  BL Add. Mss 11268, ff. 74–74v; Earle, *Sack of Panamá*, pp. 178–9.

26  Vassière, *Saint Domingue*, p. 19; Pope, *Harry Morgan's Way*, p. 210.

27  AGI Panamá 93, f. 57.

28  Exquemelin, *Buccaneers of America*, p. 172.

29  Pope, *Harry Morgan's Way*, pp. 212–14.

30  BL Add. Mss 11268, f. 75.

31  Rowland, 'Spanish Occupation of Providence', pp. 310–11; Exquemelin, *Buccaneers of America*, pp. 176–7.

32  BL Add. Mss 11268, f. 75.

33  AGI Panamá 93, f. 58; Earle, *Sack of Panamá*, pp. 184–6.

34  Earle, *Sack of Panamá*, pp. 188–90.

35  AGI Panamá 87, Don Agustin de Bracamonte to crown, 29 October 1668.

36  Exquemelin, *Buccaneers of America*, p. 181.

37  Earle, *Sack of Panamá*, pp. 192–6.

38  Ibid., pp. 198–201.

39  Exquemelin, *Buccaneers of America*, p. 189.

40  AGI EC 461B, pza x, f. 486v; Earle, *Sack of Panamá*, pp. 210–12.

41  BL Add. Mss 11268, f. 77.

42  Exquemelin, *Buccaneers of America*, p. 193.

43  Earle, *Sack of Panamá*, pp. 213–16.

44  BL Add. Mss 11268, Deposition of John Peeke, f. 79.

45  Earle, *Sack of Panamá*, pp. 219–21.

46  AGI Panamá 93, Pérez de Guzmán to crown, 19 February 1671.

47  Pope, *Harry Morgan's Way*, pp. 237–41.

48  Earle, *Sack of Panamá*, pp. 223–4, 226.

49  BL Add. Mss 11268, f. 78.

50  Pope, *Harry Morgan's Way*, pp. 242–4; Exquemelin, *Buccaneers of America*, pp. 198–9.

51  BL Add. Mss 11410, f. 160.

52  TNA CO 1/27, Browne to Williamson, 21 August 1671, p. 69.

53  Earle, *Sack of Panamá*, p. 241.

54  Ibid., pp. 228–31.

55  BL Add. Mss 11268, f. 79.

56  Exquemelin, *Buccaneers of America*, p. 207.

57  Earle, *Sack of Panamá*, pp. 245–6.

58  BL Add. Mss 11410, Lynch to Arlington, 27 June 1671, f. 183.

59 A. P. Thornton, 'The Modyfords and Morgan', *Jamaican Historical Review*, 11 (1952), 57.

60 BL Add. Mss 11410, Lynch to Arlington, 27 June 1671, f. 181.

61 Earle, *Sack of Panamá*, pp. 248–9.


## Chapter 12: French Service

1 Thornton, *West India Policy under the Restoration*, pp. 149–50.

2 Nuala Zahedieh, 'Trade, Plunder, and Economic Development in Early English Jamaica, 1655–89', *Economic History Review*, 39 (1986), 206–7.

3 TNA CO 1/28, Lynch to Arlington, 2 March 1672, ff. 46–46b; Nuala Zahedieh, 'The Merchants of Port Royal, Jamaica, and the Spanish Contraband Trade, 1655–1692', *WMQ*, 3rd Ser., 43 (1986), 575.

4 BL Add. Mss 28140, 'An Essay on the Nature and Method of Carrying on a Trade to the South Seas', ff. 24–24b; TNA CO 110/152, Brailsford Papers.

5 See C. P. Nettels, 'England and the Spanish American Trade, 1680–1715', *Journal of Modern History*, 3 (1931), 1–33.

6 Thornton, *West India Policy under the Restoration*, p. 214. See also Gilbert M. Joseph, 'British Loggers and Spanish Governors: The Logwood Trade and its Settlements in the Yucatan Peninsula' (Parts I and II), *Caribbean Studies*, 14 (1974), 7–36; 15 (1976), 43–52.

7 For a description of the life of the logwood-cutters see Dampier, *Travels*, 2, pp. 155–6, 178–9, 181ff.; Preston and Preston, *Pirate of Exquisite Mind*, pp. 56–60, 66–72.

8 *CSP* 1669–74, Nos 587, 638.

9 TNA CO 1/31, Lynch to Williamson, 6 July 1671, f. 11; CO 140/1, Modyford to Privy Council, 28 September 1670, pp. 38–9; Modyford to Arlington, 31 October 1670, No. 59; CO 1/27, Lynch to Arlington, 25 December 1671, f. 193.

10 AGI Indiferente General 2542, Junta de Guerra to crown, 31 January 1676, p. 5.

11 Apestegui, *Pirates*, pp. 173–4.

12 BL Add. Mss 11410, ff. 270–1.

13 Marley, *Pirates and Privateers of the Americas*, p. 149.

14 Thornton, *West India Policy under the Restoration*, p. 215.

15 Marley, *Pirates and Privateers of the Americas*, pp. 81–2.

16 TNA CO 389/5, Lynch to Worsley, 8 July 1673, p. 17.

17 BL Longleat Mss Coventry Papers, 124, Lynch to Arlington, 23 September 1674, p. 19; Thornton, *West India Policy under the Restoration*, pp. 217–19.

18 BL Add. Mss 25120, Coventry to Vaughan, f. 47.

19 Earle, *Sack of Panamá*, pp. 250–3, 261.

20 Israel, *Dutch Primacy in World Trade*, pp. 293–4.

21 Marley, *Pirates: Adventurers of the High Seas*, p. 66.

22 Marley, *Pirates and Privateers of the Americas*, pp. 295–7.

23 P. P. Boucher, 'The "Frontier Era" of the French Caribbean, 1620–1690', in Daniels and Kennedy (eds), *Negotiated Empires*, p. 222.

24 Lane, *Pillaging the Empire*, p. 123; Archivo Nacional de Historia, Quito, Ecuador, Series 'Popayán', caja 5 (1674).

25 Marley, *Pirates and Privateers of the Americas*, pp. 4–5.

26 *CSP* 1675–6, No. 988.

27 Haring, *Buccaneers*, pp. 214–15.

28 Ibid., p. 217.

29 *CSP* 1677–80, Nos 347, 375, 383, 1497; TNA SP Spain, vol. 65, f. 102.

30 Breverton, *Admiral Sir Henry Morgan*, pp. 110–14; Thornton, *West India Policy under the Restoration*, p. 222.

31 Apestegui, *Pirates*, p. 160.

32 TNA CO 1/40, Vaughan to Coventry, 28 May 1677, No. 93.

33 Peña Battlé, *Isla de la Tortuga*, pp. 251–2; Marley, *Sack of Veracruz*, p. 10.

34 Crouse, *French Struggle for the West Indies*, pp. 110–18, 120–1.

35 Dampier, *Travels*, I, p. 81.

36 Marley, *Pirates: Adventurers of the High Seas*, p. 69.

37 Haring, *Buccaneers*, p. 240.

38 AGI Santo Domingo 65, Padilla to crown, 12 June 1678, p. 21.

39 Marley, *Pirates: Adventurers of the High Seas*, p. 71.

40 Lucena Samoral, *Piratas*, p. 209.

41 *CSP* 1677–80, Nos 770, 815, 1516.

42 AGI Santo Domingo 65, Junta de Guerra to crown, 5 July 1678, p. 5.

43 H. G. Bensusan, 'The Spanish Struggle against Foreign Encroachment in the Caribbean, 1675–1697', PhD dissertation, University of California, Los Angeles, 1970, pp. 88–9.

44 Marley, *Pirates: Adventurers of the High Seas*, pp. 20–1; Marley, *Pirates and Privateers of the Americas*, pp. 374–5.

45 Goslinga, *Dutch in the Caribbean and the Guianas*, pp. 1–4.

46 Bensusan, 'Spanish Struggle', p. 45.

47 *CSP* 1681–5, No. 668, pp. 282–8.

48 Goslinga, *Dutch in the Caribbean and the Guianas*, p. 85.

49 *CSP* 1677–80, No. 1498. See also Gilbert M. Joseph, 'John Coxon and the Role of Buccaneering in the Settlement of the Yucatán Colonial Frontier', *Terrae Incognitae*, 12 (1980), 65–84.

50 *CSP* 1677–80, Nos 1150, 1188, 1199, 1516.

51 Marley, *Pirates: Adventurers of the High Seas*, p. 73.

52 BL Sloane Mss 2752, f. 29.

53 Biblioteca Nacional Madrid, 20066, 'Relación de la sucediddo en Portovelo y Panamá en el año 1680'.

54 TNA SP Spain, vol. 65, f. 121.

55 Marley, *Pirates: Adventurers of the High Seas*, p. 73.

56 Dampier, *Travels*, I, pp. 200–1.

57 Haring, *Buccaneers*, pp. 224–5; Bradley, *Lure of Peru*, pp. 106–7.

58 Ringrose, *Journal*, p. 307.

59 BL Sloane Mss 46B, 'Sharp's journal of a voyage to the South Seas, 1680–1682', f. 7.

60 Preston and Preston, *Pirate of Exquisite Mind*, pp. 106–16.

61 Ibid., pp. 120–40. For complete accounts of buccaneer exploits in the South Seas see P. T. Bradley, *Lure of Peru*, and P. Kemp and C. Lloyd, *Brethren of the Coast*.

62 Thornton, *West India Policy under the Restoration*, pp. 225–7.

63 Marley, *Pirates and Privateers of the Americas*, p. 164.

64 TNA CO 1/45/4, p. 11; National Library of Jamaica, MS 105, Diary of John Taylor, 'Multum in Parvo', pp. 494–7.

65 Nuala Zahedieh, ' "The Wickedest City in the World": Port Royal, Commercial Hub of the Seventeenth-century Caribbean', in Sheperd (ed.), *Working Slavery, Pricing Freedom*, pp. 4–5; Hickeringill, *Jamaica Viewed*, p. 16.

66 National Library of Jamaica, MS 105, Diary of John Taylor, 'Multum in Parvo', p. 509.

67 Zahedieh, ' "Wickedest City in the World" ', pp. 10–11.

68 TNA HCA 15/14, 'Account Book of Swiftsure'; HCA 30/664, 'Account Book of Cadiz merchant'.

69 National Library of Jamaica, MS 105, Diary of John Taylor, 'Multum in Parvo', p. 501.

70 Ibid., pp. 491–507, 589.

71 Talty, *Empire of Blue Water*, pp. 132–4. See also Mary Carleton, *New from Jamaica in a Letter from Port Royal Written by the Germane Princess to Her Fellow Collegiates and Friends in New-Gate*; J. Todd and E. Spearing (eds), *Counterfeit Ladies*; and M. J. Kietzman, *Self-Fashioning of an Early Modern Englishwoman*.

72 National Library of Jamaica, MS 159, 'History and State of Jamaica under Lord Vaughan, 1679–80', p. 61.

73 Hickeringill, *Jamaica Viewed*, p. 16.

74 TNA CO 138/4, Thomas Lynch to Jenkins, 6 November 1682, p. 115.

75 Zahedieh, ' "Wickedest City in the World" ', pp. 10–11.

76 Zahedieh, 'Trade, Plunder, and Economic Development', pp. 220–1.

**Chapter 13: Suppression**

1 *CSP* 1677–1680, No. 1361.

2 Haring, *Buccaneers*, p. 226.

3 *CSP* 1677–80, No 1420; BL Sloane Mss 2724, f. 3.

4 BL Sloane Mss 2724, f. 198.

5 *CSP* 1677–80, Nos 1425, 1462.

6 BL Sloane Mss 2724, f. 200; *CSP* 1681–5, Nos 16, 51, 144, 431.

7 *CSP* 1681–5, Nos 431, 632, 713; HMC, 7th Report, p. 405b.

8 Bradley, *Lure of Peru*, pp. 121–2.

9 Breverton, *Admiral Sir Henry Morgan*, p. 120.

10 Haring, *Buccaneers*, pp. 234–6.

11 Davies, *Royal African Company*, pp. 328–35; Burns, *British West Indies*, pp. 332–7.

12 Haring, *Buccaneers*, pp. 237–9.

13 Apestegui, *Pirates*, pp. 183–4.

14 Ibid., p. 189.

15 Marley, *Sack of Veracruz*, p. 8.

16 Lane, *Pillaging the Empire*, p. 165.

17 Apestegui, *Pirates*, p. 185.

18 Marley, *Sack of Veracruz*, pp. 11–13.

19 Ibid., pp. 15–19.

20 Ibid., pp. 23–34.

21 Ibid., pp. 35–41. Spanish reports of the sack of Veracruz are preserved in AGI Audiencia de Mexico 54, 91 (Ramo 3), 350, 366 and 864; Contractación 622; EC 229-A, 229-B, 297-C and 1044; Indiferente General 2547, 2548 and 2616; Patronato 243 (Ramo 2), and were used by Juan Juárez Moreno for his classic *Piratas y corsarios en Veracruz y Campeche*.

22 Marley, *Sack of Veracruz*, pp. 41–50.

23 AGI EC 297-A, 'Inquiry on the guilty in the entrance and looting of Veracruz by the pirate Lorenzo'.

24 Marley, *Sack of Veracruz*, pp. 51–8.

25 Ibid., p. 63.

26 Apestegui, *Pirates*, p. 186.

27 H. G. Bensusan, 'The Spanish Struggle against Foreign Encroachment in the Caribbean, 1675–1697', PhD dissertation, University of California, Los Angeles, 1970, pp. 54–5.

28 Charlevoix, *Histoire de l'isle Espagnole*, 3, pp. liv, viii, 141, 202; CSP 1681–5, Nos 1210, 1249, 1424, 1461, 1649, 1718 and 1839.

29 Apestegui, *Pirates*, pp. 187–8.

30 Marley, *Pirates and Privateers of the Americas*, pp. 13, 108.

31 Rodríguez del Valle, *El castillo de San Felipe del Golfo Dulce*, p. 35.

32 Dampier, *Travels*, pp. 152–5; Bancroft, *History of Central America*, 2, pp. 553–5.

33 Bradley, *Lure of Peru*, p. 185.

34 Apestegui, *Pirates of the Caribbean*, pp. 189–92.

35 Marley, *Pirates: Adventurers of the High Seas*, p. 79.

36 Marley, *Pirates and Privateers of the Americas*, pp. 166–7.

37 Duro, *Armada Española*, 5, pp. 273–4; *CSP* 1685–8, Nos 193, 339, 378, 778.

38 Haring, *Buccaneers*, pp. 245–6.

39 Marley, *Pirates and Privateers of the Americas*, p. 167; Marley, *Pirates: Adventurers of the High Seas*, p. 81.

40 Marley, *Pirates and Privateers of the Americas*, pp. 111–12; Marley, *Pirates: Adventurers of the High Seas*, pp. 84–5.

41 National Archives France, Series Colonies C8A/4, 67–85, Governor Bégon and Intendant Saint-Laurens of Martinique, 25 January 1685.

42 AGI Panamá 96, Consejo de Indias to crown, 11 October 1685, p. 6.

43 Breverton, *Admiral Sir Henry Morgan*, pp. 123–6; *Correspondence of the Family of Hatton* (Camden Soc. Pub.) II, p. 225; Nuala Zahedieh, 'A Frugal, Prudential and Hopeful Trade: Privateering in Jamaica, 1665–1689', *Journal of Imperial and Commonwealth History*, 18 (1990), 164.

44 CSP 1681–5, Nos 1958, 1962, 1964, 1991, 2000.

45 Ibid., Nos 668, 769, 942, 948, 1281, 1562, 1759; 1685–8, No. 558.

46 Haring, *Buccaneers*, pp. 248, 251–2.

47 *CSP* 1681–5, No. 1759 of 20 June 1684.

48 Ibid., Nos 1844, 1852.

49 Pavison and Buisseret, *Port Royal*, pp. 53–5.

50 Bensusan, 'Spanish Struggle', pp. 108–10.

51 Marley, *Pirates and Privateers of the Americas*, p. 53.

52 *CSP* 1681–5, pp. 7–8.

53 Carrión, *Puerto Rico and the Non-Hispanic Caribbean*, pp. 54–5.

54 Apestegui, *Pirates*, p. 193.

55 Marley, *Pirates: Adventurers of the High Seas*, p. 85.

56 Marley, *Pirates and Privateers of the Americas*, p. 168.

57 Apestegui, *Pirates of the Caribbean*, p. 193.

58 Duro, *Armada Española*, pp. 278–80.

59 Apestegui, *Pirates*, p. 195.

60 *CSP* 1685–8, Nos 1567, 1646, 1655, 1656, 1659, 1663, 1721, 1838, 1858.

61 Jamaica Archives, Spanish Town, Inv. 1B/11/3, Inventory of Henry Morgan, 1688, ff. 259–67.

62 TNA CO 138/6, Duke of Albemarle to the Committee of Trade, 11 May 1688, p. 118; Nuala Zahedieh, ' "The Wickedest City in the World": Port Royal, Commercial Hub of the Seventeenth-century Caribbean', in Sheperd (ed.), *Working Slavery, Pricing Freedom*, p. 14.

63 Bodleian Library, Oxford, MS Rawl A478, 'Advantages of trading with Our Plantations', pp. 65–72.

64 A. P. Usher, 'The Growth of English Shipping, 1572–1922', *Quarterly Journal of Economics*, 42 (1927–8), 467; Ralph Davies, 'English Foreign Trade, 1600–1700', *Economic History Review*, 2nd Ser., 7 (1954), 150; Minchington, *The Growth of English Overseas Trade in the Seventeenth and Eighteenth Centuries*, pp. 30–1.

65 Dampier, *Travels*, p. 160.

66 MacLeod, *Spanish Central America*, p. 362.

67 Fortune, *Merchants and Jews*, pp. 114, 116.

68 Zahedieh, 'A Frugal, Prudential and Hopeful Trade', p. 161.

69 *CSP* 1681–5, p. 521.

70 Apestegui, *Pirates*, p. 194.

## Chapter 14: The End of the Buccaneers

1 Nuala Zahedieh, 'Trade, Plunder, and Economic Development in Early English Jamaica, 1655–89', *Economic History Review*, 39 (1986), 218.

2 Dunn, *Sugar and Slaves*, pp. 156–62.

3 Pritchard, *In Search of Empire*, pp. 303, 313–14.

4 Marley, *Pirates: Adventurers of the High Seas*, pp. 109–10.

5 William Thomas Morgan, 'The British West Indies during King William's War (1689–97)', *Journal of Modern History*, 2 (1930), 383–4.

6 Marley, *Pirates: Adventurers of the High Seas*, p. 112.

7 Marley, *Pirates and Privateers of the Americas*, p. 208.

8 Marley, *Pirates: Adventurers of the High Seas*, p. 113.

9 *CSP* 1689–92, Nos 515, 616, 635, 769.

10 Ibid., Nos 873, 980, 1021, 1041.

11 Apestegui, *Pirates*, p. 196.

12 Charlevoix, *Histoire de l'isle Espagnole*, 2, pp. 215–20, 222–5; Crouse, *French Struggle for the West Indies*, pp. 177–8; Moya Pons, *Manual de historia Dominicana*, pp. 94–5.

13 Pritchard, *In Search of Empire*, p. 315; Marley, *Pirates and Privateers of the Americas*, pp. 124–5.

14 Marley, *Pirates: Adventurers of the High Seas*, p. 116.

15 Pavison and Buisseret, *Port Royal*, p. 120.

16 Sloane's Account in the *Philosophical Transactions of the Royal Society of London 1665–1800*, iii, p. 627.

17 Historical Society of Pennyslvania, Philadelphia, Norris Papers, I, Joseph to Isaac Norris, 20 June 1692.

18 Ibid., John Pike to brother, 19 June 1692.

19 Larry Gragg, 'The Port Royal Earthquake', *History Today*, 50 (2000), 28–34. See also *A Sad and Terrible Relation of the Dreadful Earth-quake that Happened at Jamaco, in the West-Indies, on the 7th of July, 1692; The Truest and Largest Account of the Late Earthquake in Jamaica, June the 7th, 1692 Written by a Reverend Divine There to his Friend in London*; Thomas Beverley, *Evangelical Repentance Unto Salvation Not to be Repented of . . . Upon the Solemn Occasion of the Late Dreadful Earthquake in Jamaica and the Later Monitory Motion of the Earth in London, and Other Parts of the Nation and Beyond the Sea*; Thomas Doolittle, *Earthquakes Explained And Practically Improved Occasioned By the late Earthquake on Sept. 8, 1692 in London, many other parts in England, and beyond Sea*; E. Heath, *A full Account of the late Dreadful Earthquake at Port Royal in Jamaica Written in two letters from the Minister of That Place From on board the Granada in Port Royal Harbour, June 22 1692*; Joan Whitrowe, *Faithful Warnings, Expostulations and Exhortations, To The Several Professors of Christianity in England, as well those of the Highest as the Lowest Quality . . . to which is added, Two Letters from the Minister of Port-Royal in Jamaica, giving a full Account of the great Destruction that came on that place (for its great sins) by the Dreadful Earthquake that was there in the Year 1692*; John Shower, *Practical Reflections On the Late Earthquakes in Jamaica, England, Sicily, Malta, &c., anno 1692 With a Particular, Historical Account of those, and divers other Earthquakes*. These titles can be read online at *Early English Books Online* – http://eebo.chadwyck.com/home.

20 Talty, *Empire of Blue Water*, pp. 72–3.

21 Dunn, *Sugar and Slaves*, p. 187.

22 Roberts, *Caribbean*, pp. 134–5.

23 *CSP 1693–6*, Nos 634, 635, 1009, 1236.

24 Morgan, 'British West Indies during King William's War', pp. 395–6.

25 *CSP 1693–6*, Nos 778, 876, 1109, 1236(1); Archives Coloniales, Corresp. Gen. de St. Dom. III. Letter of Ducasse, 30 March 1694.

26 *CSP 1693–6*, No. 1113; Charlevoix, *Histoire de l'isle Espagnole*, 2, p. 255.

27 Marley, *Pirates: Adventurers of the High Seas*, p. 120.

28 Crouse, *French Struggle for the West Indies*, pp. 192–3.

29 Pritchard, *In Search of Empire*, p. 317; Crouse, *French Struggle for the West Indies*, pp. 194–5.

30 *CSP 1693–6*, No. 1236; Crouse, *French Struggle for the West Indies*, pp. 195–6; Cundall, *Governors of Jamaica in the Seventeenth Century*, pp. 149–52.

31 *CSP 1693–6*, No. 1516.

32 Crouse, *French Struggle for the West Indies*, pp. 200–10.

33 Ibid., p. 213.

34 Charlevoix, *Histoire de l'isle Espagnole*, 2, pp. 266 ff.

35 Lucena Samoral, *Piratas*, pp. 225–6.

36 Marley, *Pirates and Privateers of the Americas*, p. 116.

37 Marley, *Pirates: Adventurers of the High Seas*, p. 119.

38 P. Bradley Nutting, 'The Madagascar Connection: Parliament and Piracy, 1690–1701', *American Journal of Legal History*, 22 (1978), 205.

39 Symcox, *Crisis of French Sea Power*, pp. 216–18.

40 William Thomas Morgan, 'The Expedition of Baron de Pointis against Cartagena', *American Historical Review*, 37 (1931–2), 238–40.

41 Marley, *Pirates: Adventurers of the High Seas*, p. 123.

42 Apestegui, *Pirates*, p. 198.

43 Morgan, 'Expedition of Baron de Pointis against Cartagena', pp. 245–6.

44 Charlevoix, *Histoire de l'isle Espagnole*, 4, pp. 123 ff.

45 Desjeans, *An Authentic and Particular Account of the Taking of Carthagena by the French*, p. 1.

46 Apestegui, *Pirates*, p. 199.

47 Marley, *Pirates: Adventurers of the High Seas*, pp. 124–5.

48 For a full account from the Spanish perspective see Enrique de la Matta Rodríguez, *El asalto de Pointis de Cartagena de Indias*.

49 Morgan, 'Expedition of Baron de Pointis against Cartagena', pp. 247–8.

50 Symcox, *Crisis of French Sea Power*, p. 219; Pritchard, *In Search of Empire*, p. 329.

51 Morgan, 'Expedition of Baron de Pointis against Cartagena', p. 253.

52 Bromley, *Corsairs and Navies*, pp. 1–2; Charlevoix, *Histoire de l'isle Espagnole*, 4, p. 106; *An Answer to Mr. Paschal's Letter* p. 5.

53 Crouse, *French Struggle for the West Indies*, p. 244.

54 Haring, *Buccaneers*, pp. 266–8.

55 Duro, *Armada Española*, 5, p. 310.

56 *CSP 1669–74*, No. 138.

57 Haring, *Buccaneers*, pp. 269–70.

58 Ritchie, *Captain Kidd and the War against the Pirates*, p. 209.

# BIBLIOGRAPHY

Alvarado Morales, Manuel, *La ciudad de México ante la fundación de la Armada de Barlovento, 1635–1643*, México, El Colegio de México-Universidad de Puerto Rico, 1993

*An Answer to Mr Paschal's letter to his friend in the countrey, stating the case of Mr Parkhurst and himself, being a vindication of the proceedings of the House of Commons, against those gentlemen commissioners for prizes, etc*, London: n.p., 1702

Anderson, R. C., *List of English Men-of-War, 1509–1649*, London: Society for Nautical Research, 1959

Andrews, Charles M., *British Committees, Commissions, and Councils of Trade and Plantations, 1622–1675*, Baltimore, MD: Johns Hopkins University Press, 1908

——, *The Colonial Period of American History*, 4 vols, New Haven, CT: Yale University Press, 1934–8

Andrews, Kenneth R., *Drake's Voyages: A Re-assessment of their Place in Elizabethan Maritime Expansion*, London: Weidenfeld & Nicolson, 1967

——, *Elizabethan Privateering: English Privateering during the Spanish War, 1585–1603*, Cambridge: Cambridge University Press, 1964

——, *The Elizabethan Seaman*, London: National Maritime Museum in conjunction with the Society for Nautical Research, 1982

—— (ed.), *English Privateering Voyages to the West Indies 1588–1595*, Cambridge: Cambridge University Press, 1959

—— (ed.), *The Last Voyage of Drake and Hawkins*, London: Cambridge University Press for the Hakluyt Society, 2nd Series, vol. 142, 1972

——, *Ships, Money and Politics: Seafaring and Naval Enterprise in the Reign of Charles I*, Cambridge: Cambridge University Press, 1991

——, *The Spanish Caribbean: Trade and Plunder, 1530–1630*, New Haven, CT: Yale University Press, 1978

——, *Trade, Plunder and Settlement: Maritime Enterprise and the Genesis of the British Empire, 1480–1630*, Cambridge: Cambridge University Press, 1984

——, Canny, N. P. and Hair, P. E. H., *The Westward Enterprise: English Activities in Ireland, the Atlantic and America, 1480–1650*, Liverpool: Liverpool University Press, 1978

Apestegui, Cruz, *Pirates of the Caribbean: Buccaneers, Privateers, Freebooters and Filibusters, 1493–1720*, London: Conway Maritime Press, 2002

Appelbaum, Robert and Sweet, John Wood (eds), *Envisioning an English Empire: Jamestown and the Making of the North Atlantic World*, Philadelphia, PA: University of Pennsylvania Press, 2005

Arciniegas, Germán, *Caribbean: Sea of the New World*, trans. Harriet de Onís, New York: Alfred A. Knopf, 1946

Armitage, David, *The Ideological Origins of the British Empire*, Cambridge: Cambridge University Press, 2000

—— and Braddick, Michael J. (eds), *The British Atlantic World, 1500–1800*, Basingstoke: Palgrave Macmillan, 2002

Avermaete, Roger, *Les gueux de mer et la naissance d'une nation*, Brussels: Dessart, 1944

Bancroft, Hubert Howe, *History of Central America*, 3 vols, San Francisco: Bancroft, 1883

Beales, Derek and Best, Geoffrey (eds), *History, Society and the Churches: Essays in Honour of Owen Chadwick*, Cambridge: Cambridge University Press, 1985

Beckles, Hilary McD., *A History of Barbados: From Amerindian Settlement to Nation-state*, Cambridge: Cambridge University Press, 1990

Bethell, Leslie (ed.), *The Cambridge History of Latin America, vol. 1: Colonial Latin America*, Cambridge: Cambridge University Press, 1984

Bindoff, S. T., Hurstfield, J. and Williams, C. H. (eds), *Elizabethan Government and Society: Essays Presented to Sir John Neale*, London: Athlone Press, 1961

Birch, Thomas (ed.), *A Collection of the State Papers of John Thurloe, Esq. Secretary to the Council of State and Afterwards to the Two Protectors Oliver and Richard Cromwell: to which is Prefixed the Life of Mr Thurloe: Containing Authentic Memorials of the English Affairs from the Year 1638, to the Restoration of King Charles II / Published from the Originals, Formerly in the Library of John Lord Somers*, London: Printed for the executor of F. Gyles, 1742

Blok, Petrus Johannes, *History of the People of the Netherlands*, vol. 3, *The War with Spain*, New York: AMS Press, 1970

Boiteux, Lucas Alexandre, *Richelieu: Grand Maître de la navigation et du commerce du France*, Paris: Ozanne, 1955

Boucher, Philip P., *Cannibal Encounters: Europeans and the Island Caribs, 1492–1763*, Baltimore, MD: Johns Hopkins University Press, 1992

Boxer, C. R., *The Dutch in Brazil, 1624–1654*, Oxford: Clarendon Press, 1957

——, *The Dutch Seaborne Empire, 1600–1800*, New York: Alfred A. Knopf, 1965

——, *Salvador de Sá and the Struggle for Brazil and Angola, 1602–1686*, London: Athlone Press, 1952

Bradley, Peter T., *The Lure of Peru: Maritime Intrusion into the South Sea, 1558–1701*, Basingstoke: Macmillan, 1989

Bray, Warwick (ed.), *The Meeting of Two Worlds: Europe and the Americas 1492–1650*, Oxford: Oxford University Press, 1994

Bréard, Charles and Paul, *Documents relatifs à la marine Normande et à ses armements aux XVIème et XVIIème siècles pour le Canada, l'Afrique, les Antilles, le Brésil et les Indes*, Rouen: A. Lestringant, 1889

Breverton, Terry, *Admiral Henry Morgan: The Greatest Buccaneer of Them All*, Cowbridge: Glyndwr Publishing, 2005

Bridenbaugh, Carl and Roberta, *No Peace Beyond the Line: The English in the Caribbean, 1624–1690*, London, New York: Oxford University Press, 1972

Bromley, J. S., *Corsairs and Navies 1600–1760*, London: The Hambledon Press, 1987

Bruijn, Jaap R., *The Dutch Navy of the Seventeenth and Eighteenth Centuries*, Columbia, SC: University of South Carolina Press, 1993

315

Burg, B. R., *Sodomy and the Pirate Tradition: English Sea-Rovers in the Seventeenth Century Caribbean*, New York: New York University Press, 1984

Burns, Alan, *History of the British West Indies*, London: George Allen & Unwin, 1965

Cadoux, Cecil J., *Philip of Spain and the Netherlands: An Essay in Moral Judgements in History*, London: Redhill, 1947

Campbell, Mavis C., *The Maroons of Jamaica, 1655–1796: A History of Resistance, Collaboration & Betrayal*, Granby, MA: Bergin & Garvey, 1988

Campbell, P. F., *Some Early Barbadian History*, Wildey, St. Michael, Barbados: Caribbean Graphics, 1993

Canny, Nicolas (ed.), *The Oxford History of the British Empire, vol. I: The Origins of Empire, British Overseas Enterprise to the Close of the Seventeenth Century*, Oxford: Oxford University Press, 1998

Capp, Bernard, *Cromwell's Navy: The Fleet and the English Revolution, 1648–1660*, Oxford: Clarendon Press, 1989

Carleton, Mary, *New from Jamaica in a Letter from Port Royal Written by the Germane Princess to Her Fellow Collegiates and Friends in New-Gate*, London: Peter Lillicrap, 1671

Carrión, Arturo Morales, *Puerto Rico and the Non Hispanic Caribbean. A Study in the Decline of Spanish Exclusivism*, Rió Piedras: University of Puerto Rico Press, 1952

Carter, Alice Clare, *Neutrality or Commitment: The Evolution of Dutch Foreign Policy, 1667–1795*, London: Edward Arnold, 1975

Cayetana, Alvarez de Toledo, *Politics and Reform in Spain and Viceregal Mexico: The Life and Thought of Juan de Palafox, 1600–1659*, Oxford: Clarendon Press, 2004

Chapin, Howard M., *Privateer Ships and Sailors: The First Century of American Colonial Privateering, 1625–1725*, Toulon: Imprimerie G. Mouton, 1926

Charlevoix, Pierre-François-Xavier de, *Histoire de l'isle Espagnole ou de S. Domingue, écrite particulierement sur des mémoires manuscrits du P. Jean-Baptiste le Pers, Jésuite, missionnaire à Saint-Domingue, & sur les pièces originales, qui se conservent au dépot de la marine*, 4 vols, Amsterdam: L'Honoré, 1733

Chaunu, Huguette and Pierre, *Séville et l'Atlantique, 1504–1650*, 8 vols, Paris: A. Colin, 1955–9

Clark, G., *The Later Stuarts, 1660–1714*, Oxford: Clarendon Press, 1956

Clarke, William, *The Clarke Papers: Selections from the Papers of William Clarke, Secretary to the Council of the Army, 1647–1649, and to General Monck and the Commanders of the Army in Scotland, 1651–1660*, ed. C. H. Firth, vol. 3, London: Camden Society Publications, 1899

Connell-Smith, Gordon, *Forerunners of Drake: A Study of English trade with Spain in the Early Tudor Period*, London: Longmans, Green, 1954

Cook, Sherburne F. and Borah, Woodrow, *Essays in Population History: Mexico and the Caribbean*, vol. 1, Berkeley, CA: University of California Press, 1971

Corbett, Julian S., *Drake and the Tudor Navy*, 2 vols, London: Longmans, 1898

——, *The Successors of Drake*, London: Longmans, 1900

Cordingly, David, *Pirates: An Illustrated History of Privateers, Buccaneers, and Pirates from the Sixteenth Century to the Present*, London: Salamander, 1996

Coward, Barry, *Oliver Cromwell*, Harlow: Longman, 1991

Craven, Wesley F., *An Introduction to the History of Bermuda*, Bermuda: Bermuda Maritime Museum Press, 1990

Cromwell, Oliver, *Letters and Speeches of Oliver Cromwell*, ed. Thomas Carlyle, London: Methuen, 1904

——, *The Writings and Speeches of Oliver Cromwell: With an Introduction, Notes and an Account of his Life*, vol. 3: *The Protectorate, 1653–1655*, ed. Wilbur Cortez Abbott, Oxford: Oxford University Press, 1989

Crouse, Nellis M., *French Pioneers in the West Indies 1624–1664*, New York: Columbia University Press, 1940

——, *The French Struggle for the West Indies, 1665–1713*, New York: Columbia University Press, 1943

Cundall, Frank, *The Governors of Jamaica in the Seventeenth Century*, London: West India Committee, 1936

—— and Pietersz, Joseph L., *Jamaica under the Spaniards. Abstracted from the Archives of Seville*, Kingston, Jamaica: n.p., 1919

Daher, Andréa, *Les Singularités de la France équinoxiale. Histoire de la mission des pères capucins au Brésil (1612–1615)*, Paris: Honoré Champion, 2002

Dampier, William, *William Dampier's Travels: Consisting of a New Voyage Round the World, a Supplement to the Voyage Round the World, Two Voyages to Campeachy and so on*, 2 vols, London: E. Grant Richards, 1906

Daniels, Christine and Kennedy, Michael V. (eds), *Negotiated Empires: Centers and Peripheries in the Americas, 1500–1820*, New York: Routledge, 2002

Davenport, Frances Gardiner (ed.), *European Treaties Bearing on the History of the United States and its Dependencies*, 4 vols, Clark, NJ: Lawbook Exchange, 2004

Davies, Godfrey, *The Early Stuarts: 1603–1660*, Oxford: Oxford University Press, 1959

Davies, K. G., *The North Atlantic World in the Seventeenth Century*, Minneapolis, MN: University of Minnesota Press, 1974

——, *The Royal African Company*, London: Longmans, Green & Co, 1957

Davis, J. C., *Oliver Cromwell*, London: Arnold, 2001

Davis, N. Darnell, *The Cavaliers & Roundheads of Barbados, 1650–1652*, Georgetown, British Guiana: Argosy Press, 1987

Deive, Carlos Esteban, *Tangomangos: Contrabando y Piratería en Santo Domingo, 1522–1606*, Santo Domingo: Fundación Cultural Dominicana, 1996

Desjeans, Jean Bernard Louis de, *A Genuine and Particular Account of the Taking of Carthagena by the French and Buccaniers, in the year 1697 ... With a preface, giving an account of the original of Carthagena, etc*, London: Oliver Payne, 1740

Dessert, Daniel, *La Royale: Vaisseaux et marins du Roi-Soleil*, Paris: Fayard, 1996

Duffy, Michael (ed.), *Parameters of British Naval Power, 1650–1850*, Exeter: University of Exeter Press, 1992

—— (ed.), *The New Maritime History of Devon. vol. I, From Early Times to the Late Eighteenth Century*, London: Conway Maritime Press, 1992

Dunn, Richard S., *Sugar and Slaves: The Rise of the Planter Class in the English West Indies, 1624–1713*, Chapel Hill, NC: University of North Carolina Press, 1972

Duro, Fernández Cesareo de, *La Armada Española*, 9 vols, Madrid: Museo Naval, 1895–1903

Du Tertre, Jean-Baptiste, *Histoire générale des Antilles habitées par les Français*, 4 vols, Paris: Thomas Jolly, 1667–71

Earle, Peter, *The Sack of Panamá*, London: Jill Norman and Hobhouse, 1981

Egerton, H. E., *A Short History of British Colonial Policy*, London: Methuen, 1908

Elliott, John H., *The Count-Duke of Olivares: The Statesman in an Age of Decline*, New Haven, CT: Yale University Press, 1986

——, *Richelieu and Olivares*, Cambridge: Cambridge University Press, 1984

Exquemelin, Alexander O. (trans. A. Brown), *The Buccaneers of America*, Mineola, NY: Dover Publications, 2000

Firth, C. H., *Cromwell's Army: A History of the English Soldier during the Civil Wars, the Commonwealth and the Protectorate*, London: Methuen, 1962

Floyd, Troy S., *The Anglo-Spanish Struggle for Mosquitia*, Albuquerque, NM: University of New Mexico Press, 1967

Fortune, Stephen A., *Merchants and Jews: The Struggle for British West Indian Commerce, 1650–1750*, Gainesville, FL: University of Florida, Center for Latin American Studies, 1984

Foster, Nicholas, *A Briefe Relation of the Late Horrid Rebellion Acted in the Island Barbados in the West Indies, wherein is contained their inhumane acts and actions . . . Acted by the Waldrons and their Abettors, anno 1650. Written at sea by Nicholas Foster*, London: T. Fisher Unwin, 1879

Gage, Thomas, *Travels in the New World*, ed. J. Eric Thompson, Norman, OK: University of Oklahoma Press, 1958

——, *The English-American: A New Survey of the West Indies, 1648*, ed. A. P. Newton, London: G. Routledge & Sons, 1928

Galenson, David W., *White Servitude in Colonial America: An Economic Analysis*, Cambridge: Cambridge University Press, 1981

Gámez, José D., *Historia de Nicaragua*, Managua: Fondo de Promoción Cultural Banco de America, 1975

Gardiner, Samuel Rawson, *History of the Commonwealth and Protectorate: 1649–1656*, vol. 2: *1651–1653*, Adlestrop: Windrush Press, 1988

Gonzalez Carranza, Domingo, *A Geographical Description of the Coasts, Harbours, and Sea Ports of the Spanish West-Indies; Particularly of Porto Bello, Cartagena, and the Island of Cuba; with Observations of the Currents, Variations of the Compass in the Bay of Mexico . . .*, London: Printed for the Editor Caleb Smith, 1740

Goodman, David, *Spanish Naval Power, 1589–1665: Reconstruction and Defeat*, Cambridge: Cambridge University Press, 1997

Goslinga, Cornelis Ch., *The Dutch in the Caribbean and on the Wild Coast, 1580–1680*, Gainesville, FL: University Press of Florida, 1971

——, *The Dutch in the Caribbean and in the Guianas, 1680–1791*, Dover, NH: Van Gorcum, 1985

Gragg, Larry, *Englishmen Transplanted: The English Colonization of Barbados, 1627–1660*, Oxford: Oxford University Press, 2003

Grancsay, Stephen, *Master French Gunsmiths' Designs of the XVII–XIX Centuries*, New York: Winchester Press, 1970

Guerra y Sánchez, Ramiro, *Manual de historia de Cuba*, Havana: Cultural, 1938

Hamilton, Earl J., *American Treasure and the Price Revolution in Spain, 1501–1650*, Cambridge, MA: Harvard University Press, 1934

Haring, Clarence H., *The Buccaneers in the West Indies in the XVIIth Century*, London: Methuen, 1910

——, *The Spanish Empire in America*, New York: Oxford University Press, 1947

——, *Trade and Navigation between Spain and the Indies in the Time of the Hapsburgs*, Cambridge, MA: Harvard University Press, 1916

Harlow, Vincent T., *Christopher Codrington, 1668–1710*, Oxford: Clarendon Press, 1928

—— (ed.), *Colonizing Expeditions to the West Indies and Guinea (1622–1667)*, London: Hakluyt Society, 1925

——, *A History of Barbados, 1625–1685*, Oxford: Clarendon Press, 1926

Harris, C. A. (ed.), *A Relation of a Voyage to Guiana; Describing the climat, scituation, fertilitie, provisions and commodities of that Country ... Together with the manners, customes, and dispositions of the people. Performed by R. H., etc. With Purchas's Transcript of a Report made at Harcourt's Instance on the Marrawini District*, London: Hakluyt Society, 1928

Hatton, Christopher (ed. Edward Maunde Thompson), *Correspondence of the Family of Hatton: Being Chiefly Letters Addressed to Christopher, First Viscount Hatton, A.D. 1601–1704*, 2 vols, London: Camden Society, 1878

Herrero García, Miguel, *Ideas de los Españoles del Siglo XVII*, Madrid: Voluntad, 1928

Hickeringill, Edmund, *Jamaica Viewed: With All the Ports, Harbours, and their several Soundings, Towns, and Settlements thereunto belonging, Together With the nature of it's Climate, fruitfulnesse of the Soile, and it's suitablenesse to English complexions, With several other collateral Observations and Reflexions upon the Island*, London: John Williams, 1661

Hill, Christopher, *God's Englishman: Oliver Cromwell and the English Revolution*, London: Weidenfeld & Nicolson, 1970

Hoffman, Paul E., *The Spanish Crown and the Defense of the Caribbean, 1535–1585: Precedent, Patrimonialism and Royal Parsimony*, Baton Rouge, LA: Louisiana State University Press, 1980

Hume, Martin, *The Court of Philip IV: Spain in Decadence*, London: Eveleigh Nash, 1907

Hutchinson, Thomas, *The Hutchinson Papers etc. (A Collection of Original Papers Relative to the History of the Colony of Massachusetts-Bay)*, The Prince Society, 1865

*Interesting Tracts Relating to the Island of Jamaica, from its Conquest, down to the Year 1702*, St. Jago de la Vega: Lewis, Lunan & Jones, 1800

I.S., *A brief and Perfect Journal of the Late Proceedings and Success of the English Army in the West-Indies, Continued until June the 24th, 1655. Together with some Queries Inserted and Answered*, London: n.p., 1655

Israel, Jonathan I., *Dutch Primacy in World Trade, 1585–1740*, Oxford: Clarendon Press, 1989

——, *The Dutch Republic and the Hispanic World, 1606–1666*, Oxford: Clarendon Press, 1982

——, *Empires and Entrepots: The Dutch, the Spanish Monarchy and the Jews, 1585–1713*, London: Hambledon Press, 1990

Ives, Vernon A. (ed.), *The Rich Papers: Letters from Bermuda, 1615–1646: Eyewitness Accounts*

*Sent by the Early Colonists to Sir Nathaniel Rich*, Toronto: University of Toronto Press, 1984

James I, *A Counter-Blaste to Tobacco*, London: Rodale Press, 1956

Jameson, James F., *Privateering and Piracy in the Colonial Period: Illustrative Documents*, New York: Macmillan, 1923

——, *Willem Usselinx, Founder of the Dutch and Swedish West India Companies*, New York: G. P. Puttnam's Sons, 1887

Juárez Moreno, Juan, *Piratas y corsarios en Veracruz y Campeche*, Sevilla: CSIC, 1972

Keeler, M. F. (ed.), *Sir Francis Drake's West Indian Voyage, 1585–86*, London: Hakluyt Society, 2nd Ser., vol 148, 1981

Kelsey, Harry, *Sir Francis Drake: The Queen's Pirate*, New Haven, CT: Yale University Press, 2000

Kemp, Peter and Lloyd, Christopher, *The Brethren of the Coast: The British and French Buccaneers in the South Seas*, London: Heinemann, 1960

Kendall, C. W., *Private Men-of-War*, London: Philip Allan, 1931

Kennedy, Paul M., *The Rise and Fall of the Great Powers: Economic Change and Military Conflict from 1500 to 2000*, New York: Random House, 1987

Kietzman, Mary Jo, *The Self-Fashioning of an Early Modern Englishwoman: Mary Carleton's Lives*, Aldershot: Ashgate, 2004.

Korr, Charles P., *Cromwell and the New Model Foreign Policy: England's Policy Toward France, 1649–1658*, Berkeley, CA: University of California Press, 1975

Kossmaul, Ann, *Servants in Husbandry in Early Modern England*, Cambridge: Cambridge University Press, 1981

Kupperman, Karen Ordahl, *Providence Island, 1630–1641: The Other Puritan Colony*, Cambridge: Cambridge University Press, 1993

Laet, Johannes de, *Iaelyck Verhael van de Verrichtinghen der Geotroyeerde West-Indische Compagnie in derthien Boecken*, 3 vols, The Hague: Martinus Nijhoff, 1931

Lane, Kris E., *Pillaging the Empire: Piracy in the Americas, 1500–1750*, New York and London: M. E. Sharpe, 1998

Las Casas, Bartolomé de, *Tears of the Indians: Being an Historical and True Account of the Cruel Massacre and Slaughters Committed by the Spaniards in the Islands of the West-Indies, Mexico Peru etc*, Baarle-Nassau: SoMa, 1980

Laurence, Anne, *Parliamentary Army Chaplains, 1642–1651*, Woodbridge, Suffolk: Boydell Press, 1990

Lavigne Sainte-Suzanne, Maurice de, *La Martinique au premier siècle de la colonisation*, Nantes: Chontreau, 1935

Leslie, Charles, *A New History of Jamaica, from the Earliest Accounts, to the Taking of Porto Bello by Vice-Admiral Vernon. In Thirteen Letters from a Gentleman to his Friend . . . The second edition*, London: J. Hodges, 1740

Ligon, Richard, *A True & Exact History of the Island of Barbadoes*, London: Peter Parker & Thomas Guy, 1673

Ligtenberg, Catharina, *Willem Usselinx*, Utrecht: A. Oost-Hoek, 1914

Linebaugh, Peter and Rediker, Marcus, *The Many-Headed Hydra: Sailors, Slaves, Commoners and the Hidden History of the Revolutionary Atlantic*, Boston, MA: Beacon Press, 2000

Lloyd, T. O., *The British Empire, 1558–1995*, Oxford: Oxford University Press, 1996

Loades, David, *England's Maritime Empire: Seapower, Commerce and Policy 1490–1690*, Harlow: Longman, 2000

——, *The Tudor Navy: An Administrative, Political and Military History*, Aldershot: Scolar, 1992

Long, Edward, *A History of Jamaica*, 3 vols, London: Frank Cass, 1970

Lucena Samoral, Manuel, *Piratas, Bucaneros, Filibusteros y Corsarios en América: Perros, Mendigos y Otros Malditos del Mar (Tierra Nuestra)*, Madrid: Mapfre, 1992

Lussan, Raveneau de, *Les flibustiers de la mer du Sud: Journal d'un voyage fait à la mer du Sud avec les flibustiers de l'Amérique, depuis le 22 novembre 1684 jusqu'en janvier 1688*, Paris: France-Empire, 1992

Lynch, John, *Spain under the Habsburgs*, vol. 2: *Spain and America, 1598–1700*, Oxford: Oxford University Press, 1969

MacCaffrey, Wallace T., *Elizabeth I: War and Politics, 1588–1603*, Princeton, NJ: Princeton University Press, 1992

MacDougall, Norman, *James VI: The Stewart Dynasty in Scotland*, Edinburgh: John Donald, 2006

McInnes, Charles M., *The Early English Tobacco Trade*, London: Kegan Paul, 1926

MacLeod, Murdo J., *Spanish Central America: A Socioeconomic History, 1520–1780*, Berkeley, CA: University of California Press, 1973

Maltby, William S., *The Black Legend in England. The Development of Anti-Spanish Sentiment, 1558–1660*, Durham, NC: Duke University Press, 1971

Mancke, Elizabeth and Shammas, Carole (eds), *The Creation of the British Atlantic World*, Baltimore, MD: Johns Hopkins University Press, 2005

Marley, David F., *Pirates and Engineers: Dutch and Flemish Adventurers in New Spain (1607–1697)*, Windsor, Ont.: Netherlandic Press, 1992

——, *Pirates: Adventurers of the High Seas*, London: Arms & Armour, 1995

——, *Pirates and Privateers of the Americas*, Santa Barbara, CA: ABC-CLIO, 1994

——, *Sack of Veracruz: The Great Pirate Raid of 1683*, Windsor, Ont. Netherlandic Press, 1993

Martin, Colin and Parker, Geoffrey, *The Spanish Armada*, Harmondsworth: Penguin, 1989

Marx, Jenifer, *Pirates and Privateers of the Caribbean*, Malabar, FL: Krieger Publishing, 1992

Matta Rodríguez, Enrique de la, *El asalto de Pointis de Cartagena de Indias*, Sevilla: CSIC, 1979

Miller, Perry, *Errand in the Wilderness*, Cambridge, MA: Harvard University Press, 1956

Mims, S. L., *Colbert's West India Policy*, New Haven, CT: Yale University Press, 1912

Minchington, W. E., *The Growth of English Overseas Trade in the Seventeenth and Eighteenth Centuries*, London: Methuen, 1969

Monson, Sir William, *The Naval Tracts of Sir William Monson*, ed. M. Oppenheim, London: Navy Records Society, vols 22–3, 43, 45, 47, 1902–14

Morales Carrión, Arturo, *Puerto Rico and the Non Hispanic Caribbean. A Study in the Decline of Spanish Exclusivism*, Río Piedras: University of Puerto Rico Press, 1952

Moya Pons, Frank, *Manual de Historia Dominicana*, Santo Domingo: Caribbean Publishers, 1995

Muldoon, James, *The Americas in the Spanish World Order: The Justification for Conquest in the Seventeenth Century*, Philadelphia, PA: University of Pennsylvania Press, 1994

Naber, S.P. L'Honoré and Wright, I. A., *Piet Heyn en de zilvervloot: Bescheieden uit Nederlandsche en Spaansche archieven*, Utrecht: Kemink & Zoon, 1928

Newton, Arthur Percival, *The Colonising Activities of the English Puritans: The Last Phase of the Elizabethan Struggle with Spain*, New Haven, CT: Yale University Press, 1914

——, *The European Nations in the West Indies, 1493–1688*, London: A. & C. Black, 1933

O'Callaghan, Seán, *To Hell or Barbados*, Dingle, Co. Kerry: Brandon, 2000

Padrón, Francisco Morales, *Spanish Jamaica*, trans. Patrick E. Bryan, Kingston, Jamaica: Ian Randle Publishers, 2003

Paige, John, *The Letters of John Paige, London merchant, 1648–1658*, ed. George F. Steckley, London: London Record Society, XXI, 1984

Paquette, Robert L. and Engerman, Stanley L. (eds), *The Lesser Antilles in the Age of European Expansion*, Gainesville, FL: University Press of Florida, 1996

Pares, Richard, *Merchants and Planters*, Economic History Review Supplement No. 4, Cambridge: Economic History Society, 1959

Parker, Geoffrey, *The Dutch Revolt*, Harmondsworth: Penguin, 1979

Parry, J. H., *The Spanish Seaborne Empire*, New York: Alfred A. Knopf, 1966

Pavison, Michael and Buisseret, David J., *Port Royal, Jamaica*, Oxford: Clarendon Press, 1975

Peña Battlé, Manuel Arturo, *La Isla de la Tortuga: Plaza de armas, refugio y seminario de los enemigos de España en Indias*, Madrid: Cultura Hispánica, 1951

Penn, Granville, *Memorials of the Professional Life and Times of Sir William Penn*, vol. 2, London: James Duncan, 1834

Pennell, C. R. (ed.), *Bandits at Sea: A Pirates Reader*, New York: New York University Press, 2001

Pepys, Samuel (eds Robert Latham and William Matthews), *The Diary of Samuel Pepys*, 10 vols, London: G. Bell & Sons, 1972

Perrin, W. G. (ed.), *Boteler's Dialogues*, London: Navy Records Society, 1929

——, *British Flags, their Early History, and their Development at Sea; with an Account of the Origin of the Flag as a National Device*, Cambridge: Cambridge University Press, 1922

Petitjean Roget, Jacques, *La société d'habitation à la Martinique: Un demi-siècle de formation, 1635–1685*, Paris: Honoré Champion, 1980

Petrovich, Sandra, *Henry Morgan's Raid on Panama – Geopolitics and Colonial Ramifications, 1669–1674*, Lewiston, NY: Edwin Mellen Press, 2001

Pezuela y Lobo, Jacobo de la, *Historia de la Isla de Cuba*, 4 vols, Madrid: C. Bailly-Baillière; New York: Baillière Hermanos, 1868–78

Phillips, Carla Rahn, *Six Galleons for the King of Spain: Imperial Defense in the Seventeenth Century*, Baltimore, MD: Johns Hopkins University Press, 1986

Pico, Fernando, *Historia General de Puerto Rico*, Rio Piedras: Huracàn, 1986

Pincus, Steven C. A., *Protestantism and Patriotism: Ideologies and the Making of English Foreign Policy, 1650–1668*, Cambridge: Cambridge University Press, 1996

Pope, Dudley, *Harry Morgan's Way: The Biography of Sir Henry Morgan, 1634–1684*, London: Secker & Warburg, 1977

Postma, Johannes Menne, *The Dutch in the Atlantic Slave Trade, 1600–1815*, Cambridge: Cambridge University Press, 1990

Preston, Diana and Michael, *A Pirate of Exquisite Mind: The Life of William Dampier*, London: Doubleday, 2004

Preston, Jean, *The Mosquito Indians and Anglo-Spanish Rivalry in Central America, 1630–1821*, Glasgow: Latin American Studies, University of Glasgow, 1988

Pritchard, James, *In Search of Empire: The French in the Americas, 1670–1730*, Cambridge: Cambridge University Press, 2004

Puckrein, Gary A., *Little England: Plantation Society and Anglo-Barbadian Politics, 1627–1700*, New York: New York University Press, 1984

Quinn, David B. and Ryan, A. N., *England's Sea Empire, 1550–1642*, London: Allen & Unwin, 1983

Ringrose, Basil, *The Dangerous Voyage and Bold Attempts of Captain B. Sharp and Others upon the Coasts of the South Sea. From the Original Journal of the Voyage*, Part 4 in William Swan Stallybrass (ed.), *The Buccaneers of America*, London: George Routledge & Son, 1923

Ritchie, Robert, *Captain Kidd and the War against the Pirates*, Cambridge: Cambridge University Press, 1986

Roberts, W. Adolphe, *The Caribbean*, New York: Bobbs-Merrill, 1940

Rodger, N. A. M., *The Safeguard of the Sea: A Naval History of Britain, 1660–1649*, London: HarperCollins, 1997

Rodríguez del Valle, Mariana, *El castillo de San Felipe del Golfo Dulce. 'Historia de las fortificaciones de Guatemala en la Edad Moderna'*, Sevilla: Ediciones de la Escuela Estudios Hispano-Americanos de Sevilla, 1960

Rodríguez-Salgado, M. J. and Adams, Simon (eds), *England, Spain and the Gran Armada, 1585–1604*, Edinburgh: John Donald, 1991

Roots, Ivan (ed.), *Cromwell: A Profile*, London: Macmillan, 1973

Rotz, J., *The Maps and Text of the Boke of Idrography Presented by Jean Rotz to Henry VIII, Now in the British Library*, ed. Helen Wallis, Oxford: Roxburghe Club, 1981

Rouse, Irving, *The Taínos: Rise and Decline of the People Who Greeted Columbus*, New Haven, CT: Yale University Press, 1992

Rout, Leslie B., *The African Experience in Spanish America, 1502 to the Present Day*, Cambridge: Cambridge University Press, 1976

Ruigh, Robert E., *The Parliament of 1624: Politics and Foreign Policy*, Cambridge, MA: Harvard University Press, 1971

Russell, Conrad, *Parliaments and English Politics, 1621–1629*, Oxford: Clarendon Press, 1979

*A Sad and Terrible Relation of the Dreadful Earth-quake that Happened at Jamaco, in the West-Indies, on the 7th of July, 1692 . . .* , [London]: Printed for P. Brooksby, J. Deacon, J. Blare, and J. Back, 1692

Sáiz Cidoncha, Carlos, *Historia de la piratería en América española*, Madrid: San Martín, 1985

323

Savelle, Maxwell H., *The Origins of American Diplomacy: The International History of Anglo-America, 1492–1763*, London: Collier-Macmillan, 1967

Scammell, G. V., *Seafaring, Sailors and Trade, 1450–1750: Studies in British and European Maritime and Imperial History*, Aldershot: Ashgate Variorum, 2003

——, *The World Encompassed: The First European Maritime Empires, c. 800–1650*, London: Methuen, 1981

Schreiber, Roy E., *The First Carlisle: Sir James Hay, First Earl of Carlisle, as Courtier, Diplomat and Entrepreneur, 1580–1636*, Philadelphia, PA: American Philosophical Society, 1984

Seitz, Don C., *The Buccaneers: Rough Verse*, New York: Harper & Brothers, 1912

Senior, C. M., *A Nation of Pirates: English Piracy in its Heyday*, Newton Abbot: David and Charles, 1976

Serrano Mangas, Fernando, *La segura travesía del Agnus Dei: Ignorancia y malevolencia en torno a la figura de Benito Arias Montano 'El Menor'*, Badajoz: Diputación de Badajoz, Editora Regional de Extremadura, 1999

Sheperd, Verene A. (ed.), *Working Slavery, Pricing Freedom: Perspectives from the Caribbean, Africa and the African Diaspora*, Kingston, Jamaica: Ian Randle Publishers, 1992

Sheridan, Richard B., *Sugar and Slavery: An Economic History of the British West Indies, 1623–1775*, Baltimore, MD: Johns Hopkins University Press, 1974

Skowronek, Russell K. and Ewen, Charles R. (eds), *X Marks the Spot: The Archaeology of Piracy*, Gainsville, FL: University Press of Florida, 2006

Smith, Adam, *An Inquiry into the Nature and Causes of the Wealth of Nations*, London: Dent, 1910

Smith, Abbot E., *Colonists in Bondage: White Servitude and Convict Labor in America, 1607–1776*, Chapel Hill, NC: University of North Carolina Press, 1947

Smith, John, *The True Travels, Adventures and Observations of Captain John Smith in Europe, Asia, Africa and America: And the General History of Virginia, New England and the Summer Isles, books I.–III.*, ed. A. E. Benians, Cambridge: Cambridge University Press, 1908

Snelders, Stephen, *The Devil's Anarchy: The Sea Robberies of the Most Famous Pirate Claes G. Compaen, and, the Very Remarkable Travels of Jan Erasmus Reyning, Buccaneer*, New York: Autonomedia, 2005

Southey, Thomas, *Chronological History of the West Indies*, 3 vols, London: Longman, Rees, Orme, Brown, and Green, 1827

Stein, Stanley J. and Barbara H., *Silver, Trade and War: Spain and America in the Making of Early Modern Europe*, Baltimore, MD: Johns Hopkins University Press, 2000

Stradling, R. A., *Europe and the Decline of Spain: A Study of the Spanish System, 1580–1720*, London: Allen & Unwin, 1981

——, *Philip IV and the Government of Spain, 1621–1665*, Cambridge University Press, 1988

Strangeways, Thomas, *Sketch of the Mosquito Shore, including the Territory of Poyais, etc*, Edinburgh: W. Blackwoods, 1822

Symcox, Geoffrey, *The Crisis of French Sea Power, 1688–1697: From the Guerre d'Escadre to the Guerre de Course*, The Hague: Martinus Nijhoff, 1974

Talty, Stephan, *Empire of Blue Water: Henry Morgan and the Pirates Who Ruled the Caribbean Waves*, London: Simon & Schuster, 2007

Taylor, S. A. G., *The Western Design: An Account of Cromwell's Expedition to the Caribbean*, London: Solstice Productions, 1969

Tenenti, Alberto, *Piracy and the Decline of Venice, 1580–1615*, London: Longmans, 1967

Thomas, Hugh, *Conquest: Montezuma, Cortes, and the Fall of Old Mexico*, New York: Simon & Schuster, 1993

Thomas, Keith, *Religion and the Decline of Magic*, New York: Charles Scribner's Sons, 1971

Thompson, I. A. A., *War and Government in Habsburg Spain, 1560–1620*, London: The Athlone Press, 1976

Thornton, A. P., *West India Policy under the Restoration*, Oxford: Clarendon Press, 1956

Todd, Janet and Spearing, Elizabeth (eds), *Counterfeit Ladies*, London: William Pickering, 1994

Tomalin, Claire, *Samuel Pepys: The Unequalled Self*, London: Viking, 2002

Torres Ramírez, Bibiano, *La Armada de Barlovento*, Sevilla: Escuela de Estudios Hispano-Americanos, 1981

Townshend, Lee Porcher (ed.), *Some Account of General Robert Venables, of Antrobus and Wincham, Cheshire; Together with the Autobiographical Memoir, or Diary, of his Widow, Elizabeth Venables*, Manchester: Chetham Society, 1871

Trevelyan, Raleigh, *Sir Walter Raleigh*, London: Allen Lane, 2002

*The Truest and Largest Account of the Late Earthquake in Jamaica, June the 7th, 1692 Written by a Reverend Divine There to his Friend in London; With Some Improvement Thereof by Another Hand*, London: Printed for Tho. Parkhurst, 1693

Vásquez de Espinosa, Antonio, *Compendium and Description of the Isthmus of America. With Wafer's Secret Report (1688) and Nathaniel Davis's Expedition to the Gold Mines (1704)*, London: Hakluyt Society, 1933

Vassière, Pierre de, *Saint Domingue, la société et la vie créole sous l'ancien régime*, Paris: Perrin, 1909

Velius, Theodoricus, *Chronyk van Hoorn*, ed. Sebastiaen Centen, Hoorn: Centen, 1740

Venables, Robert, *The Narrative of General Venables: With an Appendix of Papers Relating to the Expedition to the West Indies and the Conquest of Jamaica, 1654–1655*, ed. C. H. Firth, London: Longmans, Green, 1900

Venning, Timothy, *Cromwellian Foreign Policy*, Basingstoke: Macmillan, 1995

Vila Vilar, Enriqueta, *Historia de Puerto Rico (1600–1650)*, Sevilla: Escuela de Estudios Hispano-Americanos, 1974

Wallerstein, Immanuel M., *The Modern World-System: 1, Capitalist Agriculture and the Origins of the European World-Economy in the Sixteenth Century*, London: Academic Press, 1974

Ward, Christopher, *Imperial Panama: Commerce and Conflict in Isthmian America, 1550–1800*, Albuquerque, NM: University of New Mexico Press, 1993

Warner, Aucher, *Sir Thomas Warner: Pioneer of the West Indies: A Chronicle of Family, etc*, London: West Indies Committee, 1933

Waters, David W., *The Art of Navigation in England in Elizabethan and Early Stuart Times*, London: Hollis & Carter, 1958

Wernham, R. B., *After the Armada: Elizabethan England and the Struggle for Western Europe, 1588–1595*, Oxford: Clarendon Press, 1984

——, *Before the Armada: The Growth of English Foreign Policy, 1485–1588*, New York: W. W. Norton, 1972

——, *The Return of the Armadas: The Last Years of the Elizabethan Wars against Spain, 1595–1603*, Oxford: Clarendon Press, 1994

Whitelock, Bulstrode, *Memorials of the English Affairs from the Beginning of the Reign of Charles the First to the Happy Restoration of Charles the Second*, vol. 4, Oxford: Oxford University Press, 1853

Wilkinson, Henry Campbell, *The Adventurers of Bermuda: A History of the Island from its Discovery until the Dissolution of the Somer Island Company in 1684*, Oxford: Oxford University Press, 1933

Willan, T. S. (ed.), *A Tudor Book of Rates*, Manchester: Manchester University Press, 1962

Williams, Eric, *Capitalism and Slavery*, London: André Deutsch, 1964

——, *From Columbus to Castro: The History of the Caribbean, 1492–1969*, London: André Deutsch, 1970

Williamson, James A., *The Caribee Islands, under the Proprietary Patents*, Oxford: Oxford University Press, 1926

——, *Maritime Enterprise, 1485–1558*, Oxford: Clarendon Press, 1913

Wimpffen, Alexandre-Stanislas, Baron de, *A Voyage to Saint Domingo, in the Years 1788, 1789, and 1790*, London: T. Cadell, Junior & W. Davies, 1817

Winter, P. J. van, *De Westindische Compagnie ter kamer Stad en Lande*, 's-Gravenhage: Omslag, 1978

Worth, John E., *Timucuan Chiefdoms of Spanish Florida*, vol. 2: *Resistance and Destruction*, Gainesville, FL: University Press of Florida, 1998

Wright, I. A. (ed. and trans.), *The English Conquest of Jamaica: An Account of What Happened in the Island from May 20 1655 up to July 3 1656*, Camden Miscellany, vol. 13, London: Royal Historical Society Publications, 1923

—— (ed.), *Historia documentada de San Cristóbal de la Habana en la primera mitad del siglo XVII*, Havana: Imprenta 'El Siglo XX', A. Muñiz y hno., 1930

—— and Dam, Cornelius van (eds), *Nederlandsche Zeevaarders op de eilanden in de Caraibische Zee en aan de kust van Columbia en Venezuela, gedurende de Jaren 1621–1648(9). Documenten hoofzakelijk uit het Archivo General de Indias*, 2 vols, Utrecht: Kemink & Zoon, 1934–5.

——, *Santiago de Cuba and its District, 1607–1640, Villaverde. – Sanchez de Moya. – García Nabia. – Velasco. – Fonseca Betancur. Azevedo. – Amezqueta Quijano. – Roca de Borja. Written from Documents in the Archive of the Indies, at Seville, Spain*, Madrid: Estab. tip. de F. Peña Cruz, 1918

—— (ed. and trans.), *Spanish Documents Concerning English Voyages to the Caribbean, 1527–1568*, Nendeln, Liechtenstein: Kraus Reprint, 1967

—— (ed. and trans.), *Spanish Narratives of the English Attack on Santo Domingo, 1655*, Camden Miscellany, vol. 14, London: Royal Historical Society Publications, 1926

Zapatero, Juan Manuel, *La guerra del Caribe en el siglo XVIII*, San Juan de Puerto Rico: Instituto de Cultura Puertorriqueña, 1964

# INDEX